HITCHCOCK AND THE CENSORS

HITCHCOCK AND THE CENSORS

JOHN BILLHEIMER

UNIVERSITY PRESS OF KENTUCKY

Paperback edition 2021

Scholarly publisher for the Commonwealth,
serving Bellarmine University, Berea College, Centre
College of Kentucky, Eastern Kentucky University,
The Filson Historical Society, Georgetown College,
Kentucky Historical Society, Kentucky State University,
Morehead State University, Murray State University,
Northern Kentucky University, Spalding University,
Transylvania University, University of Kentucky,
University of Louisville, and Western Kentucky University.

Editorial and Sales Offices: The University Press of Kentucky
663 South Limestone Street, Lexington, Kentucky 40508-4008
www.kentuckypress.com

Unless otherwise noted, photographs are from the author's collection.

Library of Congress Cataloging-in-Publication Data

Names: Billheimer, John W., author.
Title: Hitchcock and the censors / John Billheimer.
Description: Lexington : The University Press of Kentucky, 2019. | Includes bibliographical references and index.
Identifiers: LCCN 2019000222| ISBN 9780813177427 (hardcover : alk. paper) | ISBN 9780813177410 (pdf) | ISBN 9780813177434 (epub)
Subjects: LCSH: Hitchcock, Alfred, 1899–1980—Criticism and interpretation. | Motion pictures—Censorship—Great Britain. | Motion pictures—Censorship—United States. | Television—Censorship—United States.
Classification: LCC PN1998.3.H58 B55 2019 | DDC 791.4302/33092—dc23
ISBN 978-0-8131-8054-0 (pbk. : alk. paper)

This book is printed on acid-free paper meeting the requirements of the American National Standard for Permanence in Paper for Printed Library Materials.

Manufactured in the United States of America.

Member of the Association of University Presses

For Wayne and Susan, my pride and joy
(or is it my joy and pride?)

Contents

Introduction

In the dining car of the *Twentieth Century Limited*, Eva Marie Saint raises her eyebrows and smiles provocatively at Cary Grant. Her lips form the words "I never make love on an empty stomach." But on the soundtrack, the audience hears, "I never *discuss* love on an empty stomach." This line from the movie *North by Northwest* is just one of hundreds of bits of dialogue Alfred Hitchcock sacrificed to the censors of the Motion Picture Production Code over the course of his career.

The Production Code shackled creativity in American movies for most of Alfred Hitchcock's productive years. The Code contained nearly four thousand words, with an initial sentence that promised, "No picture shall be produced which will lower the moral standards of those who see it." It was adopted by motion picture producers in 1930 to ward off government intervention and convince religious groups alarmed by screen sex and violence that the industry was capable of policing itself. In the early years of the Code, there was virtually no self-policing and little changed on American screens. By 1934, however, fear of federal censorship and pressure from the Catholic Legion of Decency caused producers to turn the keys to the Production Code office over to Joseph I. Breen, a sanctimonious, anti-Semitic Irish Catholic who would demand strict adherence to the Code and ensure that no picture could be released in the United States without his office's Seal of Approval.

On average, Breen and the Production Code office requested 22.5 changes to each of Hitchcock's American films. These changes ranged from the mundane to the mind-boggling, covering a wide variety of topics, including dialogue (no profanity), settings (no scenes in bathrooms), costumes (no cleavage), characters (no loose women), plots (no unpunished evildoers), and relations between the sexes (no extramarital affairs). Because Code approval was required for US release, the requested changes, which rarely improved the finished films, required Hitchcock's full attention and at least as much cleverness and ingenuity as he put into the movies themselves. According to Hitchcock biographer Patrick McGilligan, the director bucked the Code "with exceptional tenacity in the American phase of his career, pushing the boundaries of sex and violence in his films. And he usually did so deviously, rather than by direct confrontation, stalling, surrendering by degrees, swapping off one cherished transgression for another."[1]

Hitchcock gleefully layered many of his scripts with outlandish dialogue or plot points he knew to be objectionable so that they could be used as sacrificial lambs to appease censors and convince them to allow images that might otherwise have been cut. The director claimed that he actually enjoyed these negotiations, likening them to the "thrill of competitive horse trading."[2] In this give-and-take, Hitchcock was willing to surrender certain elements of his films while taking great pains to protect others. The first element to go was dialogue, followed, if necessary, by logic, plot, character, color, and the musical score. All of these would be sacrificed to protect the visual imagery that he viewed as the foundation of his movies. "I like to have the whole film complete in my mind," he wrote in an early piece, "Some Aspects of Direction." "I like to have the whole story down, shot by shot, on paper . . . before I ever enter the studio."[3]

Dialogue was much less important to Hitchcock than other elements of his films. "I have strong feelings about the art of cinema, but I don't believe in dialogue," he told interviewers. "I create suspense, and I'm trying to play with the audience like a cat with a mouse."[4] Many of Hitchcock's screenwriters were adept at creating racy dialogue, and the Production Code's reviews of his finished scripts were littered with requests that this line or that observation be omitted. These requests became fodder at the negotiating table. While Hitchcock might protect a few of the sharper quips, he was always willing to sacrifice large segments of dialogue, some of which may have been made deliberately objectionable so that they could be used as trading chips. Sometimes, as in the case of the *North by Northwest* byplay between Eva Marie Saint and Cary Grant, these sacrifices were evident on the screen.

Plot and logic were the next sacrifices Hitchcock was willing to make to preserve his precious imagery. "Nothing in the world is as dull as logic," he told interviewers. "There's something more important than logic, and that's imagination. If we insist on always thinking in logical terms, we will never use our imagination."[5] When an actress in *To Catch a Thief* asked Hitchcock who had thrown her film father over a balustrade into the sea, the director, with a typical disdain for plot details, told her, "It doesn't mat-

A FEW FORBIDDEN WORDS

"hell," "damn," "damned," "you ass," "harpie," "Oh, my God," "lived in hell," "lovers," "tramp," "for God's sake," "Lord," "proposition," "lovely," "oh, Lord," "assignation," "bastards," "tomcat," "louse," "my dear boy," "connubial," "cripes," "lecherous," "I wish to God," "sissy," "jeeze," "mistress," "impotent," "thingummy," "Fire!" "So help me God," "disorderly house," "punks," "Oh, you go and phone yourself," "frustration," "son of a ——," "bazooms," "fanny," "libido," "slut," "lousy," "stinks," "arsenic," "cyanide"

A partial list of words and phrases excised from Hitchcock films. The words *arsenic* and *cyanide* were taboo because censors feared they might give explicit aid to potential poisoners. The generic word *poison* was substituted for these specific designations. (Courtesy of Jerry Ohlinger.)

ter."[6] Although critics sometimes complained about the lack of logic in certain Hitchcock films, audiences never seemed to mind. "Hitchcock's thrillers were full of holes," Pauline Kael wrote, "but you were having too good a time to worry about them."[7]

Hitchcock was drawn to the built-in suspense of plots involving a wrongly accused man and used this theme in several films. But he was sometimes forced to use it because the Production Code would not allow criminals to escape punishment. As a result, Hitchcock's scripts sometimes absolved protagonists of crimes that they had committed in the source material, often with no regard for character consistency. Thus the script of *Rebecca* made Laurence Olivier's Maxim de Winter innocent of murdering the wife he had killed in Daphne du Maurier's novel, and the script of *Suspicion* rewrote Cary Grant's Johnnie Aysgarth so that the self-absorbed playboy did not commit any of the murders attributed to him in the book on which the film was based.

Hitchcock also made other, less obvious, accommodations to slip his cherished images past the censors. To downplay the violence in *Psycho,* he "deliberately made it in black and white to avoid showing red blood running down a bathtub."[8] When the Code office objected to the fireworks-lit seduction scene between Cary Grant and Grace Kelly in *To Catch a Thief,* Hitchcock asked the film's composer, who had originally backed the sensuous scene with a "smoky tenor saxophone," to rescore the scene "in a more conventional way, like with strings."[9] The director then managed to convince the censors that the resulting music tempered the lustful nature of the images enough to win the Code's Seal of Approval.

Like a child testing the boundaries set by his parents, Hitchcock delighted in seeing how far he could go while staying strictly within the confines set by the Production Code. The kissing scene between Cary Grant and Ingrid Bergman in *Notorious* was precisely constructed to skate around the Code's rules against "excessive lustful kissing." Unofficially, Code administrators were thought to judge kisses to be "excessively lustful" when lips were locked for more than three seconds. In *Notorious,* Grant and Bergman begin embracing on the balcony of Bergman's Rio apartment. The two lovers kiss for just under three seconds, then nuzzle, exchange short butterfly kisses, whisper in each other's ears, and move indoors without ever leaving each other's arms. The scene occupies two minutes and forty seconds, and the actors exchange at least twenty kisses —but none of them exceeds the three-second limit that would plunge them into lasciviousness.

The shower scene in *Psycho,* one of the most memorable scenes in movie history, affords another example of Hitchcock staying within strict Code limits while making a powerful cinematic statement. Like a magician, he arranged seventy-eight pieces of film in a harrowing forty-five-second, now-you-see-it, now-you-don't sequence of unparalleled violence.[10] But what did he really show the audience? Bare breasts? Pierced skin? A bloody knife? Not at all. Images flew by so fast that censors disagreed on what they were seeing. Those who initially thought they saw nudity didn't see it on the next viewing. The overall impact was devastating, but the individual images were well within Code guidelines. The Code office ultimately passed the sequence after Hitchcock agreed to cut the closing shot, in which the overhead camera pulled away from the body draped over the edge of the bathtub, briefly exposing a bare buttock.

As François Truffaut observed, Hitchcock proceeded by indirection, filming scenes of love as if they were scenes of murder, and scenes of murder as if they were scenes of love.[11] In dealing with the Production Code, the director feinted like a conjuror, showing the censors he had nothing up his sleeves and listening politely to their objections to the finished script. Then he shot the film he wanted to shoot the way he wanted to shoot it, all the while lulling the censors with soothing promises until it was time to show them the finished film. Finally, he would line up his trading chips, giving in with a great show of reluctance even when surrendering a line of dialogue or plot point that he never really intended to use. While this ritual actually improved the final film on rare occasions, for the most part it was a monumental waste of the director's time.

Hitchcock was not the only filmmaker to buck the Production Code. Every producer and director in the United States felt the pinch of the Code, and a few, like Billy Wilder and Otto Preminger, consistently pushed the boundaries of censorship, addressing such forbidden topics as alcoholism, drug abuse, homosexuality, rape, prostitution, cross-dressing, and adultery. This book chronicles the rise and fall of the Breen office, noting the work of other directors when their films produced a change in the Code or its administration. For the most part, however, the chapters focus on Hitchcock and his strategies for dealing with all forms of censorship.

Hitchcock was well versed in the art of sidestepping censorship by the time he reached America. His early films in Britain were made under the watchful eye of the British Board of Film Censors, whose members were more attuned to political and social issues than the scenes of sex and violence that occupied Production Code watchdogs. In America, the Production Code censors were joined by a variety of organizations with the power to make demands on the director, including the Office of War Information (on *Lifeboat*), the Humane Association (on *The Birds* and *Marnie*), and the Department of the Interior (on *North by Northwest*). This book also chronicles the demands of each of these ancillary watchdogs.

Once Hitchcock's films had been completed and submitted for distribution, they ran the gauntlet of scissor-wielding scolds in a variety of cities, states, and foreign countries. Ireland banned *Notorious* altogether, India cut a scene of Grace Kelly sitting on James Stewart's lap from *Rear Window,* Maryland snipped Bruno's strangling of Guy's wife from *Strangers on a Train,* and England cut portions of the murder of the U-boat captain from *Lifeboat.* Because these post-production cuts were usually made without consulting the director or his producers and had no impact on the design or creation of specific films, no attempt has been made to catalogue them extensively. Such cuts were scattered and voluminous, and although this book cites a few, for the most part they have been ignored because they had no measurable impact on Hitchcock's decision making.

A few book-length studies of Hitchcock's individual films (including *Rear Window, Psycho, Vertigo, The Birds,* and *Marnie*) have addressed the issue of censorship of these films, but no book has tracked the impact of censorship on each of the director's films. This work traces the development of film censorship in Britain and America and details the censors' objections to Hitchcock's thrillers on a film-by-film basis, documenting the director's reactions as his prominence rose and he bargained with bluenoses, giving up some Code-stretching elements and slipping in others to produce a lifetime of memorable moments.

1

The Code and the Censors

A scene from Cecil B. DeMille's *Sign of the Cross,* a film that outraged the Catholic clergy and helped to establish the Legion of Decency and strengthen the Production Code. (Courtesy of Photofest.)

1

Origins of the Code

The Motion Picture Production Code was a self-inflicted wound that took over thirty-four years to heal, affecting more than eleven thousand films, weakening most and leaving only a few stronger for the encounter.

The origins of the Production Code were grounded in a 1915 Supreme Court decision that motion pictures were "a business pure and simple," and thus not protected speech under the Constitution. This decision paved the way for censors at all levels, and by 1921 five states—Pennsylvania, Ohio, Maryland, Kansas, and New York—had established censorship boards to assuage growing fears that the immorality emanating from Hollywood might infect society at large. These states, which controlled nearly 30 percent of the ticket sales in the United States, had the power to ban individual films or snip selected scenes at will. They wielded this power with little oversight or consistency. Women could not smoke on-screen in Kansas, but they could in Ohio. Pregnant women could not appear on-screen in Pennsylvania, but they could in New York.[1] When the *New York Times* asked the first chairman of New York's Board of Censors, George H. Cobb, what principles of censorship the board followed, he replied, "So far I haven't been able to find any."[2] A few major cities also established their own censorship boards, so that a well-traveled film could experience enough cuts to render it incoherent.

Fearing that they might eventually have to march to the tune of forty-eight different state drummers, and possibly follow a conductor at the federal level, the studio heads countered the move to state censorship boards early in 1922 by forming the Motion Picture Producers and Distributors of America (MPPDA—the forerunner of today's Motion Picture Association of America). To lead the MPPDA, the studio heads selected Will Hays, who had successfully run Warren G. Harding's 1920 presidential campaign and been rewarded with the job of postmaster general. The studio heads, who were predominately Jewish, understood that in 1920s America they needed a front man like Hays, "folksy and Protestant, a Republican from Indiana, who could speak the language of the American heartland."[3] Hays's primary jobs were to stem the rising tide of state and local censorship boards and to improve the public image of the movie industry.

Hays succeeded admirably at the first of these jobs. Of the thirty-seven states with censorship bills pending before he took over as head of the MPPDA, only one, Virginia, succeeded in creating a censorship board. In Massachusetts, the bill to create such a board passed the state legislature but needed the approval of a public referendum to become law. Prior to the referendum in November 1922, Hays sent lobbyists to small-town papers and encouraged exhibitors to screen slides between movies encouraging viewers to vote against the censorship proposal. As a result, the bill was defeated by a walloping 2.5 to 1 majority.

Massachusetts eventually sidestepped the results of the vote by invoking "blue laws" that forbade immoral undertakings on the Sabbath, empowering state officials to act as censors on Sundays. Since exhibitors weren't likely to show one version of a film on Sunday and another on the other six days of the week, Massachusetts effectively became the seventh state to create a censorship board. But the state's overwhelming public vote against censorship was not lost on other states considering censorship legislation.

Hays attempted to polish the public face of the film industry in a number of ways. He encouraged studios to incorporate a morals clause in their actors' contracts, hoping to avoid scandals like the Fatty Arbuckle rape trials and the William Desmond Taylor murder case, which ruined the careers of established stars in the early 1920s. To avoid future scandals, he issued what Hollywood unofficially called "The Doom Book," a list of 117 actors deemed unfit for movie roles by reason of their personal involvement with drug use, illicit sex, or other licentious behavior.[4] To convince state agencies, civic groups, and religious organizations that they didn't have to police the industry because the industry would police itself, Hays adopted and publicized a list of thirteen screen no-nos, shown in the inset.[5]

Hays also created a Public Relations Committee (later the Studio Relations Committee) under Colonel Jason S. Joy to review plays and novels considered for screen adaptation and advise studios on those elements likely to offend local censor boards. However, there was no mechanism forcing studios to submit materials for review or requiring them to follow

Hays's Thirteen Points

Exclude Pictures Which

1. Deal with sex in an improper manner;
2. Are based on white slavery;
3. Make vice attractive;
4. Exhibit nakedness;
5. Have prolonged passionate love scenes;
6. Are predominately concerned with the underworld;
7. Make gambling and drunkenness attractive;
8. Might instruct the weak in methods of committing crime;
9. Ridicule public officials;
10. Offend religious beliefs;
11. Emphasize violence;
12. Portray vulgar postures and gestures; and
13. Use salacious subtitles or advertising.

A 1922 cartoon depicting Will Hays coming to the rescue of the motion picture industry.

the committee's recommendations. As a result, studios began withholding materials and ignoring the committee's recommendations on material that they did submit.[6] So, operating behind the shield of their burnished public image, the major studios quickly returned to business as usual, and films became more and more daring as the 1920s progressed. The introduction of sound in 1927 added another dimension to the movies and presented another potential avenue that could threaten public morality.

As films grew racier, complaints from civic groups and church organizations increased, as did threats of legislation. Sensing the need for tighter controls, Hays sent Joy to meet with the heads of state censorship boards to learn what elements were most often cut from the films they reviewed. Hays used this information to expand his list of thirteen screen no-nos to a broader program of thirty-six guidelines consisting of eleven "Don'ts" and twenty-five "Be Carefuls" (see appendix). The list of "Don'ts" included profanity, nudity, drug trafficking, sex perversion, and willful offense to any nation, race, or creed. In addition, movie makers were admonished to "be careful" when dealing with such issues as the flag, international relations, firearms, robbery, brutality, murder techniques, smuggling methods, the execution of death penalties, sympathy for criminals, sedition, cruelty to children or animals, rape, men and women in bed together, seduction, surgical operations, drug use, law enforcement, and excessive or lustful kissing.

With the revamped guidelines adopted by the MPPDA, the purview of the Studio Relations Committee was expanded from a review of potential source material to a review of scripts and finished films. But Hays's efforts were doomed to fail. The committee's function remained advisory, and studios were under no obligation to follow its advice. Nor were they under any obligation to submit films for review. By the close of the 1920s, barely half of the MPPDA members' scripts were submitted for review, and only 20 percent of finished films were submitted.[7] Those producers who followed the committee's suggestions lost customers to studios offering racier fare. Universal producer Carl Laemmle complained that his company was "losing business because of its reputation for 'namby-pamby' movies."[8] It's hardly surprising, then, that films continued to grow hotter and hotter. In 1929, Joan Crawford doffed her skirt for a sweaty Charleston in *Our Dancing Daughters*, and Renee Adoree swam nude in *Mating Call.*

As the movies heated up, so did cries for government oversight. In 1929, William Randolph Hearst directed his newspaper empire to push for federal censorship, and Iowa senator Smith W. Brookhart introduced a bill to place the movie industry under the direct control of the Federal Trade Commission.

Martin S. Quigley was another man who was concerned over the rampant immorality in motion pictures. A devout Catholic and publisher of film trade journals, Quigley had long editorialized against screen immorality and enlisted the aid of a Jesuit priest, Daniel J. Lord, to develop "a reliable yardstick and document of guidance to the appreciation of American mores and American decency." Recognizing that Hays's helter-skelter lists of "Don'ts" and "Be Carefuls" were nothing more than "isolated statements, unconnected [and] in no way complete or clear," Quigley and Lord created a code that included not only rules and regulations but a unifying philosophy.[9]

Their Code contained four thousand words, divided into two sections: a philosophical justification entitled "General Principles" followed by a series of guidelines called "Working Principles." In an abbreviated addendum designed for easy consumption by studio heads, the General Principles were summarized as follows:

1. No picture should lower the moral standards of those who see it.
2. Law, natural or divine, must not be belittled, ridiculed, nor must a sentiment be created against it.
3. As far as possible, life should not be misrepresented, at least not in such a way as to place in the mind of youth false values on life.

The Code's Working Principles contained a series of positive and negative injunctions that were far more comprehensive and logically arranged than the "Don'ts" and "Be Carefuls" of the Hays office. For example, there were specific instructions covering "Details of Plot, Episodes, and Treatment"; detailed rules regarding such plot devices as sex, passion, seduction, and murder; and extensive guidelines on such "flashpoints as vulgarity, obscenity, costume, dancing, locations, and religion." The Code, written while Prohibition was still the law of the land, contained the provision "The use of liquor in American life, when not required by the plot or proper characterization, will not be shown," a stipulation that continued to be observed long after Prohibition had been repealed.

Will Hays saw the Code as a godsend, and the MPPDA moguls signed onto its provisions in February 1930. This signing led historian Francis G. Couvares to observe that the movies were "an industry largely financed by Protestant bankers, operated by Jewish studio executives, and policed by Catholic bureaucrats."[10] Although the authors of the Code were indeed Catholic, the Code itself was largely nondenominational. However, the Catholic concepts of punishment and redemption did find their way into the practical interpretation of the Code. Sin could be shown on-screen, but only if the perpetrators repented or were appropriately punished.

A number of filmmakers took immediate advantage of this loophole. The early 1930s brought a rash of gangster films (*Little Caesar, Public*

Enemy, Scarface, I Was a Fugitive from a Chain Gang) that ran roughshod over Code admonitions against brutal killings, excessive liquor use, unrestricted use of firearms, and the depiction of crimes "in such a way as to throw sympathy with the crime as against law and justice." Gangsters were shown living well, drinking heavily, and sporting mistresses before being dispatched in a hail of bullets in the final scenes.

Cecil B. DeMille was a master at baiting the audience with a hundred minutes of titillation before offering five minutes of punishment before the closing credits. In his 1932 biblical epic, *The Sign of the Cross,* he filled the screen with pagan sacrifices of scantily clad Christians, Roman orgies, and Claudette Colbert naked in a bath of ass's milk before getting around to the burning of Rome. This movie drove a wedge between Hollywood and an outraged Catholic hierarchy that perceived, not without reason, that the movie community was going about its business as if the Production Code did not exist.

And as a practical matter it didn't, because the Studio Relations Committee, which continued to review scripts, had no real power. On the rare occasions (ten times in three and a half years following Code approval) when the committee refused to approve a film, an appeals jury would overturn its verdict. This result was hardly surprising since the jury pool consisted of three producers from competing studios who expected (and received) lenient treatment when their own films flunked the review process. So even though censorship guidelines had grown from the 385 words of Hays's original thirteen points to nearly 4,000 words, movies kept getting hotter and hotter.

In 1932 an indifferent gangster film starring George Raft introduced the movie public to a scene-stealing sex bomb who would blight the lives of censors for the rest of the decade. Mae West was an instant sensation in the film *Night After Night,* and Paramount soon announced it would feature her in the film version of *Diamond Lil,* a stage play laden with double and single entendres she had written. One of her earlier Broadway plays, with the truth-in-advertising title *Sex,* had landed her in jail for ten days on charges of "obscenity and corrupting the morals of youth." Will Hays had personally placed *Diamond Lil* on the Studio Relations Committee's list of unfilmable properties.

Diamond Lil turned out to be eminently filmable, with a new title, *She Done Him Wrong,* and the heroine Diamond Lil renamed Lady Lou. In

The first of a series of Mae West Code busters.

addition to these name changes, the Studio Relations Committee had also managed to snip a few lines of ribald dialogue, but not enough to disguise the film's heritage or keep it from being a resounding success. As Lady Lou, Mae West still boasted that she was "one of the finest women that ever walked the streets," and invited a young Cary Grant, acting in only his third film, to "come up sometime and see me." She also sang songs with such suggestive titles as "A Guy What Takes His Time" and "Easy Rider." The film clearly made hash of the Code admonitions that "impure love must not be presented as attractive and beautiful . . . must not be treated as material for laughter, and must not be made to seem right and permissible." The reactions of the Code's creators were predictable. Martin Quigley called it a "wash-out," and Father Daniel Lord, incensed that everyone knew that *She Done Him Wrong* was just "the filthy *Diamond Lil* slipping by under a new name," warned that "producers who decided to 'shoot the works' would face a 'day of reckoning.'"[11]

Paramount's day of reckoning was not quite what Lord had expected. An investment of $200,000 delivered $2 million in domestic business and another $1 million from international releases. It was almost enough to put the studio, which had been hit hard by the Depression, into the black.[12] The film would also be judged an artistic success, being nominated for the Academy Award for Best Picture. The studio wasted no time in capitalizing on this success, quickly releasing *I'm No Angel,* in which West once again invites Cary Grant, "Come up and see me," and sneaks one of her most famous lines, "When I'm good, I'm very good, but when I'm bad, I'm better," past the censors. Still incensed, Father Lord warned Hays that the "motion picture industry will be very unwise to incur the militant enmity of the Catholic hierarchy."[13]

By 1933, increasing dissatisfaction with the perceived immorality of Hollywood films manifested itself on several fronts. Father Lord's threat of action from the Catholic hierarchy found a voice in a New York speech by the pope's newly appointed representative in America, Monsignor Amleto Giovanni Cicognani, in which he called for Catholic bishops and priests to undertake "a united and vigorous campaign for the purification of the cinema, which has become a deadly menace to morals."[14] This led to the formation of the Legion of Decency, which applied its own rating system to films, assigning an A to films that were morally unobjectionable, a B to films which were morally objectionable in part, and a C to condemned films. Cincinnati archbishop John McNicholas composed a membership pledge for the Legion, which read in part:

> I wish to join the Legion of Decency, which condemns vile and unwholesome moving pictures. I unite with all who protest against them as a grave menace to youth, to home life, to country and to

> religion. I condemn absolutely those salacious motion pictures which, with other degrading agencies, are corrupting public morals and promoting a sex mania in our land. . . . Considering these evils, I hereby promise to remain away from all motion pictures except those which do not offend decency and Christian morality.

This pledge was eventually administered once a year at mass, and Catholics taking the pledge were enjoined to avoid C-rated films under pain of sin.

Although Catholics constituted little more than 16 percent of the nation's population, the threat of boycott caught the attention of the film industry. In 1934, the Detroit branch of the Legion of Decency condemned sixty-three films, forty-three of which had been passed by the Studio Relations Committee. The Chicago branch matched that with sixty-three condemned films, and Father Lord started listing five condemned films a month in his magazine *Queen's Work*. In Philadelphia, box-office receipts dropped 40 percent when Cardinal Dougherty asked parishioners to stop going to the movies altogether.[15]

The Legion of Decency wasn't the only problem facing the major studios in the early 1930s. Between 1928 and 1932, a group of social scientists funded by the philanthropic Payne Fund had been conducting an extensive study of the impact of motion pictures on children. These studies produced twelve volumes of surveys, graphs, figures, anecdotes, and jargon documenting the extent of the movie audience and the role of celluloid imagery in warping young minds. In 1933, journalist Henry James Forman summarized these findings in a single volume. *Our Movie Made Children* confirmed the gut-level suspicion that the "movies burrowed like termites into impressionable juvenile minds: girls took to rouge and tobacco, boys to backtalk and violence, and all to disrespect and deviance."[16] Forman likened Hollywood to a toxic water source that, if unregulated and unfiltered, was "extremely likely to create a haphazard, promiscuous, and undesirable national consciousness."[17]

A force even more dangerous to moviemakers than the Legion of Decency and the Payne studies surfaced in 1933 with the inauguration of Franklin Delano Roosevelt. In his first hundred days in office, FDR introduced his New Deal, creating a number of federal agencies designed to stem the tide of the Great Depression. One of these agencies was the

National Recovery Administration (NRA), which called for government-business cooperation to spur economic recovery. Along with industry and agriculture, the amusement trades fell within the purview of the NRA and raised the specter long feared by the studio heads: federal censorship.

Threatened on three sides—by the Catholic hierarchy, the New Dealers, and the Payne studies—movie moguls cast about for a scapegoat. Will Hays was suddenly faced with the loss of his $100,000 a year salary as the moguls pointed fingers at him, wondering why he hadn't compelled producers to comply with the rulings of the Studio Relations Committee. In truth, Hays was not ideally suited for the job of chief censor. A lawyer by training, he was more of a mediator. And Colonel Jason Joy, Hays's choice to head the committee, wasn't cut out to be a censor either. A movie fan, he relaxed standards for films he felt were worthwhile and prestigious, like *All Quiet on the Western Front* and *A Farewell to Arms.*

Under pressure from the Catholic hierarchy and the federal government, Hays finally found the right man for the job. And it wasn't all that hard. In December 1933, he made his personal assistant, Joseph Ignatius Breen, the acting head of the Studio Relations Committee.

Breen had been lobbying for this job, both overtly and covertly, ever since Hays hired him in 1931. A devout Catholic, he was a good friend of Martin Quigley and enjoyed the confidence of the Church hierarchy. These connections, along with his public relations background, were the chief reasons Hays had chosen him to be his personal assistant. Unbeknownst to Hays, Breen and Quigley had helped to create the current crisis by inserting remarks condemning the movies' "incalculable influence for evil" in the speech by Monsignor Cicognani that had preceded the formation of the Legion of Decency. Breen and Quigley both hoped that focusing the attention of the Catholic Church on movie decadence would force the studio heads to give the Production Code teeth.[18]

Not long after his appointment as acting head of the Studio Relations Committee, Breen met with the NRA divisional administrator assigned to regulate the motion picture industry, a loyal New Dealer named Sol A. Rosenblatt. Although Rosenblatt had speculated that the Production Code could be administered more effectively as part of the NRA, Breen convinced him that censorship should be a matter of Hollywood self-regulation rather than Washington edict, and that Joseph Ignatius Breen was just the man to clean up the movies. Within a week of the meeting, Breen's appointment as committee head became official and he was publicly endorsed by Rosenblatt.

Within the next two months, Breen rejected six films, as many as the committee had rejected in the previous three years. In four of these cases, producers bowed to Breen's objections and made the corrections he requested. In the other two, the producers appealed and the back-scratching appeals board overruled Breen.

The producer of one of the appealed films, a Fox musical with the suggestive title *Bottoms Up,* ultimately elected to remain on Breen's good side by cutting the "vulgar" scene that had led to the film's condemnation. The other film was *Queen Christina,* starring Greta Garbo, and Breen could get no cooperation from producer Walter Wanger or director Rouben Mamoulian. Breen particularly objected to a scene depicting a sexy bedroom tryst between Garbo's Queen Christina and the Spanish envoy, played by John Gilbert. The sieve-like nature of the existing review system was amply demonstrated by the fact that even before the rubber-stamp appeals jury of three producers had handed down its decision, *Queen Christina* was playing a roadshow engagement at the Astor Theater in New York.[19]

Although Breen had won five of his first six battles, he was a sore winner, grousing about the one that got away. A rabid anti-Semite, he couldn't imagine that any good could ever come of a voluntary system overseen by the studio heads, who were mostly Jewish—or "scum" and "lice," as he called them in his private correspondence.[20] He lobbied his boss, Will Hays, to revamp and strengthen the Studio Relations Committee, claiming, "It was a Board, and . . . all boards are long, and narrow, and wooden."[21]

Breen's bid to strengthen the Production Code couldn't have come at a better time. Hollywood was reeling from the prospect of a federal takeover, and Catholic boycotts in major cities were affecting box-office receipts already suffering from the effects of the Great Depression. (In 1932, only two of the eight major studios, Columbia and MGM, turned a profit.) Worse, favorable news coverage of the boycotts had Protestants and Jews threatening to join the Catholics.

Recognizing that boycotts could not last forever, the Catholic Bishops Committee on Motion Pictures scheduled a special conference to meet in Cincinnati on June 21, 1934, to consider the next step in its campaign. The chair of the committee, Archbishop John McNicholas, the author of the

Legion of Decency pledge, asked Breen's old friend Martin Quigley to develop a program of self-regulation for the committee to consider. Quigley believed that the best long-term solution to the problem was not boycotts, blacklists, or federal regulation, but rather strict enforcement of the Production Code. With Breen's help, he set out to develop such a program.

On June 13, 1934, a week before the Catholic bishops were to meet, Breen and Quigley presented the MPPDA Board with a program for empowering the Production Code. Under their plan, Breen's Studio Relations Committee would morph into a strengthened Production Code Administration. Studio participation would no longer be voluntary. Every major studio and independent producer would be required to submit both scripts and finished films to a rigorous review process overseen by Breen. Films passing muster would be awarded a Seal of Approval. Without this seal, films could not be exhibited. Any producer violating these rules and procedures would incur a fine of $25,000. (At the time, the average film cost $375,000 to produce.) To ensure that the Production Code's rulings would be observed, the appeals process would be taken out of the back-scratching hands of Hollywood producers and transferred to the executives on the MPPDA Board in New York.

The MPPDA Board approved Breen's and Quigley's vision and sent the two men to Cincinnati to sell it to the Catholic bishops, with permission to give the bishops "anything they want" in return (they hoped) for stopping the boycotts and blacklists.[22]

With Mae West's latest release, tentatively titled *It Ain't No Sin,* in the headlines, Protestants and Jews lining up to join the Catholics at the barricades, and the New Dealers threatening to take control from Washington, the bishops clearly had the upper hand. Breen eventually sweetened the deal by promising that older films he had judged to be offensive, like *A Farewell to Arms* and *She Done Him Wrong,* would be pulled from distribution and subjected to review under the new guidelines.

A few of the bishops could not bring themselves to trust Hollywood, but Archbishop McNicholas was convinced of Breen and Quigley's sincerity and their ability to enforce the Production Code. At the close of the Cincinnati conference, the bishops issued a statement expressing their confidence that forming the Production Code Administration under Breen and scrapping the producers' appeal board would "materially and constructively influence the character of screen entertainment."[23] Believing that the bishops' acquiescence meant the end of boycotts and Legion of Decency blacklists, the MPPDA Board sent instructions to the studio heads to do nothing that might rile the Catholic hierarchy. "If Joe Breen tells you to change a picture, you do what he tells you," Henry Warner wired the Warner Bros. Hollywood offices. "If anyone fails to do this, and this goes for my brother—he's fired."[24]

In the eyes of the MPPDA, the New Dealers, and the Catholic Church, Breen had become an indispensable man. Less than six months after assuming control of the hapless Studio Relations Committee, he had been granted the final cut on every movie coming out of Hollywood.

Well, not quite the final cut. The *final* final cut was reserved for the seven state censorship boards and numerous local boards that still had the power to blacklist entire movies or snip offending scenes from films approved by Breen and the Production Code Administration. So even the most powerful censors had censors, after the fashion of the Victorian poem "A Budget of Paradoxes":

> Great fleas have little fleas upon their backs to bite 'em.
> And little fleas have lesser fleas, and so ad infinitum.[25]

Most of the state and local censors operated with little guidance and more fervor than good sense. It was like turning a group of fanatics loose in a museum with paints and a set of tools and watching while they smeared black paint over the breasts of Goya's *Naked Maja* and chiseled the privates off Michelangelo's *David.*

Even after Archbishop McNicholas and the Catholic Bishops Committee on Motion Pictures approved the revamped Production Code Administration, the Legion of Decency remained a stumbling block for Hollywood. A powerful group of bishops continued to mistrust Hollywood and refused to abandon their own programs. The Philadelphia boycott continued, and Legion of Decency boards in other cities ramped up their censorship efforts. Unfortunately, there was little coordination between dioceses on what constituted grounds for condemnation. While Detroit Catholics were forbidden to see William Powell and Myrna Loy in MGM's smash comedy *The Thin Man,* Chicago's review board gave it a B (morally objectionable in part), rating it suitable for adults. *Of Human Bondage,* passed by Breen after RKO substituted tuberculosis for venereal disease in the film version, was condemned in Detroit, Pittsburgh, Omaha, and Chicago, but Catholics elsewhere were able to see it without risking the loss of their immortal souls. This inconsistency proved confusing to Catholics, and even embarrassing, as when a few dioceses condemned *Tarzan and His Mate* because a couple of priests thought Maureen O'Sullivan's costumes as Jane were too skimpy.

The Legion of Decency solved the difficulty of geographic differences at the bishops' meeting in 1935 by consolidating the production of a single rating list in their New York office. This did not satisfy Hays and Breen, who had thought that the 1934 Cincinnati meeting would lead to an end of the Legion's rating system. When their cries of "foul" fell on deaf ears, Hays set out to determine how much harm these ratings were doing to the motion picture industry by sending an emissary to interview newspaper editors, movie critics, theater owners, and local politicians in twenty American cities. He found that the Legion's listings had a negative impact on box-office receipts only in Philadelphia. In the other nineteen cities, whenever a film was banned by the Legion, ticket sales went up, even among Catholics.[26]

Hays and Breen did not publicize these findings. It was in their interest to cast themselves as industry saviors and the last line of defense against Legion boycotts and blacklists, and the two men did not want the studio heads to know that they had folded in the face of a weaker hand when they had assented to the creation of the Production Code Administration.

Even though the Legion of Decency was a less formidable adversary than was initially believed, Hays and Breen did deserve credit for eventually bringing the threat of boycotts and blacklists under control. At the same time, they also managed to take credit for a stroke of good luck that was beyond their control. In 1932 and 1933, with the national economy in the throes of the Great Depression, movie industry losses had totaled $60 million. In 1934, the year the Production Code Administration was created, the economy began to recover, and Hollywood recorded a modest profit of $9 million. In 1935, the economy continued to improve and profits totaled $30 million. While it was clear that the increase in ticket sales could be traced to the improving economy, Hays and Breen deliberately confused correlation with causation and claimed the attendance surge was proof that the public wanted cleaner films.[27] With profits increasing, studio heads saw no reason to question this analysis, and so for better (sometimes) or for worse (mostly), the Production Code Administration remained a powerful force in Hollywood for the next thirty-four years.

From the beginning, the Production Code Administration received mixed reviews in the press. While many newspapers applauded attempts to clean up the screen, other critics deplored the watering down of films and ridiculed the more outlandish decisions of censors, such as the banning of *Tarzan and His Mate.* Critic Morris Ernst, commenting in 1937 on the "early fruits of the work of the Production Code Administration," wrote that "more inane, saccharine, and spineless pictures have come from Hollywood since the setting up of the Administration than ever before."[28] Another observer wrote that "from July 1934 Hollywood films took on a decidedly conservative point of view for moral issues: Divorce was a sin, adultery was punished, 'modern living' was painted in negative terms, and virtue was rewarded. . . . Social problems might be raised, but controversial solutions were rarely offered."[29]

One of the first films to be reviewed by Breen as head of the Production Code Administration was Mae West's *It Ain't No Sin.* Breen had originally reviewed the film script under the aegis of the Studio Relations Committee and submitted many suggestions, most of which were ignored. Now, with the power of the Seal of Approval behind him, Breen enforced many of his earlier suggestions, expunging the heroine's criminal past, marrying her off in the final scene, and changing the film's ungrammatical, suggestive title to *Belle of the Nineties.*

Mae West was one of the first casualties of the newly empowered Production Code. After being the highest paid woman in the United States in 1935, with earnings of $481,000, her Code-tamed films declined in popularity and by the end of the decade she was effectively out of the movies, having been replaced as the top box-office draw by child star Shirley Temple.[30]

2

Censors at Work

Armed with the ability to deny distribution to Production Code transgressors, Joe Breen set up shop in July 1934 at 5504 North Hollywood Boulevard, on the fourth floor of the building housing the MPPDA, and began expanding his staff. He handpicked seven reviewers, all men, to help him apply Code stipulations at each step of film production. The policy of hiring only men as reviewers continued throughout the life of the Code. One of the later Code reviewers suggested that one reason was Breen's feeling that since "ninety percent of our dealings, or even more than that, were with men, that we should have men on the staff."[1] Perhaps another reason was Breen's own fondness for loose language. Although he was fiercely efficient in eliminating "hells" and "damns" from film scripts, he often laced his own language with vulgarities when talking to recalcitrant studio heads, who were known to have colorful vocabularies of their own. Nobody had to worry about muzzling himself if there were only men in the room.

Breen and his seven reviewers used the four-thousand-word Code to judge the suitability of proposed properties, story treatments, final screenplays, and finished films. These words stipulated, among other things, that evil should not be made to appear attractive; that crime and criminals must not be shown in a sympathetic light; that American institutions would not be ridiculed; that courts could not be presented as unjust; that marriage was sacred; that adultery could never be justified; that nudity, suggestive costumes, unseemly "movement of breasts," and "excessive and lustful kissing" were forbidden; that religion could not be ridiculed; that ministers of religion could not be used as villains; that methods of committing crimes should not be shown in detail; and that films must always reflect "goodness, honor, innocence, purity, and honesty."

The Code office's interpretations of these guidelines gave rise to a number of myths both inside and outside the industry. It was generally believed that the admonition against "excessive and lustful kissing" meant that lips could not be locked for more than three seconds. (One rumor set the limit at ten seconds.) Not so, according to former Code reviewer Albert Van Schmus, who says no such rule existed, that Code officials did not use stopwatches to time kisses, and that the point at which kisses crossed the line to become "excessive and lustful" was left to the judgment of individual reviewers. Another Code reviewer, Jack Vizzard, who had heard the rumor that kisses passed from chaste to lustful at the ten-second mark, dubbed the mistaken idea that Code officials used stopwatches to measure lust "the rail bird myth" because it evoked the image of clockers leaning on racetrack railings.[2]

In his memoir *See No Evil,* Vizzard also exploded a few other Code myths, such as the requirement that married couples must occupy twin beds and that couples sharing a bed must have at least one foot on the floor at all times. While these guidelines may have been invoked in individual instances, perhaps even in many instances, they were not hard-and-fast rules.[3]

The Breen office insinuated itself into every phase of movie production, offering advice on book and play acquisitions, reviewing story treatments, approving scripts, viewing finished films, and awarding the Code Seal of Approval to those films that passed muster. When a studio was considering a best-selling book or Broadway play, Breen and his reviewers stood ready to offer advice on the suitability of the property.

The Code office didn't control what studios bought, but its reviews showed producers what they would be up against. The studios would have to decide if it was possible to rework controversial material into an approvable form, and, if so, whether it was worth the money and time required to do so. Different studios made different decisions. MGM passed on purchasing the rights to James M. Cain's popular but sensational novel *Double Indemnity* in the mid-1930s because of problems cited by the Breen office. In the mid-1940s, however, Paramount turned the novel into a successful film after Raymond Chandler altered the story radically to meet Code guidelines.

In the case of Daphne du Maurier's best-selling novel *Rebecca,* the Code office advised, "The story is in violation of the Code, in its present form, on the ground that it justifies and condones and does not punish murder."[4] Producer David O. Selznick purchased the rights to *Rebecca* anyway, spending $50,000, the same sum he had paid for the rights to

Gone with the Wind, and it became Alfred Hitchcock's first directorial job when he came to America. *Rebecca*'s screenwriters brought the novel's story into compliance with the Code by recasting the book's troublesome murder as a tragic accident and soft-pedaling the "perversity" of the title character.

Whereas the Production Code's views on prospective properties were advisory, their rulings on scripts had the force of law. After July 1, 1934, all screenplays produced by American film companies had to be submitted for Production Code approval, and banks required a letter from the Code administration saying scripts were acceptable before filming could be financed.[5]

Breen and his colleagues did not consider themselves censors. What they did was not censorship but "self-regulation." In the words of one of the self-described self-regulators, Albert Van Schmus, "It was definitely *not* a case of going out as a censor and saying 'This must go.' It simply was not done that way."[6]

According to Van Schmus, incoming scripts were assigned to two readers. Readers would meet every morning, discuss anything that might be a problem, and come to a position. If scripts posed special problems, additional readers might be assigned. Once the readers had reached a position, one of the original reviewers would write a letter for Breen's signature saying whether the script met the requirements of the Production Code. If it didn't, the letter would list the detailed objections of the readers, often on a page-by-page basis, along with specific suggestions for changes and deletions. This review process would be repeated with each script revision.

During his career as an American director, Alfred Hitchcock made twenty-seven films subject to the review of the Production Code Administration, starting with *Rebecca* in 1940 and ending with *Torn Curtain* in 1966. In that time he received seventy-five letters suggesting script changes, or nearly three letters per film. The average number of changes suggested per film was 22.5, and the greatest number of comments on any Hitchcock film was fifty-nine, leveled against *I Confess.*

Script alterations were reviewed and commented on until the Production Code reviewers deemed the screenplay to be ready for filming. The average time between the initial Code letter and final approval was forty-seven days on Hitchcock's films. During that time, Hitchcock was presiding over the full range of moviemaking decisions, overseeing script changes, scouting locations, casting supporting roles, consulting with set designers, and mollifying producers as well as meeting with Production Code officials on particularly difficult screenplays. While his attention was split several ways, it is fair to say that in the course of making the twenty-seven films from *Rebecca* to *Torn Curtain* Hitchcock spent the equivalent of three and a half years with Production Code concerns on his to-do list.

Throughout the script-review process, Hitchcock would charm the Production Code reviewers, with the objective of making as few changes as possible. He lulled reviewers with promises, meeting with them in person to discuss such sticking points as the cavalier attitude toward murder in *Strangers on a Train* and the heroine's dubious morality in *Notorious.* Before filming began on *Rear Window,* Hitchcock invited Production Code officials onto the set to show them that everything happening in the apartments around the courtyard, including the dancing of the sexy Miss Torso, which concerned at least one reviewer, would be shot from the distant viewpoint of a man in a wheelchair looking out of his apartment window, and not with salacious close-ups.

Nearly every letter from the Production Code office concerning script review, including their final letter of approval, ended with the reminder: "You understand, of course, that our final judgment will be based on the finished picture."

Hitchcock was at his best in defending cherished images in his finished pictures against the objection of code reviewers. The shower scene in *Psycho* wasn't the only aspect of the finished film that challenged the Production Code. Code officials also objected to the opening scene of Janet Leigh and John Gavin in bed together, which reviewers found to be "entirely too passionate," featuring "extremely lustful intimacies, including, among other things, a quite blatant open mouth kiss."[7]

While the censors ruminated over the "now-you-see-it, now-you-don't" images of knives and nudity in the shower scene, Hitchcock made them an offer. He would remove all suggestions of nudity from the shower scene if they would allow him to keep the opening bedroom scene. When they refused, he followed with a counteroffer. "All right, if you leave the shower sequence as is, I will reshoot the opening, but I want you people on the set to tell me how you will pass it just watching it."[8]

When no one from the Production Code office showed up, Hitchcock

The Code Seal: this full-frame imprimatur of the Breen office, originally screened at the start of certified films, soon was shrunk to a small speck in the corner of a film's credits.

didn't reshoot, and the scene remained unaltered in the finished film. In the end, Hitchcock was allowed to keep both the opening scene and the bulk of the shower scene in return for eliminating a few minor lines of dialogue and a fleeting glimpse of bare buttocks.

Hitchcock's offer to let Code officials observe a reshoot may have been a consummate bluff. The Code office had an unwritten policy against having its reviewers appear on set to tell directors what they could and couldn't shoot. "We *never* insisted on being present at the shooting of any material," one reviewer said. "Joe Breen would've fired anybody who did that."[9]

Final approval for a film came in a form letter from the Production Code Administration, accompanied by a numbered certificate. In the early days of the Code Administration, studios showcased the Code Seal of Approval, an oval logo encircling the MPPDA's initials, in a separate frame preceding the title credits of a certified film. When the seal began drawing jeers and catcalls and what the *Hollywood Reporter* called "a good community hiss," the Code Seal was shrunk and mounted inconspicuously in the bottom left-hand corner of the title credits, ostensibly, according to the MPPDA, "to obviate the extra running time required by having the seal on a separate frame."[10]

In July 1934, when the Production Code Seal of Approval became necessary for film exhibition, films already in release were subjected to a crude form of triage. Films the Code office considered to pose no problems were allowed to remain in circulation. Films with a few issues, like Mae West's *I'm No Angel,* were allowed to fulfill their current exhibition contracts, but no new contracts were to be signed. A few pictures, including Barbara Stanwyck's *Baby Face,* were withdrawn immediately, even though they had met Code requirements when those requirements were self-administered.[11]

Films the studios wanted to rerelease and older films that had been withdrawn from circulation had to be resubmitted to the Production Code Administration for a seal before they could be reissued. This posed a problem for some racier pre-Code films. Behaving more like a censor than a self-regulator, Breen blocked the reissue of Mae West's *She Done Him Wrong* in 1935 and again in 1949. A few major films were reissued with minor editing. *King Kong* was deprived of a little monkeying around with Fay Wray, and *All Quiet on the Western Front* lost a nude bathing scene.

Other cuts were more substantial. When Goldwyn reissued *Arrowsmith,* they virtually deleted Myrna Loy's role as a mistress. And *A Farewell to Arms* was subjected to extensive reediting, including the crude insertion of an anonymous man's hand placing a wedding ring on a woman's finger that was supposed to legitimatize the illicit relationship between Gary Cooper and Helen Hayes, even though they were shown discussing the possibility of marriage in a subsequent scene.[12]

The Breen office was funded by dues paid to the MPPDA by the studios, which depended on the power of the Code Seal to save them from local censors and federal control. In addition, the office assessed modest fees for issuing the Code Seal. Beginning in 1934, they charged $50 for a new feature and $25 for reissues, shorts, and foreign films. Over the years, these fees increased with inflation, and by 1967, in the final days of the Code administration, they were assessed on a sliding scale ranging from $600 for films with budgets under $150,000 to $3,000 if a film's budget exceeded $1.5 million. Breen's salary also increased over the years. When he was hired by the MPPDA in 1930, he earned $18,000 per year. By 1941, when he left briefly to serve as the head of RKO, he was making a little over

$50,000 annually (valued at $1.5 million in terms of current living standards). During his time at MPPDA, Breen's salary was kept an "official secret," on the theory that studio heads might be less deferential if they knew how much they out-earned him.[13]

Breen was a great believer in the value of a paper trail. Problems should be raised and resolved at the script stages, while they were still on paper. Once translated to film, they became much more expensive to correct. Copies of all correspondence with studio representatives were retained, and meetings were rigorously documented with file memos. These files have been scrupulously maintained by the current Motion Picture Association of America (MPAA) in the Margaret Herrick Library in Beverly Hills and provide a fascinating look at the level of detail Code officials included in their instructions. Here, for example, is the Code reviewers' reaction to the suggestion that two secondary characters in *Spellbound* might have checked into a hotel with the intention of carrying on an affair.

> Page 48: The suggestion of an illicit sex affair between Fleurot and Mrs. Murchison is entirely unacceptable, and could not be approved in the finished picture. This will call for the deletion, among other things, of the dialogue "you have a reservation?" "Yes. For Mr. and Mrs. John Timothy"; the line on page 49 "Don't give your name to the police. We don't want any investigation of Mr. and Mrs. Timothy"; the line on Page 50 "No. She's here with Dr. Fleurot—for a weekend-consultation."[14]

One of the paper trails created by the Breen office eventually led nowhere. In addition to records of reviewers' all-important interactions with studios, the office maintained an internal file on every picture it reviewed, in the form of an extensive five-page checklist entitled "Analysis of Film Content," which covered the following topics:

- Portrayal of Professions (sympathetic, unsympathetic, or indifferent).
- Portrayal of Races and Nationalities (sympathetic, unsympathetic, or indifferent).
- Treatment of Liquor (amount, where consumed, portrayal of drunkenness).

- Crime Depiction (type of crime, sympathy for criminal, fate of criminal).
- Sociological Factors (depictions of violence, gambling, courtrooms, religious ceremonies, weddings, divorces, adultery, illicit sex, illegitimacy, seduction, rape).

The film-content checklists were filled out by a rank-and-file clerk, usually a woman, who screened the films along with the Code's male reviewers. The resulting data sheets were designed to be translated to punch cards for ease of tabulation. According to Albert Van Schmus, reviewers in the Hollywood office *never* consulted the completed questionnaires. Copies were sent along to the New York office of the MPPDA, just in case anyone inquired about such issues as the use of liquor in films or the treatment of specific races or the depiction of ministers. If questioned about drinking in the movies, for example, the New York office "could come up with an answer and say, 'Well, five hundred pictures were made in such-and-such a year, or last year, and there were only forty that had drinking,' . . . or something like that."[15]

As it turned out, then, the analytic checklists rarely saw the light of day, but they do reveal the mindset of the censors' office, constituting a body count in their ongoing war on immorality. Breen and his reviewers were on the front lines in that war, and their engagements with studio heads and directors helped to shape films from 1934 to 1968, for better or (mostly) worse.

It is important to remember that the film industry itself bestowed the power of the final cut on Joe Breen, because movie moguls feared that otherwise they might have faced final cuts from forty-eight pairs of scissors in forty-eight state censors' offices—or worse, one very big pair of scissors in the hands of the federal government. Neither the individual states nor the federal government were likely to be as responsive to filmmakers as the Breen office, which was supported by studio dues paid to the MPPDA.

Although Alfred Hitchcock's reputation advanced to the point where his contracts gave him the decision-making power on the final cut of his films, that power actually belonged to Joe Breen's office on twenty-seven of the films produced during the director's most productive years. In some cases, Breen's cuts were indistinguishable from Hitchcock's, and in a few instances, the censors' suggestions actually improved the final films. In more than a few cases, moreover, the perceived need to outwit the Code led the director to create memorable film sequences.

No matter whether the Production Code's interventions helped or hurt Hitchcock's films, in every case they imposed a drain on the director's energy and attention. It's impossible to say whether Hitchcock would have made more or better films if he hadn't had to contend with the Breen office. What we can do, though, thanks to the relentless record keeping of the Breen office and the custodial efforts of the Margaret Herrick Library, is look at the demands imposed by the censors on each film and the director's response to these demands, which provide valuable insights into Hitchcock's methods and mindset, as well as the times in which he lived and worked.

II

The British Years (1922–1939)

Hitchcock in his cameo role as a photographer in *Young and Innocent*.

3

The British Board of Film Censors

Whereas film censorship in America largely dealt with matters of sex and morality, British censors were more concerned with political and social issues. The British Board of Film Censors was the unintended offspring of the Cinematograph Act of 1910, which Parliament passed to ensure that movie theaters and peepshow parlors adhered to fire laws. However, the act was so loosely worded that the local licensing authorities charged with keeping theaters safe from fire decided they could keep them safe from disturbing images and ideas as well, and local censorship boards sprang up throughout England. By 1912, the separate rulings of these boards were so idiosyncratic and disparate that members of the film industry formed the British Board of Film Censors (BBFC), predating Hollywood's initial attempts at self-regulation by ten years.

Although the Home Office had approved the formation of the BBFC, it disavowed any open participation in staffing and censorship decisions. However, it was generally understood that if the BBFC decisions were unacceptable to the government of the day (with an eye on public opinion), Parliament reserved the right to replace the organization with a legal body.[1]

The BBFC was nominally led by a president selected by the film industry, but the day-to-day operations were run by a full-time secretary. From 1913 to 1948, a period that included Alfred Hitchcock's British moviemaking, that secretary was Joseph Brooke Wilkinson, a dapper and efficient man with a knack for satisfying both critics on the right, who wanted stricter controls, and critics on the left, who wanted more liberal films. With all his talents, "Brooksie" Wilkinson had an unfortunate drawback for a man charged with movie censorship: for at least twenty years of his term he suffered from failing eyesight.

Wilkinson was assisted by four censors whom he chose personally.

Two censors viewed each submitted film and those approved for distribution were classified either U, meaning suitable for general viewing, or A, acceptable for those over sixteen. Because the BBFC's rulings were strictly advisory, local boards retained the power to ban approved films or, conversely, to allow screenings of films banned by the agency. At first, therefore, the creation of the BBFC did little to relieve the chaos imposed by local censorship. However, local boards gradually accepted central control, and by 1921 the London City Council had made BBFC approval a prerequisite for films playing within the city.[2]

Unlike the Breen office, with its four-thousand-word Production Code, the BBFC censors began with only two specific rules—no materialization of Christ and no nudity. Over the years, the censors themselves, the secretary, and incoming presidents increased this number of no-no's. The second BBFC president, T. P. O'Connor, a Liberal M.P., introduced forty-three rules forbidding such things as "indecorous dancing" and "references to controversial politics," along with a catchall restriction that rejected any "scenes tending to disparage public characters and institutions."[3]

Two of the added rules had a huge impact on what could be shown on British screens: the first forbade films "calculated to wound the susceptibilities of foreign people," and the second banned all references to "relations between capital and labour," by which was meant the "screening of anything which suggested conflict between employers and the employed."[4]

The rule cautioning against wounding "the susceptibilities of foreign people" resulted in some curious decisions at the BBFC. Starting in 1933, the board refused to pass any films that might upset the Nazi regime in Berlin. This reluctance stayed in place until just before the outbreak of World War II and affected two of Hitchcock's British anti-espionage films, *The 39 Steps* and *The Lady Vanishes.* Both of these films featured Teutonic villains who were presumably in the service of the Third Reich, but the BBFC would approve them only if the villains' nationalities were not specified.

The BBFC's refusal to allow any hint of discord "between capital and labour" also led to some unfortunate bans. The Russian movie *Battleship Potemkin,* directed by Serge Eisenstein and regularly ranked among the top ten films of all time, was banned by the BBFC from its release in 1926 until 1954, not because of the bloodletting in its justifiably famous Odessa Steps sequence but because of the implicit fear that its depiction of a successful uprising against authority might inspire mutinies on the high seas, working-class revolts, or other acts of rebellion against established political entities.

Although banned from public showings, *Potemkin* was initially made available for screenings by the Film Society, a private organization formed in 1925 by Ivor Montagu and Sidney Bernstein to show imported films that were unlikely to receive a general release. Both men were friends, and eventually producing partners, of Alfred Hitchcock, who often attended screenings sponsored by the society. The Film Society's members, which included Bertrand Russell, Julian Huxley, John Maynard Keynes, and George Bernard Shaw, frequently opposed the BBFC, which H. G. Wells characterized as "a gang of mystery men."[5]

Two years after the BBFC banned *Potemkin,* Ivor Montagu, a member of the British Communist Party, tried to sidestep the ban by appealing directly to the London City Council. However, the council upheld the ban and Montagu's failed end run aroused the attention of the Conservative government. Immediately following the council's ruling, Scotland Yard officials visited *Potemkin*'s distributors, who thereafter refused to supply prints to the Film Society or any other private entity without written permission from the home secretary. No such permission was ever issued, and the film remained banned from both private and public viewing until 1954.

The enforcement of the *Potemkin* ban highlighted the close ties between the BBFC and the British government, which gave the BBFC the upper hand in most dealings with the Film Society. Although the society and its individual members might oppose the stance of the BBFC on specific films, they tended to agree that censorship was necessary for the uneducated majority, if not for themselves and their kind. Montagu himself held the elitist view that "popular mainstream films required more stringent censorship than those intended for the enlightened few."[6]

Of the forty-three rules introduced by T. P. O'Connor, seven were overtly political and aimed at perpetuating the social status quo. O'Connor's immediate successors, Sir Edward Shortt and Lord William Tyrrell, maintained his political focus and made it their business not only to censor films that opposed government policy but also to keep alternative policies from reaching the screen. By 1937, Lord Tyrrell was able to announce with satisfaction to a gathering of British film exhibitors, "We may take pride in observing that there is not a single film showing in London today which deals with any of the burning questions of the day."[7] By the end of the 1930s, the number of rules and regulations imposed by the BBFC had increased to ninety-eight, causing producer Victor Saville to complain that if he abided by all the BBFC's rules he wouldn't even be able to film *Cinderella.*[8]

Whereas the focus of British film censorship was largely political and that of the American Production Code was largely moral, the importance of the American market to British filmmakers, and vice versa, meant that each country tended to honor the other's restrictions. Thus American filmmakers shied away from characterizing Nazis as villains during the years between the First and Second World Wars. This voluntary ban, which also reflected a dollars-and-cents concern for the German market, ended for one studio in 1938 when Joe Kaufman, a Jewish representative of Warner Bros. in Germany, was clubbed to death by thugs in a Berlin back alley. With the aid and encouragement of FBI chief J. Edgar Hoover, Warner's subsequently produced the propaganda film *Confessions of a Nazi Spy,* which had no trouble labeling the masters of the Third Reich as villains.[9]

Even though its chief concerns were political, the BBFC rules had a few moral guidelines that went beyond those of Hollywood's Production Code. One rule insisted that married couples occupy twin beds. The problem first surfaced in the 1938 Barbara Stanwyck mystery *The Mad Miss Manton,* which the BBFC refused to pass because of a scene in which a caretaker and his wife were shown sleeping in a double bed when he got up to investigate an outside noise. RKO solved the problem by darkening the scene so much that the sleeping arrangements were not easily distinguished. After that incident, American producers routinely provided twin beds for married couples, giving rise to the legend that the requirement stemmed from a provision of the MPPDA Production Code.[10]

By the end of the 1930s, when Alfred Hitchcock decamped for America, the importance of the US market to British filmmakers meant that the MPPDA Production Code, as enforced by Joe Breen's office, had at least as much influence on the moral tone of films made in Britain as the BBFC, which continued to focus on political concerns.

Because the BBFC's London offices were destroyed by a direct hit from Luftwaffe bombers in 1941, no firsthand records of the censors' interactions with Alfred Hitchcock's British films survive. However, personal accounts suggest that the director was just as crafty with British censors as he was later with Production Code officials in the United States. In Britain, Hitchcock was allowed to sit with the secretary of the BBFC when his films were scrutinized, and by the time the director's Gaumont thrillers were under review, Brooksie Wilkinson's eyesight had deteriorated so far that he had to wear glasses with one opaque lens. According to Hitchcock, whenever an "offending piece of film approached, I said, 'Mr. Wilkinson—.' He turned his head toward me and the scene went by on the screen without his seeing it."[11]

In his first British thriller, the silent movie *The Lodger,* Hitchcock ran into a form of censorship that had nothing to do with the BBFC. Hitchcock cast matinee idol Ivor Novello as a sinister man renting a room in a London household at a time when the city was terrorized by a series of Jack the Ripper–like murders. In the novel on which the film is based, the lodger is revealed to have almost certainly been the killer stalking the city, and he manages to elude the police and disappear. This ending was forestalled by front-office demands that Novello had to be cleared at the end of the film to protect his image with his legions of female fans. Hitchcock acceded to the demands, but he subsequently told François Truffaut that he would have preferred that the ending follow the book, with the lodger going off into the night so that the viewer never really knows whether or not he was responsible for the serial killings. "But with the hero played by a big star, one can't do that," he told Truffaut. "You have to clearly spell it out in big letters 'He is innocent.' . . . These are the problems we face with the star system. Very often the story line is jeopardized because a star cannot be a villain."[12]

Hitchcock faced a similar problem with his producers over the ending of *Blackmail,* Britain's first sound film. In the film, a young woman stalks off after having an argument with her boyfriend, a police inspector, and is picked up by an artist, who takes her to his apartment and tries to rape her. To defend herself, she stabs him with a bread knife and flees the scene. Her policeman boyfriend, assigned to the murder investigation, finds his girlfriend's glove at the scene of the crime but does not share the information with his superiors. A friend of the artist, who had seen the girl enter his apartment, finds the other glove and tries to blackmail both the girl and the policeman. The blackmailer runs afoul of the law, is chased by the policeman, and dies when he falls through a skylight in the British

Museum. The policeman uses the blackmailer's shady past and association with the artist to frame him for the murder. Unaware of this, the girl, wracked by guilt, shows up at the police station to confess, but is interrupted by her boyfriend before she can incriminate herself.

In Hitchcock's preferred ending, the guilt-ridden girl confesses the crime, and her boyfriend has to lead her away in handcuffs. The picture would then close with an end-of-the-workday scene that mirrors one of the earliest scenes in the picture, in which the policeman's partner asks him as he is washing up whether he has plans to spend the evening with this girlfriend, and the policeman answers, "Not this evening." Hitchcock told François Truffaut that the producers found the revised ending "too depressing," and they may have been right.[13]

In Hitchcock's view, a happy ending wasn't always necessary. "If you get a solid grip on the audience," he told Truffaut, "they will follow your reasoning. Providing there is sufficient entertainment in the body of the film, people will accept an unhappy ending."[14] As a practical matter, however, Hitchcock's British producers rarely allowed him to test this theory.

Hitchcock's own accounts of his interactions with British censors confirm the observation that the BBFC was more interested in politics than morality. In an extensive 1938 interview with *Film Weekly* entitled "The Censor Wouldn't Pass It," the interviewer characterized the director's most recent film, *The Lady Vanishes,* as formulaic and asked Hitchcock "why he had never used his brilliant technique to dramatize real events in our national life." "Because," said Hitchcock, "circumstances have forced me into the realm of fiction. I have always wanted to make films with some sociological importance—but I never have been allowed to do so. You must remember . . . that my chief appeal is an ability to work people up into a state of excitement. . . . It is my love of the dynamic that has forced me into the fields of fiction."

Hitchcock gave the interviewer two examples of his attempts to dramatize real events.

> Soon after the general strike in 1926 I wanted to put the whole thing into a film. I saw in this subject a magnificently dynamic motion picture. When I suggested the idea to my production chief, he approached the British Board of Film Censors, who immediately vetoed it.

> I should, no doubt, have been allowed to make a wishy-washy picture about the general strike, but in this form the subject no longer appealed to me. I wanted to show fistfights between strikers and undergraduates, pickets and all the authentic drama of the situation.

The director observed that much the same thing happened when he wanted to put the Sydney Street siege on the screen in *The Man Who Knew Too Much.* "When the idea was submitted for approval to the Home Office they informed me that I mustn't show the militia being called out and the house in Sydney Street surrounded by machine guns. All that I was allowed to do was depict the policemen being handed rifles and shown how to use them. Again and again I have been prevented from putting on the screen authentic accounts of incidents in British life."

Hitchcock went on to outline the subterfuge necessary to get a story approved by the BBFC. "If you imply 'It can't happen here'—if you set your story in Central Europe or even make your villain a foreigner—officialdom raises no objections. But if your picture is too obviously a criticism of the social system, Whitehall shakes its head."[15]

At the time of this interview, Hitchcock still had forty-two years and thirty brilliant thrillers ahead of him. Although there is no telling what sort of socially significant films the director might have made if it weren't for the censors' objections, the BBFC may have done him, and the world of cinema, a favor by steering him into fiction and a lifetime of thriller production.

4

The British Gaumont Thrillers

By 1933, following the unsuccessful reception of the musical costume drama *Waltzes from Vienna*, Hitchcock's career was at a low ebb. This all changed when he joined his friend and mentor Michael Balcon at Gaumont British Studios and embarked on a series of contemporary thrillers, starting in 1934 with *The Man Who Knew Too Much*. In the space of four and a half years prior to his departure for America, he turned out seven thrillers and established an international reputation as a master of suspense films.

Although the BBFC had first cut at the finished form of these thrillers, the Luftwaffe's bombs in 1941 ensured that the only surviving evidence of the organization's cuts is anecdotal. By 1934, however, Joe Breen had installed the Production Code's offices in Hollywood, and the Code Seal of Approval was required for all films seeking a US release. At first, Breen's reviewers simply imposed additional cuts on Hitchcock's thrillers before they were allowed to play in America. Because copies of the original British releases survive, these additional cuts did little lasting harm. American filmgoers during this period may not have realized they were seeing edited versions of Hitchcock's thrillers, just as visitors to the Louvre during World War II didn't know they were seeing a plaster copy of the Venus de Milo, since the French had hidden the original when the Nazi occupation of Paris appeared imminent.

As the 1930s wore on, the Production Code office insinuated itself deeper into Hitchcock's British productions, suggesting script changes that affected the form of the finished films. The nature of these changes shows how the concerns of Breen's reviewers differed from those of their British counterparts, and foreshadows the types of objections Hitchcock would face when he emigrated to America and encountered Breen personally.

The Man Who Knew Too Much (1934)

Synopsis. *In St. Moritz a group of spies led by a man named Abbott (Peter Lorre) kidnaps the daughter of a vacationing British couple to keep the two* *from revealing what they have learned about a plot to murder a visiting diplomat in London. Afraid to go to the police, the couple track the spies to their London hideout and thwart an assassination attempt in Albert Hall. The alerted police then launch a siege of the gang's hideout, kill the spies, and rescue the kidnapped girl.*

***

Hitchcock viewed *The Man Who Knew Too Much* as the film that reestablished his prestige and marked the real beginning of his career.[1] In its initial review of the shooting script, the BBFC noted several concerns, including the fact that the head of the spy ring, played by Peter Lorre, was allowed to escape the final shootout. The BBFC requested that the screenwriters eliminate two instances of *bloody* from the dialogue and alter the ending so that the spymaster is appropriately punished. In keeping with its political focus, the BBFC's primary concern was with the final shootout, which echoed the Sydney Street siege of 1911 in which English bobbies, traditionally unarmed, were issued weapons prior to storming a house occupied by two anarchists. The actual six-hour siege, which was overseen by the then home secretary Winston Churchill, cost the life of a fire commissioner as well as the lives of the anarchists.

The British censors' stated concern with the film depiction was that the armed English police misrepresented standard procedures. Gaumont British Studios sent its script supervisor to meet with a representative of the BBFC, the same half-blind Mr. Wilkinson whom Hitchcock was sometimes able to distract during their joint viewing sessions.

After Wilkinson outlined the BBFC's position, the script supervisor agreed to work out an ending that did not require armed policemen, but asked that backup troops could be armed with rifles, as the Scots Guards had been in the actual siege. Hitchcock got around this agreement by inserting dialogue noting the bobbies' customary lack of weapons and the decision of a police inspector to obtain rifles from a private gunsmith. Following a scene showing the police being issued the gunsmith's rifles from the rear of a truck, the director proceeded to film the shootout as planned.

The shootout also troubled Breen's Production Code office when *The Man Who Knew Too Much* was submitted for the approval necessary for US distribution. Although Hitchcock's alterations passed Mr. Wilkinson's failing eyesight, Breen's Hollywood censors trained at least four good eyes on the film, and they were appalled at what they saw. In an initial letter,

Breen said that they were unable to approve the film under the provisions of the Code. There was simply "too much slaughter; too much gunplay; too much murdering of policemen."[2]

In a letter to his boss, Will Hays, justifying his judgment, Breen wrote that the "final two reels of the film present a slaughter the likes of which we have not seen since the days of SCARFACE." In Hitchcock's film "a mere handful of assassins hold off the British police for what is indicated to be a long period of time, at the close of which twenty or thirty of the policemen are killed, and all of the assassins." Breen's body count estimate is somewhat high. Only four policemen are actually shown receiving mortal wounds, but he makes the valid point that "we cannot forbid our own people to do certain things and then approve those same things in films made abroad. Any such stupidity on our part is certain to compromise the work of our administration and lead to considerable disorder."[3]

Breen followed his initial observations to the film's producers with a detailed letter specifying the deletions needed to get the Production Code Seal. These deletions included the excision of all profanity and the elimination of a close-up showing a gloved hand covering the mouth of the kidnapped child, a request "in line with our general procedure in eliminating all details of kidnapping."[4]

Most of the deletions identified in Breen's follow-up letter, made to "soften and play down this shooting business," effectively emasculated the final shootout. Specifically, Breen asked that the producers "cut immediately after the first platoon of policemen start to rush the criminals' hideout. Eliminate scenes in which policemen are shown being cut down, also scenes of various people appearing at windows, attracted by sound of gunfire." Subsequent directions stipulated the deletion of "all scenes of gangsters firing" as well as all scenes of policemen being shot.[5]

Gaumont British complied with the requests of the Breen office, cutting a little over five minutes from the British version's seventy-five minutes, and the film received the Production Code Seal of Approval. Even with the deletions, the film was a huge hit with both the critics and public in America, establishing Hitchcock's reputation as the premier director of suspense films on both sides of the Atlantic.

The 39 Steps (1935)

Synopsis. *Following a London music hall act featuring Mr. Memory, an* *attractive foreigner asks Canadian Richard Hannay (Robert Donat) to take her to his home. There she tells him she is being pursued by enemy agents from an organization called the 39 Steps because she has evidence of a major British security leak. When she is murdered later that evening, Hannay goes on the run from the police, who suspect him of her murder, and the enemy agents, who fear that she may have confided her secrets in him. Fleeing to Scotland, he is captured by the agents and handcuffed to a young woman, Pamela (Madeleine Carroll), whom they believe may be his accomplice. The two escape while handcuffed together and spend the night at a country inn, where Pamela overhears their pursuers planning to leave the country with Mr. Memory, whose mind has become the repository for stolen secrets. Hannay and Pamela arrive at the theater in time to expose the plot and clear Hannay's name.*

***

In Hitchcock's next thriller, *The 39 Steps,* it was sex, not violence, that proved to be a stumbling block. Code reviewers balked at the byplay between Robert Donat and Madeleine Carroll when they spend the night handcuffed to one another in the bedroom of a rural inn. Although the couple are at odds with each other and never exchange so much as a friendly word, let alone a chaste kiss, the Code censors requested the following deletions, which misidentify the Donat character Hannay as Hammond.

1. Close-up shot of the girl taking off her stocking while handcuffed to Hammond.
2. Dialogue: "Now for the operating table," spoken by Hammond.
3. Two shots of Hammond rolling over and placing his hand on the girl's leg.
4. All profanity, including three "damns" and one "hell."[6]

Shortly after receiving the Code letter, Gaumont British replied that it had made all of the requested deletions except #3, in which Hannay rolls over and places his hand on Pamela's leg, because making the cut would lead to "a very bad break in the action" and "impair the value of the production." They therefore asked that the Code office reconsider its request.[7]

Although Hannay is sound asleep when he rolls over onto Pamela, and Pamela extricates herself immediately, the Code censors insisted that the deletion be made, adding that their first thought had been "to delete the

The Production Code Office insisted that the British producers cut key portions of this scene, in which Madeleine Carroll eventually releases herself from the handcuffs linking her to Robert Donat, because the two are shown in bed together, even though they are fully clothed and anything but amorous.

whole sequence where the girl and man are on the bed, and would have done so had we had the opportunity to examine the script prior to the shooting of the scene."[8]

Once the requested cuts were made, the film was released in America, where the critics and public received it as eagerly as they had in Britain. In the *Sunday Times,* Sydney Carroll had written, "In *The 39 Steps,* the identity and mind of Alfred Hitchcock are continuously discernable, in fact supreme. There is no doubt Hitchcock is a genius. He is the real star of the film."[9] And in America, *New York Times* columnist Andre Sennwald wrote of Hitchcock: "A master of shock and suspense, of cold horror and slyly incongruous wit, he uses his camera the way a painter uses his brush, styling his story and giving it values which the scenarist could hardly have expected."[10]

Secret Agent (1936)

Synopsis. *During World War I, British secret agent Richard Ashenden (John*

Gielgud) is sent to Switzerland to kill a German spy with the help of Elsa Carrington (Madeleine Carroll), an agent posing as his wife, and an assassin known variously as "the General" and "the Hairless Mexican" (Peter Lorre). At first Ashenden's reluctance is offset by Elsa's enthusiasm, but both have second thoughts when they kill the wrong man. Ashenden is about to resign when he learns that Elsa is leaving Switzerland with the real spy, an American playboy named Richard Marvin (Robert Young). Ashenden and the General follow the pair onto the Constantinople train. Allied bombs destroy the train and mortally injure Marvin, who shoots the General just before he dies.

***

With Hitchcock's previous British thrillers, the Breen office's first exposure to the material was the finished film as it was presented for the Seal of Approval. With *Secret Agent,* however, Gaumont British submitted the shooting script for approval first, reasoning that it would be simpler and less costly to respond to requested changes before the offending elements were committed to film. Breen had suggested this earlier participation in his correspondence concerning the handcuffed bedroom byplay in *The 39 Steps*, and British Gaumont's acceptance gave the Production Code office far more control over Hitchcock's British films.[11]

The Code office wasted no time in exercising its increased latitude and responded to the screenplay with a detailed letter: four single-spaced pages of suggested revisions. Perhaps out of deference to British sensibilities—or, more likely, out of concern for foreign markets—Breen's reviewers were at least as considerate of the feelings of foreigners as the BBFC. Although the Germans were clearly identified as villains in World War I, the Code office objected to a speech in which a German agent was characterized as "playing the old game—working for both sides. He's ready to talk if we pay him enough." On the grounds that "in its present form it will be offensive to the German government," the line was omitted from the finished film.[12]

Breen's censors were also concerned that depictions of scenes in the Swiss café, the village square, and the train station be carefully treated "to obviate giving offense to a foreign nation." One of their chief concerns in this regard was that Peter Lorre's character, identified as the Hairless Mexican, "should not be definitely characterized as a Mexican."[13] The characterization arose from the primary source material for the movie, two short stories by W. Somerset Maugham, "The Hairless Mexican" and "Triton." In the final film, the potentially offensive characteristic was explained away by Ashenden's superior as follows: "We call him the 'Hairless Mexican,' chiefly because he's got a lot of curly hair and isn't really a Mexican. You can call him 'The General.' He isn't a general, but he'll appreciate the compliment."

The Code office's concern for matters of the flesh resurfaced in its script review. The next issue, after the denaturalization of the Hairless Mexican, was that "the portrayal of the rooms in the hotel in which Ashenden and Elsa reside should be done in such a way as to clearly establish that they live in separate rooms, with no action taking place in a bathroom." Code reviewers also objected to certain bits of potentially off-color dialogue, suggesting that the word *sweetheart* be substituted for *lover,* and that the word *connubial* be eliminated altogether. They also proposed that "the running 'gag' of the Mexican throwing coins and chocolates to girls in such a way that they drop down inside the dresses of the girls and then offering to retrieve them should be modified in such a way as to cut all business of the coins slipping inside the dresses."[14] In the final British print, Elsa clearly establishes the separate sleeping arrangements by insisting that Ashenden use the couch, but the word *connubial* remains, as does the running gag of the non-Mexican dropping coins and candies down nearby bosoms, although he never offers to retrieve them.

Six months after submitting comments on the shooting script of *Secret Agent,* the Breen office reviewed the first cut of the film for the Production Code Seal of Approval. Reviewers found that "thematically the picture appears to be in conformity with the provisions of the Production Code," except for "a sequence and a few minor details which, in our considered judgment, should be modified or deleted in order to meet the requirements of the Code." The sequence the Code office found objectionable portrayed the initial meeting of the four key characters in the Swiss hotel, during which several of them pass in and out of the bathroom. According to the Code office, "It is our policy to eliminate from scripts and pictures scenes and sequences played in, and in connection with, bathrooms."[15] The Code's bathroom bugaboo plagued Hitchcock on several subsequent films—until he finally broke through with a vengeance in *Psycho.*

Other Code objections to the initial cut were relatively minor, involving one instance of profanity (the word *God*), a scene of Britain's head of intelligence naked from the waist up in a steam room, a silhouette of three bodies hanging from a gibbet, and a close-up shot of Peter Lorre placing his gun against Robert Young's body prior to shooting him.

In the initial cut of the film, the German spy played by Robert Young is mortally injured in the train wreck and John Gielgud's Ashenden shrinks back from strangling the dying man. When Young requests a drink of brandy from Peter Lorre, Lorre provides the brandy from a vest-pocket flask, but shoots Young while he is drinking it, causing the Gielgud and Madeleine Carroll characters to recoil in horror. Both the BBFC and the MPPDA Production Code expressed concern over this ending, largely because it allowed the Peter Lorre character to "walk off free" after murdering two people. Although Hitchcock preferred this ending, he changed it in deference to the two censor boards. In the final cut, the mortally injured Robert Young, trapped in the train wreckage, requests a drink of brandy after Gielgud's hero has failed to strangle him. When the assassin played by Peter Lorre sets his gun down to retrieve his vest-pocket flask, Young picks up the gun and shoots him. A few critics have interpreted Lorre's gesture with the gun as "the traditional invitation to the enemy to take his own life," but in the finished film it looks more like carelessness than chivalry, and ensures that the Lorre character will not get away with murder.[16]

Producer Ivor Montagu protested the censors' preferred ending to no avail, arguing that if Lorre is killed as the censors demanded, the hero and heroine become "a couple of irresolute cissies whose shilly-shallying results in the death of their unwaveringly dutiful colleague."[17] Kerzoncuf and Barr argue in their book *Hitchcock Lost and Found* that both versions show the hero and heroine to be "irresolute cissies" who leave their colleague to do the "dirty but necessary work of killing," and that the film's coda, which shows the Allied advance toward victory, supports the lesson, strong in both versions, that the elimination of the German agent "is the kind of thing that has to be done to win a war."[18]

Sabotage (1936)

Synopsis. *An anarchist, Karl Anton Verloc (Oscar Homolka), operates an Islington cinema with his wife Winnie (Sylvia Sidney). Suspecting that he is under Scotland Yard surveillance, Verloc gives his young brother-in-law a* *timebomb to deliver to Picadilly Station. The unwitting boy is killed when he is delayed in transit and the bomb explodes. Guessing that her husband was responsible for her brother's death, a dazed Winnie stabs him with a carving knife and escapes punishment when one of Verloc's cohorts destroys the crime scene with a bomb.*

***

Sabotage, released in America as *The Woman Alone,* passed the Production Code review with no more than a few relatively minor profanity deletions.[19] Code reviewers were silent on the scene that Hitchcock always said he regretted, the death of the young brother of the saboteur's wife. The boy dies when a bomb he has been given by his brother-in-law explodes before he has a chance to deliver it. Although the scenes showing the boy unknowingly carrying the bomb generated a great deal of suspense, they also created sympathy for the boy, so that the audience was resentful when he was killed. "It was a grave error on my part," Hitchcock told François Truffaut.[20]

Although the Production Code office had objected to the death of each policeman killed in the climactic shootout in *The Man Who Knew Too Much,* and even demanded the deletion of a scene showing a kidnapper placing his hand over the mouth of his young victim in the same film, the office passed the bombing death of the innocent young boy in *Sabotage* without a comment. The office also had no comment on the memorable sequence in which the boy's sister dispatches her saboteur husband with a carving knife. While the Production Code office had relatively few objections to *Sabotage,* the Brazilian government banned the film altogether, fearing that "the film was capable of goading the docile citizenry to acts of affray, or at least of disrespect."[21]

Although British critics and the public never warmed to *Sabotage,* it found an appreciative audience in the United States, where Mark Van Doren, writing in the *Nation,* praised Hitchcock as "the best director now flourishing" in the English language.[22]

Young and Innocent (1937)

Synopsis. *The body of an actress strangled with the belt from a raincoat is found on the beach by screenwriter Robert Tisdale (Derrick De Marney), a friend of the victim whom the police suspect of the murder when he reports his raincoat is missing. He goes on the run, aided by Erica Burgoyne (Nova*

Pilbeam), the daughter of the local police chief. The two fugitives locate an old tramp who has been given a beltless raincoat by a man with a twitching eye and follow the lead to the murderer, the actress's estranged husband.

***

Although the censors required relatively few cuts in *Young and Innocent* (one "Oh, God," one "I wish to God," and one "damn"), the film, retitled *The Girl Was Young* for its American distribution, was inexplicably cut in the United States to reduce its eighty-minute running time.[23] The scene cut was one that Hitchcock considered "the essence of the film." The young protagonists on the run stop at the home of the girl's aunt, where a game of blindman's bluff takes place at a children's birthday party. Although the girl's aunt becomes suspicious, the couple escape her groping clutches when she is blindfolded for the children's game and continue their flight. Hitchcock called the scene a "deliberate symbol" in which only the children see clearly while all the adults in the film, particularly the police, are fumbling in the dark.[24] Unfortunately, the symbolism, and the charm and suspense of the blindman's bluff scene, were lost for American audiences when it was cut to save ten minutes of running time.

After the relatively somber stories of *Secret Agent* and *Sabotage, Young and Innocent* marked a return to the sly, suggestive humor of *The 39 Steps* and did better with British critics and the public than its two darker predecessors. Through both darker and lighter offerings, though, Hitchcock's position as the foremost British film director remained unchallenged.

The Lady Vanishes (1938)

Synopsis. *A kindly elderly governess, Miss Froy (Dame May Whitty), seemingly disappears from a fast-moving train traveling across the Continent to England. When her young friend Iris Henderson (Margaret Lockwood) investigates, none of the passengers admit to having seen her. Iris finally convinces a traveling musicologist, Gilbert Redman (Michael Redgrave) of Miss Froy's existence, and he agrees to help her search the train. The search leads to a baggage-car fistfight and a shootout with a group of spies before Miss Froy is found and her disappearance is explained.*

***

The Lady Vanishes is one of the two best known and most popular of

Hitchcock's British thrillers, along with *The 39 Steps*. In filming this classic, the director seamlessly integrated comic relief, romance, bright dialogue, and the crumbling map of Europe into the fast-paced action of a topical thriller. The chief concern of the Production Code was the adulterous relationship of the couple cited in the credits as Mr. and "Mrs." Todhunter. In addition to the credits, several lines of dialogue make it clear that the man and woman are each married to someone else, and Breen's reviewers asked to have all of these lines deleted in order to "remove the adulterous relationship, which is apparently unnecessary to the plot."[25] Far from being unnecessary, it is the fear that their illicit affair will be exposed that causes the Todhunters to join the other passengers in lying about having seen the vanished Miss Froy aboard the train. Removing every trace of their illicit relationship from the film also removed their motive for lying.

The Production Code censors also demanded the removal of several of the cleverest lines from the screenplay written by Frank Launder and Sidney Gilliat, who went on to establish themselves as a first-rank writing, directing, and producing team on the strength of the success of *The Lady Vanishes*. One of the screenwriting pair's lines that the Code didn't want to cross the Atlantic was Michael Redgrave's comment to Margaret Lockwood when he decides to help her find Miss Froy: "My father always taught me never to desert a lady in trouble . . . he even carried it as far as marrying my mother."

The Production Code's squeamishness regarding toilets resurfaced as reviewers asked the producers to delete the phrase "a private thingummy," the way two Britishers request a private toilet at the overcrowded hotel where they are waiting for the delayed train.

Deletions notwithstanding, *The Lady Vanishes* was a critical and popular success in both Britain and America, and the New York Film Critics honored Alfred Hitchcock with their Best Director award.

Jamaica Inn (1939)

Synopsis. *In the early 1800s, a young Irish orphan, Mary Yellan (Maureen O'Hara), is sent to Cornwall to live in Jamaica Inn with her uncle Joss, who leads a band of pirates that lures ships onto the nearby rocks, plunders them, and kills their crews. When the band is about to hang Jem Trehearne (Robert Newton), a naval officer sent to obtain evidence against the cutthroats, Mary rescues him and they seek protection from the local magistrate, Sir Humphrey*

Pengallan (Charles Laughton), but find out too late he is the brains behind the pirates' plundering.

***

Jamaica Inn is the last and least satisfying of the British thrillers Hitchcock made before leaving for America. With an eye on the American market, the film's co-producer, Erich Pommer, involved Hollywood's Production Code Administration at every step of production, sending it a review copy of the Daphne du Maurier best seller on which the film is based, and using the Code's comments in shaping the screenplay, which was also submitted for Code approval.

The focus of the *Jamaica Inn* novel is the orphan Mary Yellan, who is shocked to learn of her uncle's involvement with pirates and shares that knowledge with a kindly vicar, who in du Maurier's book turns out to be the leader of the cutthroats. The Breen office's chief objection to the book was the character of the vicar. "The Production Code specifically states that ministers of religion, in their role as ministers, shall not be portrayed as comic characters or villains," the Code office advised Pommer, adding that when the vicar's villainy is unmasked, he "indulges in a number of exceedingly blasphemous statements which cast reflection upon all religions." As a result, the Breen office recommended "that you portray the character in some role other than minister."[26]

Pommer willingly acceded to this suggestion and shifted the villain's occupation from vicar to magistrate. The co-producer and star of the film, Charles Laughton, acknowledged this shift with an effusive letter thanking the Code for its guidance. "At the time your forbidding the clergyman was a very great blow," Laughton wrote. "However, it was only another sinister figure. Actually, with the squire I think I am going to have the part of my life."[27]

Hitchcock had known Laughton since the late 1920s, and had agreed to direct *Jamaica Inn* in response to a request from his old acquaintance. However, it was Hitchcock's first experience with a Method actor, and he found the experience exasperating. Laughton did not take direction, and struggled for days trying to find a walk that suited his character. Until he found that walk, he advised Hitchcock not to film him below the waist.[28] Although Hitchcock liked Laughton personally and the two men had much in common, including middle-class origins, Catholic upbringing, and excessive girth, he had little patience with the actor professionally, finding him childish, self-indulgent, and undisciplined.[29] "Directors can't direct a Laughton picture," Hitchcock complained. "The best they can hope for is a chance to referee."[30]

Laughton's power as co-producer and star also changed the shape of the film. Whereas du Maurier's book had been written as a whodunit, with the identity of the pirate mastermind withheld until the last chapter, Hitchcock rightly perceived that the presence of Laughton in the role of the duplicitous magistrate would be a dead giveaway. As the director remarked, "It would be like making a whodunit with Laughton playing the butler and not expecting everyone somehow to guess that the butler did it."[31] As a result, Hitchcock revealed Laughton's duplicity early in the film, and the noted author J. B. Priestly was hired to build up Laughton's role, further distancing the film from du Maurier's book, which focused on the plight of the relocated orphan girl played by Maureen O'Hara.

The Production Code's advice to the British producers was not limited to changing the occupation of the primary villain. Its review of the script warned against excessive brutality on the part of the pirates, dictated the deletion of all profanity, stressed the importance of minimizing the consumption of intoxicating liquor ("Yo-ho-ho and a *half* bottle of rum?"), cautioned against the "pansy" characterization of the pirate Dandy, asked that an incident of domestic violence between Mary's aunt and uncle be toned down, and reminded the producers that when Mary discards her dress to swim away from danger, her undergarments "must cover her body adequately."[32]

The Production Code office devoted a full page to a consideration of the demise of Laughton's double-dealing squire, who leaps to his death after being chased up the topmast of a ship's rigging. The censor's concern was the Code provision that "suicide, as a solution of problems occurring in the development of screen drama, is to be discouraged as 'morally objectionable' and 'bad theater.'" It was important to the Code administrators that Laughton's squire be clearly depicted as a madman, rather than a cornered suicide, and that "the scene immediately preceding his fatal jump definitely establish his unbalanced mental condition."[33]

To make sure that this point would not be missed, Maureen O'Hara, who has been captured by Laughton and carried to the harbor, twice screams, "Don't shoot! He's mad. He can't help himself!" before Laughton releases her and climbs the mast, shouting down to his pursuers, "I shall be down to you before you are up to me!" Swaying on the mast, Laughton politely asks those below if they would "be kind enough to give me room," before shouting, "Make way for Pengallan!" as he jumps to his death.

Hitchcock was not pleased with his experience in making *Jamaica Inn,* and was even less pleased with the results. "I'm still unhappy over it," he told François Truffaut, even though the film became a box-office hit, thanks largely to the reputations of Hitchcock and Laughton.[34] Although the public responded favorably, the film did not please the critics, one of whom called it a "singularly dull and uninspired picture—highly lackadaisical melodrama."[35] Nor did it please Daphne du Maurier, who called it a "wretched affair" and advised her publisher not to see the picture.[36]

The unsuccessful experiences of *Jamaica Inn* and *Waltzes from Vienna,* the film that preceded Hitchcock's run of British thrillers, left the director wary of costume melodramas. He confessed he had no feel for this form of historical storytelling, being unable to intuit what the characters inside the costumes were thinking or feeling—or envision them using the bathroom.[37]

Even though *Jamaica Inn* was a British picture, Joe Breen's Hollywood office dictated the occupation of the villain, the level of violence in the pirate encounters, the incidence of profanity, and even the mind-set of the villain in his final scenes. The influence of the Production Code on the finished film constituted a preview of coming attractions as Hitchcock decamped for America to film another Daphne du Maurier novel, *Rebecca.*

III

The Selznick Years (1940–1947)

Alfred Hitchcock and David O. Selznick. (Courtesy of Jerry Ohlinger.)

5

Hitchcock and Selznick

By the time he finished *Young and Innocent,* Hitchcock had become England's best known and most respected film director. But the British film industry was in decline, and America offered superior production facilities, sounder financing, bigger stars, and international recognition. Tired of being a big fish in a small pond, Hitchcock resolved to leave England for America following a rash of British film industry bankruptcies in late 1936. He began seriously exploring options through his American agent, Myron Selznick, in 1937. The director made his first trip to America in the summer of that year and Selznick arranged contacts with a number of studio representatives, including his brother, David O. Selznick, head of Selznick International, who was so preoccupied with plans for filming *Gone with the Wind* that he spoke with Hitchcock only by phone.

When no firm offers resulted from his first American visit, Hitchcock returned to England to film *The Lady Vanishes.* The week after completing that film, he traveled to Hollywood at his own expense to meet personally with David O. Selznick and other producers. This trip bore fruit, although the fruit was neither as juicy nor as sustaining as Hitchcock had hoped. In July 1938, the director signed a contract with Selznick International to produce one picture for $50,000, with a Selznick option for one Hitchcock picture per year through 1943. After taxes, the $50,000 fee for one Selznick picture was not significantly more than the director had earned for *The Lady Vanishes,* and there was no guarantee of employment beyond the first year's work. But it was Hitchcock's ticket to America, and Myron Selznick pointed out that the contract terms left the director available to freelance for other producers once he had fulfilled his one-picture deal with Selznick International.

At the time he signed Hitchcock, Selznick stated publicly that the director's first American project would deal with the sinking of the *Titanic.* Shortly afterward, the producer acquired the rights to Daphne du Maurier's novel *Rebecca,* and announced that this property would be the subject of

Hitchcock's second American film. A number of considerations helped *Rebecca* leapfrog *Titanic* to become Hitchcock's first film for Selznick International. These included a form of censorship that has always existed but is rarely documented: British ship-owning interests brought strong pressures to bear against the making of a *Titanic* film. Hitchcock acknowledged these pressures in a November 1938 interview. After noting that the *Titanic* story made "a marvelously dramatic subject for a motion picture," he went on to say that "the shipping companies are trying to prevent me making the picture. They seem to think that if I recapture all the horror and violence of the situation, it will stop people going on cruises."[1]

In addition to commercial pressures, Charles Barr, in his work on Hitchcock's *Titanic* project, lists a number of other factors that pushed *Rebecca* ahead of the *Titanic* on Selznick's production schedule.[2] Among these were the producer's unhappiness with a film treatment submitted by English novelist Richard Blaker, the desire to cash in as soon as possible on the success of *Rebecca* as a novel, Selznick's failure to obtain a real ocean liner, the *Leviathan,* to represent the *Titanic,* and the outbreak of war in Europe. All these considerations conspired to make *Rebecca* Hitchcock's first American film and confine the *Titanic* project to the dustbin of what might have been.

After finishing *Jamaica Inn,* based on another du Maurier novel, in late November 1938, Hitchcock wanted to start his new project as soon as possible. But Selznick was fully occupied with *Gone with the Wind* and informed Hitchcock that he couldn't possibly begin *Rebecca* until March or April 1939. A delayed start date would leave Hitchcock with no income for the three or four months between the end of *Jamaica Inn* and the beginning of *Rebecca,* so the director asked Myron Selznick to find him a quick job to cover that period. When Paramount stepped in with a job offer, David O. Selznick refused to give his consent, insisting that his contract gave him the right to produce Hitchcock's first American picture.

The problem was resolved when the New York Film Critics named Hitchcock the Best Director of 1938 for his work on *The Lady Vanishes.* Fearing that the award would make the freelancing Hitchcock more attractive to rival studios, Selznick proposed contract amendments that would tighten his hold on the director. The amendment gave Selznick International the exclusive rights to two Hitchcock pictures a year, one of which could be a loan-out, provided that both parties agreed. To sweeten the pot for Hitchcock and alleviate his immediate money worries, Selznick increased the director's annual salary to $100,000, which would be paid regularly rather than on a per-picture basis, with payments beginning in April 1939. Hitchcock agreed, and made arrangements to sail for America on March 4.

The amended contract represented a measurable improvement over Hitchcock's British salaries, but it was not especially lavish by Hollywood standards. A 1938 survey showed that at least forty Hollywood directors made $100,000 or more per year at that time.[3] The list of survey respondents earning as much or more than Hitchcock was filled with journeyman directors who couldn't approach his talent. And many of Hollywood's most talented directors failed to respond to the survey. By way of comparison, in 1940 the highly respected director George Stevens had a one-year contract with Columbia that brought him $200,000 and a 15 percent share of profits.[4]

In practice, Selznick took advantage of the loan-out clause in the amended contract more often than not. He would rent Hitchcock out at double or triple his contracted salary and pocket the difference. The apparent inequity of this one-sided profit taking irritated Hitchcock, but the director welcomed the loan-outs, since they freed him from Selznick's meddling supervision on the films made for Selznick International.

Hitchcock and Selznick were a mismatched pair. Both men were highly talented in their own right, passionate about film, and used to getting their own way. But there the similarities ended. Selznick was an extrovert, while Hitchcock was subdued and secretive; Selznick was explosive and overbearing, while Hitchcock hated conflict and disagreement; Selznick worked round the clock, fueled by amphetamines, while Hitchcock kept strict office hours, shutting down the set in time to make dinner with his wife, Alma; and Selznick was "chronically disorganized but relentlessly verbal, throwing long-winded memoranda at a chaos he sometimes helped to create," while Hitchcock was a methodical planner, plotting scenes and camera angles in advance and communicating clearly through illustrated storyboards.[5]

Selznick and Hitchcock also differed in their approach to censorship. Selznick engaged in open warfare with the Breen office, fighting to retain Rhett Butler's farewell speech in *Gone with the Wind,* and openly expressing his view that "this insane, inane, and outmoded code" was strangling the industry.[6] Hitchcock was more circumspect, avoiding direct confrontation, proceeding by indirection and, in the end, manipulating censors as slyly as he manipulated moviegoers.

The well-organized Hitchcock resented the last-minute barrage of memos from his producer. At that time, though, producers, not directors, dominated the Hollywood system, and Selznick had the final cut on those films made for Selznick International. Here Hitchcock repaid a bit of the frustration he had suffered in coping with Selznick's memos. Hitchcock shot his films efficiently, minimizing excess footage and "cutting with the camera" to achieve the montage effects sketched in his storyboards. This process left little leeway for last-minute interference from Selznick in the cutting room, and the producer constantly complained about the director's "goddamn jigsaw cutting."[7]

In spite of their differences, the collaboration between Hitchcock and Selznick was mutually beneficial. Hitchcock proved to be just as prolific during his initial years in America as he had been in his final years in England. Between 1939 and the end of his Selznick contract in 1947, Hitchcock directed ten films, including five that rank among his finest work: *Rebecca, Foreign Correspondent, Shadow of a Doubt, Lifeboat,* and *Notorious.* Of this list, only *Rebecca* was actually made under Selznick's supervision at Selznick International. Three were made on loan to other studios, and Selznick sold the entire *Notorious* package to RKO and ceded the final cut to Hitchcock because *Duel in the Sun* demanded the producer's full attention at the time. The remaining five films, *Mr. and Mrs. Smith, Suspicion, Saboteur, Spellbound,* and *The Paradine Case,* were all high-gloss studio productions, with all but one, *Saboteur,* featuring top-rank stars, and all but another, *The Paradine Case,* profitable at the box office.

After leaving Selznick, Hitchcock went on to create more masterpieces, while Selznick never topped *Gone with the Wind* and went into decline, divorcing his wife, marrying Jennifer Jones, and devoting the rest of his days to furthering his new wife's career before dying of a heart attack at age sixty-three. Historians have interpreted these facts to mean that "Selznick needed Hitchcock more than Hitchcock needed Selznick." Yet Selznick gave Hitchcock his ticket to America and the financial support and star access he needed to make first-rate films. In return, Hitchcock gave Selznick award-winning films and a positive bottom line. In the end, it seems true that "Hitchcock did not succeed *despite* Selznick any more than Selznick succeeded *because of* Hitchcock. The dynamic served both men, not only as artists but—of equal importance to them—as Hollywood professionals."[8]

6

Rebecca (1940)

Synopsis. *An unnamed young American girl (Joan Fontaine) who is visiting Monte Carlo as the paid companion of a social-climbing dowager meets wealthy widower Maxim de Winter (Laurence Olivier). Although intimidated by his brusque manner, she accepts his marriage proposal and they return to his Cornish mansion, Manderley, where the sinister head housekeeper, Mrs. Danvers (Judith Anderson), keeps the memory of de Winter's deceased first wife Rebecca alive. Mrs. Danvers consistently undermines the second Mrs. de Winter's attempts to replace her beautiful predecessor, even suggesting suicide as a remedy for her frustrations.*

When the stormy seas off the Cornish coast yield up Rebecca's body, the boat she died in is found to have been deliberately scuttled and Maxim is accused of murder. He confesses to his second wife that he hated Rebecca, who died accidentally while taunting him with tales of her infidelities and claiming to be pregnant with a child that wasn't his.

In an attempt to provide the coroner's inquest with a motive for Maxim's alleged murder of Rebecca, her most recent lover, Jack Favell (George Sanders), leads the investigators to a Dr. Baker (Leo G. Carroll), who, Favell expects, will testify to Rebecca's pregnancy. Instead, Dr. Baker reveals that Rebecca was dying of an incurable cancer, leading the inquest to return a verdict of suicide that clears Maxim's name. Maddened by the verdict, an enraged Mrs. Danvers sets fire to Manderley, perishing in the flames.

***

Rebecca was Hitchcock's first American film under his new contract with David O. Selznick and his first direct contact with the man who would prove to be his nemesis in the Production Code office, Joseph I. Breen. Of all the sources adapted by the director and his screenwriters, Daphne du Maurier's book was the most popular and most successful as a novel. When the book was first published in 1938, Hitchcock expressed an interest in purchasing the rights, but could not compete in a bidding war with larger producers. One such producer was David O. Selznick who, with his story editor Val Lewton, submitted a synopsis to the Production Code office for analysis before deciding to make an offer on the book. Selznick and Lewton were concerned about the possibility of Code acceptance because, in the novel, Maxim de Winter actually kills Rebecca, shooting her in response to her taunting, but fake, claim that she is carrying another man's child. In the original du Maurier version, de Winter opens the sea-cocks on Rebecca's boat and sends the craft carrying her dead body out to sink in the bay. When the coroner's inquest reveals that Rebecca's body was actually heavy with cancer rather than a child, her death is judged to be a suicide, and Maxim gets off scot-free. In the judgment of Breen's office, this was "a clear violation of the Production Code, since it apparently justifies and condones murder."[1]

In spite of the Code warning, Selznick purchased the rights to *Rebecca* for the then exorbitant sum of $50,000, the same amount he paid for *Gone with the Wind,* which was in production at the time he began filming *Rebecca.*

Hitchcock arrived in America carrying a film treatment of *Rebecca* he had developed with his wife Alma, his secretary Joan Harrison, and British writer Michael Hogan. In the first of many skirmishes that marked their eight-year association, Selznick rejected Hitchcock's treatment with a three-thousand-word memo that clearly contradicted his statement that he was "shocked beyond words."[2] Hitchcock would remark thirty years later that Selznick's memo "was so long that I've just finished reading it."[3]

Because both men wanted full control of their projects, Hitchcock and Selznick formed an edgy but mutually reinforcing collaboration. In retrospect, Selznick's rejection of Hitchcock's initial treatment seems more than justified. In an attempt to enliven du Maurier's humorless story, the director tried to imbue the nameless and insecure protagonist of the novel not only with a name, but also with some of the spunkiness of the British heroines of *The 39 Steps* and *The Lady Vanishes,* thereby undermining the self-conscious characteristics of the second Mrs. de Winter that Selznick admired.

In Selznick's view, Hitchcock's treatment also sullied the portraits of the novel's other characters, detoxifying Mrs. Danvers, demystifying Maxim de Winter, and vulgarizing Beatrice, de Winter's sister. "We bought *Rebecca* and we intend to make *Rebecca,*" Selznick dictated, demanding a revised treatment from Hitchcock's team and hiring playwrights Philip MacDonald and Robert E. Sherwood to help shape the final product.[4]

Hitchcock's first direct contact with the Production Code office took place following the submission of the initial *Rebecca* script, when the director and Val Lewton met with Joe Breen and his assistant Geoffrey Shurlock at the Victor Hugo restaurant. As they had warned prior to the purchase of *Rebecca,* Breen and Shurlock reiterated that because "this man murders his wife, covers up the evidence, identifies another body as his wife's, remarries, and finally goes off scot-free, it is a story of high lighted, unpunished murder and . . . cannot be approved."[5]

In a follow-up memorandum to the Production Code files, Breen states hopefully that "it would appear that we are on our way to a solution of the difficulty. Briefly, this solution is suggested by Mr. Hitchcock's thought that it will be contrived in a dramatic way so that there will be no murder of the wife by her husband. She will die as the result of an accident, but the circumstances will be such . . . that the husband, panic-stricken, will do all the things he now does in the story, even though he has not murdered his wife."[6]

At the time of Hitchcock's first meeting with Breen, Selznick was consumed with the cutting and marketing of *Gone with the Wind.* This extravaganza had its own problems with the Production Code, not the least of which was the fight over Rhett's farewell speech to Scarlett, culminating in the memorable line, "Frankly, my dear, I don't give a damn." Selznick held the Code in open contempt and was not pleased with the proposal that Rebecca's death be accidental. "The whole story of *Rebecca* is of a man who has murdered his wife," Selznick complained, "and it now becomes the story of a man who buried a wife who was killed accidentally!"[7] Given the producer's antipathy toward the Code and his view that treating Rebecca's death as an accident was absurd, the next script submitted for Code review still depicted Maxim de Winter as a murderer.

The reaction of the Code office was predictable. Breen wrote Selznick that "the material, in our judgment, is definitely and specifically in violation of the Production Code and that, because of this, it cannot be approved." Breen went on to list three specific objections:

1. As now written, it is the story of a murderer, who is permitted to go off "scot free."
2. The quite inescapable inference of sex perversion.
3. The repeated references, in the dialogue, to the alleged illicit rela-

> tionship between Favell and the first Mrs. de Winter, and the frequent references to the alleged illegitimate child-to-be.

The letter goes on to document, by page number, a catchall of words and phrases to be eliminated, including "damned," "you ass," "for God's sake," "Oh, lord," "lived in hell," "harpie," "lovers," and "Oh my God."[8]

In order for the script to receive Code approval, Breen stipulated, it would be necessary either to "establish the fact that the first Mrs. de Winter died as the result of an accident" (as suggested some weeks back in the meeting with Hitchcock and Lewton), "or that the murderer, de Winter, be punished for his crime."[9]

After receiving Breen's letter, the production company began altering the script during shooting and sending the revisions to Breen on a daily basis. Lewton apologized to Breen for this hurry-up arrangement, but the shooting schedule and the constant flow of memos from Selznick made it necessary.[10]

Of the three key objections listed by Breen, only the first, the absolution of de Winter by rendering Rebecca's death accidental, was completely incorporated in the final film. The references to Rebecca's affair with Jack Favell remained an integral part of the film, although the force of the "phantom" pregnancy was blunted somewhat by upgrading the doctor played by Leo G. Carroll from an abortionist in the book to a respectable physician in the movie.

The "quite inescapable inference of sex perversion" also remained in the film, at least insofar as Mrs. Danvers's lesbian attraction to Rebecca was concerned. From the standpoint of the present day, this attraction remains "inescapably clear to all but the most innocent of viewers."[11] It was certainly clear to Hitchcock and to Breen, who specifically objected to Mrs. Danvers's description of Rebecca's physical attributes" and her handling of Rebecca's "various garments, particularly the nightgown."[12]

It may be true that to the present-day viewer, "the implications of a lesbian relationship between Rebecca and Mrs. Danvers are, in fact, considerably clearer in the film than in the novel."[13] It's not at all certain, though, that this relationship was clear to the average 1940 moviegoer. When asked years later whether she portrayed the character of Mrs. Danvers to emphasize a possible lesbian relationship, Judith Anderson said, "Why no, we never thought of such things at that time."[14] While the

Mrs. Danvers (Judith Anderson) encourages the second Mrs. de Winter (Joan Fontaine) to commit suicide by jumping from the window to the cliffs below.

actress may not have thought of such things, it seems clear that her director did. Reports from the set indicate that Hitchcock "assumed the character in rehearsals and showed Anderson how to position herself for optimum camera effect. 'I knew I was in the presence of a master,' she said afterward. 'I had utter trust and faith in him.'"[15]

So, although the censors expunged all references to a lesbian relationship from the film's dialogue, Hitchcock managed to suggest it implicitly through Danvers's fondling of Rebecca's lingerie and the tone of her recollections of the first Mrs. de Winter. Hitchcock also cleverly managed to film Maxim's account of Rebecca's death in a manner that leaves some room for doubt regarding his culpability and masks the absurdity of the contrived accident. Instead of using a standard flashback when Maxim recounts the specifics of Rebecca's death, Hitchcock causes the camera to pan across the room where she died, following Rebecca's path without her being present. The camera starts from the divan with its ashtray full of cigarette butts, moves past the tea table, and ends focusing on the block and tackle where, in Maxim's narration, after daring her husband to kill her, she stumbles and strikes her head. By foregoing the standard flashback and telling the story visually in this way, Hitchcock achieves two objectives. First, he avoids showing Rebecca, who never appears physically on-screen even though her presence is felt throughout the film. Second, he leaves open the possibility, particularly for readers of the book, that Maxim may be lying.

The Code-inspired deviations from the plot of the book did not affect the film's popularity. *Rebecca* was an enormous critical and commercial success. Reviewers were overwhelmingly positive. The *New Yorker* found the film "even more stirring than the novel," and *Theater Arts* pronounced it "a piece of suspenseful Hitchcock magic."[16] *Time* called *Rebecca* a "splendid job," and devoted a third of its review to praise for the director's beautifully orchestrated "confession scene."[17] One reviewer, James Shelley Hamilton, objected to the late turnaround in Maxim's character, noting, "A plot surprise, in a mystery story, is one thing, a character surprise, with all its upsetting of emotional attitudes, is another."[18]

The film's popularity was reflected in the Academy Award selections for 1940, with *Rebecca* winning Oscars for both Best Picture and Best Cinematography. Hitchcock received the first of five nominations for Best Director and suffered the first of five losses, this time to John Ford for *The Grapes of Wrath.* Joan Fontaine was nominated for the Best Actress award, but lost to Ginger Rogers's portrayal in *Kitty Foyle.*

The film returned a profit of $700,000 to Selznick International Pictures, after subtracting a cost of just over $1 million. This pleased Hitchcock, whose previous British films had not earned nearly that much, but disappointed Selznick, who was hoping for another blockbuster on the order of *Gone with the Wind.* Still, both men had every right to be proud of the film. It's fair to say that, in spite of their pronounced differences and disagreements, each man learned from the other. Although Selznick's meddling memos "certainly ruffled Hitchcock, they benefitted *Rebecca* and helped form the Englishman's reputation for efficiency."[19] Whereas Hitchcock thought in visual terms and sometimes connected images with broad leaps that ignored plot and characterization, Selznick often tolerated unimaginative visuals in an attempt to remain faithful to the source material. Whereas Selznick was a man who wanted to "use all the pieces," Hitchcock understood that certain pieces mattered more than others, and it was the director's visual ingenuity in filming Maxim's confession scene that helped the audience accept the incredible Code-inspired contrivance of Rebecca's fatal accident.[20]

In an interview years later with the critic Richard Schickel, Hitchcock summarized the two men's contrasting points of view regarding novel adaptation, characterizing Selznick's approach as the belief that a novel should "be followed meticulously, especially if it was a best seller, because the public, having read the scene, would want to see it come to life on the screen." In Hitchcock's view, however, "When you consider the vast world audience, a best-seller—I don't care how big it is—doesn't reach anything like the same number of people or meet the same conditions as a film. . . . So my instincts are to go with the visual and not follow the words of the novel. Follow the story line if you wish, but retell it in cinematic form."[21]

The sheer numbers bear out Hitchcock's argument. In the years between 1938 and 1965, Daphne du Maurier's novel *Rebecca* never went out of print, selling 2,829,313 copies. Selznick and Hitchcock's film version of the novel reached over twice that number in its initial release, without considering rereleases, TV airings, and DVD recordings. On the strength of those numbers, the lasting images of *Rebecca* are formed not by du Maurier's words, but rather by Judith Anderson as the malicious Mrs. Danvers, Laurence Olivier as the imperious Maxim de Winter, and Joan Fontaine as the insecure second Mrs. de Winter. And, of course, the visual imagery of Alfred Hitchcock.

In spite of their differences, Hitchcock and Selznick remained friends throughout the remainder of their lives. The same cannot be said for Hitchcock and Breen, although the director's reaction to his first joust with Breen was not unfavorable. Hitchcock reported that the "spirited give and take" with the Production Code office had "all the thrill of competitive horse trading." As an example, he told an interviewer, "Breen wants Rebecca to die of cancer and I want her to be shot with a gun." Depicting himself as the soul of reason, the director added, "In the middle of the argument, I suggested that we get together on a hammer murder."[22]

Breen's chief worry over *Rebecca* was that Maxim de Winter might go unpunished for the murder of his first wife. A reporter, concerned about the impact of the Code on de Winter's fate, asked the director, "Would it be necessary to kill him?" "You mean Breen?" Hitchcock responded. "I don't think so."[23]

7

Foreign Correspondent (1940)

Synopsis. New York Globe *reporter Johnny Jones (Joel McCrea) is asked to change his name to Huntley Haverstock and travel to Europe to assess the threatened outbreak of world conflict. In London, he meets an elderly Dutch diplomat named Van Meer (Albert Basserman), one of the few people who might be able to prevent war. At a conference in Amsterdam organized by the head of the Universal Peace Party, Stephen Fisher (Herbert Marshall), Van Meer is kidnapped while a double is assassinated as a decoy.*

Johnny flags down a car driven by fellow reporter Scott ffolliott (George Sanders), whose passenger happens to be Fisher's beautiful daughter Carol (Laraine Day). They follow the assassin to the Dutch countryside, where they lose track of him until Johnny spots a windmill turning in the wrong direction. He investigates while Carol and Scott go for help. Inside the windmill, he finds the real Van Meer, drugged and held captive. But Van Meer's captors manage to escape with their prisoner, and no one believes Johnny has seen him alive.

Carol and Johnny fall for each other, but Johnny discovers an attempt on his life was ordered by Carol's father and that his Peace Party is a front for an organization of spies intent on fomenting war. Carol refuses to believe him, and he and Scott cannot convince Scotland Yard either. On the day war is declared, Fisher, fearing exposure, leaves London with his daughter on a Clipper plane, which Johnny and Scott also manage to board. The plane is shot down over the ocean, and Fisher sacrifices himself to save the other survivors, including Johnny, Scott, and Carol.

Now reconciled, Johnny and Carol return to London where, during a blackout in the midst of a German bombing, Johnny carries on an overseas broadcast, asking America to "hang on to your lights, they're the only lights left in the world."

***

In making *Foreign Correspondent,* Hitchcock challenged both the Production Code and the Neutrality Acts put in place by the US Congress between 1935 and 1938 to limit US involvement in future wars. They reflected a widespread disillusionment and increasing isolationism following World War I as well as the belief that America had been pushed into that conflict not to make the world safe for democracy, but to make profits for bankers and munitions makers. Will Hays and Joe Breen were only too happy to reflect the isolationist sentiments of the Neutrality Acts in interpreting the Production Code, since the MPPDA was reluctant to offend any country, including Nazi Germany, which provided its studio membership with significant box-office receipts.

Foreign Correspondent was based on *Personal History,* a combination of memoir and historical analysis by war correspondent Vincent Sheean that won the National Book Award in 1935. Sheean wrote about his firsthand experience with the Bolshevik Revolution, the rise of Mussolini and Hitler, and the Spanish Civil War, and predicted a coming world war against the Nazis. Producer Walter Wanger acquired the rights to the book in 1936 and put a series of writers to work adapting it for the screen. An early 1938 treatment submitted for Production Code review led to the admonition that a film version of *Personal History* "might arouse audience feeling against the present German regime."[1] A revised treatment was also rejected by the Code office because it "raises issues regarding the present Civil War in Spain and the treatment of the Jews in Germany."[2]

Discouraged by the Production Code responses, Wanger postponed production plans for *Personal History. Variety* speculated that the postponement reflected box-office concerns, reporting that "the shelved script is known to contain highly controversial angles as well as direct pokes at certain governments which the producer feels will cut the foreign take."[3]

Meanwhile, Hitchcock had begun filming *Rebecca.* He was, however, already looking ahead to his next project, hoping to find one that would free him from David O. Selznick's perpetual meddling. Still busy with *Gone with the Wind,* Selznick had no other projects lined up for Hitchcock after *Rebecca.* This left the director free to accept an offer from Wanger, who had long admired Hitchcock. Wanger offered the director a free hand in developing a new approach to *Personal History,* and when Hitchcock agreed to take on the project, the producer cut a deal with Selznick, paying him $5,000 a week for Hitchcock's services. Since Hitchcock's salary was only $2,500 per week, this represented a $2,500 weekly profit for Selznick. At the same time, Wanger agreed to pay Alma Hitchcock $2,500 a week, which she would earn free and clear of Selznick, to help with project development. So, while Hitchcock concentrated on *Rebecca,* his wife, Alma, and his secretary Joan Harrison began adapting *Personal History.*[4]

By Christmas 1939, the Hitchcocks' first Christmas in America, Alma and Harrison had molded *Personal History* into a treatment worthy of the master of suspense that sidestepped the censors' concerns. The two women had replaced Sheean's formless memoir with a world of spies, traitors, assassination attempts, a plane crash, and an American hero, a street-smart New York newspaper reporter turned fledgling foreign correspondent whose name, Johnny Jones, is upgraded to Huntley Haverstock by his editor to make him sound more experienced.

A parade of fourteen writers wound up working to turn the adventures of Jones/Haverstock into a finished screenplay. The first of these was Hitchcock's British screenwriter Charles Bennett, followed by a group that included novelist James Hilton and humorist Robert Benchley, who was eventually given a part in the film. At the end of the parade, the only element retained from the Sheean memoir was the opening setting, Holland.

Because of the Neutrality Acts, any producer undertaking an explicitly anti-Nazi film ran the risk of incurring State Department displeasure. And Wanger had already run afoul of the Production Code's restrictions on offending foreign governments and the MPPDA's unwillingness to write off the German-speaking market. The Breen office not only objected to depicting Germany as a haven for spies, it also didn't want villains speaking identifiable German. Having encountered this obstacle in *The Lady Vanishes,* Hitchcock adopted the ploy he had used in that film and had the villains speak in a made-up vernacular, ostensibly created by reciting German backward.[5] Since Germans could not be depicted as villains, the primary enemy in the film, the sponsor of the nest of spies, is identified as the mythical country of Borovia. Hitler is mentioned only once in the film, when the novice Johnny is looking for leads. "How about Hitler?" he asks, "Don't you think it might be a good idea to pump him? He must have something on his mind." When the war the fictional spies have been trying to foment finally comes, though, it is war with Germany, which had actually been at war with Britain for over a year when the film was released. Even though the villains in *Foreign Correspondent* were artfully disguised as Borovians and never identified as Germans, "the contrivance was so clever," as writer Mark Glancy pointed out, that "the audience in 1940 would have had no trouble decoding the story, and they may not have noticed that they had to decode it."[6]

One of Hitchcock's parade of screenwriters, a young man named Richard Maibaum who later helped to script the early James Bond films, complained to the director that the screenplay wasn't very logical. "Oh, dear boy," Hitchcock replied, "don't be dull. I'm not interested in logic. I'm interested in effect. If the audience ever thinks about logic, it's on their way home after the show, and by that time, you see, they've paid for their tickets."[7]

The effects Hitchcock created in *Foreign Correspondent* are among his most famous. Joel McCrea pursues an assassin through a black sea of bobbing umbrellas in a rain-drenched Amsterdam square and follows him to a country windmill whose blades are turning in the wrong direction to signal a circling plane. As McCrea hides from the assassins inside the creaking works of the windmill, Hitchcock teases the audience by having the hero's coat caught in the ponderous wooden gears connected to the wrong-way blades. And the film's final scenes include a realistic plane crash at sea in which the doomed plane's downward flight is followed through rear projections of the pilot's view until it hits the ocean and a hundred gallons of water burst through the rear projection screen into the cockpit and fill the plane's cabin as the frightened passengers struggle to keep their heads above water.

None of these effects were cheap. The reproduction of the rainy Amsterdam square covered ten acres and required an elaborate drainage system. And the final crash required a complete plane as well as an underwater system of rails to control the drift of the broken wing and tail sections clung to by survivors. Wartime conditions also increased the costs when a ship containing cameras and second-unit footage of London and Amsterdam was torpedoed and sunk. The budget of $1.5 million made *Foreign Correspondent* Hitchcock's most expensive film up to that time and was more than double the average cost of Wanger's previous films. But the producer admired and trusted Hitchcock, and "accepted the expensive sets and special effects as the cost of doing business with the Englishman."[8]

With the villainous enemy consigned to Borovia, the Production Code office found little to criticize in the script of *Foreign Correspondent* prepared by Hitchcock's team of writers. In a letter to his boss, Will Hays, Joe Breen noted that Hitchcock's script bore no relationship to the version of

Sheean's memoir that had given the office trouble two years earlier.[9] Breen subsequently logged only minor comments to Wanger, cautioning against excessive brutality in the treatment of the captive Van Meer and advising that the injection of drugs into Van Meer's wrist should not be photographed.[10] Breen also warned Wanger that the local "censor boards almost invariably delete the actions showing guns pointed into the backs of characters" and asked that specific references to God, rude driving, and sex be eliminated from the script.[11]

In addition to the thinly disguised Borovians, Hitchcock and Wanger managed to sneak other political commentary past the Production Code. In the final scenes, the script casts the Neutrality Acts in opposition to the Bill of Rights. When the American captain of the ship that rescues the crash survivors tries to use the arguments of the Neutrality Acts to keep Johnny from reporting on the plane's being shot down, the foreign correspondent argues that this violates the freedom of the press and tricks the captain by repeating the news loudly within earshot of an open line to his New York newspaper office.

With most of *Foreign Correspondent* completed, Hitchcock made a quick, unpublicized trip to England. While in London, which was anxiously preparing for imminent visits from the Luftwaffe, Hitchcock tried unsuccessfully to persuade his mother to relocate to the United States, checked on the availability of his English funds, agreed to make war propaganda films for England's Ministry of Information, and helped to arrange for the evacuation of a group of orphans to the safer side of the Atlantic.

Hitchcock returned to the United States determined to alert America to the plight of an England living under German bombsights. To this end, he met with Walter Wanger and screenwriter Ben Hecht to develop an up-to-the-minute ending for *Foreign Correspondent.* Hecht wrote the ending in a day, echoing Churchill in a ringing plea for action delivered into a microphone by Joel McCrea with bombs dropping on London.

> Hello America! I've been watching a part of the world being blown to pieces. A part of the world as nice as Vermont and Ohio, Virginia, California, and Illinois lies ripped and bleeding like a steer in a slaughterhouse. And I've seen things that make the history of the savages look like Pollyanna legend.

Bombs explode outside and the lights are cut off, forcing McCrea to continue without his prepared speech. He describes the carnage in London and ends with a plea delivered as the national anthem plays, imploring the United States to

> keep those lights burning. Cover them with steel, ring them with guns! Build a canopy of battleships and bombing planes around them. Hello America! Hang onto your lights! They are the only lights left in the world!

This tacked-on ending was unjustified dramatically, out of sync with the rest of the film, seemingly in violation of the Neutrality Acts, and out of place in a Hitchcock thriller. But it was prescient. The scene was filmed on July 5, 1940, and just five days later the first German bombs fell on London.

Mindful of the Neutrality Acts, Hecht had carefully worded *Foreign Correspondent*'s new ending so that Hitchcock could argue that it wasn't anti-isolationist but rather pro-preparedness, urging that Americans stand ready to repulse any incursion. While the Production Code accepted this interpretation, not everyone did. Harry Hopkins, President Roosevelt's unofficial emissary to Winston Churchill, sent Hitchcock a congratulatory telegram, and Joseph Goebbels, Nazi Germany's minister of propaganda, reportedly praised *Foreign Correspondent* as a "masterpiece of propaganda."[12]

Criticism of the final speech came from a surprising source. When the movie was released in England, a group of prominent British film figures led by producer Michael Balcon, Hitchcock's onetime mentor, signed a letter in the *Documentary Newsletter* denouncing McCrea's inspirational speech as the blatherings of "an irresponsible American newshound" whose call to US arms was "an insult" to the British "army of civilians" who, they predicted, would inevitably turn the tide on Hitler.[13]

A few weeks earlier, Balcon had been widely quoted in London and New York newspapers denouncing the "famous directors" of England who were hiding out from the dangers of war in Hollywood "while we who are left behind shorthanded are trying to harness the films to our great national effort." Without mentioning Hitchcock's name, Balcon left no doubt about who he had in mind, citing "a plump young junior technician" whom Balcon himself had promoted upward "from department to department."[14]

Joel McCrea and Laraine Day listening to bombs dropping as McCrea prepares to deliver the final speech of *Foreign Correspondent* from a blacked-out London broadcasting studio. (Courtesy of Jerry Ohlinger.)

Balcon's hurtful comments were not the only abuse aimed at the absent Hitchcock in the English press. British screenwriter and actor Seymour Hicks had publicly scoffed at those English filmmakers "gallantly facing the footlights" abroad and proposed a film satirically titled "Gone with the Wind Up" to be directed by Hitchcock and starring fellow expatriates Charles Laughton and Herbert Marshall.[15]

These comments were deeply upsetting to the Hitchcocks. Encouraged by Selznick and his wife, Hitchcock uncharacteristically issued a press release in which he ascribed Balcon's remarks to jealousy over the producer's own failed experience in Hollywood and added, "The manner in which I am helping my country is not Mr. Balcon's business."[16]

The image of Hitchcock as a shirker could not have been further from the truth. In making *Foreign Correspondent,* he had flouted both the Breen office and the Neutrality Acts to publicize Britain's plight. Even if he had wanted to return to England, he was shackled to the United States by his contract with Selznick. He would go on to honor his pledge to make propaganda films for England and contribute generous amounts of time and money to wartime causes. As one biographer noted, "From the very beginning of the war, he was wholeheartedly involved, and to the end of his life the full extent of his involvement was never publicized."[17]

Michael Balcon and his compatriots were just about the only viewers who didn't like *Foreign Correspondent.* It was popular with the critics and the public on both sides of the Atlantic. *Time* called it "easily one of the year's finest pictures," and Otis Ferguson, writing in the *New Republic,* said, "If you want a seminar on how to make a movie travel the lightest and fastest way, in a kind of beauty that is peculiar to movies alone, you can see this once, and then again to see what you missed, and then study it twice."[18] Bosley Crowther added in the *New York Times* that Hitchcock "has packed about as much romantic action, melodramatic hullabaloo, comical diversion and illusion of momentous consequence as the liveliest imagination could conceive."[19]

When the film opened in London, Dilys Powell wrote in the *Sunday Times,* "With so much that is brilliant—the realism of the wrecked plane, the beautiful scenes in the darkness of the windmill amid the turning wheels, the superb melodramatic shot of the torturers' faces seen by the victim under the arc lamp—I scarcely noticed the blemishes. This film is worth fifty *Rebeccas.*"[20]

The film did well at the box office, but, because of its high costs, it lost $370,000. It was nominated for six Academy Awards, including Best Picture, Best Special Effects, Best Writing (Charles Bennett and Joan Harrison were credited, with dialogue by James Hilton and Robert Benchley), and Best Supporting Actor (Albert Basserman). None of the nominees won Oscars, but the other Hitchcock film that came out in 1940, *Rebecca,* won Best Picture.

Foreign Correspondent was a success as both entertainment and propaganda.[21] By the time it was released, the war in Europe was causing the Production Code to relax its views on social and political issues in films. After stating in 1938 that "the industry has resisted and must continue to resist the lure of propaganda," Joe Breen's boss Will Hays had changed his tune by 1940 and was praising movies "that dramatize present-day social conditions," including "issues of war and peace."[22]

After making two films in America, Hitchcock was learning that the Production Code office could be manipulated. The office could be lenient and responsive to artistry and argument once images made it to the screen. But the real problem with the censors was their power over what made it to the screen in the first place. As Otis Ferguson observed at the time, the Code's "influence on what can be taken up as a subject, what can be written into a movie script, what can be made with cameras, is insidious and final. . . . Many things have been allowed and passed over with a sort of bought tolerance. But many things have died in the initial stages before you ever heard about them."[23] As a case in point, the original scenario for Vincent Sheean's *Personal History* never made it to the screen after the Breen office raised the specter of German disapproval in 1938.

Between 1939 and 1941, isolationists in Congress estimated that Hollywood produced approximately fifty films, including *Foreign Correspondent,* which they considered anti-Nazi in theme and/or content. The highest number of these films came from Warner Bros. after one of its representatives in Germany, who was Jewish, was clubbed to death by thugs in a Berlin back alley. Politicians were "appalled at the possibility that five or six movie company presidents could be influencing foreign policy through propaganda films seen by a movie-going public of eighty million people a week." Joseph P. Kennedy, US ambassador to Great Britain and a leading isolationist, visited Hollywood in November 1940 and insisted at a private dinner for motion picture industry leaders that anti-Nazi films must stop because, in his view, the fall of England was inevitable and the United States would eventually have to make peace with Hitler. Noting that many industry leaders were Jewish, Kennedy allegedly suggested that "their fate might eventually be as tragic as that of European Jews if they were not more careful in their pro-Allied film treatments."[24]

A number of isolationist senators shared Kennedy's views, and one, Burton K. Wheeler, the chairman of the Senate Committee on International Commerce, instigated a subcommittee investigation of propaganda in films on September 9, 1941. The subcommittee heard testimony from senators who were afraid that a small number of filmmakers could exert a great influence on the public's opinion of foreign policy. It balanced these views with testimony from four Hollywood executives, represented by counsel Wendell L. Willkie, who had just lost the presidential election to Roosevelt in 1940. During the testimony, Willkie observed that one of the hoped-for results of the pressure of the Senate investigation was to influence the industry to alter its policies so that they were more in accord with isolationist views, concluding, "The industry is prepared to resist such pressure with all of the strength at its command."[25]

Foreign Correspondent was mentioned twice in the course of the subcommittee hearings. The subcommittee adjourned on September 26, 1941. On December 7, 1941, the Japanese bombed Pearl Harbor, and declarations of war with Japan and Germany rendered the terms of the Neutrality Acts and the wishes of the isolationist senators irrelevant. Hitchcock and Hecht's closing plea for the alliance of America and Great Britain had been answered, and worries about hurting the feelings of the Nazi government would never again trouble the Production Code.

8

Mr. and Mrs. Smith (1941)

Synopsis. *Ann and David Smith (Carole Lombard and Robert Montgomery), a well-off couple living in New York, have been bickering over David's ill-advised statement in a truth-telling game that he doubts whether he would marry Ann again if he had his life to live over. When they learn that a legal technicality has rendered their marriage invalid, David decides he would definitely marry his wife again, but she is not so sure she wants him.*

Attempting to win Ann all over again, David takes her to Mamma Lucy's, the restaurant where he had asked her to marry him. But the restaurant is now so run down that the scruffy cat that invades customers' tables refuses to eat the house soup. When the gambit fails, David is forced to spend a night at his men's club, the Beefeaters.

Enjoying her newfound independence, Ann reverts to her maiden name and takes a job as a sales clerk in a department store. David contrives to have her fired after learning that she had a date with the store owner. Undeterred, Ann encourages the attentions of David's law partner, Jefferson Custer (Gene Raymond), who has always liked her.

Jefferson's parents take Ann's interest in their son seriously and invite the couple to stay with them at the Lake Placid ski resort. David follows the pair to Lake Placid, pretending to be suffering from pneumonia induced by lovesick drinking bouts. After a series of misunderstandings, during which David is found to be perfectly healthy and Ann asks Jefferson to marry her, Ann and David realize they are made for each other and decide to stay together.

***

After finishing *Foreign Correspondent,* Hitchcock, on loan to RKO, made his most atypical American film, the screwball comedy *Mr. and Mrs. Smith.* While the movie did little to advance Hitchcock's reputation as an auteur, it did help him learn a little more about how to deal with the Production Code censors. The director told François Truffaut that he decided to direct it in a "weak moment" as a favor to the star Carole

Lombard who, with her husband, Clark Gable, had become good friends with Hitchcock and Alma.[1] The promise of a $15,000 bonus from Selznick if he could complete two RKO films within a year undoubtedly helped the cash-strapped director to overcome any reluctance he might have felt about the assignment.

The script was already completed when Hitchcock accepted the project. It was written by Norman Krasna, who already had several successful comedies to his credit, including *Hands across the Table,* which also starred Carole Lombard. Krasna would go on to win an Oscar in 1943 for writing *Princess O'Rourke.* Hitchcock did nothing to alter the screenplay because, as he told Truffaut, he felt he "really didn't understand the type of people portrayed in the film." Consequently, all he tried to do was to "photograph the scenes as written."[2]

Mr. and Mrs. Smith was lighter fare than most of Hitchcock's films, but the Production Code office was just as diligent in finding fault with this comedy as with his suspenseful thrillers. The Code reviewers found the basic story acceptable, but cited eighteen unacceptable items in Norman Krasna's screenplay. These items included the words *stinks, old bat,* and *bedroom slippers*, a derogatory reference to the Girl Scouts, and matters of dress for both Ann and David. "Ann should not be shown 'clad in scant panties and brassiere,' but should be wearing a negligee," the censors wrote. And David should be wearing an undershirt in one scene, and in another, "should not be shown unhooking the top of his trousers," presumably so that there is "nothing sex suggestive about David's reactions . . . getting ready for bed."[3]

Krasna was noted for his racy dialogue and the censors objected to the underlined words in the following three exchanges on the grounds that their context made them "sex-suggestive or otherwise unacceptable":

> ANN (*to Jefferson, after he declines to kiss her because he has a cold*): That's another difference between you and David. Colds never stopped him. He got the measles once. How I never got the measles I'll never know.

> DAVID (*to his friend Chuck after speaking with a blind date on the phone*): She liked my voice.

CHUCK: That's not all she'll like.

ANN (*to Jefferson on a horse-drawn sleigh ride*): I love the smell of snow!
JEFFERSON (*sniffing the air and wincing*): That's the horse.[4]

Krasna changed the line "That's the horse" to "That's not the snow" but retained the other objectionable lines. Still, he made enough changes in the second draft of the script to whittle the censors' objections down to three:

1. The second draft of the screenplay showed David doodling Ann's maiden name, Miss Ann Krausheimer, changing it to MisTress Ann Krausheimer. The censors responded, "The gag on the use of the word 'mistress' is unacceptable."
2. The line "That's not all she'll like" had survived the script revision but was marked for omission as "sex suggestive."
3. "The gag with the plumbing must *NOT* suggest the flushing of the toilet."[5]

Hitchcock and Krasna effectively ignored these objections and the initial print of the film included the "mistress" gag, the "sex suggestive" line, and the sound of a flushing toilet.

Upon viewing the rough cut, the censors required three changes before they could award the Code's Seal of Approval. These were:

1. The elimination of a "revealing shot of the camera panning between Miss Lombard's legs."
2. The omission of a reference to Mamma Lucy's "big bazooms."
3. The cutting of "three sounds of the toilet flushing."[6]

Hitchcock and Krasna made changes 1 and 2 and substituted clanging pipes for the sound of a toilet flushing. It would be another twenty years before the director would crack the Code's bathroom barrier by not only showing a toilet on-screen in *Psycho,* but also filming the actual flushing of evidence.

More than half of the lines the Code office objected to in the original script remained in the finished film. Early in his American career, Hitchcock was learning to make relatively few changes in response to the censors' early script suggestions and wait for their reactions to the film itself. If the censors still objected to what appeared on the screen, he would bargain with them, surrendering a line here or a scene there in order to protect cherished images.

Krasna's script was wildly uneven, and so is the picture. A few bits, like the nightclub scene, which begins with Robert Montgomery pretending to be the escort of an attractive woman at the table next to him and ends with a self-inflicted nose bleed, elicit laughter, but too many fall flat. Nonetheless, Lombard is delightful throughout. She is clearly enjoying herself, and her wit and intelligence shine through her performance. On the set, her prankish sense of humor mirrored Hitchcock's own. Reacting to the director's often misquoted observation comparing actors to cattle, she greeted him on the first day of shooting by installing a small corral with three stalls on the set and filling each stall with a calf carrying the name of one of the film's three stars tied around its neck with a red ribbon. Lombard also teased her costar Robert Montgomery, a staunch Republican, by sneaking off during filming and plastering his car with Roosevelt stickers.

Before coming to America, Hitchcock had told an interviewer that he would like to cast Lombard "not in the type of superficial comedy which she so often plays, but in a much more meaty comedy-drama, giving her plenty of scope for characterization."[7] Although the star clearly fit the role of the icy Hitchcock blonde, she would never have the chance to work with the director again. Tragically, she made only one more movie after *Mr. and Mrs. Smith, To Be or Not to Be,* for Ernst Lubitsch, before she was killed in a plane crash while touring the United States promoting the sale of war bonds.

Cashing in on Lombard's popularity, *Mr. and Mrs. Smith* earned a $670,000 profit for RKO. Reviews were mixed. *Newsweek* found it "extremely funny in spots," but Theodore Strauss in the *New York Times* called it a "chucklesome comedy that fails to mount into a coruscating wave of laughter," and John Mosher of the *New Yorker* wrote it off as "as commonplace a film as one may find anywhere."[8]

The poor reviews didn't hurt Hitchcock's image in Hollywood. He was learning to deal with the censors and had demonstrated his versatility by taking on a screwball comedy and finishing it in eight weeks. He was earning a reputation as an efficient director and had completed the first half of the two-film RKO loan-out that would earn him a promised bonus. He turned his attention to the second of the two films, *Suspicion.*

9

Suspicion (1941)

Synopsis. *Ne'er-do-well playboy Johnnie Aysgarth (Cary Grant) meets and pursues wealthy country girl Lina McLaidlaw (Joan Fontaine). Against the wishes of Lina's father (Sir Cedric Hardwicke), who knows of Johnnie's disreputable past, the two marry and move to an elaborate home on the Sussex coast. Shortly after their marriage, Lina catches Johnnie in a series of lies and learns that he has been sacked for embezzling £2,000 from his employer. Her suspicions of her husband's misdeeds extend to murder when their friend Beaky (Nigel Bruce) dies under mysterious circumstances after entering a business deal with Johnnie. Lina begins to fear for her own life when Johnnie begins inquiring about the efficacy of various poisons and she learns that he has secretly taken out a large insurance policy on her life.*

Worried that Johnnie intends to kill her while driving on a treacherous mountain road, Lina bolts from their car. Johnnie catches her and confesses that he had purchased poison while contemplating suicide, but has decided to face his creditors. When Johnnie assures Lina he had nothing to do with Beaky's death, the two return home together.

***

Suspicion affords an example of a film that was greatly altered by the taboos of both the Production Code and Hollywood studios. The film is based on the novel *Before the Fact* by Francis Iles (Anthony Berkeley Cox), which RKO purchased in 1933 without producing a satisfactory script until David O. Selznick loaned Alfred Hitchcock to the studio in 1940. In the book, which is told from Lina's point of view, Johnnie Aysgarth is not only a philanderer and embezzler but a murderer as well, having successfully killed his wealthy father-in-law. When Lina realizes that her husband has added murder to his list of misdeeds, she willingly drinks a glass of milk she knows he has poisoned to avoid exposing the love of her life as a murderer. Successful murderers were a Production Code no-no, but the original novel contained many other red flags for the censors; both Johnnie and Lina were involved in extramarital affairs and Lina was pregnant at the time of her death, compounding the immorality of her suicidal decision to drink the poison.

The red flags waved by censors often affected Hitchcock the same way that red flags waved in the arena affect bulls. He set out to subvert the strictures of the Code, conceiving an ending in which Lina willingly downs the poisoned milk, but only after writing a letter to her mother explaining that she is desperately in love with Johnnie and doesn't want to live knowing that he is a killer. To ensure that Johnnie will not go on killing, however, she asks him to mail the letter to her mother when he offers her the fatal glass of milk. In Hitchcock's version, after Lina drinks the poison, the final scene of the movie shows Johnnie whistling happily as he deposits the incriminating letter in the mailbox.

Hitchcock was confident he could dodge the censors' red flags by offering a few minor concessions in return for Lina's voluntary poisoning and Johnnie's presumed imprisonment once the incriminating letter is opened. He proved to be right in this assessment, at least insofar as the guardians of the Production Code were concerned. After Hitchcock made a show of scrapping most of the novel's taboo elements, including marital infidelity, the father-in-law's murder, and Lina's pregnancy, the censors were able to muster only a few relatively trivial objections to the initial shooting script. These objections addressed concerns over the possible exposure of Lina's breasts in a low-cut ball gown, the presence of multiple liquor bottles in a scene in which a toast is proposed, a few references to a brothel, the mannish appearance of a female dinner guest, and the explicit use of the word *arsenic.*[1] All of these objections were either easily addressed or swept aside.

While Hitchcock was successful in his horse trading with the Production Code, Code officials weren't the only obstacles blocking the director's vision of the film. The higher-ups at RKO decided that it would be a mistake to let Cary Grant play a villain. The director had run into this reasoning once before, when Gainsborough executives decided that Ivor Novello was too popular a property to play a murderer in *The Lodger.* Hitchcock had increased in stature since he filmed *The Lodger,* and he may have hoped he could convince his friends in the RKO front office to go along with his proposed ending. This hope vanished when RKO president George Schaefer fired Hitchcock's front-office contacts and replaced them with the director's nemesis, Joseph Breen, who left his position with the Production Code to become RKO's head of production.

Cary Grant and the potentially fatal glass of milk, which Hitchcock illuminated by inserting a tiny light in the glass.

Breen arrived at RKO in mid-June 1941, just as the studio was testing the initial version of *Before the Fact* (as it was still called) at a preview screening in Pasadena. In accordance with the wishes of the front office, the initial film version did not feature Cary Grant as a murderer. As in the book, Johnnie brings a glass of milk to his suspicious wife, who recites a suicidal prayer and drinks it, expecting to die. When the drink proves to be harmless, she realizes she was wrong about her husband and seeks him out, only to find him preparing to take poison himself in reparation for his wastrel ways. She arrives in time to stop him, and they resolve to go on living together.

The preview audiences panned the jerry-rigged ending. "Trial audiences booed it, and I don't blame them," Hitchcock told the *Herald Tribune*. "They pronounced the girl stupid to willfully drink her possible destruction. With that I don't agree. But I do agree that the necessary half-reel of explanation following the wife's survival was deadly."[2] With the rest of the film completed, Hitchcock conferred with his screenwriters, his wife, Joan Harrison, and Samuel Rafelson, to consider alternative endings. A number of options were suggested, including one in which Johnnie joins the RAF, and two were submitted for Production Code approval in mid-July.

In the version that was finally filmed, Lina views the glass of milk brought by Johnnie warily, fearing that it might be poisoned. She leaves the glass untouched on her nightstand and announces the next morning that she is going to visit her mother. Johnnie insists on driving her and they take off on a wild ride on a winding road high above the sea. Convinced that Johnnie is trying to kill her, Lina opens the car door to leap out, only to be grabbed by Johnnie at the last instant. When the car slews to a stop, she runs from it, pursued by Johnnie. He catches her and confesses that he has been contemplating suicide because of his mounting debts, but has resolved to face his accusers and the possibility of prison. Lina is persuaded by his confession, and in the final shot of the film, the car circles back toward home and Johnnie puts his arm around his wife.

This version had the advantage of requiring little in the way of additional footage. Hitchcock had already filmed a scene in which Lina believes Johnnie attempts to push her out of a speeding car high above the Sussex coast.[3] This scene originally came before the scene with poisoned milk, contributing to Lina's growing suspicions. All Hitchcock had to do was reposition the scene so it followed the refusal of the milk and add roadside dialogue explaining that Johnnie was only trying to keep her from falling out of the car, that he had been contemplating suicide, and that he'd had nothing to do with Beaky's death. Then all that was needed was a wide U-turn in the middle of the road as the couple returned home.

This cobbled-together ending, barely a cut above "It was all a dream," satisfied the Production Code but not the new RKO head of production. With Hitchcock away in New York, Joseph Breen's second-in-command, a producer named Sol Lesser, sabotaged the film by cutting out all deaths and removing any indication that Cary Grant might possibly be a killer.[4] This inane manifestation of the censor's mind at work left the film with a running time of fifty-five bland minutes that might more appropriately have been titled *Unsuspicious.* On his return from New York, an apoplectic Hitchcock managed to convince Breen's boss, George Schaefer, that the lugubrious results of Lesser's cutting were unmarketable and received permission to restore the film to its previous condition.

When Hitchcock's restored version was released, the clumsy ending didn't bother the moviegoing public. *Suspicion* became RKO's highest-grossing film of the year and was nominated for an Academy Award for Best Picture. Although it lost to *How Green Was My Valley,* Joan Fontaine won the Oscar for Best Actress. Although most critics praised the movie—Howard Barnes of the *Herald Tribune* called it "a far finer film than *Rebecca,*"—a few came down hard on the ending. Bosley Crowther of the *New York Times* observed that "the ending is not up to Hitchcock's usual style," and the *Hollywood Reporter* objected to the "sop of a happy ending dragged in by the heels."[5]

Given the constraints imposed on the filmmakers by the Production Code and RKO executives, the last-minute tacked-on ending was probably the best of a bad lot, and better for the box office than Hitchcock's preferred ending with Johnnie whistling at the mailbox. Although Hitchcock's ending had the benefit of a surprise twist, it required moviegoers to believe that Lina would voluntarily drink milk she believed poisoned, an action that was hooted down by the preview audiences and was in direct violation of the Code rule against suicide. It's also quite possible that the RKO executives were right in assuming that the public would not have accepted Cary Grant as a murderer. Grant himself subsequently observed, "I'm sure I didn't do it. My character wasn't that sort of chap at all. He couldn't possibly have murdered her. My character was a rogue, not a rat."[6]

The *Cahiers du cinéma* crowd, for whom Hitchcock could do no wrong, came out strongly in favor of the film's ending, arguing that it was ambiguous enough that the viewer could imagine Johnnie driving Lina back home and doing her in after the credits rolled.[7]

In his celebrated book about Hitchcock, François Truffaut argued that the ending of the film "has an edge over the novel because it allows for subtler nuances of characterization," and observed that "the film version, showing a woman who mistakenly believes her husband is a killer, is less far-fetched than the novel, which is about a woman who accepts the fact that her husband is a murderer" and ultimately drinks the poisoned milk he brings her. In Truffaut's view, "Hollywood's unwritten laws and taboos" actually improved *Suspicion*'s story line.[8] Thus Breen and his RKO lieutenants, although totally wrongheaded in their attempt to rid the movie of every suggestion that Cary Grant might be a murderer, actually did Hitchcock a favor, commercially if not artistically, by insisting that, in the end, Grant could not be a murderer, and especially not a successful murderer.

Joseph Breen's tenure at RKO was short-lived. As head of the Production Code he had exercised control over hundreds of films. As RKO's head of production, however, he found it difficult to control even the output of a single studio.[9] He returned to his post at the Production Code within a year and would joust with Hitchcock in that role for another thirteen years until his retirement.

10

Saboteur (1942)

Synopsis. *Suspected of sabotage after a fire at a California aircraft factory kills a coworker, Barry Kane (Robert Cummings) goes on the run in pursuit of the real saboteur, Frank Fry (Norman Lloyd). Barry traces Fry to the ranch of respected millionaire Charles Tobin (Otto Kruger), the head of a group of spies, who turns him over to the police.*

Barry escapes and seeks shelter in the rural cabin of a blind composer, Phillip Martin, who trusts him, and his niece, Pat Martin (Priscilla Lane), who doesn't. Barry and Pat set out for Soda City, a ghost town near Boulder Dam, following a lead obtained at Tobin's ranch. When their car breaks down they find refuge with some circus performers, who take them in their caravan to Soda City.

The pair find evidence that Tobin's spies intend to blow up the dam, and Pat, who now trusts Barry, goes off to tell the local police while Barry introduces himself to two of the would-be saboteurs as the man responsible for the California aircraft factory fire. Hoping to find Fry, he tells the saboteurs that Tobin has sent him and they agree to help him escape by driving him across the United States to their New York headquarters.

Barry's cover is blown when Tobin arrives in New York at the home of the wealthy socialite fronting for the band of spies. Tobin locks Barry up, but he escapes and finds Fry, the original saboteur, in a newsreel van set up to explode a ship being launched in Brooklyn Harbor.

Barry thwarts the explosion and follows Fry to the Statue of Liberty, where he chases the saboteur up to the platform surrounding Liberty's torch. Fry tumbles backward over a safety rail and Barry tries to save him by grabbing his sleeve. The sleeve rips and Fry falls to his death, but not before providing enough information to clear Barry's name.

***

With the war in Europe raging in 1941, Hitchcock had an idea for a film patterned after *The 39 Steps,* in which an innocent man is pursued across Great Britain while trying to clear his name of a murder charge. In

Hitchcock's update, the locale would be the United States, and the crime would be sabotage, perpetrated by a group of rich isolationists resembling the America Firsters, an antiwar group infiltrated by German agents, whom the director believed represented a real threat on the home front. Hitchcock's personal assistant, Joan Harrison, prepared a treatment, which the director took to David O. Selznick. Selznick, who had just raised Hitchcock's salary to $3,000 per week, was cool to the idea of a sabotage movie but nonetheless eager to capitalize on his director's popularity. So the producer assigned a novice screenwriter, Peter Viertel, to turn the treatment into a screenplay and packaged the resulting screenplay and Hitchcock into a two-picture deal that he sold to Universal Studios for $120,000 and 10 percent of the gross, with the 10 percent contingent on Hitchcock's ability to complete the picture within a tight $750,000 budget.

The initial script of *Saboteur,* whose episodes were "held together by the slenderest of threads" and which Hitchcock himself criticized as undisciplined and "cluttered with too many ideas," covered a lot of ground, taking the hero from a California aircraft factory to a high-society party in New York to the memorable climax on the Statue of Liberty.[1] In an attempt to introduce some continuity and wit to Viertel's screenplay, Hitchcock hired a noted member of the Algonquin Round Table, Dorothy Parker. The famous poet and critic brought her ironic humor to the project but also, as a confirmed left-winger, "peppered the script with anti-establishment zingers aimed at the American upper class and capitalism in general."[2]

The timing of *Saboteur* was propitious. Hitchcock was having his first meeting with production designer Robert Boyle when the Japanese bombed Pearl Harbor. As a result, the film's script, which a year earlier would have raised the hackles of the Production Code as anti-Nazi propaganda, was freed from the constraints of the Neutrality Acts. Even so, the Code officials still found fault with several of the barbs Dorothy Parker had leveled at rich American socialites and fascist sympathizers. Following its initial review of the script, the Code office warned Universal, "There is a disturbing element which appears from time to time throughout the script, and that is the great number of seemingly anti-social speeches and references. It is essential that these speeches be rewritten to avoid giving this flavor."[3]

Examples of the antisocial comments cited by the censors included Barry Kane's observation regarding the archvillain Tobin, "Just because he's got a big ranch and a fancy house and a million-dollar swimming pool, that doesn't say he's a good guy." The Code office also objected to a few of the remarks emanating from Pat's blind uncle: "My dear, the police are always on the alarmist side. They seem to believe that frightening people is the first step toward protecting them" and "I have my own ideas about my duties as a citizen. They sometimes involve disregarding the law."[4] Along the same lines, the censors found fault with a similar remark voiced by the leader of the circus troupe that votes to shelter Barry and Pat: "I have always prided myself that never yet have I served as an instrument of the police." Another antisocial comment flagged by the censors came from a spectator watching fire trucks arrive at the home of the wealthy fifth columnist sheltering Tobin's spies after Barry has touched off an alarm by lighting a match under the sprinkler system: "Yeah, look how fast the engines got there. *They wouldn't do that for you and me.*"[5] The Production Code Administration underlined the objectionable portion of the comment in its letter to Universal to make sure the studio understood the source of its discontent.

Hitchcock went ahead and filmed most of the antisocial lines cited by the Production Code, but his script supervisor flagged them for potential elimination. In the give-and-take that followed, many of the objectionable lines were cut, but Barry's observation that Tobin's riches did not necessarily make him a good guy remained in the finished film, as did Pat's uncle's boast that he sometimes disregarded the law as a matter of his civic duty.

The final film confrontation between the aristocratic Charles Tobin and the democratic Barry Kane "sums up all the class-conscious Parker touches that have gone before" and was passed uncut by the Production Code.[6] Tobin refers to the masses of Americans as the "moron millions" and argues that the "competence of the totalitarian nations is much higher . . . they get things done." Kane responds, "Yes, they get things done. They bomb cities, sink ships, torture and murder—so you and your friends can eat off gold plates." The hero then launches into a rousing call to arms that never would have passed the neutrality-obsessed censors a year earlier, promising to fight back and "win if it takes from now till the cows come home."

In addition to antisocial remarks, the censors objected to the standard complement of offensive words and phrases, including "jeeze," "lousy," "hell," "punks," and "When you've got to go, you've got to go."[7] They also cautioned against using the national anthem as background music because "it is illegal in many states to use this Anthem unless played fully."[8] Additionally, they expressed two concerns regarding potential audience reactions to *Saboteur:* "In view of present conditions, it is highly inadvisable to make use of the sound of sirens in motion pictures for the obvious reason of avoiding any cause of audience panic."[9] And, regarding a scene in the Radio City Music Hall in which shots are fired and an audience member is wounded, "Such scenes as this, we feel, are very dangerous in that they might excite a panic among the audience viewing the picture."[10]

Both the sirens and the Music Hall shooting remained in the picture. No instances of audience panic were reported.

The Production Code censors weren't the only ones worried about the scenes showing the saboteur exchanging shots with the police during a film in the Music Hall theater. The owners of the Music Hall, where *Saboteur* premiered, demanded cuts in the sequence to avoid any possibility that the theater might be identified. The producers made the requested cuts, but restored them when the film was rereleased in 1948.

The Navy Department also had a hand in shaping the finished film. When Hitchcock was shooting on the Universal lot, the news came that the French ship *Normandie,* the largest ocean liner in existence, had caught fire and capsized in the New York harbor. The opportunistic director sent a Universal newsreel crew to film the wrecked ship and worked it into the plot of *Saboteur,* cutting its image into the film when the villain Fry is escaping from the Brooklyn Navy Yard in a taxi. Hitchcock had Norman Lloyd, the actor playing Fry, glance out the window of the taxi. Then the director cut to the hulk of the damaged *Normandie* lying on its side and cut back to a close-up of Lloyd, who, after seeing the wrecked ship, has a self-satisfied smirk on his face.

The navy, which had publicly denied that the *Normandie* had been sabotaged, objected to the message implied by the smirking saboteur and asked that the sequence be removed from the film. Universal complied with the request, although it restored the cut footage, along with the excised Music Hall material, in the postwar rerelease of *Saboteur.*

Besides freeing Hitchcock and his screenwriters from the shackles of the Neutrality Acts, the US entry into the war impacted the making of

Sequence of photos suggesting that the saboteur had been responsible for the *Normandie* wreckage. The navy, which had reported that sabotage was not involved, asked that the sequence be deleted.

Saboteur in other ways. Concern for real-life sabotage caused the government to limit access to Boulder Dam, so that the filmmakers were forced to use stock footage and a backdrop painting to represent the dam in the movie.

Hitchcock himself was not happy with the finished film. In addition to the cluttered screenplay, he felt that the lead actors were weak. He had wanted Gary Cooper and Barbara Stanwyck to play the leads, but early in his American career major stars viewed thrillers as second-class vehicles. The director told François Truffaut that in a chase film such as *Saboteur,* "whenever the hero isn't portrayed by a star, the whole picture suffers . . . because audiences are far less concerned about the predicament of a character who's played by someone they don't know." Although some second-choice leads, like Joel McCrea in *Foreign Correspondent,* had served Hitchcock well, Robert Cummings was definitely a drawback in *Saboteur.* He had the rubbery face of a light comedian and an annoying assortment of inappropriate grins, so that "even when he's in desperate straits, his features don't convey any anguish."[11]

Hitchcock also felt that he had made a mistake in the film's most famous sequence, the climax on the Statue of Liberty, when the real saboteur's life literally hangs by a thread as the hero grabs his sleeve to keep him from falling from Liberty's torch. The director felt that "if we'd had the hero instead of the villain hanging in mid-air, the anguish would have been much greater."[12] But the dangling villain serves an important plot function, clearing the name of the hero before plunging to his death.

Other criticisms of the film include the split focus on two villains, one of whom, the mastermind Tobin, slips by the Production Code unpunished. One writer also questioned the credulity of the long list of common folk who help the wrongly accused saboteur escape when he has nothing to recommend his innocence except his personality, which, in Cummings's portrayal, is somewhat off-putting.[13] The list of those who give aid includes the mother of the sabotage victim, a blind man, a truck driver, circus people, and the love interest, played by Priscilla Lane. This list might also stretch the credulity of the audience, were it not for the fact that Hitchcock keeps things moving so fast.

Saboteur performed well with audiences but not with critics. The film grossed $1.3 million domestically against overrun, but still low, production costs of $780,000, netting Hitchcock a bonus of $18,000 in profit participation. The deal also worked out well for Selznick, who realized a net profit of over $100,000 on his contract with Universal, even after paying his director the increased salary he had more than earned.[14]

The critics were not kind to the film. The *Nation* called it "wild without being exciting," and Bosley Crowther of the *New York Times,* after observing that "there is no logic in this wild-goose chase," notes, "Apparently, Mr. Hitchcock has endeavored to imitate his own 'The 39 Steps.' But the going is not so even. He trips too often in his headlong ascent."[15] Even Hitchcock's friend Dilys Powell damned the director with faint praise in the *London Sunday Times:* "This is Hitchcock at his most Hitchcock, which does not necessarily mean at his best."[16]

With isolationist sentiment still strong in 1941 America, Hitchcock had set out to make a thriller warning the United States of the dangers of internal sabotage and the pro-German leanings of the America First Party. By the time *Saboteur* was released in May 1942, America was at war and the Production Code no longer stifled Hitchcock's anti-Nazi sentiments, which permeate the film and culminate in the hero's promise that the United States will "fight standing on our own two feet . . . till the cows come home."

11

Shadow of a Doubt (1943)

Synopsis. *When wealthy Uncle Charlie (Joseph Cotten) comes to stay with his sister's family in Santa Rosa, California, his niece, Young Charlie (Teresa Wright), expects his presence will lift the family out of the doldrums. But the family is unaware that he is the "Merry Widow Murderer," a serial killer fleeing the police.*

Young Charlie begins to suspect that her uncle may be the Merry Widow Murderer. A detective, Jack Graham (Macdonald Carey), who's in love with her, shares her suspicions, which are confirmed when Uncle Charlie gives her a ring engraved with the initials of the latest murder victim. Young Charlie confronts her uncle with the evidence and agrees not to inform the police if he will leave town to avoid disgracing her mother. Uncle Charlie agrees, but reneges when another man suspected of the same murders is killed while trying to escape from the police, closing the case.

Safe from police pursuit, Uncle Charlie sees his namesake as the only obstacle to his freedom and stages two "accidents" in unsuccessful attempts to kill her. Fearing for her safety, Young Charlie threatens to take the evidence of the engraved ring to the police if her uncle doesn't honor his promise to leave town.

Uncle Charlie agrees to leave. As his train departs the station, he tries again to kill his niece by wrestling her off the observation platform between cars, but loses his footing and falls under the wheels of an oncoming engine. When the citizens of Santa Rosa give him a hero's burial, Young Charlie remains silent about her uncle's guilt for the sake of her mother.

***

Shadow of a Doubt has been called "a brilliant success," Hitchcock's "first great American masterwork," and the director's "best Hollywood film."[1] Hitchcock himself praised it as "a most satisfying picture," and more than once called it his "favorite."[2] The censors had relatively little impact on the film, compared with the impact of the war effort, which clamped down on production materials and forced Hitchcock to film as much as possible on location in Santa Rosa, adding greatly to the small-town realism of the finished picture.

The basic idea of evil coming to a small American town originated at a lunchtime discussion with novelist Gordon McDonell, who, at Hitchcock's urging, turned it into a six-page synopsis. Hitchcock took the synopsis to Universal, which approved the concept, originally titled "Uncle Charlie," as the second film in the studio's two-picture deal with David O. Selznick. For the second picture, Selznick raised the fee for eighteen weeks of Hitchcock's work to $150,000, with $50,000 going straight to the director.

To turn McDonell's six pages into a screenplay with the feel of small-town America, Hitchcock sought the services of dramatist Thornton Wilder, who had won a Pulitzer Prize for his portrayal of small-town life in *Our Town*. Wilder was paid $15,000 for five weeks of work, the amount of time he had before he was due to report for duty in the Army Air Force Intelligence Service. Hitchcock and Wilder got along famously, and spent a part of their working time visiting Santa Rosa, the small California town to be used in the picture, meeting with city officials, soaking up the local atmosphere, and scouting locations for on-site shooting. The most important location was the white frame house in which the heroine, Young Charlie, lives with her family. Hitchcock and Wilder found the home they wanted and negotiated terms with the owner. When the director returned to do the actual shooting, he was surprised to find "the owner was so pleased that his house was going to be in a picture that he had it completely repainted. So we had to get his permission to paint it dirty again. And when we were through, naturally, we had it done all over again with bright, new colors."[3]

The script wasn't quite finished when Wilder had to leave for his army duty, so Hitchcock and producer Jack Skirball accompanied him on the train and completed a first draft somewhere between Los Angeles and the East Coast. Hitchcock was so happy with his experience working with Wilder that he gave the playwright a special acknowledgment in the main credits of the movie.

The Production Code office was also happy with the completed script—at least it found very little to question as a result of its initial review. The censors asked that the words *lousy* and *hell* be cut from the script, and that the word *cyanide* be replaced by the generic word *poison* to avoid giving specific aid to any would-be poisoners in the audience. They also wanted to be sure that "young Charlie's nightdress will be adequate" and cautioned that "care must be taken in the casting of the Rev. Dr. MacCurdy," a minor character, "so as not to offend religious groups."[4]

Finally, the censors worried that "the reference to the 'A & P' will be objected to by exhibitors on the grounds of direct advertising" and recommended that it be changed.[5] In the light of today's omnipresent product placement strategies, where frame after frame of popular films are filled with recognizable brand names, this worry seems nearly as naïve as objections to the words *lousy* and *hell*.

Hitchcock easily accommodated the Code's objections. The restrictions of different production concerns had a somewhat greater impact on *Shadow of a Doubt*. To preserve resources for the war effort, the War Production Board put a ceiling of $5,000 on set construction using new material in Hollywood pictures. This led Hitchcock and producer Skirball to shoot all exteriors and some interiors on location in Santa Rosa, contributing to the realistic feel of the finished film.[6]

The main set constructed for *Shadow of a Doubt* came in well under the $5,000 limit. A replica of Young Charlie's Santa Rosa home was built on the Universal lot for $1,987. The set, built by production designer Robert Boyle to accommodate Hitchcock's camera setups, was "quite a phenomenon," according to the *New York Times*. "As the camera moves into, out of, and through the house to record the action, windows come apart, the porch stands aside, the roof bends over, the kitchen walks away."[7]

Hitchcock was well served by his actors, particularly Teresa Wright as Young Charlie. But everyone, from the leads to the Santa Rosa residents, who were paid $5 per day as extras, helped to create a believable portrait of small-town family life. *Shadow of a Doubt* was the "rare occasion when suspense and melodrama combined well with character," Hitchcock said. "You know, the family can be so frightening. I do not give my first priority to character, but when good characters come through, it makes me very happy."[8]

The film made a small profit, bringing in $1.2 million domestically against a cost of $813,000. Critics were generally positive. Archer Winston wrote in the *New York Post*, "There is much honesty of observation herein, as well as the amusement of recognition rather than that of the joke."[9] In the *New York Times*, Bosley Crowther praised Hitchcock for "bringing in another bumper crop of blue-ribbon shivers," but complained that "the moral is either anti-social or, at best, obscure," citing Young Charlie's concluding observation that the world is a horrible place and her young detective's response that "sometimes it needs a little watching."[10]

The *London Times* praised Hitchcock's films in general as "one of the greatest treats the cinema has to offer" and predicted that "*Shadow of a Doubt* will long stay in the mind as a film of tense and cumulative interest."[11] Although the reviews were largely positive, the film was "seen by most critics as a modest crime thriller." Since its release in 1943, however, "*Shadow of a Doubt* has grown and keeps growing in critical esteem."[12]

Part of the reason for the growth in esteem is Hitchcock's oft-quoted remark naming *Shadow of a Doubt* as his favorite film. He backed off on this claim in his conversation with François Truffaut, telling his interviewer, "I wouldn't say that *Shadow of a Doubt* is my favorite picture; if I've given that impression, it's probably because I feel that here is something that our friends, the plausibles and logicians, cannot complain about."[13] Hitchcock's fondness for *Shadow of a Doubt* may also have been affected by the pleasure he took in working with Thornton Wilder or the relative freedom from the interference of both the Production Code and David O. Selznick. Whatever the reasons, "For most critics it remains one of the finest films he ever made. Such is the verdict of posterity."[14]

12

Lifeboat (1944)

Synopsis. *A survivor from a ship sunk by a German U-boat, columnist Constance Porter (Tallulah Bankhead), wearing a mink coat, high-heeled shoes, and a Cartier diamond bracelet, helps other survivors to board a lifeboat off the coast of Bermuda. The survivors represent a sampling from all walks of life: ship's engineer John Kovac (John Hodiak), radio operator Stanley Garrett (Hume Cronyn), injured seaman Gus Smith (William Bendix), millionaire manufacturer Charles S. Rittenhouse (Henry Hull), an African American steward, "Joe" Spencer (Canada Lee), a nurse, and a hysterical Englishwoman holding her dead baby.*

The last survivor to be picked up is a burly German, Willi (Walter Slezak), from the sunken U-boat. At first, he claims to be an ordinary seaman and to speak only German. The other passengers debate whether to throw him overboard, but decide to let him stay. They come to learn he speaks fluent English and was the U-boat's captain. He gradually takes over the lifeboat, claiming to sail toward Bermuda while using a secret compass to take the passengers to a Nazi supply ship.

As the days go by, hunger and thirst cause tensions to rise. The leg of the injured seaman, Gus, becomes gangrenous, and Willi, a surgeon in private life, amputates it successfully. Tossing and turning while everyone but he and Willi are asleep, Gus sees that Willi has a secret supply of water, and the U-boat captain throws him overboard before he can share this information. The next morning, Willi tells the remaining survivors that Gus committed suicide during the night. Guessing the truth, they mob the Nazi, beating him and tossing him into the ocean.

Drifting on the course set by the U-boat captain, the survivors are approaching the German supply vessel when an American warship appears and sinks it. As they wait to be rescued, a young German sailor boards the lifeboat, brandishing a gun. He is quickly disarmed, and the surviving passengers decide to let him live as the rescue ship approaches.

***

With *Lifeboat,* Hitchcock had an idea for a film treating the survivors of a U-boat attack as a portrait of the war in microcosm. When he was unable to interest either David O. Selznick or Universal Studios in the project, he found himself working for a new studio, Twentieth Century Fox, under the scrutiny of an additional watchdog, the Office of War Information.

Farming Hitchcock out once again, Selznick charged Fox $9,000 a month for the director's services, pocketing the difference between that sum and Hitchcock's monthly $3,000 salary. The disparity rankled Hitchcock, but he was happy to be free from Selznick's meddling supervision. And Darryl Zanuck of Fox was excited not only by the prospect of working with Hitchcock but also by the idea of *Lifeboat,* since he had been encouraged by the Merchant Marine to make a film about the North Atlantic convoys threatened by German U-boats.

Because Hitchcock had had such success working with Thornton Wilder on *Shadow of a Doubt,* he asked Zanuck's permission to hire a big-name author to turn his *Lifeboat* concept into a film treatment. Zanuck, who was about to leave for a tour of duty with the Army Signal Corps, concurred, and Hitchcock approached Ernest Hemingway with the idea. When Hemingway was too busy to accept, the director turned to John Steinbeck, who had seen Twentieth Century Fox turn his novel *The Grapes of Wrath* into a successful film three years earlier.

Steinbeck accepted the job and turned in a forty-thousand-word novella told from the point of view of a shipwrecked merchant seaman. In Steinbeck's story, the German U-boat captain speaks no English and is far from the capable plotter Hitchcock had envisioned as a representative of the master race. Finding Steinbeck's work unsuitable for filming, Hitchcock worked with veteran screenwriter Jo Swerling to turn out a script closer to the director's original concept, in which, as he told François Truffaut, representatives of the democracies must "put their differences aside temporarily and . . . gather their forces to concentrate on the common enemy."[1] The end result was a screenplay that bore little resemblance to Steinbeck's novella. So little, in fact, that when controversy arose, the author tried, unsuccessfully, to have his name removed from the film.

Steinbeck wasn't the only one offended by Hitchcock's allegorical concept of a lifeboat mirroring the current world situation and showing "at that moment there were two world forces confronting each other, the democracies and the Nazis, and while the democracies were completely disorganized, the Germans were clearly headed in the same direction."[2] The newly formed Office of War Information (OWI) also had several problems with *Lifeboat*'s plot and characterizations. The OWI was created six months after war was declared to consolidate existing government information services and deliver propaganda both at home and abroad. A branch of the OWI, the Bureau of Motion Pictures, was charged with "assuring that all films coming out of Hollywood served, or at least did not undermine, the war effort."[3]

On reviewing the *Lifeboat* script, the OWI wrote Zanuck complaining that the screenplay presented "more serious problems than any script of yours which has been reviewed by this office," because "the group of Americans in the lifeboat present a picture which the Nazi propagandists themselves would like to promote."[4] The letter found fault with practically every one of the representatives of democracy. The journalist Connie Porter was seen as a "selfish, predatory, amoral, international adventuress"; the millionaire Rittenhouse was "an unfairly unsympathetic businessman"; the ship's engineer Kovac had Communist leanings and apparently cheated at poker; and Joe, the African American steward, was a former pickpocket who, because he didn't participate in discussing the fate of the German, was evidently "unaccustomed to the franchise" of voting.[5]

Worst of all, the OWI wrote, "The only hero is the Nazi," and they found it disgusting that the German would be beaten and drowned by an unruly mob of distasteful Americans.[6] Unlike the Production Code office, the OWI's function was strictly advisory, and its members did not have the power to block the release of films they found objectionable. However, its Office of Censorship was able to deny export licenses to such films, a power that could hit producers where they were most vulnerable, in the box office.

When Zanuck returned from his war duties to resume his position as Fox's head of production, he found the OWI letter waiting for him. A lifetime foe of censorship who had brought such controversial films as *I Was a Fugitive from a Chain Gang* and William Faulkner's *Sanctuary* to the screen, Zanuck had hopes of establishing a long-term relationship with Hitchcock and passed the OWI's observations along to the director without insisting that any action be taken. He said only that, while he did not agree with all of the criticisms, he felt that they should be taken into account.[7] Hitchcock duly took the criticisms into account and then ignored them all.

Hitchcock also failed to act on many of the demands imposed on *Lifeboat* by the Production Code office. The censors sent a series of five letters to Fox after their review of the original script and its revisions. Several bits of dialogue were mentioned more than once in these letters as they recurred in successive versions of the script without being cut. Examples of dialogue earning repeated objections from the Code office included:

- Kovac's explanation that when the torpedo hit "I was caught with my—I was washing my hands."[8]
- Connie Porter's observation that "we weren't a mob when we killed him."[9]
- "The broken expression 'son-of-a——' must either be eliminated or finished inoffensively."[10]

All of the above bits of dialogue slipped by the censors and found their way into the finished film. When Breen realized nearly two months after *Lifeboat*'s release that the cut-off expression "son-of-a——" remained in the film, he asked the studio to remove it from all prints. When Fox agreed, Breen sent a telegram to his boss, Will Hays, announcing their agreement, and followed with a letter admitting, "We slipped up badly, but immediately the error was drawn to our attention, we proceeded, with the excellent cooperation of the studio, to correct it."[11]

The censors also asked for other changes:

- The characters should indicate "disgust and remorse" for the brutal way in which they gang up on the German to kill him.
- Dialogue should be inserted to indicate that Mrs. Porter had a husband to remove the "present suggestion that she had been a kept woman."[12]
- The words *fanny, punk, louse, sissy,* and *Lord* should be omitted.
- Prior to the dissolve following the storm, "Kovac should not be lying on top of Mrs. Porter or in a suggestive position."[13]

Breen's office also cautioned against undue brutality and gruesomeness, and twice warned the producers to avoid exposing Mrs. Porter's breasts.[14] As it turned out, breast exposure wasn't the problem with Tallulah Bankhead's portrayal of Connie Porter. The star, known to be opposed to using undergarments, often exposed her opposition, to the delight of some and the disgust of others. When the cameraman complained to Hitchcock that this penchant was ruining some shots, the director reportedly asked, "Should I call wardrobe, makeup, or hairdressing?"[15]

Hitchcock's selection of Tallulah Bankhead, a well-known prima donna, to play a prima donna on screen was inspired, and Bankhead was recognized by the New York Film Critics as best actress of the year for her work in *Lifeboat.* Her performance covers a much greater range than the one-note "selfish adventuress" characterized by the OWI. She becomes less and less selfish as the script deprives her of her worldly possessions; she loses her camera, mink coat, typewriter, and wardrobe before finally offering up her diamond bracelet as bait for the ocean's fishes.

The remaining cast was excellent as well, particularly Walter Slezak as Willi, the conniving German, and William Bendix as Gus, the injured sailor. The NAACP joined the OWI in complaining that the characterization of Joe, the African American steward played by Canada Lee, was a stereotype. John Steinbeck, miffed at Hitchcock for the many changes the director made in bringing the writer's novella to the screen, echoed this criticism, claiming that Hitchcock and Swerling had turned his dignified representative of the black race into a "stock comedy Negro."[16] Steinbeck's observations, along with those of the NAACP and OWI, seem a bit off the mark. In Hitchcock's film, Joe is far from a Stepin Fetchit caricature. He is introduced as the heroic rescuer of a drowning mother and child, is shown to be deeply religious as well as a devoted family man, and is the only passenger who refuses to participate in the mob murder of the German U-boat captain.

Although *Lifeboat* was shot entirely on a sound stage, filming did not go smoothly. Two lifeboats were used. One was built on a rocker that could simulate the tossing of the waves, and the second was moored to the bottom of a tank fed by four chutes capable of dumping huge amounts of water on its passengers. Hume Cronyn recalled that the actors "were frequently wet, cold, and covered with diesel oil," and that "there was a large demand for anti-seasickness pills." Tallulah Bankhead wrote that she was "black and blue from the downpours and the lurchings" and came down with bronchial pneumonia, halting production for several days.[17]

The shooting was also slowed by Hitchcock's insistence on filming scenes sequentially to allow the actors (and the director) to shape the performances as the film progressed. When Zanuck returned from his tour of duty with the Signal Corps, delays and costs appeared to be spiraling out

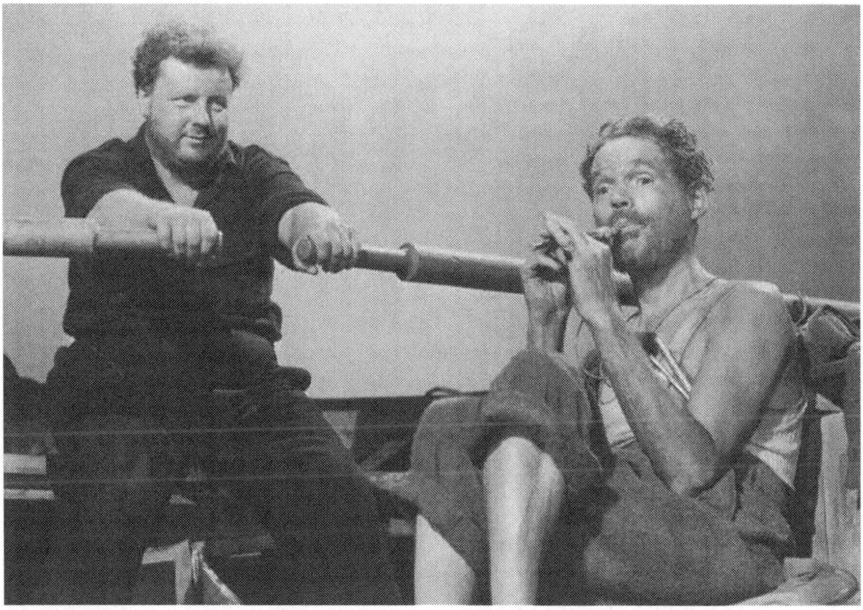

The German U-boat captain Willi (Walter Slezak) and C. S. Rittenhouse (Henry Hull), an American millionaire. As representatives of fascism and capitalism respectively, they incurred the wrath of the Office of War Information because the captain was so much more competent than the millionaire and other representatives of the democracies.

of control and he had several arguments with Hitchcock, who grudgingly agreed to make minor cuts in several scenes.

Initial reviews of *Lifeboat* were positive. Howard Barnes of the *New York Herald Tribune* called it "a memorable film, a bitterly absorbing and pictorially beautiful show, stacking up impressively as entertainment or work of art."[18] Bosley Crowther of the *New York Times* conceded that Hitchcock had "turned out a consistently exciting and technically brilliant drama of the sea." He then had second thoughts and concluded that he had "a sneaking suspicion that the Nazis, with some cutting here and there, could turn '*Lifeboat*' into a whiplash against the 'decadent democracies.' And it is questionable whether such a picture, with such a theme, is judicious at this time."[19]

Crowther then followed his second thoughts with third and fourth thoughts that were in concert with the OWI view that the movie glorified the Nazi "superman" at the expense of the quibbling and ineffectual representatives of democracy. He followed his initial review with two Sunday columns condemning the "appalling folly" and insidious nature of *Lifeboat.* Having been supplied a copy of the Steinbeck's original novella by the author, Crowther publicly assigned the blame for all that was bad about *Lifeboat* to Hitchcock, absolving Steinbeck of any culpability.[20] Since little of Steinbeck's creation made it to the film, it seems appropriate to assign any blame, and any praise as well, to the director.

Dorothy Thompson, the globetrotting columnist for the *Herald Tribune* who was the prototype for Tallulah Bankhead's character in *Lifeboat,* was also of two minds about the film. She lauded the movie as "brilliant" from the "point of direction and entertainment," but condemned it as a work that, "translated into German, could be presented in Berlin as a morale builder for the Nazis' war, with only minor changes."[21]

Not all critics agreed that the German's competence cast a slur on the merits of democracy. Richard Winnington observed, "A Nazi surgeon U-boat commander with a secret supply of food tablets, water, and compass would make a formidable companion in any lifeboat."[22] And David Lardner of the *New Yorker* chided those critics who would wish to see an enemy "described as ignorant and blundering when it patently is not."[23]

The critical controversy fueled behind-the-scene complaints to Fox about the perceived pro-Nazi propaganda slant of the film, causing Daryl Zanuck to cut back on advertising and support. After a strong opening, *Lifeboat* sank at the box office, earning only $1 million against its cost of $1.7 million. It was Hitchcock's first major American failure, and guaranteed that he would direct no more films for Twentieth Century Fox.

Controversy notwithstanding, *Lifeboat* earned three Academy Award nominations, for Hitchcock's direction, Glen MacWilliams's black-and-white photography, and John Steinbeck's story (what was left of it). None of these three nominees earned an Oscar, with Hitchcock losing to Leo McCarey's direction of *Going My Way.*

With *Lifeboat,* Hitchcock encountered a new censorship group in the form of the OWI. Since this group had no power to block the release of the film, the director ignored its objections, along with many of the suggestions offered by the Production Code office, and made the movie he wanted to make. Unfortunately, the OWI's concerns that the movie presented the Nazi as too capable, especially as compared with the representatives of democracy, continued to haunt the film after its release, lowering the box-office receipts.

Following the defeat of Germany and the disbanding of the OWI in 1945, the passage of time has erased any concern over the depiction of Walter Slezak's Nazi as a superman. As with most of Hitchcock's films, critical appreciation of *Lifeboat* has risen over the years. Hitchcock biographer Patrick McGilligan praises the film as "dazzling," concluding that it "is as original and searching as any picture made in Hollywood during World War II."[24]

13

Spellbound (1945)

Synopsis. *Dr. Constance Petersen (Ingrid Bergman) is a hardworking psychiatrist on the staff of the Green Manors insane asylum run by Dr. Murchison (Leo G. Carroll), who is about to retire. When Dr. Murchison's successor, Dr. Edwards (Gregory Peck), arrives, Constance immediately and uncharacteristically falls in love with him. However, she quickly learns that her new lover is really an amnesiac who is convinced that he has killed the real Dr. Edwards.*

Faced with this knowledge and fearing discovery, "Edwards" runs away from the clinic, but Constance, convinced of his innocence, manages to track him down. Narrowly avoiding the police, she takes him to the home of her mentor, Dr. Alex Brulov (Michael Chekov), who will help her analyze the amnesiac's dreams and curious aversion to parallel lines on a white background. Piecing together clues from the dreams of "Edwards," Constance and Dr. Brulov learn that he has always felt responsible for the accidental death of his younger brother and is suffering from the shock of witnessing the death of the real Dr. Edwards in a similar fashion on a ski slope.

The dream-based clues lead Constance to confront Dr. Murchison, who killed Edwards so that he could stay on as the head of Green Manors. Faced with this evidence, Murchison first threatens Constance with the murder gun and then uses it to commit suicide, leaving the psychiatrist and the cured amnesiac, whose real name is John Ballantyne, to start a new life together.

***

Spellbound marked the second film Hitchcock made for Selznick International under the direct supervision of David O. Selznick. Its start was delayed for eight months as the director made two short propaganda films in London as a tribute to the French Resistance for his friend Sidney Bernstein, head of Britain's Ministry of Information. Before leaving for England, Hitchcock had talked with Selznick about the possibility of building a film around the fledgling field of psychoanalysis. Most producers had shied away from this topic, feeling that it was too vulnerable to censorship to survive the scrutiny of the Breen office and too far removed from the experience of the general public to succeed commercially. But Selznick, in the midst of a midlife crisis over the breakup of his marriage and his affair with Jennifer Jones, was undergoing psychiatric treatment himself and was enthusiastic about the idea.

Hitchcock had optioned the screen rights to a novel, *The House of Dr. Edwardes,* by Francis Beeding, in which a madman runs an insane asylum, and recommended it to Selznick, who okayed the project. Hitchcock began developing a treatment and script, working first with Angus McPhail during his London sojourn, and then with Ben Hecht on his return to America. The director and his collaborators added a love story to the novel's mystery plot and scrapped nearly everything else except the basic concept of a madman taking over an asylum.

Once again, Hitchcock found himself facing extra layers of censorship. In addition to the Production Code and the Office of War Information, Selznick hired his own psychoanalyst, Dr. May Romm, to act as psychiatric advisor on the project. Dr. Romm's job was to ensure that the methods of psychoanalytic treatment were accurately and understandably reported and she made it her mission to seek out and destroy any instances of phallic symbolism.

In its initial review of the script, the Breen office approved the basic story of *Spellbound* but added still more layers of censorship by recommending that Selznick consult both with the British Board of Film Censors and the Federal Bureau of Investigation. Breen warned Selznick that the BBFC had "steadfastly refused to license pictures dealing with lunatic asylums or insane people." And FBI oversight was warranted because one of the men pursuing the fleeing "Dr. Edwards" was a federal agent.[1]

In reaction to the script itself, Breen recommended the deletion of a number of words and phrases, including *frustration, playing tomcat, lecherous, libido, sex maniac, seduction complex, narcissism,* and *Good Lord.* He also found fault with a number of wisecracks, such as "We'll spend our honeymoon in one of the padded cells" and "A friend of mine eloped with a man who turned out to be a woman, with a moustache." A reference to the "mating of two psychoanalysts" was marked for deletion as well.[2]

Breen also warned that the "suggestion of an illicit sex affair" between one of the staff psychoanalysts, Dr. Fleurot, and Mrs. Murchison, the wife of the outgoing asylum head, "is entirely unacceptable and would not be approved in the final version." But Breen and his censors were far more worried about the suggestion of an illicit affair between Constance and "Dr. Edwards." They insisted that both parties remain fully dressed when they share a train compartment, cautioned against any deviation from the doctor-and-patient relationship, and stated flatly that "any possible suggestion of illicit sex" between Constance and "Dr. Edwards" "would render the finished product unacceptable."[3]

Responding to Breen's letter, Hitchcock eliminated the character of Murchison's wife altogether and submitted to nearly all of the suggested dialogue changes. The deletion of words had always been less important to him than the censoring of images.

In reviewing the second draft of the script, Breen expressed satisfaction with the changes, but still found the "mating of two psychoanalysts" objectionable. The censors continued to warn against any inferences of "sex suggestiveness" between Constance and "Dr. Edwards," but shifted their focus to Miss Carmichael, the asylum inmate played by Rhonda Fleming in her first major movie role. They asked that the filmmakers "take care to avoid any characterization of Miss Carmichael as a woman sexually obsessed, or anything bordering on nymphomania." In this regard, they asked that the studio rewrite the speech in which Miss Carmichael "recounts in detail her infidelities" so as to omit "all the details of her sexual irregularities." Finally, the censors asked that the studio "avoid any gruesomeness" in the scene in which "Dr. Edwards" recalls the accidental death of his younger brother.[4]

By the third draft of the script, the "mating of two psychoanalysts" had been watered down to the "wedding of two psychoanalysts," which still failed to pass muster with Breen, who objected in his letter to the "welding [*sic*] of two psychoanalysts." The censors' final script review ordered the omission of Dr. Brulov's line characterizing Constance and "Dr. Edwards" as "just two people who have agreed to legalize the libido," and added that they presumed that the "kissing bug" portrayed by Rhonda Fleming in the dream sequence would be properly clothed.[5]

Spellbound's dream sequence commanded the attention of the press, the Production Code office, and psychiatric advisor May Romm. Hitchcock had asked Selznick to hire the Spanish surrealist Salvador Dalí to design the sequence. Selznick assumed Hitchcock had requested Dalí primarily for publicity purposes, but the director denied this, saying, "I felt that if I was to have dream sequences, they should be vivid. I didn't think that we should resort to the old-fashioned blurry effect that they got by putting Vaseline around the lens."[6]

Selznick was concerned both about the cost of Dalí's services and potential censorship issues. One studio memo addressing the possibility of censorship from religious groups stated, "We would, of course, get kicks against the pricks from the Holy Men who are undoubtedly convinced by now that Mr. Dali is a very unsavory character."[7] But studio analysts estimated that Dalí's name would be worth roughly $50,000 in publicity and guarantee free coverage in national magazines. Armed with this information, Selznick took advantage of the painter's desire for film exposure to bargain his price down from $5,000 to $4,000.

But the price of Dalí's conceptual designs didn't include the cost of committing them to film, and Selznick balked when the studio estimated that this could run as high as $150,000. The producer relented only after Hitchcock assured him that he could film Dalí's images in the studio for only $20,000 using miniatures and rear projections.

Dalí's concepts for the dream sequence involved four separate scenes.

1. A gambling house with a backdrop of large eyes in which the Peck character is playing cards with a bearded man who holds faceless cards and is accused of cheating by a faceless proprietor.
2. A high, sloping roof with the faceless proprietor hiding behind a chimney and holding a misshapen wheel as the bearded man falls to his death.
3. A ballroom with pianos suspended from the ceiling in which Peck and Bergman dance and kiss before Bergman turns into a statue.
4. A flat, steep slope, down which Peck tries to outrun the beating wings of a flying statue.[8]

In the gambling house scene, the "kissing bug" played by Rhonda Fleming circulates from table to table kissing the gamblers while dressed in a Dior negligee that Dalí had cut to shreds. The tattered attire was too much for Breen, who told Selznick that Fleming must be "more covered . . . there must be more rags around her midriff, considerably more rags to cover the inside of the left thigh, and . . . to cover the breasts properly."[9] Wardrobe made the adjustments, which are barely noticeable in the finished film, since Fleming flits about the upper right-hand quarter of the screen for less than five seconds. To minimize any harm that Breen's

Rhonda Fleming as the "kissing bug" in Dalí's dream sequence. First Dalí cut her costume to shreds, and then Breen caused most of her part to be cut. (Courtesy of Jerry Ohlinger.)

demands might have done to Dalí's vision, Gregory Peck's voice-over informs the audience that Fleming's "kissing bug" is "scantily clad."

For the ballroom scene, Dalí wanted to hang fifteen heavy pianos from the ceiling so that they swung very low over the heads of the dancers. Selznick's cost-consciousness dictated the substitution of miniature pianos for real ones. To correct for the perspective problems imposed by the miniatures, the studio dressed forty dwarfs in black and deployed them to dance in the scene. But not even Hitchcock could disguise the fact that the dancers were dwarfs, and he and Dalí decided to abandon the dangling pianos.

In place of the pianos, a variety of objects were suspended from the ballroom ceiling, including a long tubular sack of coal that vaguely connoted genitalia to May Romm and had to go. The psychiatric advisor also warned Selznick that Peck and Bergman "dancing in a dream is a symbol of sexual intercourse" and asked, "Is that what you want?"[10] Selznick nixed the dancing. With no dangling pianos and no dancing principals, little was left of Dalí's ballroom vision, and the entire scene was cut.

Dalí's vision for the scene in which the Peck character outruns a winged statue down a steep slope originally included a gigantic pair of pliers. But Dr. Romm decided that these were too obviously phallic and "might prevent whatever possible endorsement we might otherwise get from a psychiatric society." Hitchcock fought to retain Dalí's imagery, arguing that the audience would follow the action, not the objects, but Selznick respected Romm's opinion, and the frame was cropped so that only the handles of the pliers were visible.[11]

Hitchcock had succeeded in remaining free from Selznick's interference during most of the shooting of *Spellbound.* When the producer visited the set, Ingrid Bergman recalled, the director "simply stopped the camera, announced a 'mechanical fault,' and stopped production."[12] Once the director had completed principal photography, however, he left for England almost immediately, and control over cutting, dubbing, and reshooting reverted to Selznick. Frustrated with his lack of control during shooting, the producer set about cutting with a vengeance and eliminated an estimated twenty minutes of Hitchcock's footage.

Never comfortable with Dalí's dream sequence, Selznick reshot elements and cut nearly a minute from Hitchcock's version, trimming the total screen time to just under two minutes. Those minutes no longer featured the bare thighs banished by Breen, the phallic symbols spotted by Romm, or the extra footage cut by Selznick, but neither the producer, the director, nor the artist was happy with the result.

The dream sequence is accompanied by a Gregory Peck voice-over that tells the audience what they are seeing on the screen and is followed by a scene in which Constance and her mentor, Dr. Brulov, interpret bits of the dream. The card player is the real Dr. Edwards, the steep roof is a ski slope, and the winged pursuer is Constance herself, a ministering angel. The remaining parts of the puzzle, linking the misshapen wheel to a revolver and unmasking Dr. Murchison as the faceless proprietor and killer of Dr. Edwards, are not pieced together by Constance until the final scenes.

The simplistic view of dream analysis is of a piece with the unrealistic behavior of the principal characters throughout the movie. It's preposterous that a psychoanalyst as dedicated and straightlaced as Constance would fall instantly in love with her new boss and then, when she discovers he is an imposter and possible murderer, abandon all semblance of professional behavior by running away with him in an attempt to cure his amnesia. When Ingrid Bergman found the love-at-first-sight conceit so unbelievable that she asked to have it rewritten, Hitchcock's response was "Fake it."[13]

The Production Code's official objections to *Spellbound* eased somewhat in the summer of 1944 when Joe Breen turned the responsibility for monitoring the movie over to Geoffrey Shurlock, his "less irascible and more liberal" lieutenant.[14] Shurlock and Hitchcock got along well, and their affinity may account for the fact that Miss Carmichael, the inmate of questionable morals played by Rhonda Fleming, made it to the screen with her sexual neuroses intact.

Another point that seemed to escape the censors' notice was the culminating suicide of Dr. Murchison. The Code explicitly forbade the use of suicide to avoid prosecution for one's crimes. A year after *Spellbound* opened, Michael Balcon, British producer of the film *Nicholas Nickleby,* raised this issue in a cable to his New York office:

> PLEASE EXPLAIN UNDER WHICH SECTION OF CODE DOCTOR IN SPELLBOUND COMMITS SUICIDE THUS THWARTING JUSTICE WHILST WE ARE CALLED UPON TO MODIFY RALPH NICKELBYS SUICIDE IN OUR FAITHFUL ADAPTATION OF WORLD FAMOUS CLASSICAL SUBJECT.[15]

Breen answered that the "doctor's suicide in SPELLBOUND was permitted as being the act of a demented person. In one or two other cases of this sort we have approved this treatment of suicide, provided that the person was obviously of unsound mind."[16] One of those instances was Hitchcock's *Jamaica Inn,* in which the Code Office insisted that Maureen O'Hara twice exclaim loudly, "He's mad. He can't help himself!" in advance of Charles Laughton's suicidal leap from the topmast of his ship.

In the final analysis, Breen's office had only minimal comments to make on the finished print of *Spellbound* and readily awarded its Seal of Approval. On the psychological front, Dr. May Romm "found no technical inaccuracies, and approved the body of the film with whole-hearted enthusiasm." And the Office of War Information gave the film high marks for its positive contribution to public opinion, commenting that this was especially relevant "because of the increasing importance of psychiatric treatment, particularly in relation to the problems of returning servicemen the world over."[17]

Critical reviews were mixed. Bosley Crowther of the *New York Times* praised "Miss Bergman and her brand of treatment" as a "guaranteed cure for what ails you, just as much as it is for Mr. Peck."[18] And *Newsweek* found the movie "a typical Alfred Hitchcock exercise in crime and astonishment and, as such, a superior and suspenseful melodrama."[19] But James Agee, writing in the *Nation,* disagreed: "Alfred Hitchcock's surprisingly disappointing thriller about psychoanalysis is worth seeing, but hardly more," noting that it "reveals just as much of the Id as could be safely displayed in a Bergdorf Goodman window."[20] Manny Farber was even harsher in the *New Republic,* calling *Spellbound* "slow moving and unbelievable": "The plot is worked out with excessive care to give each step some degree of logic, but it is a logic you never believe in and you don't feel that its director does either."[21]

The mixed reviews didn't hurt the box office. Hitchcock and Bergman proved to be big draws at home and abroad, and the film grossed $4.7 million domestically against a cost of $1.7 million, making it Selznick's most profitable black-and-white film, trailing only the color epics *Gone with the Wind* and *Duel in the Sun. Spellbound* was also well represented at the 1946 Academy Award ceremonies, receiving nominations for Best Picture, Best Director, Best Supporting Actor (Michael Chekov), Best Black and White Cinematography, Best Special Effects, and Best Musical Score. The only winner among these nominees was Miklos Rozsa for his musical score.

As psychoanalysis has become more and more a part of the American scene, *Spellbound*'s treatments of its methods have become less and less believable, and it is one of the few Hitchcock films that have not enjoyed resurgence in critical appreciation over time. In his extended interviews with Hitchcock, François Truffaut volunteered that he "found the picture something of a disappointment," and Hitchcock downplayed it as "just another manhunt story wrapped up in pseudo-psychoanalysis."[22] Film historian David Thomson was somewhat less diplomatic than Truffaut. He characterized *Spellbound* as "a grotesque mess, half-baked in its view of psychoanalysis, and the worst example of producer David O. Selznick's interference with his director."[23] All in all, *Spellbound* is a case of too many tasters overseeing at least one too many cooks making an unpromising recipe.

14

Notorious (1946)

Synopsis. *At the end of World War II, Alicia Huberman (Ingrid Bergman), the fast-living daughter of a convicted American traitor, is approached by government agent T. R. Devlin (Cary Grant) with a proposition that she use her father's contacts to investigate a group of Nazi collaborators at large in Brazil. Alicia agrees, and Devlin accompanies her to Rio de Janeiro, where they fall in love while awaiting specific orders. When those orders come, they cause a serious rift in the romance. Alicia is asked to "get close to" Alex Sebastian (Claude Rains), a Nazi agent who had once been in love with her.*

Alicia soon becomes a regular visitor to Sebastian's mansion, which is run by his domineering mother (Leopoldine Konstantin) and houses a group of five Nazi agents. Against his mother's wishes, Sebastian proposes marriage to Alicia. When an embittered Devlin fails to object, she agrees to the match.

As the new mistress of Sebastian's household, Alicia becomes suspicious of the one room closed to her, a wine cellar to which Sebastian holds the only key. Alicia surreptitiously obtains the key and she and Devlin explore the cellar, where they discover uranium hidden in fake wine bottles. Sebastian surprises Alicia and Devlin in the wine cellar and realizes he has married an American agent. At his mother's insistence, he begins poisoning Alicia, hoping to hide his blunder from his Nazi colleagues by making it appear that Alicia is slowly wasting away.

Concerned for Alicia's well-being, Devlin surreptitiously enters Sebastian's mansion and finds his way to Alicia's room. He declares his love and carries the weakened Alicia to the head of the mansion's ornate stairway, where they are accosted by Sebastian and his mother. Devlin threatens to tell Sebastian's Nazi colleagues that he has been in league with an American spy if he does anything to block their exit. Sebastian agrees and the two men help Alicia down the stairs under the watchful eyes of the Nazi collaborators. When they help Alicia into Devlin's waiting auto, he locks the door and drives off, leaving a distraught Sebastian to face the now-suspicious eyes of his collaborators.

***

Notorious is one of the few Hitchcock films that were actually improved by the involvement of the Production Code. The film is very loosely based on a 1921 *Saturday Evening Post* story by John Taintor Foote entitled "Song of the Dragon."[1] In this two-part serial, a young actress volunteers to seduce a German spy headquartered in Manhattan during World War I with the aim of exposing him and breaking up the ring of saboteurs under his leadership. She succeeds in her mission, but later fears that her wartime activities will come to light and cause her to be rejected by the wealthy parents of the love of her life, an army captain who has proposed marriage. To forestall this, she persuades the Broadway producer who helped to recruit her to explain her actions to the parents and, with the help of a presidential commendation, wins their approval.

This somewhat sappy story, which focused on the young woman's marital quandary, seemed an unpromising source for a Hitchcock movie, but producer David O. Selznick owned the rights and sought to interest Hitchcock and screenwriter Ben Hecht, who had worked together effectively on *Spellbound,* to turn the material into a vehicle for Ingrid Bergman. Hitchcock and Hecht accepted the challenge and set about spinning the leaden *Saturday Evening Post* serial into cinematic gold. By the time they finished, the only recognizable element surviving from the source material was the concept of an amateur spy conscripted to sleep with the enemy.

In converting the *Post* serial into a promising screenplay, Hitchcock and Hecht ran afoul of the FBI, the Office of War Information, and the Production Code Administration. Seeking a plot point, or Macguffin, to serve as a focus for the espionage story, they explored the possibility of using an explosive device whose existence was only rumored in early 1945, an atomic bomb. At the time Hitchcock and Hecht began writing, the bomb was still under development and protected by top-secret clearances. So when the pair showed up in the Cal Tech offices of Dr. Robert A. Millikan, the first American-born physicist to win the Nobel Prize, and asked, "How big is an atomic bomb?" the scientist initially panicked and responded, "Do you want to be arrested?" and "Do you want me to be arrested too?"[2] Once Millikan had regained his composure, he tried to talk Hitchcock and Hecht out of incorporating such a concept into a movie, and dutifully reported their inquiries to the proper federal authorities after the meeting ended. Hitchcock subsequently reported that he was under FBI surveillance for three months.

Millikan's initial reaction and rumors of Nazi research with heavy water convinced the director that a uranium-fueled bomb would make a plausible hook for a conflict between FBI agents and Nazi subversives. Selznick was skeptical at first, but the possibility of enlivening the movie with special effects showing the testing of such a bomb persuaded him to allow Hitchcock and Hecht to use it as a plot device. Exploding the bomb "makes the whole thing real," he told the director, "and will give the picture size and spectacle."[3]

Selznick set about securing the necessary approvals for a film script involving an FBI agent and an atomic bomb. Following Breen's advice, he approached J. Edgar Hoover's office directly and learned through a Hoover aide that, while the atomic bomb was a "ticklish subject for [a] picture," because the Germans and not the Americans were the putative inventors of the bomb in the scenario, the material seemed acceptable.[4] But Hoover himself had other concerns regarding *Notorious.* The FBI director objected to the portrayal of its agents' tactics in the script and the relatively blunt sexual subtext, fearing that the movie might subject both the bureau and the producers to "some criticism on the grounds of morality."[5] But the depiction of FBI agents on Brazilian soil proved to be an even greater concern. Officially, the bureau was charged with catching spies in the United States, not spying on enemy agents abroad. Ironically, in June 1940 the FBI had secretly established a "Special Intelligence Service" to round up German spies in Latin America. This unit was still operating five years later when Selznick submitted the *Notorious* script to Hoover's office. As with the uranium ore Macguffin, Hitchcock and Hecht had stumbled a little too close to the truth. To protect the reputation of his agency and the secrecy of his Brazilian operation, Hoover had no choice but to object to the role the FBI played in *Notorious.* Hitchcock complied and eliminated all references to the bureau from the film. The agents played by Grant and Louis Calhern were referred to simply as "intelligence men" representing the American embassy in Rio de Janeiro.[6]

The OWI wasn't as upset about sexual subtexts or references to an atomic bomb as about the implication that the death of the lead Nazi spy eliminated all danger to the Western democracies. On reading the script, the OWI liaison wrote Selznick, "This is the kind of over-simplified attitude which would make overseas audiences question our political maturity and our understanding of the true nature of Fascism."[7]

The OWI's views were merely advisory and could be ignored. But the views of the Production Code Administration could keep *Notorious* off the screen. Hitchcock and Hecht went through several drafts of the *Notorious* script, including one in which Devlin, the agent played by Cary Grant, dies in the end, before settling on one they thought would satisfy the censors. In the version initially submitted for Code approval, Alicia Huberman, the Ingrid Bergman character, does not survive, presumably as partial atonement for a life of loose living.

The death of the heroine was not enough to satisfy the Code administration. In a letter to David O. Selznick, Joe Breen wrote,

> I regret to be compelled to advise you that the material, in its present form, seems to us to be definitely unacceptable under the provisions of the Production Code.
>
> This unacceptability is suggested principally by the characterization of your lead, Alicia, as a grossly immoral woman, whose immorality is accepted "in stride" in the development of the story and who, eventually, is portrayed as dying a glorious heroine.
>
> There is, too, in contrast with her immoral characterization, an almost complete absence of what might be called "compensating moral values."[8]

Breen did offer a few suggestions for softening the characterization of Alicia that ultimately improved the movie remarkably:

> It is our thought that it might be possible to tell this story if you were to establish it early that Alicia is, possibly, a lady who lives by her wits—a gold-digger, perhaps, but not specifically a prostitute. It might be indicated that motivation for this characterization is prompted by her total loss of faith in her father, which leads her to sour on society in general, and, instead of becoming a kept woman of loose morals, such souring process might be evidenced by her determination to get what she can out of life, without paying any personal price for it.[9]

In response to Breen's letter, Hitchcock and Hecht met with Breen lieutenants Geoffrey Shurlock and T. A. Lynch and " agreed that the characterization of the female lead would be changed in such a way as to avoid any direct inference that she is a woman of loose sex morals." Shurlock noted in a file memo that Hecht had indicated that future drafts would leave Alicia alive at the end and free to marry Devlin. In Shurlock's view, Alicia's survival would make it "absolutely necessary to avoid any suggestion of sex promiscuity or looseness on her part," since the script would no longer suggest that such promiscuity could be fatal.[10]

Following the Shurlock meeting, Hitchcock and Hecht set about sponging down Alicia's character without entirely whitewashing her. However, the next Code review still found that "the present characterization of the girl, as a woman of loose sex morals, is unacceptable, and could not be approved in a story of that sort."[11] This review made seventeen specific suggestions for changes, including the elimination of five separate instances of the use of the word *tramp* as applied to Alicia.

All but two of the seventeen suggestions were aimed at softening Alicia's image. The two outliers involved the elimination of the words *cyanide* and *arsenic.* This was a particular bugaboo of the Code administrators, who feared that the use of such specific terms might serve as alluring product placement and "how-to" advice for would-be poisoners.

At this point, several events outside of Hitchcock's control overtook the project. Selznick, distracted by the disintegration of his marriage and mounting fiscal and production problems on *Duel in the Sun,* decided he had to sell the rights to *Notorious* to continue with *Duel,* which starred the love of his life, Jennifer Jones. So he created a package consisting of Hitchcock, Bergman, and the *Notorious* script and looked for buyers. Producer Hal Wallis was interested, but passed because he regarded the idea of a superbomb as "a goddamn foolish thing to base a movie on."[12] RKO was more than happy to purchase the package for $800,000 in cash and 50 percent of the net profits. Selznick realized almost $500,000 from the sale, and Hitchcock, for the first time, became the de facto producer on one of his own movies.[13]

Another event testified to Hitchcock's prescience and the foolishness of producers skeptical of the *Notorious* reliance on uranium as a plot device. Less than a month after RKO took over the project in July 1945, the United States dropped atomic bombs on Hiroshima and Nagasaki, leading to the unconditional surrender of Japan, the end of World War II, and the dismantling of the Office of War Information.

Hitchcock and Hecht continued to adapt the *Notorious* script, incorporating some of the Code's requests and ignoring others. The next full-scale Code review of the script came in mid-September 1945 and included fourteen specific requests, mostly involving dialogue changes, including a reiteration of the request that Devlin's characterization of Alicia as "a tramp, ready to die for her country" be deleted.

Once again, Breen's review included a suggestion to "get away from the present flavor that these officials know they are hiring a promiscuous woman." He proposed that the officials' discussion be rewritten to indicate that they decided to hire Alicia "because they know that Sebastian was once in love with her, omitting all innuendo as to her previous character."[14] Hitchcock and Hecht followed this suggestion insofar as Sebastian was concerned, which had the added benefit of making him a more sympathetic character, but were reluctant to remove all traces of Alicia's past affairs from the script, since to do so would make it difficult to explain Devlin's skepticism and bitterness when she accepts the assignment to pursue Sebastian. The incorporation of a past history with Sebastian also added believability to Alicia's acceptance of his marriage proposal and made her mission of "sleeping with the enemy" less distasteful and more acceptable to the censors.

Script changes continued to be made piecemeal and submitted for Code approval even after shooting began in mid-October. Breen's written comments dwindled once shooting started, although one November suggestion affected the portrayal of Devlin and his boss Prescott, played by Louis Calhern. In a scene following the party in which Devlin and Alicia discover uranium in Sebastian's wine cellar, Devlin confesses to Prescott that he has a "pain in the gut that he can't stand" from the way the situation with Alicia has developed and asks Prescott to reassign him. Prescott observes that Alicia's assignment "can't last much longer . . . then maybe you can assist the Sebastians in a nice clean divorce."

Breen objected to this exchange on the grounds that the idea of a "nice clean divorce is very questionable, particularly when spoken by an officer of the United States government."[15] Hitchcock and Hecht cut the scene, which not only contained the questionable divorce reference, but also Devlin's first acknowledgment of the pain Alicia's assignment is causing him as well as the fact that Prescott is aware of that pain.

Breen's correspondence during the script review typically ended with the admonition, "Our final judgment, as you know, will be based on the finished picture." In its reaction to the first cut of the finished picture, the Code office requested several specific changes. The most important of these involved the first reel of the film; the censors asked that the producers delete the "entire scene between Alicia and Ernest, . . . to get away from the suggestion that Ernest and Alicia have been having an illicit sex affair" and "reduce the drinking and drunkenness as much as possible throughout. The drunken couple should be eliminated."[16] In addition, the Code administrators asked that four specific lines of dialogue impugning Alicia's character be changed or omitted.

After a conference with Selznick and Hitchcock, Breen agreed to issue a Production Code Seal of Approval subject to the following deletions and changes:

1. The entire sequence between Alicia and Ernest in the Miami bungalow will be deleted.
2. The drinking and drunkenness, as well as the shot of the drunken couple on the couch at the Miami party will be reduced in footage.[17]

So, in return for jettisoning the minor character of Ernest, who was clearly living in sin with Alicia, Hitchcock got to keep most of the drinking footage at the Miami party. It is not clear how much of the party footage was finally reduced, but the shot of the drunken couple on the couch, a sight gag replicating the pose of Michelangelo's Pietà, remained, as did the offending lines of dialogue concerning Alicia's character later in the film, including Prescott's admiring observation, "The young lady knows how to make friends with gentlemen" and the not-so-admiring observation of Prescott's superior, "I don't think any of us have any illusions about her character."

The strictures and guidance of the Production Code definitely enriched *Notorious* artistically, not only concerning the depiction of key characters but also with regard to individual scenes and the manipulation of audience sympathy. The Code's insistence on reforming the prostitute of the initial script and recasting Alicia as a woman who lived by her wits was a definite improvement. The Alicia of the finished film is no better than she needs to be, as reflected in Prescott's observations and Devlin's skepticism and frustration, but she was never in the business of selling herself for money. She may have been willing to sleep with the devil to atone for her father's sins or her own slightly checkered past, but she wouldn't be demanding payment for services rendered.

In addition to improving the narrative, the recasting of Alicia "from a woman who lived by her body to one who lived by her wits" made sense from a marketing standpoint.[18] Ingrid Bergman was one of the most popular actresses of her day, but her public image had been formed by a series of portrayals of nuns and "good girls" and a purportedly happy marriage to Dr. Robert Lindstrom. While Bergman herself was "tired of playing saints" and only too happy to broaden her roles as an actress, it's clear that the moviegoing public was not ready to accept her as a prostitute. Witness the public outrage just four years later when she abandoned her husband to have an affair and a child with the Italian director Roberto Rossellini. Her relocation to Italy and subsequent divorce left her ostracized at home and earned a scathing denunciation in the *Congressional Record* from Democratic senator Edwin C. Johnson of Colorado.[19]

One of the most famous scenes in the Hitchcock canon is the kiss shared by Alicia and Devlin as they await Alicia's assignment in Rio de Janeiro. The scene makes it plain that the two have fallen in love since their arrival, and was precisely constructed by Hitchcock to skate around the strictures of the Production Code, which explicitly forbade any "excessive lustful kissing, lustful embraces, suggestive postures and gestures." Unofficially, the Code administrators judged kisses to be "excessively lustful" when lips were locked for more than three seconds. (Code administrators denied this, but their clock-watching image was clearly imbedded in the minds of directors, even though the exact limits of lustfulness may have varied from director to director.)

Mindful of the alleged three-second limit, Hitchcock constructed a scene that begins with Alicia and Devlin embracing on the balcony of Alicia's Rio apartment. The two lovers embrace, kiss for just under three seconds, then nuzzle, exchange short butterfly kisses, whisper, and move inside, never leaving each other's arms, so that Devlin can phone his hotel for messages. Devlin completes his call while nuzzling and kissing Alicia, receives his phone message, and announces that he must leave for a meeting, occasioning more nuzzling and kissing before he exits. Two minutes and forty seconds elapse from the first embrace on the balcony to the time the door closes behind Devlin, and the couple exchange at least twenty kisses, none of which exceed the three-second limit that would label them as "excessively lustful."

To lessen the chance that the censors would object to the scene, Hitchcock, who always prized images above dialogue, abandoned Hecht's script at the last minute and had Grant and Bergman improvise their dialogue. Instead of Hecht's repartee, which was laced with double entendres, the two lovers discuss plans for a chicken dinner between their chaste (by Code definition) kisses. When Hecht saw the finished scene on film for the first time, his response was, "I don't get all this talk about a chicken."[20] "We kept moving and talking, so that the seconds [we spent kissing] were always interrupted," Bergman recalled.[21] In this way, Hitchcock snuck nearly three minutes of passionate love play past the watchful eyes and ears of the censors and created one of the most memorable and famous screen kissing scenes of all time. Roger Ebert noted that the three-second rule actually "led to a *better* scene; an actual 180-second kiss might look like an exercise in slobbering, and the interplay of dialogue and lip and eye contact is electric."[22]

The portrayal of the Alex Sebastian character was also greatly improved by the suggestions and strictures of the Production Code: first, by Joe Breen's suggestion that the plot would be well served if Sebastian had at one time been in love with Alicia, and second, by the fact that Alicia's mission of "sleeping with the enemy" could most easily be carried out under the Code if she were to marry Sebastian. These two elements combined to make Alex Sebastian one of the most sympathetic villains in Hitchcock's works. The fact that he is so smitten with Alicia as to propose marriage shows him to be outwardly far more caring than Devlin, who is too bullheaded to object to the marriage. The marriage also puts Sebastian at odds with his domineering mother, adding conflict to the plot and generating more sympathy for his character.

Hitchcock himself recognized the attractiveness of Claude Rains, who played Alex Sebastian, as a villain, telling François Truffaut, "Claude Rains is a rather appealing figure, both because his confidence is being betrayed and because his love for Ingrid Bergman is probably deeper than Cary Grant's."[23] It seems likely that Hitchcock and Hecht took this attractiveness into account when concocting the film's ending. They rejected endings involving shootouts and car crashes in favor of the final scene in which Alex Sebastian is left to face his Nazi colleagues, alone and exposed, as one

The ending of the *Notorious* kissing scene, in which Ingrid Bergman and Cary Grant exchange nearly twenty kisses, none of which exceeded the supposed three-second limit that would have plunged the scene into obscenity.

who has brought a spy into their midst. Audience sympathy for the Sebastian character greatly heightens the emotional effectiveness of this scene.

Notorious was an immediate success both critically and commercially. James Agee reported in the *Nation*: "Hitchcock has always been as good at domestic psychology as thrillers, and many times here he makes a moment at a party, a lovers' quarrel, or a mere interior shrewdly exciting in ways that few people seem to know. The shots of Rio de Janeiro are excellent and one late-afternoon love scene is equally remarkable in its special emotion and the grandeur of excitement it gets away with, and in communicating the exact place, weather, and time of day."[24] And Bosley Crowther wrote in the *New York Times,* "Mr. Hitchcock has directed in brilliant style a romantic melodrama which is just about as thrilling as they come—velvet smooth in dramatic action, sharp and sure in its characters, and heavily charged with the intensity of warm emotional appeal." Crowther also paid tribute to the balcony nuzzling of Grant and Bergman: "We do not recall a more conspicuous—yet emotionally delicate—love scene on the screen than one stretch of billing and cooing that the principals play in this film."[25]

Not everyone was pleased with the final film. In spite of the Production Code Seal of Approval, Ireland banned *Notorious* on the grounds that "the ignoring of the moral law by the casual treatment of marriage in this film makes it undesirable for general presentation."[26] But the Irish censors were in the minority. The public embraced the film at the time of its release and it grossed $4.8 million domestically for its producers, against a cost of $2.4 million. It has held up well over time and has gone on to be venerated in the top ranks of Hitchcock's masterpieces. François Truffaut called it the "very quintessence of Hitchcock," and rated it as his favorite black-and-white Hitchcock picture.[27] David Thomson called it Hitchcock's "first deeply personal and fully achieved picture," and the American Film Institute (AFI) included it among the top one hundred romantic movies of all time.[28] Very few films on that AFI list involved prostitutes, so it's safe to assume that the Production Code's whitewashing of Alicia Huberman's past, along with its upgrading of Alex Sebastian to a sympathetic love interest, went a long way to ensuring the film's lasting appeal.

15

The Paradine Case (1947)

Synopsis. *Maddalena Paradine (Alida Valli), a beautiful woman with a checkered past, is accused of murdering her blind husband, Colonel Paradine, for his considerable estate. Her married defense attorney, Anthony Keane (Gregory Peck), falls in love with his client and convinces himself of her innocence. When he learns that Mrs. Paradine has had an affair with her husband's valet, Andre Latour (Louis Jourdan), he tries to pin the murder on him.*

The presiding judge, Lord Horfield (Charles Laughton), is a lecher who verbally abuses his own wife (Ethel Barrymore) and enjoys sending women to the gallows. He has long lusted after Keane's wife, Gay (Ann Todd), and is openly hostile to the defense lawyer throughout the trial.

When the valet Latour takes the witness stand, Keane badgers him mercilessly until he admits betraying his master by having an affair with Mrs. Paradine. Burdened by this betrayal, he subsequently commits suicide. Word of Latour's suicide reaches the court when Mrs. Paradine is in the dock. Distraught over the news, she admits to murdering her husband and publicly lashes out at Keane for driving her lover to his death. A humbled Keane apologizes to the court and withdraws from the case. With his career and illusions shattered, he returns to his loyal wife.

***

The Paradine Case was the last picture Hitchcock made under his seven-year contract with David O. Selznick. Easily the worst of their joint ventures, the project seemed doomed from the start. It was based on a 1933 novel by Robert Hichens that Selznick had encouraged MGM to acquire as a vehicle for Greta Garbo shortly after he joined that studio in that same year. He made several attempts to develop the project while at MGM, but was discouraged by Garbo's lack of interest and the warnings of the Breen office. Joe Breen wrote MGM in 1935 to caution against filming a script based on the Hichens novel. "Your leading character is an adulteress and a murderess who is acquitted of the murder of which she is charged. The acquittal is achieved through perjured testimony. Later, when the truth comes out, she gets out of her predicament by committing suicide."[1]

Breen objected to the perjured miscarriage of justice, the use of suicide to avoid punishment, and the sympathy the story bestowed on the murderess. He also found "the characterization of the presiding judge as a man who revels in his power to inflict the death penalty and who enjoys seeing people suffer" to be highly questionable. All of this made *The Paradine Case* "a dangerous story for screen presentation."[2]

Selznick never lost faith in the basic story, however, and thirteen years later, as head of Selznick International, he acquired the rights from MGM for $60,000, more than he had paid for either *Gone with the Wind* or *Rebecca.* He offered the project to Hitchcock, who accepted and began working on a treatment with his wife, Alma.

Casting proved to be a stumbling block. After Garbo, Selznick had tried unsuccessfully to attract either Ingrid Bergman or Vivien Leigh to the role of Maddalena Paradine, but settled for Alida Valli, an Italian actress he hoped to mold into the next Bergman. To make her seem more exotic, Selznick billed her as Valli, using only her last name. Hitchcock and Selznick's first choice for the role of Anthony Keane, the British barrister, was Vivien Leigh's husband, Laurence Olivier, who was busy preparing to film *Hamlet.* Second and third choices were two other British actors, Ronald Colman and James Mason, but the producer and director settled for Selznick contract player Gregory Peck on the strength of his popularity with American audiences. The role of Judge Horfield was first offered to Claude Rains, but went to Charles Laughton after Rains turned it down.

Years after the movie was filmed, Hitchcock told François Truffaut that he considered the major casting flaw to be Louis Jourdan. In the book, Mrs. Paradine's lover was a groom, and Hitchcock felt he should have been played by a rougher, "manure smelling stable hand,"—someone like Robert Newton, whose "horny hands" made him a much grittier choice than the traditionally handsome Jourdan, another Selznick contract player.[3] In the film, though, the Jourdan character was upgraded to a valet who had served with Colonel Paradine before and during the war, so that the actor's appearance was more in keeping with his assigned role.

None of these second and third choices were fatal to the movie. All performed creditably, even Gregory Peck, miscast as a British barrister, and Charles Laughton, who hammed his way through the role of the lecherous judge. The real problem with the film turned out to be the script, which was bedeviled both by Selznick's interference and the Production Code's demands.

At Hitchcock's suggestion, Selznick had hired James Bridie, a Scottish physician turned playwright, to turn the director's treatment into a finished script. Bridie had little feel for logical structure or motivation, and he got off to a poor start when Selznick's employees failed to meet him at the Los Angeles airport. Miffed, the playwright returned to Scotland and wrote the script there, communicating with Hitchcock by phone. Selznick found the resulting effort unacceptable and set about improving it himself, with occasional uncredited help from Ben Hecht. Selznick was in no position to take on such a task, since he was heavily involved in marketing *Duel in the Sun* and struggling with the breakup of his marriage. He was still fussing with the script when filming began, causing the production to fall behind schedule as he often stayed up all night dictating changes for the next day's shoot. These changes had to be read and absorbed by the cast and crew and then rushed to the Breen office for approval before shooting could begin. The producer's last-minute adjustments sometimes delayed actual filming until after lunch.

These delays might have been justified if Selznick had actually been improving the script. But for the most part, the producer was simply regurgitating the pages of the book, restoring "whole stretches of Robert Hichen's wordy dialogue, drowning the drama in a sea of verbiage."[4] The effect was demoralizing for Hitchcock. The director would "see those blue pages in the morning and he would just retreat to his bungalow," Gregory Peck recalled. "In all fairness to Hitch, the dialogue was invariably worse, not better."[5]

The Breen office had raised problems with the *Paradine* script long before the hectic shooting schedule began. Reacting to an early draft of Bridie's screenplay, the censors found one aspect totally unacceptable—"the indication that your lead, Mrs. Paradine, escapes justice by committing suicide." As a result, Breen wrote, "This phase of your story will have to be changed before the picture can be approved."[6]

In addition to this major flaw, the censors found fault with an unusually large number of objectionable words in the screenplay. These included eight instances of *damned,* two each of *Good God! Oh God! damn,* and *hell,* and single sightings of *God knows, For God's sake,* and *Good Lord.* They also asked that the words *impotent, lover,* and *smut* be deleted, along with references to a "disorderly house" and "quiet little flat," which could be "unduly pointed references to prostitution." Other problems with the script included the depiction of a toilet in Mrs. Paradine's cell and several specific mentions of cyanide as the method by which Colonel Paradine was dispatched, both recurring bugaboos. Regarding cyanide, Breen suggested that "it might be well to take protection shots using the general word, poison."[7]

Selznick and Hitchcock made the major script change identified by the censors before shooting began. Maddalena Paradine no longer followed her perjury-enabled release from prison by committing suicide. Instead, Judge Horfield sentenced her to hang with lip-smacking satisfaction after the suicide of her lover led her to confess to murdering her husband. The other changes suggested by the Breen office were all made eventually as part of Selznick's helter-skelter rewrites during shooting.

Just before shooting began, Breen wrote Selznick acknowledging the change in Mrs. Paradine's scripted fate, stating that her murder conviction removed "the basic difficulty under the code" and reiterating the remaining changes recommended in his initial letter. He also added two new concerns, asking that the producer take care to ensure that "the intimate parts of the body—specifically the breasts of women—be fully covered at all times," and noting that, in a later bathroom scene, "it would be advisable to omit any showing of Keane in the bath, even by suggestion, in order to avoid showing a man and a woman in the bathroom at the same time."[8]

In their eagerness to see justice done to Mrs. Paradine, the censors overlooked the potentially homoerotic subtext involving Andre Latour. While taking Keane to the Paradines' country house to meet Latour, the carriage driver twice refers to the valet as a "queer one." Although the remark could be construed as a British synonym for "odd," Latour's torment on the witness stand over having betrayed the master he had served for so long, and whom he characterized as "the best man I ever knew in all my life," would support a different interpretation. And Louis Jourdan's handsome features are a close fit to the then prevalent stereotype of gay men as "pretty boys."

Hitchcock required ninety-two days of principal photography, a record for him, before he could deliver Selznick a rough cut of the verbose script that ran just under three hours. Selznick managed to cut the film to

131 minutes for its opening in Los Angeles and New York on the last day of 1947, just in time to qualify for the 1948 Academy Awards. Still not satisfied, Selznick continued cutting the film before it went into nationwide distribution.

Among the final frames to be cut were courtroom shots of Valli, who had tested poorly with preview audiences; an early scene showing Keane successfully defending an accused killer and earning an admonition from Judge Horfield for his courtroom histrionics; and a scene between Horfield's abused wife, played by Ethel Barrymore, and Anthony Keane in which she begs the barrister to get Mrs. Paradine off because her husband so loves to hang women that he is randy and uncontrollable when he comes home after pronouncing death sentences on female defendants. This last scene reflected one of the earliest concerns of the Breen office, which considered the novel's "image of a justice who revels in his power to inflict the death penalty" unsuitable for film treatment.[9]

Selznick's rush to open *The Paradine Case* in time to qualify for the Academy Awards bore fruit only in the case of Ethel Barrymore, who received a nomination as Best Supporting Actress. Ironically, the producer's last-minute cuts kept one of the actress's most powerful scenes from receiving nationwide distribution.

Curiously, Selznick's final cuts left Ann Todd, who played Anthony Keane's faithful wife, with nearly as much screen time as Valli, the femme fatale and the ostensible star of the film. This may have happened because Selznick, always alert to public preferences, found that preview audiences reacted more positively to Todd than to Valli. It's also been suggested that the producer, whose real-life affections were split between his wife and Jennifer Jones, was guiltily giving more time to the point of view of the movie's loyal wife, and padding Todd's time with speeches expressing sympathy for the obsessed and guilt-ridden husband.[10] "Just because a man, a husband, fancies another woman, you don't treat him as a criminal. . . . It's very painful, but it's painful for him too."

The Selznick-induced production delays pushed the cost of the film and its advertising to $4.3 million, almost exactly as much as the producer spent on *Gone with the Wind.* But the fault was not all Selznick's. Hitchcock oversaw the creation of an exact replica of London's Old Bailey for the trial scenes, and lavished money on the country-house sets. By the start of filming, the cost of sets alone was $275,000, $100,000 more than the cost of sets for *Gone with the Wind.*[11] Even with Selznick pouring more money into advertising than he had for any of his other films, there was no chance that *Paradine* would ever earn a profit. Worldwide income eventually totaled $2.2 million, roughly half of the film's cost. Allowing for inflation, *The Paradine Case* was the most expensive movie Hitchcock ever made.[12]

Reviews varied, with many critics expressing ambivalent opinions. *Time* noted that the film had "high polish and intelligence," but added that the characters "are lifeless participants in a rigid, theatrical dance."[13] A few reviewers blamed Selznick for the picture's faults, absolving Hitchcock of any culpability. Bosley Crowther of the *New York Times* wrote that "David O. Selznick and Alfred Hitchcock have put upon the screen a slick piece of static entertainment in their garrulous 'The Paradine Case.'" Crowther went on to pan Selznick's script as tedious and not too well written while praising Hitchcock's direction, noting that "Mr. Hitchcock has made the best of a difficult script and has got as much tension in a courtroom as most directors could get in a frontier fort."[14]

John McCarten of the *New Yorker* was particularly hard on Selznick: "One picture may be worth a thousand words, but you'll never prove it by David O. Selznick." He went on to excuse, but not absolve, Hitchcock: "It is with great reluctance that I am compelled to announce that 'The Paradine Case' was directed by Alfred Hitchcock," adding, "The Selznick script must have caught him nodding." Selznick subsequently banned McCarten from press previews, and wrote a letter to *New Yorker* editor Harold Ross accusing the critic of being drunk and distracting at screenings.[15]

In apportioning blame for the failure of *The Paradine Case,* some consideration should be given to the Breen office. As with *Rebecca,* the censors forced the studio to change the original ending of the novel so that no one got away with murder and, with *Paradine,* so that suicide was not introduced as a means of thwarting justice. There's no way of knowing whether the novel's perjured testimony and subsequent suicide would have played better than the movie's witness-box confession spawned by a lover's suicide, but the book's plot introduces more conflict, is more believable, and has the added advantage of stemming from the background and motivations of the characters created by the novel's author.

The Paradine Case represented the low point in Hitchcock and Selznick's collaboration. The blame for the failure of what might have been a much better movie is generally assigned to Selznick. Appropriately, he took the financial hit of more than $2 million, while Hitchcock emerged with his salary and reputation intact. By 1948, Selznick's companies had shut down, and he was divorced and $12 million in debt. Free of Selznick's oversight, Hitchcock was on his way to his own production company and the perils of risking his own money on his artistic choices.

IV

The Transatlantic Years (1948–1949)

Hitchcock in a publicity shot for *Rope,* Transatlantic's first independent production. (Courtesy of Photofest.)

16

Hitchcock and Transatlantic

The completion of *The Paradine Case* marked the end of Hitchcock's contractual obligations to David O. Selznick. Casting about for an alternative, the director turned to his old friend Sidney Bernstein. In London at the end of the war, the two men had discussed the formation of a company, Transatlantic Pictures, that would employ the best talent available in England and America. Hitchcock began working on the new company while preparing to shoot *The Paradine Case* in London, devoting his "days to *Paradine* and his nights to Transatlantic."[1]

When Selznick got wind of Hitchcock's plans, he offered the director a new long-term contract that would pay him $100,000 per picture. In theory, the two men complemented each other, with Selznick's understanding of story values balancing Hitchcock's technical artistry. In practice, however, both men needed to be in complete control, and Hitchcock rankled under Selznick's domineering interference. As Transatlantic co-producer with Bernstein, Hitchcock would have complete control over casting, budgets, and subject matter as well as directorial details. Although Selznick could promise financial security, he couldn't match the autonomy that Hitchcock would enjoy with Transatlantic, and the director turned down his offer.

Starting Transatlantic from scratch, Hitchcock and Bernstein needed to find investors, stars, properties, and a distributor. They first struck an agreement with Warner Bros. to distribute their films in America. On the strength of this agreement and Hitchcock's reputation, Bernstein was able to get Bankers Trust to agree to finance the firm's first two films up to a total of $5 million. Hitchcock then contacted his old friends Cary Grant and Ingrid Bergman, who tentatively agreed to perform for Transatlantic.

With distribution, funding, and star power in place, Hitchcock and Bernstein set about finding properties to film. This proved to be a little more difficult, since they were competing with major studios that had large teams of evaluators searching for promising properties—as well as bigger bankrolls to secure them. With a limited budget and only one employee, the two men decided to concentrate on British plays and novels, reasoning that they would be less expensive and more likely to escape the notice of American studios.

One of the first properties Transatlantic obtained was *Under Capricorn,* a melodrama set in nineteenth-century Australia. The novel was written by Helen Simpson, a friend of Hitchcock's who had worked with him on the British production of *Murder!* Hitchcock negotiated a favorable price, and *Under Capricorn* was announced as Transatlantic's first picture, to star Ingrid Bergman.

When Bergman's busy schedule forced production delays, another British property, *Rope,* based on a 1929 play by Patrick Hamilton, became Transatlantic's first picture. Although Hamilton's play had been successful on both sides of the Atlantic, major studios had shied away from it because of its homosexual overtones. Although Hamilton denied the connection, the play mirrored the notorious Leopold-Loeb murder case in 1924 Chicago.

So the first two properties to be filmed by Hitchcock under the Transatlantic banner were *Rope,* based on a murder committed by two homosexuals, and *Under Capricorn,* a costume melodrama set in 1830s Australia. The two properties proved to be exceptionally poor choices. They were available at bargain prices not because they had been overlooked by the major studios, but rather because the major studios had looked hard at them and used good judgment in passing them up.[2]

In the past, Hitchcock had been able to shore up weak story lines and inferior properties with his bravura style. "The subject doesn't count," he said. "You get your satisfaction through your style of treatment. I'm not interested in content."[3] Unfortunately, Hitchcock elected to film Transatlantic's first two properties in a style that used long, uninterrupted takes and played against his skills in cutting and creating memorable scenes. The weaknesses of the properties themselves, coupled with Hitchcock's experiments with linear storytelling, doomed the fledgling company.

17

Rope (1948)

Synopsis. *One summer afternoon in an apartment overlooking Manhattan, two wealthy young intellectuals, Brandon Shaw (John Dall) and Philip Morgan (Farley Granger) strangle a friend for the thrill of demonstrating their superior status. Although it is never explicitly stated, the pair are homosexual lovers. Immediately after the murder, they throw a party in which food and drinks are served from the top of a chest containing the victim's corpse.*

Guests at the party include the victim's father and fiancée as well as a publisher, Rupert Cadell (James Stewart), a former teacher who had introduced the murderous pair to the Nietzschean concept of the Superman who is above the law.

The film plays out in real time, as if done in one long take. As the party progresses, the murderers attempt to impress their mentor by disclosing bits of the truth about the fate of their friend. Before the evening is over, the publisher has pieced together the bits of information, discovered the body in the chest, and summoned the police.

***

In Hollywood in the 1940s, both prevailing morality and the Production Code made it impossible to make a film about gay men. This made the filming of a movie based on Patrick Hamilton's play *Rope*, which mirrored the notorious Leopold-Loeb murder case in 1924 Chicago, a particularly tricky endeavor. The case, in which two University of Chicago students in a homosexual relationship kidnapped and murdered a fourteen-year-old boy to demonstrate their intellectual superiority, had received national coverage and been dubbed "the crime of the century." Recognizing that the Breen office would challenge any overt intimations of homosexuality in the film's dialogue or actions, Hitchcock worked to keep all such hints below the surface. Far from ignoring them, though, he hired a gay screenwriter and cast gay actors in the two lead roles.

Screenwriter Arthur Laurents called this approach "very Hitchcock."

"It tickled him that Farley was playing a homosexual in a movie written by me, another homosexual; that we were lovers; that we had a secret he knew; that I knew he knew. . . . All titillating to him, not out of malice or a feeling of power but because they added a slightly kinky touch, and kink was a quality devoutly to be desired."[1]

In addition to Farley Granger as the weaker of the gay pair of killers, Hitchcock's concept of ideal casting envisioned the rising star Montgomery Clift as the mastermind of the murderous lovers, and Cary Grant as Rupert Cadell, the former prep school master, another gay man, who had introduced the pair to Nietzsche's theory of the "Superman." Even though the sexuality of the three leads was not explicitly defined, the script had enough homosexual implications (Brandon wore cologne and was mother-fixated, two gay stereotypes of the times) to frighten both Clift and Grant. "Since Cary Grant was at best bisexual and Monty was gay," Laurents recalled, "they were scared to death and wouldn't do it."[2] In place of Montgomery Clift, Hitchcock cast John Dall, another rising young gay actor who had been nominated for an Oscar for his supporting role in *The Corn Is Green,* and who was not worried about *Rope*'s homosexual subtext.

Instead of Cary Grant, the key role of Rupert Cadell, the murderous pair's mentor, went to Jimmy Stewart. This posed a problem in Laurent's view, because he felt Stewart was so asexual that nobody (presumably including Stewart) "knew he was supposed to have a 'relationship' with the boys."[3] A few modern critics have agreed with Laurents that Stewart, whose image at the time was that of a folksy everyman, was miscast. It's difficult to credit this argument, however, since the gay subtext was so subtle it would have slipped by 90 percent of the 1940s viewing audience, who certainly would not have been aware of the sexual preferences of Dall and Granger.

The gay subtext was also downplayed on the studio lot. "The play is basically about the Leopold-Loeb murders," Laurents said, "which nobody mentioned and nobody admitted. It dealt with these two homosexual boys and their homosexual teacher, which nobody also admitted. Nobody used the word 'homosexual;' it was referred to as 'it' by Hitch, by the studio, by everyone. They just pretended it wasn't there, but they wanted it there."[4]

The gay subtext of the work was so subtle it also eluded the Breen office, at least in its first review of the play itself. While still working days on *The Paradine Case* and nights trying to get Transatlantic Pictures started, Hitchcock had sent a copy of Patrick Hamilton's play to Joseph Breen, asking that he review it from the standpoint of the Production Code. Breen responded with a letter stating that the material basically seemed "to meet the standards of the Production Code."[5]

Breen mentioned two concerns in his letter, neither of which involved homosexuality. One cautioned about the "emphasis on and dialogue about liquor and drinking." The other warned that the proper moral values that the play finally asserts might be undermined by earlier speeches ridiculing these values and the Ten Commandments themselves.[6]

The Breen office finally caught up with the issue of *Rope*'s homosexuality in its review of the initial script, citing the similarity between the two murderers and Leopold and Loeb. Noting a "possible flavor in some of the dialogue that a homosexual relationship existed between Brandon and Philip," the censors pointed out that "such a treatment would not be acceptable under the terms of the Production Code."[7]

In a subsequent meeting, Transatlantic assured the Breen office that the studio was "equally as adverse to such a flavor coming through" and agreed to "change any specific lines of dialogue that might reflect a homosexual relationship between the two characters."[8] To fulfill this promise, Laurents excised a few of the English idioms, such as "my dear boy," that had survived his transposition of Hamilton's English play to Manhattan and were considered vaguely homosexual.

The Breen office review of the revised script found only one instance of potentially dicey dialogue, suggesting cutting the word *lovely* from Brandon's claim to "have a lovely excuse." The reviewers were more interested in the "rather pointed emphasis on liquor and drinking," the explicit detail in the strangling scene that opens the film, and the "unacceptable" action of Brandon wiping a glass free of fingerprints, which could potentially serve as instruction for would-be murderers in the movie audience.[9]

Additional script changes were reviewed by the Breen office a month later and found to be acceptable, although it asked once again that the "continuous references to liquor and drinking" be cut down during the shooting of the picture. The letter of acceptance closed with the standard admonition that "our final judgment will be based on the finished picture."[10]

As shooting began, Transatlantic made an unusual request of the Breen office. Because it was "photographing the picture one reel at a time without any cuts," the studio feared that any comments Breen and his censors "might have to make when the picture is completed might well be calamitous." Accordingly, Transatlantic asked that the censors view the individual reels before they were finalized and advise the studio immediately of any objectionable features. While the studio promised to "submit the completed film for your verdict in the usual way," it felt it would be of great advantage "to get your guidance as the film goes along."[11]

In the end, it would be Hitchcock's decision to film *Rope* in long uninterrupted takes, rather than any hint of homosexuality, that would seal the fate of the film. Hitchcock had conceived the idea of filming in "real time," rather than cinematic time, as early as 1940 when he was working on *Saboteur.* Patrick Hamilton's play afforded an ideal testing ground for the technique, since it covered events in a single setting over the course of an evening, breaking only for intermissions.

In theory, the plan to capture action in real time with long takes could have provided significant savings in the usual ten to twelve weeks required for principal photography and "affirmed Hitchcock's reputation as a bankable filmmaker in solid touch with economic realities."[12] In practice, the long-take approach had several limitations. One of these was the length of film reels, which could capture only nine to ten minutes of action before running out. This led to the creation of artificial "cuts" disguised by passing the camera closely behind the back of a character or closing in on a piece of furniture before changing reels.

The limitations in reel length proved to be the least of the technical problems imposed by real-time shooting. Elaborate sets had to be constructed with movable walls and furnishings so that the bulky Technicolor cameras could follow characters as they moved through doors and around furniture. Camera movements had to be carefully choreographed in advance, and the movements and set alterations were often so noisy that sound had to be recorded separately. At one point, James Stewart observed, "The only thing rehearsed around here is the camera."[13]

The strain of ten-minute camera takes was hard on everyone. James Stewart recalled, "Each time the company neared the end of a take, the actors became 'sort of glassy eyed.' All of us were thinking, 'Oh, God, don't let me go up on my lines now! If I do we'll have to go back and do the whole thing again.'"[14]

Rope was Hitchcock's first Technicolor film, and the last five reels had to be reshot to overcome problems with the dusk and sunset effects outside

James Stewart confronts the two thrill killers, John Dall and Farley Granger, with evidence of their crime.

the apartment window. Even with the reshoots and the cast on edge, principal photography was completed in three weeks, with eleven takes ranging from just under five minutes to over nine minutes in length. So the anticipated production savings were realized, albeit at the expense of pacing and cinematic values. The resulting film was cold and clinical because "the moving camera never paused long enough to discover the characters' humanity."[15]

Hitchcock had experimented with long takes on *The Paradine Case* but was dissuaded by Selznick, who realized that the technique robbed him of control of the final cut and downplayed Hitchcock's scene-making skills. *Rope*'s co-producer, Sidney Bernstein, may have recognized this problem, but didn't try to stem Hitchcock's enthusiasm for the experiment. Although Bernstein theoretically had the "final say" on Transatlantic's pictures, he recognized "that the moment I exercise it, it's the end of the partnership."[16] Besides, Bernstein saw the long-take experiment as a means of recording current British theater productions on film for a wider audience.

Transatlantic and Warner Bros. poured $450,000 into a promotional campaign for *Rope,* and the film turned a modest profit on its $1.5 million budget. Reviews varied. *Time* praised it as a "rattling good melodrama."[17] The *Hollywood Reporter* said it was "Hitchcock at his best, tense, exciting, and thrilling," even though the reviewer found the drama a "superficial study whose momentum is achieved by theatrical artifice rather than a subtle analysis of personality."[18] At the low end of the scale, Bosley Crowther, writing for the *New York Times,* called it "possibly the dullest picture ever made."[19]

Those reviews that mentioned the long uninterrupted takes and real-time storytelling weren't entirely sold on the concept. The *Hollywood Reporter* called the technique "bold and imaginative—compelling in its own fashion and always interesting to watch." The reviewer added, however, that "it is not always interesting to hear, for in achieving completely fluid camera action the screenplay is obliged to pad the piece with superfluous dialogue that amounts to so much small talk."[20] And Bosley Crowther in the *New York Times* was even harder on what he called Hitchcock's "little stunt": "With due regard for his daring . . . one must bluntly observe that the method is neither effective nor does it appear that it could be. For, apart from the tedium of waiting for someone to open that chest and discover the hidden body . . . the unpunctuated flow of images becomes quite monotonous."[21]

Whispers of "the love that dare not speak its name" reached a few ears upon release of the film. Barney Balaban, the New York–based president of Paramount Pictures, wrote privately to Jack Warner, urging him to disassociate himself from the film's distribution, because it "too closely evoked the Leopold-Loeb case, with its portrait of two killers clearly homosexual and, worse, Jewish."[22]

Warner wrote back that Hitchcock had assured him that the film had "nothing whatever to do with the Loeb-Leopold case. Furthermore, the action takes place in New York and no Jewish characters are portrayed in the picture." However, he went on to tell Balaban confidentially that "had you or someone else called my attention to this case and the picture before the picture was made, Warner Bros. would not have made any deal to release the picture." After its initial push, Warner Bros. subsequently put little enthusiasm or effort into *Rope*'s distribution.[23]

Few of the major reviewers (*Motion Picture Daily* and *Variety* were rare exceptions) mentioned the Leopold-Loeb case, and certainly none raised the issue of the carefully disguised homosexual subtext. Still, letters echoing Balaban's concerns poured in from the Anti-Defamation League, film betterment councils, and other citizen organizations.[24] In Chicago, the scene of the Leopold-Loeb murder, police shut down the film on the grounds that it was "not wholesome entertainment." When Warner's appealed the decision, the locals allowed the picture to be exhibited with an "adults only" classification as a sales booster.

Municipal authorities in Worcester and New Bedford, Massachusetts; Spokane and Seattle, Washington; Atlanta, Georgia; and Memphis, Tennessee, also banned showings of the film. All seven of the existing state censorship boards passed the film, although Maryland and Ohio cut Brandon's admission that he felt exhilarated by the murder and his argument that the power to kill could be "just as satisfying as the power to create." Pennsylvania joined these two states in excising the initial strangulation scene.

Rope was banned outright in France, Italy, and Holland. While the French and Italians may have cracked the subtext code, the Dutch based their ban on the fact that the film "put forward a justification for the elimination of persons of inferior intellect." Foreign, state, and local censorship boards generated enough activity to prompt a *New York Times* article entitled "Censorship Ties *Rope* in Knots." The article wondered why the tale of a thrill killing attracted so much attention when "any number of other crimes have gotten by without arousing the censors."[25]

Missing the subtext entirely, the *New York Times* writer failed to come up with an explanation for the censors' attention and concluded by expressing his bewilderment. "Although it is not unusual for pictures to meet with official protests in certain areas—Boston, it will be remembered, considered some of the dialogue in *Henry V* too pungent for its citizens to hear on Sundays but quite all right on other days—it is not often that a picture runs into such difficulty on the scale that *Rope* has up to the minute. Especially is this true when, as in the case of *Rope,* there have been no pronounced objections voiced by religious groups."[26]

From the standpoint of the present day, *Rope*'s gay subtext is more legible. But it is easy to see how it eluded most viewers and reviewers in 1948. It would take at least twenty more years before the demise of the Production Code could free Hollywood to make movies that revolved around openly gay characters. Looking back, the screenwriter Arthur Laurents felt *Rope* was one of the "most sophisticated movies ever made" on the subject of homosexuality, largely because Hitchcock was so wary of stereotypes that he treated the characters as people. "What he liked was not that they were homosexual, but that they were homosexual murderers. If they were just homosexual, he wouldn't have been interested. If they were just murderers, he wouldn't have been interested."[27]

In the final analysis, *Rope* is inferior Hitchcock not because the homosexuality was underplayed or James Stewart was miscast, but because Hitchcock's long takes worked against his strengths as a director, emphasizing linear movement and dialogue rather than pacing and montage. It's as if Babe Ruth had decided to play a season batting right-handed. There's no doubt he could have done it, but he wouldn't have put up Ruthian numbers.

18

Under Capricorn (1949)

Synopsis. *In 1831, the Honorable Charles Adare (Michael Wilding) moves from Ireland to Australia, where his uncle has been named governor. At a party he meets Lady Henrietta (Ingrid Bergman), an alcoholic who had been friends with his sister as a child. By all appearances, Lady Henrietta is unhappily married to former stable boy and ex-convict Sam Flusky (Joseph Cotten), who has become a successful businessman. Flusky's young housekeeper, Milly (Margaret Leighton), is secretly in love with him, a fellow commoner, and has been surreptitiously encouraging his wife's drinking. Adare falls in love with Henrietta and attempts to rehabilitate her, countering Milly's designs.*

Enflamed by the housekeeper's malicious gossip, Flusky becomes jealous of Adare, accidentally shooting and seriously wounding him. To protect her husband from another prison sentence, Henrietta reveals that she had been guilty of the original shooting that had caused Flusky to be deported to Australia. Upon recovering from his wound, Adare refuses to press charges and, respecting Flusky's long-standing sacrifice and love for Henrietta, sees that he must move on and leave Australia.

***

In *Under Capricorn,* Joe Breen and his fellow censors were much less concerned with the morality of the movie than with the morality of the star, Ingrid Bergman. The movie itself, the second feature under the Transatlantic banner, proved to be a disaster in almost every respect. The humorless script was based on a lackluster novel and provided few thrills and no suspense from a director who specialized in suspenseful thrillers. Hitchcock told François Truffaut later that he had "no special admiration for the novel" and probably wouldn't have adapted it if Ingrid Bergman hadn't agreed to star in the movie. Since Bergman was one of the most popular and accomplished actresses in Hollywood at the time, he viewed her participation as a "tremendous feat" that would reaffirm his reputation and secure Transatlantic's place among the major studios. Unfortunately, the married star's off-screen romance with an Italian director proved to be a distraction and a detriment to an already burdened film. In retrospect, Hitchcock admitted his infatuation with Bergman was "bad thinking" and characterized his own behavior as "almost infantile."[1]

The director should have heeded the advice of his *Rope* screenwriter, Arthur Laurents, who not only turned down Hitchcock's offer to have him write the *Capricorn* screenplay, but also had the audacity to question the wisdom of bringing the novel to the screen in the first place. Undaunted, Hitchcock gave the job of adapting the novel to his old friend Hume Cronyn, who had little screenwriting experience.

The movie also suffered from a few poor casting decisions. The lead actor, Joseph Cotten, was miscast as a former stable boy. Hitchcock said he would have preferred someone with a more "earthy" presence, like Burt Lancaster, who was unavailable at the time. The British press also scolded Hitchcock for casting "our most promising young screen leading lady, Margaret Leighton," in the role of the shrewish housekeeper.[2] And Michael Wilding's foppish love interest was no match for Ingrid Bergman, although that problem had as much to do with the script as with casting.

Hitchcock didn't help his own cause by carrying on the experimentation with long takes that he had begun with *Rope.* As in the case of *Rope,* this decision hobbled the director's editing strengths. Although there were only three such takes in *Under Capricorn,* they slowed the action; one critic said the camera seemed "indifferent, as if actors had to keep talking until the film ran out."[3] Hitchcock subsequently told Truffaut that "as an experiment, *Rope* may be forgiven, but it was definitely a mistake when I insisted on applying the same technique in *Under Capricorn.*"[4]

As with *Rope,* the actors found the pressure of rehearsing and delivering lines for the seven to nine minutes required by the long takes to be annoying and frustrating. "What a nightmare!" Bergman told a writer years later. "The continuous shots and moving cameras were very hard on everybody. We rehearsed for days, and then at last we put on makeup and had a try at a reel. We had perhaps six minutes just fine and then suddenly something went wrong and the whole reel had to begin again. Hitch just insisted." The actress continued, "Then the prop man had the job of moving all the furniture while the camera was rolling forward and backward, or from this side to that, and the walls were flying up into the rafters as we walked by, so that huge Technicolor camera could follow us. It just drove us all crazy."[5]

The frustrated actress erupted one day, telling Hitchcock off with a stream of expletives. Hitchcock first tried to mollify her with a method that had worked in the past, reminding her, "Ingrid, it's only a movie."[6] When that failed to stop the invective, the director, who hated arguments and confrontation, just left and went home when Bergman's back was turned. Witnesses reported that the actress went on ranting for twenty minutes without realizing Hitchcock had gone.[7]

Joe Breen's Production Code office found little fault with the treatment and script for *Under Capricorn.* Its review cited the standard complement of unacceptable profanity (several *damn*s, the word *slut,* and one insufficiently reverent "So help me God"). The censors also objected to the local minister's disapproving look when the Irish Adare made the sign of the cross, and the accusation that a minor character had "got a girl in trouble." Finally, the censors expressed the hope that Ingrid Bergman would be "attired in something more than a nightgown" during a scene in Lady Henrietta's bedroom.[8]

Transatlantic responded quickly, acceding to all of Breen's demands and assuring him that in the bedroom scene Miss Bergman would "be properly covered and her nightgown will be made of very heavy material."[9]

But the vetting of the *Under Capricorn* script and the awarding of the Production Code Seal of Approval did not mark the end of Joe Breen's interactions with the production, or at least with the production's star. In the midst of shooting *Under Capricorn* in August 1948, Ingrid Bergman and her husband had taken her thirty-third birthday off to fly to Paris and meet with the Italian director Roberto Rossellini, whom the actress had written in the hope that they might make a movie together. The actress and director met again in Hollywood early in 1949, and Bergman left Hollywood in March to film *Stromboli* with Rossellini in Italy. By April 1949 the two were at the center of what Breen termed "the most shocking scandal which even Hollywood had had to contend with in many years."[10] When *Stromboli* finished shooting in August, Bergman remained with Rossellini, and in February 1950 the pair announced the birth of their illegitimate son, born while Bergman's divorce was still pending.

The Bergman/Rossellini affair was particularly distressing because the actress's public image bordered on sainthood as a result of roles as a nun in *The Bells of St. Mary's* and, most recently, as the Maid of Loraine in *Joan of*

Arc, a movie that Breen himself had uncharacteristically favored with a glowing review. The fact that Bergman had also had an affair with *Joan of Arc*'s director, the sixty-four-year-old Victor Fleming, was not known either to the general public or to Breen, whose ear was usually acutely attuned to Hollywood gossip.

On hearing rumors of the Rossellini affair, Breen took it upon himself to write Bergman, professing his hope that the press reports were untrue and warning her that such reports could "*very well destroy your career as a motion picture artist*" and "result in the American public becoming so thoroughly outraged that your pictures will be ignored, and your box-office value ruined." He pleaded with the actress to deny the rumors and "state, quite frankly, that they are not true, that you have no intention to desert your child or divorce your husband, and that you have no plans to marry anyone," adding, "I make this suggestion to you in the utmost sincerity and solely with a view to stamping out these reports that constitute a major scandal and may well result in *complete disaster to you personally.*"[11]

Writing from Italy, Bergman responded graciously to Breen's letter. By that time she had publicly confirmed the news that Breen had asked her to disavow. She wrote that she was "deeply sorry to have hurt my friends involved in the pictures I have already made," and that she hoped "with all my heart they will not have to pay for my fault."[12]

As Breen predicted, the American press and public lost no time in reviling the actress. "Letters of condemnation for Ingrid poured in by the thousands and tens of thousands."[13] By the time *Under Capricorn* opened in September 1949, the media storm had abated, but public opinion was still incensed and Bergman elected not to cooperate in any promotion of the movie. Some Catholic organizations reacted to the affair by banning the Hitchcock film, and "many cinema owners were sufficiently outraged to follow suit."[14]

Animosity toward Bergman resurfaced when *Stromboli* was released in America in mid-February 1950, just after the birth of the couple's illegitimate child. Breen sliced thirty minutes from the film's running time before issuing a Code Seal, an act Rossellini called a "laughable hatchet job" that made him look ridiculous.[15] The producers claimed that the cuts didn't harm the film and ran an advertising campaign that tried to cash in on the notoriety of the star and director. In spite of this, the film did little business, not because of any on-screen immorality (not much remained after Breen's cuts) but because critics judged it to be "feeble, inarticulate, uninspiring, and painfully banal."[16]

Bergman's reappearance in the public eye earned her an official condemnation from the floor of the US Senate. Senator Edwin C. Johnson, a Colorado Democrat, called her a "free-love cultist" and an "apostle of degradation."[17] Johnson went on to schedule a hearing to probe Hollywood morals and propose a bill that would require actors, actresses, producers, and films to be officially licensed according to their moral decency.

The idea that actors and actresses might have to have licenses that could be cancelled for private indiscretions or public infamy set off alarms within the MPPDA and the Production Code office. Recognizing that such a procedure would seriously threaten the motion picture business, Joe Breen and his boss, Will Hays's successor, Eric Johnston, quickly arranged a meeting with Senator Johnson in Washington. At first, the senator was adamant in his insistence that film actors should be licensed, in the same way that taxi drivers, plumbers, bartenders, and anyone who could do public harm should be licensed. There was no question in his mind that the deep influence actors had on the lives of their fans carried with it the potential for public harm.[18]

Breen argued that the Production Code ensured that Hollywood operated on a high moral plane and presented his exchange of letters with Ingrid Bergman as evidence that the MPPDA even tried to interfere on a personal level with performers when it appeared that they were likely to endanger public morality.

Convinced by Breen, the senator said he would withdraw his licensing bill and call off his morality hearings if the MPPDA would adopt new regulations to "ban the use of advertising that exploits the misconduct of screen personalities." Breen and his boss readily agreed to the deal, and within a month the MPPDA Board of Directors met in New York and adapted its Advertising Code to accommodate the proposed ban.[19]

Hitchcock and Bernstein had been counting on Ingrid Bergman to affect the box-office receipts of *Under Capricorn,* and she did, although not in the way they had expected. Even if the actress had remained scandal-free and actively promoted the film, though, it's unlikely that the picture would have been a success.

Reviews were uniformly bad on both sides of the Atlantic. The *Hollywood Reporter* wrote that "one had to wait one hundred and five minutes for the first thrill of the picture."[20] Howard Barnes in the *New York World Telegraph* observed simply that Hitchcock had "stumbled," and Bosley Crowther of the *New York Times* wrote that neither Hitchcock nor Bergman had chosen well in "tangling here with stuff of penny dreadful substance and superficial demands."[21] The film did no better with London reviewers. The *Tattler* called the movie "ponderous," while the *Times* reported that *Under Capricorn* "takes a long time to pose its problem and an even longer time to solve it."[22] Each of these London papers praised the long take in which Ingrid Bergman recalls her early love for her husband and reveals that she had committed the murder for which he served seven years, one of the few moving moments in the film.

In the end, *Under Capricorn* did not come close to recovering its $2.5 million cost, and the Bankers Trust reclaimed the film. The failure marked the end of Transatlantic Pictures as an independent producer. The next Hitchcock film, *Stage Fright,* began as a Transatlantic production, but was taken over by Warner Bros., which would produce the director's next four movies. Hitchcock and Bernstein continued to discuss future projects, but script and budget problems, along with Bernstein's declining interest in producing, caused them to dissolve their partnership early in 1953.

In *Under Capricorn,* Breen and the Code didn't have much input on an already bad film, but the chief censor's attempt to influence the private life of the movie's star paradoxically helped to scuttle further federal regulation of the film industry.

V

The Warner's Years (1950–1954)

Hitchcock with Farley Granger and a double bass in the director's cameo in *Strangers on a Train*. (Courtesy of Jerry Ohlinger.)

19

Hitchcock and Warner Bros.

Warner Bros.' agreement to serve as a distributor for Transatlantic films included a provision that Hitchcock was to direct one Warner's film for each Transatlantic film. When Transatlantic foundered after producing two films, Warner's restructured Hitchcock's contract. Under the terms of the new agreement, Hitchcock would continue to be his own producer, and would be paid $3,000 a week for 333 weeks to direct four films for Warner Bros. He would also receive points on those films that turned a profit. This million-dollar deal worked out to $250,000 per film, a considerable increase over the $50,000 that Selznick paid Hitchcock for directing *Rebecca.*

While Hitchcock fulfilled his obligations to Warner's, Sidney Bernstein struggled to keep Transatlantic alive, searching for promising properties and commissioning film treatments. With the partnership deeply in debt, the risks and pressures of the movie business eventually wore on Bernstein, and he resigned in 1953 to return to England, formally shutting the doors on the Transatlantic venture.

Although Hitchcock's try for true independence died with Transatlantic, his deal with Warner Bros. placed him among the best-paid directors in Hollywood. And Warner's got good value for its money. In addition to the director himself, the studio also inherited the rights to the two projects Transatlantic had in development. These were a book by English mystery novelist Selwyn Jepson called *Man Running,* which would become *Stage Fright,* and an obscure 1902 French play, *Nos deux consciences* (Our Two Consciences), which eventually became the Hitchcock film *I Confess.*

Although Jack Warner made Hitchcock a producer, he did not surrender complete autonomy over the director's productions, retaining the right to approve scripts and casting. Warner exercised his casting control on each of the four pictures made under the contract, rejecting Hitchcock's suggestion of Tallulah Bankhead for the role of the diva in *Stage Fright* in favor of Marlene Dietrich, and selecting Warner's contract player Farley Granger over Hitchcock's choice of William Holden for the part of the tennis player in *Strangers on a Train.*

Warner had different reasons for overruling Hitchcock's choice of Swedish actress Anita Björk for the lead female role in *I Confess*. After the actress had been approved and signed for the role, she showed up in Hollywood accompanied by her lover and their illegitimate baby daughter. Fearing another scandal similar to that surrounding Ingrid Bergman, Warner insisted that Björk be paid off and replaced. Hitchcock protested, but Warner persisted, and Anne Baxter got the starring role.

Warner also balked at Hitchcock's recommendation that Cary Grant play the blackmailing villain in *Dial M for Murder.* Grant was willing, but Warner feared that the public would not accept the popular actor in an unsympathetic role, an objection that both Hitchcock and Grant had faced before, on *Suspicion.* Hitchcock believed that Warner's real objection was to Grant's high salary, but accepted the less expensive Ray Milland in the villain's role.[1]

Aside from David O. Selznick, Hitchcock got to know Jack Warner better than any of Hollywood's major studio heads. But with Warner there was none of the friction the director had experienced with Selznick. Hitchcock and Warner shared a mutual respect and were able to work out most differences of opinion politely and amicably.[2]

Hitchcock's years at Warner Bros. were dark years for Hollywood. The Supreme Court consent decree that forced the major studios to divest their theater chains changed the nature of the business and closed off a key revenue stream. But television was the major source of the studios' woes. During the four years Hitchcock was with Warner's, television ownership increased and annual theatrical attendance in the United States dropped from 3.1 billion to 2.3 billion, a significant decline from its peak of 4.7 billion in the pre-TV year of 1947.

Warner's was not immune to the industry problems. During Hitchcock's tenure, the studio's annual profits dropped from $10.3 million to $2.9 million.[3] It trimmed its roster of contract players, losing such longtime stars as Bette Davis and James Cagney, and cut loose respected director Michael Curtiz, who was responsible for such hits as *Casablanca* and *Mildred Pierce,* after twenty-six years.

Hitchcock was one of the few bright spots for Warner's over this period. His four films all made money, reversing the downward trend the director had experienced following the consecutive box-office failures of *The Paradine Case*, *Rope*, and *Under Capricorn*. And Jack Warner had every reason to be happy with his end of the deal. For Warner, "Hitchcock was a triple achiever; a man with an audience track record, a consistent awards contender, and a publicity asset."[4]

20

Stage Fright (1950)

Synopsis. *Dashing young actor Jonathan Cooper (Richard Todd) begs his friend, drama student Eve Gill (Jane Wyman), to help him escape from the police. As Eve, who is infatuated with Jonathan, drives him to safety, he explains in an extended flashback that he has been having an affair with musical comedy star Charlotte Inman (Marlene Dietrich) and the police suspect him of killing her husband because he tried to help the star, who he claims actually did the killing, dispose of a bloodstained dress.*

Eve hides Jonathan at the home of her father (Alastair Sim) and returns to London, hoping to obtain evidence that will exonerate Jonathan. While tailing Charlotte's dresser, she meets the chief inspector on the case, Wilfred Smith (Michael Wilding), who is immediately attracted to her. Concealing her mission from Smith, she bribes the dresser to feign illness and takes her place in Charlotte's household, posing as a Cockney maid.

When Inspector Smith discovers Eve's meddling, he is furious, but comes around when he hears a secretly miked backstage conversation in which Eve tells Charlotte that she has her bloodstained dress. When Charlotte offers to buy the dress back, Smith steps in and arrests the actress. Meanwhile, the police apprehend Jonathan and bring him to the theater. Not knowing that Charlotte has been arrested, he bolts and takes Eve captive, admitting that he has been lying all along and actually killed Mr. Inman. Eve frees herself and Jonathan is killed trying to escape when an iron safety curtain falls on him.

***

Stage Fright was the first picture Hitchcock produced under his new contract with Warner Bros. Filmed in England, it features lyrics by Cole Porter, Marlene Dietrich as a femme fatale, and a controversial flashback seeded with misinformation. The primary concern of the censors was Dietrich's rendition of Porter's song "The Laziest Gal in Town." The Breen office, finding both the song and the performance offensive, had the chutzpah to edit the lyrics of one of the most accomplished songwriters of the day.

Cole Porter had written "The Laziest Gal in Town" in 1927, but it had been recorded only once when Hitchcock suggested it be used as a showcase for Marlene Dietrich in *Stage Fright.* In the song, Dietrich explains her disinclination to misbehave by arguing that it's not because she wouldn't, or shouldn't, or, "Lord knows," that she couldn't—she declines merely because she's "the laziest gal in town." Although the song's lyrics were the very first elements of the film to be submitted for Production Code review, the lyrics, along with Dietrich's interpretation of them, were the final sticking points to be resolved before the Code office would award its production Seal of Approval.

In their initial review, Breen's censors determined that the song was "unacceptable under the requirements of the Code by reason of its objectionable sex suggestiveness" and decreed that certain lines would have to be rewritten. The opening verse originally ended with Dietrich saying, "No!" to the invitation to misbehave. Even though the singer resisted temptation, however, the censors determined that the words "let's misbehave" would have to be rewritten. Furthermore, the censors declared, "The word, 'Lord,' which occurs twice in the refrain, will have to be changed."[1]

In response, Porter rewrote the opening verse entirely, banishing the Lord from the refrain by changing the offending lines from "And Lord knows, it's not 'cause I couldn't" to "And *you* know, it's not 'cause I couldn't."

These changes appeared to satisfy the censors. However, they remained "very apprehensive" that in the finished picture the revised lyrics might come through as "offensively sex suggestive." To help forestall this, Breen recommended that "consideration be given to keeping this lyric entirely away from 'romance' so that the lines '. . . I wouldn't . . . I shouldn't . . . I couldn't' would not in any way infer sex suggestiveness."[2] Thankfully, Porter ignored this guidance and didn't rework the lyrics so that the offending lines implied cooking, housekeeping, or exercising.

Breen was also concerned about the costume Dietrich's character, Charlotte, would be wearing during the song. Noting that the initial script called for Charlotte to be clad in a nightgown, he suggested, "It would be well if, before shooting this picture, you would send us a description of the various numbers done by Charlotte," reminding the producer that "the Production Code makes it mandatory that the intimate parts of the body—specifically the breasts of women—be fully covered at all times."[3]

Mindful of this admonition, Hitchcock had his costume designer dress Dietrich entirely in white from head to toe in a billowing, floor-

Marlene Dietrich, clad from head to toe in white, in deference to Production Code oversight, as she sings "The Laziest Gal in Town."

length nightgown covered by a flowing white dressing gown with a feathery trim. Viewers seeking titillation had to be satisfied with a glimpse of a bare ankle or a discreet triangle of flesh above a neckline that barely left her diamond choker visible.

Upon viewing the rough cut of the film, Breen found no fault with Dietrich's costume, but he was outraged over her performance. The day after viewing the cut, he wrote Jack Warner to say that his office found the performance "quite offensive" and asked that Warner "take the time to give this problem your personal attention" in the hope that he could "find some way to cut this whole business down to a minimum."[4]

Whatever objections Breen had were still unsettled when his office prepared its Seal of Approval, which contained the contingent notice that it was "issued with the understanding that in all release prints the number 'It's Not 'Cause I Couldn't' will be cut exactly as re-reviewed by us today."[5]

The precise bits of film that outraged Breen have not survived. Presumably, they involved some erotic gymnastics as Dietrich vamped her way between three on-stage lounges. By at least one report, "Dietrich gave a full-throttle performance before an audience of rapt extras whose presence she demanded," and who, not surprisingly, "gave her a standing ovation."[6]

In the final print, Hitchcock's camera cuts away from Dietrich several times to record separate reaction shots from Jane Wyman and Richard Todd. He also films the audience over her shoulder and at one point pulls his camera backstage so that only Dietrich's legs are visible kicking above the lounge cradling her performance. These cuts satisfied Breen, who wrote a letter to Warner congratulating him on the "utterly superb" job done by the editor Mac MacCord in eliminating Dietrich's worrisome "background action."[7]

Cole Porter wasn't the only famous songwriter to suffer at the hands of the Production Code censors. In his memoir *See No Evil,* Jack Vizzard, one of Breen's lieutenants, recounts the story of his appearance on the set of the film *Neptune's Daughter* to ensure that the delivery of the Frank Loesser song "Baby, It's Cold Outside" did nothing to offend or inflame the audience. The duet, in which an eager swain tries to persuade the object of his affection to stay for "maybe just a half a drink more" was sung by the film's stars, Ricardo Montalban and Esther Williams. According to Vizzard, when he and a fellow Code official made a few suggestions to tone down some of the more pointed lines, Montalban accepted the changes willingly, but Esther Williams bridled and "asked in a brittle manner, 'Say, do you guys know how babies are made?'"

When Vizzard reported the incident to Joe Breen, his boss fumed and demanded to know, "What did you say to her in return?"

"Nothing particularly," Vizzard replied, "I just kept my dignity."

"Dignity!" Breen scoffed. "If she'd said that to me I'd have said, 'No madam, I don't know. Would you like to show me?' And by God, if she took me up on it, I'd have insisted she do it right on the spot."[8]

The censors' objections to the *Stage Fright* script weren't limited to their concerns over Dietrich's production number. Noting that the script called for at least one passionate kiss, Breen cautioned producer Jack Warner to "make certain that in the various kissing scenes here and elsewhere the kisses are not lustful, prolonged, or open-mouthed." A number of dialogue changes were also suggested, including the elimination of the words *assignation* and *bastards* as well as the phrase, "Oh, you go and phone yourselves," which was recognized as "a paraphrase of offensive vulgarism and, accordingly, is unacceptable."[9]

The Code censors also warned against showing the female stars in "short panties" or "underwear," effectively thwarting Hitchcock's plans to make *Stage Fright* sexier by "taking advantage of theater traditions of casual backstage undress."[10]

One element of *Stage Fright* that proved to be more important to the critics than what Dietrich and other female characters did or didn't wear was the veracity of the extended flashback that opens the film. In narrating the flashback while on the run from the police, Jonathan Cooper claims that Charlotte Inman killed her husband and that he was guilty only of helping her to get rid of incriminating evidence, a bloodstained dress. In the film's climax, though, Cooper admits that the narrated scenes were a lie and he actually killed Charlotte's husband in response to her goading.

In the novel on which the film is based, *Man Running* by Selwyn Jepson, Charlotte is guilty not only of murdering her husband but also of trying to implicate Jonathan. The film's original screenwriters, Hitchcock's wife, Alma, and Whitfield Cook, argued strongly that Jonathan's innocence should be maintained in the film. They felt that the false flashback was likely to leave the audience feeling cheated.[11] By insisting on Jonathan's guilt, Hitchcock found himself in the unfamiliar position of setting up a "wrong man" who is actually guilty.

Over the years, critics and film scholars have offered differing opinions regarding the false flashback. When the film was released, the *London Times* reviewer suggested that Hitchcock "dealt the opening hand with an unfair ace up his sleeve."[12] In their 1957 treatment of Hitchcock's first forty-four films, Eric Rohmer and Claude Chabrol, who subsequently became famous directors themselves, defended the director by arguing that the images on the screen during the flashback are accurate portrayals of the action, so that the only false notes are in Jonathan's voice-over narration.[13] This would be an interesting point if it were true, but it isn't. The visual inaccuracies begin with the opening scene of the flashback, which shows Charlotte arriving at Jonathan's house with her dress soaked in blood. Jonathan later admits that her dress received only a light splattering of blood during the actual murder, and that he had augmented the smear after Charlotte had removed the dress to make her appear guilty in Eve's eyes. Moreover, since Jonathan was at the scene of the murder, Charlotte's arrival at his house is also a lie. Critic Richard Schickel diplomatically takes both sides of the argument. "Is that flashback a flaw in the movie or is that its most brilliant stroke? This, to me, is an open question. I really don't have an answer for it."[14]

It's not as if characters in a movie can't lie in flashbacks. *Rashomon,* which came out the same year as *Stage Fright,* depicts three differing points of view in flashback. The 1995 film *The Usual Suspects* is built on a series of flashback lies, and Hitchcock himself had inserted one in his silent film *Champagne,* using it to depict an imaginary assault. The real problems with the fake flashback in *Stage Fright* are its placement and length. The flashback starts one minute into the film, before the audience has met the characters and had a chance to gauge their reliability, and runs for fourteen minutes, by which time only the most attentive viewer will recognize that the flashback has stopped and the ongoing narrative has restarted.

Hitchcock himself felt that he'd made a mistake with the flashback. He told François Truffaut, "I did one thing in that picture that I should not have done; I put in a flashback that was a lie."[15]

The Production Code censors were much less concerned with veracity than modesty in the flashback. In their review of the script's first draft, they cautioned, "It will not be acceptable for Charlotte to remove her dress in the immediate presence of Jonathan; and . . . the scene of her embracing Jonathan when she is evidently clad only in underthings is particularly objectionable. Before this scene could be approved, it will be necessary for her to change her dress out of sight of both Jonathan and the audience."[16]

Hitchcock solved the problem by filming a close-up of Charlotte's face as she changes dresses against a blue screen and cutting in a shot of Jonathan looking out a window with his back turned until she is fully dressed. The director than replaced the objectionable embrace with two quick neck nuzzles that Charlotte, consumed with her own problems, barely acknowledges.

Stage Fright opened to mixed reviews and initially lost money domestically, but eventually proved to be profitable due to a large British turnout and the drawing power of the director and his two female stars. The *Times* reviewer found it less of an "exercise in dramatic suspense" than a "diverting comedy brilliantly served by its supporting cast" and called the ending "ingenious," even though noting that Hitchcock had unfairly palmed an ace in dealing out the opening scenes.[17] In the *New York Times,* Bosley

Crowther found "very little sustained excitement or suspense" in this "helter-skelter film," and voiced his suspicion that "Hitchcock was much less interested in his overall story than in individual scenes."[18]

This charge could be levied at many Hitchcock films, but in his best efforts the individual scenes more than make up for any story deficiencies. It's telling that the most memorable scene in *Stage Fright* doesn't involve suspense, but rather features Marlene Dietrich in a performance that was badly mangled by Breen and his censors. Even with Breen's cuts, Dietrich's interpretation of Porter's song remains a highlight of the film, and the star, who had objected to Hitchcock's insistence on its use, subsequently included it as a staple in her stage repertoire.

21

Strangers on a Train (1951)

Synopsis. *Two strangers, tennis player Guy Haines (Farley Granger) and psychopathic playboy Bruno Anthony (Robert Walker), meet on a train. Guy is in love with a senator's daughter (Ruth Roman), but his estranged wife, Miriam (Laura Elliott), will not grant him a divorce. Bruno suggests they "swap" murders, with Bruno killing Miriam and Guy disposing of Bruno's despised father. Although Guy does not take the offer seriously, Bruno does: he follows Miriam to an amusement park, where he strangles her.*

Guy is horrified when Bruno demands that he fulfill his part of the "bargain," and his tennis future and hopes for a political career are threatened when he cannot provide an alibi for his whereabouts at the time of Miriam's death.

When Bruno realizes that his imagined deal has fallen through, he decides to plant Guy's monogrammed cigarette lighter at the scene of Miriam's death, establishing proof of the tennis player's guilt. Guessing Bruno's intent, Guy rushes through an important tennis match and races to the amusement park, where he and Bruno fight on a runaway merry-go-round. The carousel crashes, killing Bruno with the incriminating lighter still in his possession, and Guy is cleared.

***

The process of converting *Strangers on a Train* from novel to film resembled the child's game of "telephone," in which a story is whispered from person to person and inevitably altered enough to make the final version barely recognizable. The original story was Patricia Highsmith's first novel, which Hitchcock read while returning to California on a train after attending the New York opening of *Stage Fright.* Excited by the basic premise of the crisscrossed murders, he was able to obtain the rights from the then unknown author for the relatively low sum of $6,000 (plus an additional $1,500 for any script work) by keeping his identity as the buyer secret until the deal was signed.[1]

With the help of Whitfield Cook, who had worked with Hitchcock on the script of *Stage Fright,* the director developed a sixty-five-page treatment of Highsmith's book. Retaining the basic premise of the proposed murder swap, Hitchcock and Cook made several changes to the novel. Guy Haines, the book's hero, is converted from an architect to a tennis champion with political ambitions. Bruno Anthony, the villain, is transposed from a physically grotesque alcoholic to a dapper and charming psychopath. The setting is shifted from Florida and the Southwest to the Northeast Corridor linking New York and Washington. Two changes in the treatment were made with an eye on the Production Code. The homoerotic element that Highsmith hinted at in Bruno's attraction to Guy is retained in the treatment but downplayed by applying coded stereotypes then in vogue to Bruno, making him a mama's boy who speaks French and wears flamboyant clothing.

But the most important change anticipated the Code objections to a hero who is allowed to get away with murder. In Highsmith's book, Guy is blackmailed into murdering Bruno's father, completing the crisscross. Hitchcock and Cook eliminated the second murder, having Guy refuse to carry out his part of the demented "bargain."

In reviewing Hitchcock and Cook's treatment, the Production Code office objected to the cavalier attitudes toward marriage, divorce, murder, and the illicit pregnancy of Guy's unfaithful wife. The homoerotic subtext was so subtle the censors missed it entirely, although they did object to Bruno's relationship with his mother, which seemed "to infer a perverted attitude on his part."[2]

With the reviewed treatment in hand, Hitchcock went shopping for screenwriters. At least eight candidates, including John Steinbeck and Dashiell Hammett, turned him down. "None of them thought it was any good," Hitchcock told François Truffaut.[3]

Then someone suggested Raymond Chandler, who at that time was second only to Hammett in the ranks of successful mystery novelists and who had worked with Billy Wilder on *Double Indemnity.* Chandler agreed to take on the project, even though he thought it was a "silly enough story," partly because "I thought I might like Hitch," and partly because "one gets tired of saying no and someday I might want to say yes and not get asked."[4]

The terms of Chandler's contract were generous, paying the author $2,500 a week, with $50 a week for secretarial services, for a guaranteed period of five weeks. It also allowed Chandler to work at his La Jolla home overlooking the Pacific, so that Hitchcock and his associate producer Barbara Keon had to make limousine trips over one hundred miles south for script conferences.

It soon became obvious that Hitchcock and Chandler were not ideal partners. Chandler preferred to write alone and get right to the point in meetings, while Hitchcock enjoyed socializing with random conversation. Chandler wanted characters to have clear motivations and plot twists to be plausible, while Hitchcock thought in terms of visual images and simply wanted a writer to connect those images. Chandler wrote a friend that Hitchcock was "too ready to sacrifice dramatic logic (insofar as it exists) for the sake of a camera effect."[5]

The two men were also divided over the importance of the Code office's reaction to Hitchcock and Cook's story treatment. As soon as Chandler was hired, Findlay McDermid of the Warner Bros. front office wrote him summarizing the censors' concerns.

> As set up at present, Guy and all of our sympathetic characters are the ones who are pressing for a divorce. If, instead, Miriam had wanted the divorce and Guy had made some attempts to hold the marriage together but had then accepted the situation, the Breen Office would find this phase of the plot more acceptable. Guy, returning to see Miriam, would find that she had changed her mind again and would still have the same reaction. The Breen Office is also concerned about two other elements, the rather bald way in which the treatment shows Bruno's home life as a fairly literal oedipal situation and the equally bald manner in which Ann, Barbara, and other sympathetic characters disclose the point that there is latent murder in everyone. . . .
>
> I pass these things on to you with the assurance that you can cope with such problems. STRANGERS ON A TRAIN will, I know, be a much more impelling, convincing drama after it receives its transfusion of Chandler dialogue and characterization.[6]

Not being used to Hitchcock's give-and-take relationship with the Code office, Chandler took this letter to mean the story treatment would require significant changes. Hitchcock disagreed, feeling that they should make the best possible film independent of the censors' suggestions and bargain later.

Working relationships in La Jolla deteriorated rapidly. Chandler continued to strive for plausibility, resisting Hitchcock's suggestions and saying at one point, "Well, if you can puzzle it out, what do you need me for?"[7]

Accounts of the final La Jolla meeting differ, but it seems clear that Chandler had been drinking heavily and once referred to Hitchcock as a "fat bastard" within earshot of the director. Hitchcock pointedly refused to contribute to the script discussion, leaving that to Barbara Keon, and finally stood up and left the house with Chandler in mid-rant, hefting his bulk into the limousine as his assistant struggled to catch up. The director remained silent for most of the trip north to Burbank, breaking the silence at one point to say, "He's through."[8]

Hitchcock began searching for another screenwriter, although he allowed Chandler to continue on the project because he feared that firing the author might set off alarms in Warner's front office. Left alone, Chandler finished the script with no input from the director, who never even acknowledged receiving the finished product.

Trying to stay on schedule, the director submitted Chandler's script for Production Code review while shooting background footage in Washington, DC. Shortly after sending the script to the censors, he hired Czenzi Ormonde, a novice screenwriter who had been working as Barbara Keon's assistant, to replace Chandler. When Ormonde came on board, Hitchcock made a show of holding his nose over Chandler's script as he dropped it into a wastebasket and announced that they would start over from page 1.[9]

The Code censors had fewer problems with Chandler's script than Hitchcock and deemed the story to be acceptable—with one key reservation. They felt that the treatment of Guy's marriage to Miriam was "unacceptably light" and recommended that the element of Miriam's extramarital pregnancy be eliminated. Aside from this, they made minimal demands, suggesting that the studio excise the word *jeez,* replace the word *arsenic* with the generic word *poison,* and eliminate Anne's speech saying that she would have stuck by Guy even if he had murdered Miriam. The censors believed that this speech might be interpreted as condoning wrongdoing. They also cautioned that the fight scene between Guy and Bruno must be "handled with care to avoid excessive brutality."[10]

After submitting their written findings, Code representatives met with Hitchcock, his staff, and Warner's officials to discuss the movie's treatment of divorce. It was agreed that the script would be rewritten to indicate that the "principal blame for the breakup will be on Miriam and not, as in the present version, on our sympathetic lead, Guy." To this end, it was also agreed that one cause of the divorce could be the "fact that Miriam had become pregnant by another man." Finally, it was agreed that Bruno's philosophizing about murder would be toned down, specifically by eliminating his observation that it was "not against the law of nature."[11]

The next version of the script to be submitted to the censors was written by Czenzi Ormonde. The young screenwriter must have retrieved Chandler's script from the wastebasket, because she retained some scenes from his original, notably the opening shots tracking two sets of feet proceeding toward the tracks in Washington's Union Station and ultimately touching toes in the parlor car of the New York–bound train. While Ormonde excised most of Chandler's dialogue, she unaccountably failed to alter those elements of the script that Hitchcock had agreed to change in his meeting with the censors.

In their review of Ormonde's revised script, the Code office expressed disappointment that the agreed-upon changes had not been made and reiterated its suggestions that Bruno's philosophizing be omitted and that it be Miriam who originally asked for the divorce.[12] Among other Code observations:

- Professor Collins, the witness who failed to validate Guy's alibi, "should not be offensively drunk."
- Bruno's cocktail party "demonstration" of strangling should not "show any objectionable details."
- The shot of Bruno kicking Guy's knuckles in the fight scene could not be approved on account of its excessive brutality.
- The exclamation "Thank God" of a mother in the crowd when her son survives the carousel crash "must be delivered reverently."
- Since the final scene in which a minister interrupts Guy and Anne on their train trip home is intended for a laugh, it would be better if the character "is not connected with the church."[13]

Hitchcock had no trouble meeting most of these relatively minor suggestions. He made Miriam the divorce seeker, excised the relieved mother's thanks to the deity, and "reluctantly" cut Bruno's observation that murder was "part of the natural law" after filming it. He experimented

Bruno Anthony (Robert Walker) strangles the wife of Guy Haines in what Bruno hopes will be the first death in his "crisscross" murder scheme. The State of Maryland scissored this crucial scene as being too violent. (Courtesy of Jerry Ohlinger.)

with alternate endings, but retained the encounter with the minister, making sure that the prelate's characterization was in no way comical. Having attended to these modest plot and dialogue changes, he was allowed to keep the close-up of Bruno kicking at Guy's knuckles on the out-of-control carousel.

Hitchcock was undoubtedly relieved that the censors, usually alert to any suggestions of homosexuality, were so intent on Bruno's murder musings and Miriam's divorce deliberations that they failed to detect Bruno's homoerotic fascination with Guy. This fascination was clear in Highsmith's novel and indicated more subtly (at least for the 1950s audience) in the foppish and mother-centric characteristics assigned to Bruno in the film treatment.

There is little doubt that Hitchcock intended for Bruno's attraction to Guy to come through on the screen. Hitchcock biographer Patrick McGilligan noted that the director made "Bruno's sexuality a fascinating subtext of the film, for anyone who cared to notice it (so long as that someone was not a studio or censorship official)."[14] In a 1963 interview, director Peter Bogdanovich asked Hitchcock directly, "Was Bruno a homosexual?" and Hitchcock answered, "Oh, I would think so."[15]

Although Hitchcock was clear in his desire to plant subtle hints regarding Bruno's sexuality on the screen, he did not share this intention with every member of his cast and writers. Farley Granger recalled, "We never discussed any homoerotic attraction Walker's character had for me, but I think Hitch did that with Walker and just asked me to act normal and not be aware of too much undercurrent. Of course, Hitch understood all of this, and he knew what he could do and what we could do."[16] Hitchcock also failed to mention the erotic subtext to screenwriter Czenzi Ormonde, and in her opinion, "It doesn't exist in the script or the film."[17] Ormonde's screenwriting predecessor, Raymond Chandler, was certainly aware of the subtext. In one of the lines scrapped from his script, Guy tells Bruno that "his type" is always theatrical and Bruno asks, "What type?"[18] But it was Ormonde, not the censors, who cut the line from the final script. The censors not only missed every hint in the treatment and the two scripts, they also asked that one line suggesting Bruno might be straight be deleted from Chandler's script. The line was spoken by Bruno's mother, who, when asked to account for Bruno's presence when he was off killing Miriam, speculated that he was probably "going to spend a weekend with some girl."[19]

Hitchcock's intention, however, was not lost on all critics at the time of the film's release. Writing in the *Nation,* Manny Farber observed that the movie "is built around the travestied homosexuality of the murderer."[20] In the years since the movie's release, general awareness of the coded traits has increased, and Bruno's repressed feelings for Guy have become an article of faith with critics. Hitchcock biographer Donald Spoto characterized the relationship as a "homosexual courtship," and Roger Ebert mentioned the "homoerotic undertones" in Bruno's manner.[21]

The film was a success at the box office, returning $1.8 million domestically on a $1.2 million investment, even though the critics of the day were ambivalent in their responses. Manny Farber called it "great fun," but qualified his judgment by adding, "if you check your intelligence at the box office."[22] Dilys Powell of the *London Times* felt that the film "went off the rails after an exhilarating start," but still was "the best thing Hitchcock has done for a good many years."[23] In the *New York Times,* Bosley Crowther admired such Hitchcock "touches" as the reflection of Miriam's murder in her dropped glasses and the runaway merry-go-round, but wrote that the "basic premise of fear fired by menace is so thin and so utterly unconvincing that the story just does not stand."[24]

Reactions of those who knew both Highsmith's novel and Hitchcock's film were also mixed. Highsmith herself was initially pleased with the film, especially with Robert Walker's portrayal of Bruno. Later, however, she said she felt Hitchcock had drained the work of its shock value by having Guy fail to carry out his part of the bargain. She was also quite critical of Ruth Roman, saying it was "ludicrous" that Guy was "supposed to be in love with that stone angel."[25]

Not surprisingly, Raymond Chandler had a low opinion of both the script and the finished film. On reviewing Ormonde's shooting script, he wrote Hitchcock, "What I cannot understand is your permitting a script which after all had some life and vitality to be reduced to such a flabby mess of clichés, a group of faceless characters, and the kind of dialogue every screen writer is taught not to write."[26] On seeing the released version of the film, he wrote a friend, "The picture has no guts, no plausibility, no characters, and no dialogue, but of course, it's Hitchcock, and a Hitchcock film always does have something."[27]

The primary Code impact on the film occurred even before the script was prepared, when Hitchcock and Whitfield Cook, anticipating the Code objections if the hero was allowed to get away with murder, excised the second murder in their treatment of Highsmith's book. The censors' actual objection to the two scripts and the finished film were relatively minor and easily handled by Hitchcock, and their initial feeling that the treatment showed Bruno's attitude toward his mother to be "perverted" was rendered moot by the casting of Marion Lorne, whose pleasantly ditzy performance as the mother erased any question of an oedipal attraction.

Hitchcock himself was ambivalent about the results. He told François Truffaut he was "quite pleased with the over-all form of the film and with the secondary characters." He particularly liked Laura Elliott as Guy's estranged wife and Marion Lorne as Bruno's mother, who is "just as crazy as her son." But he felt the picture's flaws were the "ineffectiveness" of the romantic leads, Farley Granger and Ruth Roman, and the "weakness of the final script," which he faulted for its lackluster writing and dialogue, two elements that Chandler might have improved. However, the director did agree with Truffaut's observation that *Strangers on a Train* represented a "spectacular comeback" after the consecutive artistic failures of *Under Capricorn* and *Stage Fright.*[28]

22

I Confess (1953)

Synopsis. *Quebec priest Father Michael Logan (Montgomery Clift) is suspected of murdering a well-known lawyer. The priest knows that the real murderer is his church sexton, Otto Keller (O. E. Hasse), but cannot reveal his identity because the man has admitted his guilt to him in the confessional.*

Police inspector Larrue (Karl Malden) has reason to suspect Father Logan. The murderer was spotted leaving the scene wearing a priest's cassock, and the murdered lawyer happened to be blackmailing Ruth Grandfort (Anne Baxter), the wife of a local politician, over a long-ago liaison with Father Logan before he became a priest.

When the seal of the confessional prevents Father Logan from identifying the murderer or providing a complete alibi for his own time, he is arrested and brought to trial. Although the jury acquits him, the circumstantial evidence and the revelation of his past indiscretion have turned public sentiment against him, and he is attacked by an angry mob upon his release. To stop the mob, Keller's wife, Alma (Dolly Haas), starts to accuse her husband of the murder when he shoots her and flees to a nearby hotel. The pursuing police shoot Keller, who openly confesses his guilt as he dies in Father Logan's arms.

***

Based on a 1902 play, *Nos deux consciences* (Our Two Consciences) by Paul Anthelme, the plot of the film *I Confess* was pushed beyond plausibility by the demands of Warner Bros. and the Production Code. Hitchcock first saw the play in the early 1930s and obtained the rights inexpensively for Transatlantic in 1947. The wrong-man theme and Catholic background appealed to him so much that he briefly explored turning it into a ghost-written novel under his own name. When that proved infeasible, the property was announced as the third Transatlantic film, to follow *Rope* and *Under Capricorn.*

While under development as a Transatlantic film, *I Confess* went through several treatments, including one by Hitchcock's wife, Alma, who transferred the setting to Quebec. All of the early treatments contained two elements that proved problematic for Warner Bros., the eventual distributor. In a subplot introduced by the Hitchcocks, the priest had unknowingly fathered an illegitimate child prior to his ordination. Warner's also objected to the ending of the play and the original film treatments, in which the priest is hanged for murder when he fails to break the silence of the confessional.

In a reading of one of the early treatments, Production Code reviewer Geoffrey Shurlock found that "the only thing wrong with the present version was the wiping off of the fingerprints" following the murder. He did caution, however, that "the picture's acceptability under the Code would depend on its containing nothing that would be offensive to the Catholic Church."[1]

When Transatlantic foundered under the failures of *Rope* and *Under Capricorn,* Hitchcock volunteered to sidetrack the production of *I Confess* in favor of *Stage Fright,* a move that pleased Warner's, whose doubts about the wronged-priest film were well known. The production of *I Confess* was postponed further when Hitchcock went to work on *Strangers on a Train.* During this time, Sidney Bernstein took over the development of *I Confess,* supervising still more treatments but retaining the plot elements involving the priest's illegitimate child and eventual hanging.

Upon completing *Strangers on a Train,* Hitchcock took a sabbatical in early 1951 and then assigned two writers to develop a script for *I Confess.* He finally had a script that satisfied him in the spring of 1952, and he submitted it for Code review.

The reviewers for the Code office were Geoffrey Shurlock and Jack Vizzard, a former Catholic seminarian. They found two problems with the script. First, the "indirect use which the priest makes of confessional knowledge" by leading the detective to the scene of the crime, and second, "the suggestion that the priest, before entering Holy Orders, had had an affair with a girl, by whom he had a child, about which he does not know." In an attempt to work out these problems, Vizzard met with Hitchcock, Bernstein, and Monsignor Devlin of Los Angeles and suggested solutions to the issues dealing with the priest's use of confessional knowledge. Hitchcock and Bernstein agreed to accept his suggestions and asked for more time to find a solution to the issue of the illegitimate child.[2]

At the time the Production Code office was reviewing the script, Hitchcock and Bernstein visited Quebec with screenwriter George Tabori to promote local cooperation, scout locations, recruit local actors for secondary roles, and seek the approval of religious authorities. To this end, they employed a local priest with a doctorate in theology, Father Paul La Couline, as a technical consultant. Father La Couline facilitated the discussions with local Church officials who, surprisingly, found *I Confess* to be supportive of Catholicism, since the priest, even with his illegitimate child and wrongful execution, was treated sympathetically in the script.[3]

While seeking guidance from the Production Code and Quebec Church authorities, Bernstein also asked Martin Quigley, the Catholic coauthor of the Code, to review the film treatment used in preparing the script. Quigley had the same objection as Vizzard to the priest's leading the detective to the scene of the crime and felt that "the indictment of bastardy against the character who eventually became a priest" would "tend toward alienating and antagonizing millions of Catholic people who might be expected to be patrons of a picture with the Catholic background of this subject."[4]

Although the Production Code Administration eventually logged more suggestions regarding *I Confess* (fifty-nine) than any other Hitchcock film, neither the Code's Jack Vizzard, Quebec's Father La Couline, nor Code coauthor Martin Quigley objected to the priest being unjustly hanged, a holdover from the original play that Hitchcock viewed as an argument against capital punishment. But Warner's, long unhappy with the ending, stepped in and forced Hitchcock to abandon both the wrongful execution and the illegitimate child. In place of the hanging, the true villain would be revealed and captured following a final chase. Instead of an illegitimate child, the priest and his former girlfriend would be blackmailed for having spent one stormy night together prior to his ordination.

Casting proved to be a problem. Hitchcock had proposed Laurence Olivier for the lead role, but Warner's insisted on a major American star, and they settled on Montgomery Clift, who was at the peak of his popularity, having just finished *A Place in the Sun* and signed on to appear in *From Here to Eternity.* Clift agreed to appear in *I Confess* after reading the original script and was unhappy with the changes that left him childless and alive at the end of the film.

Hitchcock's choice for the role of the leading lady was Scandinavian actress Anita Björk. Warner's approved of her signing in the hope that her billing might help to recapture European markets lost during the war. When Björk arrived in Hollywood, however, she was accompanied by her lover and their baby daughter. Having just rid the script of an illegitimate baby, Jack Warner was now faced with one in real life, and he feared another scandal similar to the one that had erupted around Ingrid Bergman. Against Hitchcock's wishes, Warner insisted that Björk be paid off and sent home, to be replaced by Anne Baxter.[5]

With Warner making all of the major decisions, he offered to buy out Transatlantic's interest and make *I Confess* a 100 percent Warner Bros. production. Hitchcock and Bernstein agreed, and Bernstein resigned as producer.[6]

Script revisions reflecting Warner's insistence on the priest's acquittal and the elimination of the illegitimate child were drawn up and submitted for Code review. The censors' review of the revised script focused primarily on technical issues regarding the sacramental seal of secrecy. Reviewers pointed out that the priest was not bound by the seal concerning events that transpired *before* the murderer began his confession. Thus the priest would not perjure himself by answering no to the prosecutor's scripted question as to whether he talked to anyone on the night of the murder. To avoid giving away the murderer's presence in the church, the censors recommended that the screenwriters remove all references to the priest's knowledge before the actual confession.[7]

Code reviewers were also concerned about the propriety of the flashback showing the priest, before his ordination, spending the night with his former sweetheart. Reviewers stipulated that "Michael Logan could not be shown as a man who had decided to become a priest" and that scenes between Michael and Ruth must "avoid too much intimate physical contact" so that the two would be seen as indiscreet rather than adulterous.[8] In a subsequent letter, Breen emphasized that "it must be positively established that Ruth and Michael did not have a sex affair."[9] Of course, the more the overnight liaison is represented as an innocent encounter, the less reason there is for it to be the source of blackmail required by the plot.

The censors also made several minor points regarding the use of the words *God* and *affair,* the modesty of the dresses worn by actresses, and the "look of rivalry" when Father Michael sees Ruth's husband in the courtroom. Reviewers also recommended that Father Michael's response

Montgomery Clift and Anne Baxter, caught in the rainstorm that will lead to a blackmail attempt made implausible by censorship demands. (Courtesy of Jerry Ohlinger.)

to prosecutorial questions threatening to break the seal of the confessional, such as "Have you any idea who [the murderer] might be?" be "I cannot answer that question" rather than a flat "No."[10]

Every letter from the Code office regarding the succession of *I Confess* scripts addressed technical aspects of the confessional so arcane as to be outside the experience of most Catholics and of interest primarily to liturgical scholars. Although each of the letters was signed by Joseph I. Breen, he was recovering from lung cancer treatments at the time and appeared in the office for short periods of only one or two days a week.[11] Coded numbers in the signature section of the letters make it clear that the technical observations regarding the confessional were composed by the ex-seminarian Jack Vizzard rather than by Breen himself. A sampling of these observations follows:

- The priest would never ask the name of the murder victim.
- The priest would never address the penitent by name.
- The priest should not look sharply at the murderer or his wife during the trial.
- The priest cannot speak to the murderer about the crime outside of the confessional.
- The murderer does *not* have to turn himself in to the police to receive absolution.
- The script must make it clear that the restitution of the stolen money *is* necessary for absolution.[12]

It's safe to say that no non-Catholic and relatively few Catholics would have recognized these details as gaffes had they been left in the film, and a few, such as Father Michael not looking at the murderer during the trial, would have denied Hitchcock one of his chief techniques for building suspense.

In his discussions with François Truffaut, Hitchcock said that the trouble with *I Confess* was "We Catholics know that a priest cannot disclose the secrets of the confessional, but the Protestants, the atheists, and the agnostics all say 'Ridiculous! No man would remain silent and sacrifice his life for such a thing.'"[13]

Truffaut agreed that the general non-Catholic public "was irritated with the plot because they kept on hoping that Montgomery Clift would speak up," and asked Hitchcock, "Would you consider that a weakness in the screenplay?"

Hitchcock answered, "It certainly is a disadvantage. If the basic idea is not acceptable to the public, it compromises the whole picture . . . to put a situation into a film because you yourself can vouch for its authenticity . . . simply isn't good enough."[14]

Truffaut felt that the bigger problem with the screenplay was the "extraordinary coincidence at the beginning" in which the murderer who has killed a man in order to rob him "should happen to confess his crime to the very priest who was being blackmailed by the dead man."[15]

Plausibility was never high on the list of Hitchcock's concerns. He generally kept the plot moving so fast and filled the screen with such ravishing images that the viewer was having too much fun to worry over coincidences and plot connections. Unfortunately, *I Confess* didn't move fast enough to cover all its implausibilities. Bosley Crowther of the *New York Times* wrote that the "obviously padded script" tended to "drag, sag, and generally grow dull," and cited one implausibility that could be traced to the insistence of the Code censors and Jack Warner that the subplot of the illegitimate son be replaced by a harmless assignation. In Crowther's view, the romance between the hero and his ladylove before he became a priest was so "blissfully innocent" that it was difficult to see "how it should ever serve as a reasonable basis for blackmail."[16]

The *Los Angeles Times* agreed with Crowther that "the whetted knife of Hitchcock's direction blunts itself again and again on a ponderous, equivocal situation."[17] But not all reviews were negative. The *Hollywood Reporter*'s reviewer wrote that "taking murder and the sanctity of the confessional as the main theme, Alfred Hitchcock has evolved a thrilling motion picture that achieves a peak of suspense from the very start and maintains it consistently throughout its 95 minutes."[18] And the film was "generally well received by the Catholic Church."[19] Robert Kass in the *Catholic World* called it "enormously interesting" and a "thoughtful adult drama," even though the Legion of Decency rated it "Morally Objectionable for Adults."[20]

Surprisingly, the Province of Quebec was the source of an unexpected stumbling block for the film. An obscure member of the Government Censor Bureau cut nearly three minutes from the film, excising Anne Baxter's declaration of love for Montgomery Clift and that part of the flashback showing that the two spent the night together, obliterating even the most tentative motive for blackmail. In view of the time Hitchcock had spent to ensure the support of the Quebec archdiocese, these cuts infuriated the director. "There will be one version for the Province of Quebec," he exploded in a Canadian Broadcasting Corporation interview, "and one for the rest of the world."[21] And there was no version for Ireland at all. The Republic of Ireland initially banned the film because it showed a priest having a relationship with a woman, even though that relationship occurred before he had even decided to become a priest. An appeals board subsequently overturned the ban, but only after cutting over five minutes from the film, including a scene of Montgomery Clift and Anne Baxter dancing and kissing before he leaves for the war, Baxter's statements of her continuing love for Clift, and a juror's speculation that there "must have been many more" meetings between the pair after his ordination.[22]

In the final analysis, though, Hitchcock was less concerned with critical reviews, plausibility, and censorship than with box-office receipts, and *I Confess* turned a $400,000 profit for Warner's, justifying the director's persistence in pursuing what seemed to everyone but him to be a most unlikely project.

23

Dial M for Murder (1954)

Synopsis. *Former tennis star Tony Wendice (Ray Milland) discovers that his rich wife, Margot (Grace Kelly), is having an affair with an American mystery writer (Robert Cummings). Afraid of losing both his wife and her money, Wendice blackmails an old acquaintance with a criminal record, C. A. Swann (Anthony Dawson), into killing her. In the carefully worked-out plan, Wendice will establish an alibi by attending a late celebration at a local club after leaving a key to his flat under a stair carpet. Swann will use the key to enter the flat after Margot is asleep and hide until a phone call from Wendice wakes her and brings her to the phone, where Swann will strangle her.*

The plan backfires when Margot struggles in the strangler's grasp and kills him with a pair of scissors. Arriving home, Wendice rigs the murder scene to make it appear that Margot was being blackmailed by Swann and the killing was premeditated. His improvisation works, and his wife is arrested, tried, convicted of murder, and sentenced to hang.

Police inspector Hubbard (John Williams) is initially taken in by Wendice's story, but eventually spots a crucial flaw in the staging of the evidence against Margot, tricks Wendice into revealing his guilt, and arrests him for what was very nearly a perfect crime.

***

Dial M for Murder was made quickly and efficiently in thirty-six days, with few deviations from the source material, a successful play by Frederick Knott, and minimal interference from Production Code officials. Hitchcock characterized it as a "run for cover" film that allowed him to recharge his batteries and "play it safe" after the disappointing critical response to *I Confess.*[1]

Knott's play was first shown on BBC TV and then became a stage hit in London in 1952. It was equally successful on Broadway, and Hitchcock saw it shortly after he completed *I Confess.* Alexander Korda had purchased the rights to the play for £1,000 after seeing it on TV and resold them to Warner Bros. at thirty times that price. Warner's purchased it for

Hitchcock, planning to film the movie in 3-D, which was popular at the time and required a bulky two-camera setup to capture the separate images that were reconciled in the theater through glasses supplied to the viewers. The fad, which filled theaters in the early 1950s with images of spears, fists, and chairs thrown directly at the audience, was fading by the time Hitchcock made *Dial M for Murder*, and the film, although shot in 3-D, was primarily distributed as a two-dimensional "flattie."

The film was the fourth and final effort owed to Warner Bros. under Hitchcock's Transatlantic contract, and Warner's exercised its control over casting, which had not always served the director well. Cary Grant had advertised an interest in playing the role of the scheming Tony Wendice, and Grant would always be Hitchcock's first choice. But the studio backed away, fearing, as RKO had ten years earlier on *Suspicion*, that the public would not accept Grant as a villain. Warner's was also reluctant to accept Grant's salary demand of 10 percent of the gross, and the role went to Ray Milland, who was more than creditable in the part and joined the list of suave and charming Hitchcock villains. The role of Margot went to Grace Kelly, then a relative unknown, in the first of her three career-making roles with Hitchcock. John Williams and Anthony Dawson reprised their stage roles admirably, and the sole clinker in the cast was Robert Cummings, who was variously described as stiff, "negative," and "uninteresting" in the part of the nominal hero.[2]

Frederick Knott adapted his own play for the screen and stuck closely to his stage script, which was heavy on dialogue and took place on a single set, the Wendice apartment. Neither he nor Hitchcock tried to open the play up by shooting too many scenes in other locations. When director Peter Bogdanovich commented on this, Hitchcock said, "If you have a hit play, just shoot it, don't open it up." Recalling this comment, Bogdanovich observed, "When Hitchcock says 'just shoot it,' he means just shoot it the way he would." *Dial M for Murder* "is a triumph of shooting a talky play . . . you don't really leave the apartment very much and it is riveting."[3]

Since Knott's screenplay followed his own successful script so closely, it elicited relatively few comments from the Production Code office. The censors suggested that a few *hell*s and *damn*s be omitted, asked that the expression "Thank God" be delivered with proper reverence, and warned Warner's that it should take "the greatest possible care in the selection and photographing of the costumes and dresses of your women" so that "the intimate parts of the body" are "fully clothed at all times." The Code officials also commented that the "meticulous elimination of fingerprints is a type of detail of which we have consistently been unable to approve" and suggested that "any difficulty on this score might be automatically eliminated" if the Swann character "might be wearing gloves."[4]

Hitchcock followed these suggestions scrupulously, color-coding Grace Kelly's wardrobe so that she wears demure white outfits with her husband, red gowns with her lover, and clothes that grow drabber and less revealing as she is first accused and then convicted of murder. Ray Milland thoughtfully provides the would-be murderer Anthony Dawson with gloves to wear in his apartment once Dawson has agreed to the murder, although Milland still makes a show of wiping Dawson's prints off the brandy glass he uses before he agrees to the scheme. And Dawson has the foresight to wear gloves on the night of the unsuccessful murder attempt.

In their reviews of both the initial and final scripts, the censors cautioned that "care be taken in both the strangling and the stabbing to avoid objectionable gruesomeness."[5] In reviewing the final script, they suggested that Hitchcock take some protective shots covering the strangling of Grace Kelly and the stabbing of Anthony Dawson, since "some political censor boards are extremely sensitive to the type of action" shown in these scenes and might delete any material they found objectionable.[6]

Hitchcock spent a full week of the thirty-six shooting days filming the aborted strangling of Grace Kelly and subsequent stabbing of Anthony Dawson. The attempted murder scene is one of the most memorable in the Hitchcock canon and easily raises *Dial M for Murder* above the typical filmed play. The lead-in to the sequence marks one of the director's few trips outside the apartment set. He follows Ray Milland and Robert Cummings to a stag celebration where Milland will establish an alibi for his whereabouts by making the 11 p.m. phone call that sets the murder of his wife in motion. Hitchcock teases the audience, upping the suspense as Milland's watch stops, causing him to miss the calling time and eliciting viewer sympathy for the villain as he tries to get to a phone before the killer leaves his apartment. There is more suspenseful teasing as Grace Kelly answers the phone, not knowing that the killer is behind her, holding his scarf stretched out to encircle her neck. After a few unsuccessful attempts to talk to the caller, she starts to lower the phone, clearing the path to her neck, and the killer raises the scarf, only to lower it as she raises the phone

Anthony Dawson is ready with the scarf as soon as Grace Kelly puts down the phone.

again to her ear, shielding her neck as she makes one last try to connect with the caller. When Kelly finally lowers the phone, the killer loops the scarf around her neck and leans her backward over the desk, where she struggles with one outstretched hand groping toward the 3-D camera and a pair of scissors. Her hand finds the scissors, and the scissors find the back of the shocked assassin, who straightens, does an operatic turn, and falls backward onto the scissors, driving the blades deeper into his back.

The scene of the failed strangling and successful stabbing passed muster with the Production Code but was nearly scrapped by the French Film Standards Commission, one of the political censor boards of concern to the Code office. François Truffaut, who was still a film critic with *Cahiers du cinéma* when *Dial M for Murder* was released, reported, "The representatives of various ministries, Justice, National Education, etc. . . . were asking for the scene of the murder to be cut." Since everyone realized that "the film loses its entire *raison d'être* if this scene is amputated, professional indignation reached its height." He added that "it took another replay of the murder scene to convince these gentlemen finally, and . . . the movie obtained its visa in the end, with the exception of one vote."[7]

The short but memorable murder scene had the desired effect on viewers. *Dial M for Murder* was the first Hitchcock film I'd ever seen, and I saw it over and over while working as an usher at the Keith-Albee Theater in Huntington, West Virginia. I can attest that the final plunge of the blade into the back of the falling killer never failed to elicit an audible gasp from the audience.

Audience appreciation extended to the box office, where the film grossed $2.7 million domestically, making it the most profitable of Hitchcock's four films for Warner Bros. It was a critical success as well. Bosley Crowther of the *New York Times* called it a "technical triumph," lauded Hitchcock for managing "the tensing of interest and excitement with just a handful of people in a room" and praised the actors, particularly John Williams as the detective who solves the case.[8] The American Film Institute (AFI) included *Dial M for Murder* in its list of the top one hundred thrillers of all time. Hitchcock has nine films on the list, with eight, including *Dial M,* in the top fifty.

In spite of its box-office performance and its inclusion in the AFI's list, *Dial M for Murder,* perhaps because it is "just" a filmed version of a stage play, is considered "minor Hitchcock." Hitchcock himself told François Truffaut, "There isn't much we can say about that one."[9] But the film has a spellbinding murder scene, a tightly knit plot, superior acting and, in Peter Bogdanovich's words, is a "perfect version of a very effective play."[10] At the very least, it is memorable as a fitting farewell to Warner Bros. and an admirable stepping-stone to Hitchcock's glory years at Paramount.

VI

The Glory Years (1954–1968)

Hitchcock directing Kim Novak in *Vertigo.* (Courtesy of Jerry Ohlinger.)

24

Hitchcock in Ascendance

In 1954, Alfred Hitchcock left Warner Bros. for Paramount under a new contract that increased his salary, gave him a percentage of gross profits, afforded him more freedom and autonomy, and put him on a par financially with any director in Hollywood. His agent, Lew Wasserman, bargained for a unique clause that went almost unnoticed at the time but ultimately pushed Hitchcock's earnings well beyond those of his peers. The clause stipulated that the ownership of the pictures he produced and directed for Paramount would revert to Hitchcock eight years after their initial release.

Using his newfound freedom to select his own properties and hire big-name stars, Hitchcock embarked on the most productive phase of his career. In ten years he produced eleven films, including such masterpieces as *Rear Window, Vertigo, North by Northwest,* and *Psycho.*

But Wasserman did more than ensure Hitchcock's creative and financial independence. In 1955, he convinced the director to produce *Alfred Hitchcock Presents,* the weekly TV series of suspense stories that ran for ten years and made him an international celebrity. Hitchcock not only introduced each story with his puckish humor, he directed seventeen half-hour episodes and two one-hour episodes himself.

Hitchcock's film and TV work made him easily the most recognized director of his era, but his suspense films were considered mere "entertainments," so that the deeper appreciation and industry awards that went to directors of more "serious" films continued to elude him. This began to change in the mid-1950s, when *Cahiers du cinéma,* the magazine supporting the New Wave of French films, started to take him seriously as an artist. In 1957, two *Cahiers* journalists who would later become successful directors themselves, Claude Chabrol and Eric Rohmer, published *Hitchcock,* the first extended appreciation of his work. And, in that same period, François Truffaut made the initial contact that would lead to his definitive study of the director's films in 1967.

As Hitchcock's star ascended, the influence of Joe Breen and the Production Code declined. TV cut into movie attendance, and the number of weekly moviegoers dropped from 90 million in 1946 to 45 million in 1954. In the search for scapegoats, some insiders felt that the strictures of the Code, which had not changed in the twenty years since its implementation, should share the blame for the box-office decline. Producers and directors started to lobby for Code upgrades. Addressing the Theater Owners of America, Samuel Goldwyn said, "It is my firm belief the time has come to bring the Code up to date, to conform to the changes that have taken place during the years since it was first adopted." Director William Wyler echoed this sentiment, declaring that the Code was "due for revision" to enable the production of "more mature pictures."[1]

A few producers didn't have the patience to wait for Code revisions. When the Breen office refused to give its Seal of Approval to the Otto Preminger comedy *The Moon Is Blue* in 1953, United Artists resigned from the MPAA and released it without a seal. The film, a relatively tame comedy of manners, had been condemned for its lecherous tone and the use of such terms as *pregnant, seduce,* and *professional virgin.* In the absence of controversy, the film might have been expected to gross around $1.2 million, but with the Code opposition and the Legion of Decency condemnation boosting sales, it grossed over $4 million. The box-office response and the attendant publicity, which focused on the Code's objections to a few relatively harmless words, showed Breen to be out of step with both critics and the public. Breen's biographer Thomas Doherty noted that the brouhaha over *The Moon Is Blue* "was a public relations fiasco. . . . Breen had seemingly chosen to go to the wall not over a cornerstone of the Code or even a brick, but a meaningless chip, a rock-headed decision that further squandered the fast-depleting moral capital of the Production Code Administration."[2]

Breen's health had been failing since he was diagnosed with lung cancer in 1951, and he was further worn down by increasing criticism of the Code and the tussle over *The Moon Is Blue.* At the Academy Award ceremonies in 1954 he was given an honorary Oscar "for his conscientious, open-minded, and dignified management of a difficult office." The golden statue, along with a golden parachute of $20,000 per year for work as an "emeritus adviser," served as the industry's retirement gifts, and Breen officially stepped down on October 14, 1954, his sixty-sixth birthday.

Breen was replaced by his longtime assistant Geoffrey Shurlock. In contrast to Breen, Shurlock was soft spoken, cultured, fluent in three languages, and a life-long student of drama. He was more lenient than his predecessor and gradually expanded the limits of the Code, both by formal upgrades and by what his fellow Code administrator Jack Vizzard called "reverse English." Shurlock was more disposed than Breen to compromise, but if no compromise could be reached, Vizzard said, he would "frequently give in just to gauge the reactions of critics and the public."[3]

Even in his weakened state during his final years as Code administrator, Joe Breen had clung to the original Code language as if it had been engraved on tablets from Sinai. As he stepped down, the pressure to update the Code intensified, and the first official changes came in late 1954. Labeled as technical clarifications, these changes removed the ban on miscegenation, relaxed restrictions on liquor use and smuggling that had been written during the Prohibition era, and admitted some words long forbidden as vulgar, including *damn, hell, fanny, hold your hat, nerts,* and *tomcat.* The lifted restrictions on the words *damn* and *hell* came with the admonition that they would still be considered offensive if used without moderation.

The technical clarifications of 1954 gave way to a major makeover in 1956 with the rescinding of flat bans on illegal drugs, abortion, white slavery, and kidnapping. Like students testing a substitute teacher, producers and directors who had previously accepted the rigid Code rules dictated by Breen pressed to find openings in the new boundaries set by his successor. With the autonomy granted by his new Paramount contract, Alfred Hitchcock "took a front seat in the row of naughty boys," leading the push to expand the limits on sex and violence in American films.[4]

25

Rear Window (1954)

Synopsis. *A news photographer, L. B. Jefferies (James Stewart), confined to a wheelchair by a broken leg, spends his days watching his neighbors across the courtyard of his Greenwich Village apartment. Both his tart-tongued nurse Stella (Thelma Ritter) and his fiancée Lisa Fremont (Grace Kelly), a high-fashion executive, chide him for his idle voyeurism. Jeff is wary of marriage, fearing that Lisa's society background is incompatible with his itinerant life-style. His attitude toward marriage is also colored by the unhappy relationships he views among his neighbors, particularly the dysfunctional union of a salesman, Lars Thorwald (Raymond Burr), and his nagging wife. When the wife disappears, Jeff suspects she has been murdered, but is unable to convince either Stella or Lisa that his suspicions have merit.*

Both women eventually come to believe Thorwald is a murderer, and Lisa breaks into his apartment in search of the wife's wedding ring, incriminating evidence that they have seen Thorwald remove from a handbag. When Thorwald catches Lisa in the act, Jeff calls the police, who arrive in time to arrest Lisa and take her to the safety of the local stationhouse. Alerted to Jeff's surveillance, Thorwald visits the photographer and wrestles him out of his apartment window before the returning police can rescue him. Jeff emerges with a second broken leg, along with new respect for Lisa and hope for their future.

***

Rear Window was the first of six pictures Alfred Hitchcock would produce and direct for Paramount under the contract negotiated by Lew Wasserman. It was also the first of four films he would undertake with screenwriter John Michael Hayes, who brought a knack for smart dialogue and an optimistic outlook to their joint ventures.

Rear Window's plot was based on a short story by Cornell Woolrich, first published in 1942 under the title "It Had to Be Murder." In the short story, a man house bound with a broken leg watches his neighbors through his rear window and begins to suspect that one of them, a traveling salesman, has murdered his nagging wife. With the help of his African American houseman and a detective friend, he proves these suspicions, deduces the location of the wife's body, and helps to bring the killer to justice.

Hitchcock and his young screenwriter embellished this basic tale by giving the house-bound voyeur played by James Stewart a love interest, Grace Kelly, and a group of neighbors who serve as counterpoints to this pair of lovers. In addition to the murderous salesman and his wife, these neighbors include a honeymooning couple who spend most of their time in bed, a ballerina, Miss Torso, who juggles a stream of suitors, and a single woman, Miss Lonelyhearts, who is desperate for male attention.

In their initial review of the script, Joe Breen and his censors found fault with nearly every aspect of the production, from the nurse's wisecracks to the courtyard neighbors and the central couple's relationship. The censors took issue with the "toilet humor" of Stella, the insurance nurse played by Thelma Ritter, particularly her claim to have predicted the 1929 Crash when a major corporation executive in her care was too nervous to control his bowels. "When General Motors has to go to the bathroom ten times a day, the whole country's ready to let go."[1]

The censors also objected to the portrayal of the neighbors surrounding the courtyard. They found "the entire element of the newly married couple as seen through the window of their apartment from time to time" to be "an unacceptable play on the sexual aspects of a honeymoon." Miss Torso's costumes, sometimes showing too much cleavage in public and consisting of "only black panties" in private, were unacceptable because they gave "the entire action the flavor of a peep show." Even the primly clad Miss Lonelyhearts came in for criticism when a man she invited back to her apartment became "excessively sex seductive," with one hand "doing something with the slide fastener at the back of her dress."[2]

But Breen's reviewers reserved their strongest criticism for the ongoing dialogue that suggested a sexual relationship between the two lead characters, Jeff and Lisa. They objected to the display of sexy lingerie that accompanied Lisa's decision to spend the night with Jeff, and would have been much happier if she had decided to stay over "merely because of the mystery that had arisen at this point in the story"—not with any hanky-panky in mind.[3]

For all the objections levied at the script, one element that escaped the censors was the central fact of voyeurism, even though that had been

The elaborate *Rear Window* set, one of the largest ever constructed indoors, helped to ease the worries of Code officials regarding the acceptability of the script.

a hot-button issue for the Breen office ever since the inception of the Code.

Hitchcock teamed with Luigi Luraschi, Paramount's liaison with the Breen office, to formulate a plan for dealing with the Code objections. As a first step, the two men invited Code officials to visit Paramount and view the *Rear Window* set firsthand.

Hitchcock and the studio were justifiably proud of the indoor set, which depicted the rear of a five-story Greenwich Village apartment complex with thirty-one units, twelve of which were fully furnished. To get the height required for the apartment building and the Manhattan skyline behind it, workers had to cut the first floor out of a warehouse on the Paramount lot and dig so far below the surface that they actually struck water.[4] At the time, it was the largest set ever constructed on the Paramount lot.

Hitchcock invited Code officials to the set prior to filming to show them that everything happening in the apartments across the courtyard, including the dancing of the sexy Miss Torso and the assault on Miss Lonelyhearts, would be shot from the viewpoint of a man in a wheelchair looking out of his apartment window, not with salacious close-ups. An understanding of the perspective this somewhat distant observer would lend to the filming helped to reduce the worries of the Code reviewers, who "readily agreed that the camera location and the nature of the rather extraordinary set eliminated much of the concern we felt in reading the script material."[5]

However, the set visit failed to eliminate all of the Code concerns. In a file memo documenting the results of the visit, the reviewers noted that they had reminded Hitchcock that the running gag of the honeymooning groom's coming to the window in his underwear for a breath of fresh air and drawing the shade when he is called back to bed by the offstage voice of his bride was still "unacceptably suggestive," regardless of the distance of the observer from the window.[6]

To prepare for the Code review of the finished film, Hitchcock captured several views of Miss Torso, filming her once topless from behind, once in a white negligee, and once in black. The topless version was intended as bait for the reviewers, to be replaced if needed by the protective negligee footage. Having eased many of the reviewers' worries through the preliminary visit to the apartment set, he stayed close to the original script in shooting the remainder of the film.

In its review of the film's first cut, the Breen office found the movie "unacceptable from the Code viewpoint," citing three major failings. To no one's surprise, the first involved Miss Torso, who had one scene in what "appeared to be her underwear, rather than a dancing costume," and two brief scenes in which she was shown "nude from the waist up," with "her posterior offensively exposed."[7]

The censors continued to worry over the honeymooning couple's sexual appetites, finding the action of the recuperating groom responding to the offstage voice of his wife by turning from the window and lowering the shade "unacceptably sex suggestive."[8]

Finally, the Code reviewers were concerned that the negligee modeled by Grace Kelly when she spent the night in James Stewart's apartment was "too suggestive and too boldly unconventional."[9] Hitchcock himself may have contributed to the Code concern over Grace Kelly's negligee. Worried that Kelly was too flat chested to do justice to the ensemble, he quietly suggested to costume designer Edith Head that the presentation might benefit from the use of falsies. Retiring to the dressing room, Head and Kelly made a few tucks and adjustments, sans falsies, and when Kelly reappeared on the set "standing as straight as possible," she reported, "Hitchcock looked at me and at Edith and said 'See what a difference they make?'"[10]

In response to the Code's objections, Paramount phoned the Breen office immediately to assure the censors that all shots showing Miss Torso nude from the waist up would be eliminated completely, that the footage of Grace Kelly in the negligee would be reduced considerably, and the shots of the honeymooning couple would be edited to "remove the action of the young man pulling down the shade."[11] Hitchcock then inserted the protective footage of Miss Torso, limited the views of Grace Kelly's negligee to those necessary to the plot, and cut the shot of the honeymooners' shade being pulled down. Even though the shade was not lowered onscreen, the groom's weary reaction to his wife's call remained, and the sound of the shade being lowered could be heard on the soundtrack as Hitchcock cut to James Stewart's bemused expression.

On viewing the protective footage of the suitably clad Miss Torso, the Code office awarded *Rear Window* its Seal of Approval. By dangling the topless footage of Miss Torso as bait, Hitchcock had distracted the censors enough so that no further mention was made of the dialogue issues and other problems cited in their earlier script review, so that Stella's salty remarks slid by unedited.

Upon its release, *Rear Window* was a critical and commercial success. The *Hollywood Reporter* called it a "directorial masterpiece," while the *New York Times* praised it as a "tense and exciting exercise."[12] The *New Yorker* offered one of the few dissenting reviews, calling the film "claptrap" and objecting to Jeff's voyeurism.[13]

The film grossed $5.3 million on its initial release in 1954, $4.5 million on its 1962 reissue and, finally, another $12 million on its 1983 rerelease, making it Hitchcock's most commercially successful film. It received four Academy Award nominations, for direction, screenplay, sound editing, and color photography. Although it didn't win any of these categories, the Mystery Writers of America honored John Michael Hayes's screenplay with an Edgar Award.

The film has grown in stature over time. Film historian David Thomson ranked Hayes's script "among the most perfect ever written."[14] Hitchcock himself called it the "most cinematic" of his films, with so much of the story conveyed visually through cuts leading from Stewart to the object of his gaze and returning for his reaction. François Truffaut praised it, with *Notorious,* as one of his two favorite Hitchcock films. Certainly it is one of his warmest films, satisfying both as a love story and a plausible mystery, equally successful as both a "great film and great entertainment."[15]

26

To Catch a Thief (1955)

Synopsis. *John Robie (Cary Grant), once a successful cat burglar, earned a prison parole for serving in the French Resistance during World War II. He is retired and living on the Riviera when a rash of jewel robberies mimicking his modus operandi cause the French police to suspect he has come out of retirement. He escapes the police with the help of Danielle (Brigitte Auber), the daughter of one of his former Resistance cohorts, who takes him to Cannes, where he hopes to prove his innocence by catching the real thief. To this end, he convinces Lloyds of London agent H. H. Hughson (John Williams) to give him a list of wealthy clients who are likely burglary targets. At the top of Hughson's list are an American oil millionairess, Mrs. Jesse Stevens (Jessie Royce Landis), and her daughter Francie (Grace Kelly). Posing as an American lumberman, Robie meets the pair and soon finds himself in a deepening relationship with Francie, who guesses his real identity and offers to help him prove his innocence. She has reason to regret this offer when, after a night of lovemaking accompanied by symbolic fireworks, her mother's jewels disappear.*

When Danielle's father is killed near the mansion of a wealthy target, the French police, anxious to allay the fears of rich tourists, falsely identify him as the cat burglar. On the basis of the police report, Francie apologizes to Robie for suspecting he stole her mother's jewels. After Robie explains that Danielle's father had a wooden leg and could not possibly have been the cat burglar, she helps him catch the real culprit by creating a diversion at a masquerade ball attended by many of the targets on Hughson's list. The diversion enables Robie to stake out the roof of the mansion where the ball is held and capture the real jewel thief, Danielle, who was working with her father and his former Resistance cohorts.

***

To Catch a Thief was adapted from a 1952 novel by David Dodge. Hitchcock had purchased the rights to the book prior to publication, presumably attracted by the thriller plot, the romantic overtones, and the Riviera locale, which was one of the favorite vacation spots of the Hitchcock family. The director and screenwriter John Michael Hayes simplified the plot but retained many of its implausibilities, including the gullibility of the Lloyds of London agent who shares a list of potential robbery targets with the prime suspect, and the willingness of the French police to turn that suspect loose so that he can clear his name.

As in the book, the real cat burglar is the daughter of one of John Robie's Resistance cohorts, although in the novel she escapes prosecution by returning the stolen jewels to their owners. In one of the movie's dangling plot points, the identity of the person who murdered the real burglar's father is never revealed. When Brigitte Auber, the actress playing the burglar, asked Hitchcock who killed her film father, Hitchcock, with a typical disdain for plot details, told her, "It doesn't matter."[1]

After viewing the film, the book's author claimed that all that survived of his work in the movie were "the title, the names of some of the characters, and the copyright, which was mine."[2] One of the biggest differences between the book and the movie is the emphasis on the romance between Robie and Francie Stevens. In the book, the romance is overshadowed by the plot and comes into focus only once the mystery is solved. In the movie, the romance is front and center from the time Francie surprises Robie with a kiss at the door of her hotel room. In his second collaboration with Hitchcock, John Michael Hayes spiced the romance with clever banter featuring double entendres so smooth that many slipped right by the censors.

The script went through several alterations during the location shooting, reflecting problems with budget, weather, locations, language difficulties, the actors themselves and, of course, the Production Code.

Following the Code review of the first draft of the script, Joe Breen logged a number of objections, including:

- Excessive bottom pinching.
- Bikini beachwear and "undue breast exposure."
- Sexual innuendo in the dialogue.
- Attempts to justify Robie's past career as a thief.
- The casino scene in which Robie drops a chip down the cleavage of a woman gambler.
- A repeated gag in which the French police are shown ogling salacious French postcards.

- Just about everything connected with the fireworks scene, including the dialogue, the out-of-frame caressing, subsequent discussions, and all suggestions of an illicit sex relationship.[3]

Hayes's rewrites failed to dispel many of these objections. In a July 9, 1954, letter reviewing the final shooting script, Breen reiterated the Code's concerns regarding the use of bikinis and "excessive exposure" in the beach scenes. Regarding the casino scene in which Robie loses a chip in a woman's cleavage, the Code reviewers worried that Robie's "poised fingers" would suggest that "he might possibly attempt to retrieve the lost chip by himself," rendering the scene "unacceptably suggestive." Breen stayed firm in his judgment that "any suggestion that the two detectives are looking at French postcards will be unacceptable." But his greatest concern remained the suggestion of illicit sex in the fireworks scene. He cautioned that the final embrace between Robie and Francie must "not be unduly suggestive," and asked that the fireworks themselves be eliminated, feeling that their symbolism was just too "pointed."[4]

Throughout the shooting, Hitchcock continued to reassure the Production Code office that all its objections would be resolved in the final print. Time proved to be on his side, because Joe Breen retired before the final print was ready for review, leaving the friendlier and more accommodating Geoffrey Shurlock in charge of negotiations. With shooting completed, the director coolly "stacked up the violations" and began horse trading with Shurlock. First to go, after a suitable show of resistance, was the scene of the French police ogling salacious postcards. When the film's composer, Lynn Murray, asked, "Why would you take that out? It's charming," Hitchcock explained, "The picture doesn't stand or fall on one little shot. . . . Besides, if I take that out, they won't complain so much about the fireworks scene."[5]

In the hope of protecting the fireworks scene, Hitchcock also agreed to cut a few lines of dialogue. Even so, much of the dialogue cited as objectionable in Breen's script reviews survived, and many of the banter and double entendres created by Hayes were so cleverly written and delivered that the censors missed them completely. Thus the director shortened Francie's question during the fireworks scene, "Ever had a better offer in your life? One with everything—diamonds, excitement—me?" by cutting the last three words, but left in Robie's observation that what Francie needs is "two weeks, with a good man, at Niagara Falls" over the censor's objections. And the censors raised no objections to the byplay between Francie and Robie when they case a villa, elude the police after a harrowing chase, and picnic at a picturesque site overlooking the French Riviera. Among the exchanges that passed inspection were Francie's request on opening the picnic basket as to whether Robie would prefer "a leg or a breast," and Robie's response, "You make the choice."

One line of dialogue that raised the censors' hackles was actually improved in the final shooting script. When her mother's jewels disappear after the fireworks scene, Francie blames Robie and reveals his identity to her mother, characterizing him as "a low, worthless thief." In the original script, her mother observes, "At least I didn't offer him my treasures in a semi-darkened room." The censors objected to this line on the grounds that it implied an "intimate relationship" between Francie and Robie.[6] In response to their objection, Hitchcock and Hayes scrapped the line, replacing it with the more succinct observation, "Just what did he steal from you?" which better reflects the acerbic character of Francie's mother.

Even with the sacrificed French postcard sequence and the dialogue cuts, the censors remained concerned about the lovemaking in the fireworks scene, and Shurlock finally issued the Code Seal of Approval with the proviso that "in all prints . . . the love scene between Cary Grant and Grace Kelly, in Miss Kelly's hotel room . . . will be terminated by a dissolve before the couple lean back toward the corner of the sofa."[7] Instead of altering the sequence as requested, Hitchcock went to composer Lynn Murray, who had scored the fireworks scene with "very sensuous" music dominated by "a smoky tenor saxophone to accent the romantic mood," and asked him to rescore the scene "in a more conventional way, like with strings."[8] The director then managed to convince Shurlock that the resulting music tempered the lustful nature of the images enough to overcome the need for any changes in the shots themselves. Thus, in return for an unimportant shot, a few lines of dialogue, and a more sedate music score, Hitchcock protected the carefully constructed sequence of sensual images comprising the fireworks scene, along with the fireworks themselves—which, the director later admitted, were "a visual metaphor for sex."[9]

Traces of the censored French postcard sequences remain in the completed film, as if the censors left messy fingerprints on the finished product. When the two policemen pursue Francie and Robie along the winding roads above Cannes, the policeman in the passenger seat can be seen

Hitchcock cut Francie's offer of "diamonds, excitement—me" from the fireworks seduction scene—but not the fireworks.

showing the driver a postcard. Without the excised setup, however, the viewer has no way of knowing what the postcard depicts.

One shot of questionable propriety involving the car chase above Cannes escaped the notice of the Production Code. The chase ends when the policemen pursuing Grace Kelly and Cary Grant crash trying to avoid a chicken crossing the road. While the frustrated police are making a distressed call to headquarters, the chicken pirouettes and daintily leaves a tiny deposit in the middle of the road. As a teenage usher in the Keith Albee Theater in Huntington, West Virginia, where *To Catch a Thief* originally played, I would leave my post at the theater door when I heard the noise of the police car crash just to smile at what I perceived to be Hitchcock's way of thumbing his nose at the censors. I also earned the admiration of my friends for my perceptive insider's knowledge of the art of filmmaking.

The shot of the chicken defiling the road can still be seen in the original theatrical prints of the film, although it takes a quick eye to spot it on smaller TV screens playing the DVD version. While the Code officials missed it in their review, they did warn the producers to "consult with Dr. Wesley Young of the American Humane Association as to all scenes in which animals are used."[10]

Critics were divided on the plot, although nearly everyone praised the scenery and Robert Burks won an Academy Award for his cinematography. Both *Variety* and the *Hollywood Reporter* weighed in with unfavorable reviews, but the *New Yorker* praised the movie as a "fine bubble-bright and sleekly machined suspense and romance with Cary Grant and Grace Kelly handsomely and cooly rivaling a stunning expanse of mouthwatering French Riviera scenery."[11] While Bosley Crowther praised both the film and its stars in the *New York Times,* he reserved most of his positive comments for the scenery.[12]

Although *To Catch a Thief* suffers by comparison with its predecessor, *Rear Window,* it performed nearly as well as the earlier film during its initial run, producing $4.5 million in North American box-office returns.[13] Even so, while *Rear Window* is rated as one of Hitchcock's masterpieces, *To Catch a Thief* is generally considered "lesser Hitchcock," reflecting the director's own characterization of it as "light entertainment."[14] Still, the Riviera scenery and romantic chemistry between Cary Grant and Grace Kelly continue to make the movie a pleasure to watch.

27

The Trouble with Harry (1955)

Synopsis*. The trouble with Harry is that he's dead. Three shots ring out in a resplendent Vermont countryside and a young boy, Arnie (Jerry Mathers), comes across Harry's body. At least three residents of the local village have reason to believe they have been responsible for Harry's death: a retired tugboat operator, Captain Wiles (Edmund Gwenn), fired three shots, mistaking Harry for a rabbit; a local spinster, Miss Ivy Gravely (Mildred Natwick), clobbered Harry with her hiking boot while repelling unwanted advances; and Arnie's mother and Harry's long-estranged wife, Jennifer Rogers (Shirley MacLaine), hit Harry with a milk bottle when he tried to end their estrangement.*

A series of misunderstandings ensues, during which Harry's body is interred and disinterred four times with the help of a local artist, Sam Marlowe (John Forsythe), before Harry is discovered to have died of natural causes. In the aftermath of the misunderstandings, deeper understandings and marriage plans develop between Sam and the widowed Jennifer, as well as between Captain Wiles and Miss Gravely.

***

The Trouble with Harry represented a departure for Hitchcock, a black comedy in which the consistently dry humor undercuts any suspense. The most English of Hitchcock's American films, it is based on the first novel of British author Jack Trevor Story, adapted by John Michael Hayes in his third collaboration with Hitchcock.

Hayes embellished the draft script with his characteristic wit, which gave the Code administrators characteristic fits. But the biggest stumbling block for the Code office was the illegitimacy of the young boy Arnie. The official correspondence from the censors noted that "one major element which could not be approved" was "the fact of the illegitimate child, which is treated with no semblance of the moral values required by the Code."[1]

Another element of the story that the censors found to be "totally unacceptable" was Jennifer's description of her wedding night with Harry.[2]

In the first draft of the script, Jennifer tells Sam that she left Harry because on their wedding night he had dressed up as his brother Robert, Jennifer's lost first love and Arnie's father, and asked her to imagine she was making love to Robert.

The Code reviewers also took exception to some of John Michael Hayes's saltier humor. In discussing Miss Gravely, the artist Sam tells the captain, who has taken an interest in the spinster, "Do you realize you'll be the first man to cross her threshold?" The captain responds, "She's a well-preserved woman," after a pause, adding, "Of course, you have to open preserves some day." The Code office found that both Sam's observation and the captain's response contained "an offensive sex suggestive implication and should either be omitted or changed."[3]

To address the major concern of the Code office, the script was altered so that Arnie's parents were married before his father was killed, eliminating the issue of illegitimacy as a concern. The "totally unacceptable" description of Jennifer's wedding night was also altered by having Harry fail to show up to consummate the marriage. According to the revised script, her new groom was dissuaded by a horoscope he read in the hotel lobby warning him "not to start any new projects on that day." Jennifer left him immediately, fearing that their married life might be blighted if Harry's future horoscopes kept him from other tasks as well, like doing the dishes. This more amusing but less believable account of Jennifer's breakup with Harry avoided any messy wedding-night descriptions and satisfied the Production Code.

Having given in on the issues of Arnie's illegitimacy and Jennifer's wedding night, Hitchcock gave himself a little more bargaining room by shooting alternative takes of the scene in which the captain leans his left elbow on the shoulder of the buxom ship's figurehead in his dining room.[4] In each take, the captain's left hand dangles successively closer to the figurehead's right breast, until it finally makes contact. In the final print, the captain's cupped fingertips come to rest about an inch from the statue's breast.

Hitchcock may have used the dangling hand as a negotiating ploy to retain some of John Michael Hayes's winking dialogue in the final print. He did agree to cut some bits of dialogue, including the dread word *cripes* and the potentially offensive observation "I hear there's good money in Evangelism." In addition, he softened Miss Gravely's description of the dazed Harry's attack on her virtue. In the end, his negotiations managed to salvage some of Hayes's best lines, including Sam's exchange with the captain about crossing thresholds and opening preserves, which had raised the censors' eyebrows at the script stage.

The lines about opening preserves made it past the censors, but as delivered by Edmund Gwenn, who was seventy-seven years old and had first worked with Hitchcock thirty-three years earlier in *The Skin Game,* they sounded more wistful than lecherous. Gwenn had other problems during the shooting. Hurricane Carla brought enormous storms to the region that caused his arthritic joints to stiffen painfully. The storm also stripped trees of the autumn foliage that had attracted Hitchcock to the Vermont setting, forcing him to finish shooting on Paramount's Hollywood lot after importing enough russet maple leaves to create the trees needed for the remaining scenes.

Hitchcock was not well served by the lead actors in *The Trouble with Harry.* Edmund Gwenn, stiff with arthritis, was "too old and tired to inject the necessary life" into Hayes's "genuinely witty lines."[5] Acting in her first film, Shirley MacLaine, although hardly arthritic, appeared somewhat stiff, showing little of the life she would exude as her career progressed. And John Forsythe came off more as a frat boy on vacation than a crotchety and penniless artist. Overall, the acting was adequate, but not up to the high standards Hitchcock was blessed with on his other Paramount films.

Absent big-name stars, the black comedy of *The Trouble with Harry* did not play well in 1955 America, but was a big hit across the Atlantic. It ran for six months in Paris and was well received in Great Britain, where the population was more attuned to Hitchcock's dry sense of humor. Reviews tended to reflect the nationality of the reviewers. Bosley Crowther of the *New York Times* reported that "the pace is leisurely, almost sluggish, and the humor frequently is strained."[6] The *London Times* reviewer, on the other hand, felt that the "sheer absurdity of the proceedings carries the day."[7]

The failure at the domestic box office could have been explained by a number of factors, including the understated British humor, the lack of characteristic Hitchcock suspense, the absence of recognizable stars, and Paramount's limited release strategy, which confined the film to first-run theaters in major cities. Reflecting on *The Trouble with Harry* years later, Hitchcock characterized the film as "an expensive self-indulgence."[8]

Mildred Natwick, Edmund Gwenn, Jerry Mathers, Shirley MacLaine, and John Forsythe pose with Harry. The lack of big-name stars (it was MacLaine's first film) did not help the US box office.

In spite of the film's poor reception, or perhaps because of it, Hitchcock often listed *The Trouble with Harry* among his favorite films. As he was finishing it, he was also developing his TV series, *Alfred Hitchcock Presents*, and he gave an early cut of the movie to James Allardice, the man he had hired to write the monologues he would use in introducing each episode, as an example of the type of tone he wanted in the series. *The Trouble with Harry* was not only a template for *Alfred Hitchcock Presents*, but, given its sardonic humor and leisurely pace, the story might have played better as an entry in the future series than as a feature-length film.

28

The Man Who Knew Too Much (1956)

Synopsis*. On holiday in Marrakech, Dr. Ben MacKenna (James Stewart), his wife, Jo (Doris Day), a former musical star, and their young son Hank witness the murder of a Frenchman, Louis Bernard (Daniel Gelin). The Frenchman dies in Ben's arms and whispers the sketchy details of a planned political assassination in London. To silence Ben, a British couple involved in the assassination plot, the Draytons (Bernard Miles and Brenda De Banzie), kidnap Hank and take him to London. The MacKennas follow, hoping to rescue Hank and prevent the political murder.*

In London, Ben and Jo follow a convoluted set of clues to the Albert Hall, where a foreign ambassador is to be murdered under the cover of a clash of cymbals during a concert. Jo foils the attempt by screaming just as the assassin is about to fire.

The grateful ambassador invites Ben and Jo to a reception at the embassy, where Hank is being held by the Draytons and the country's prime minister, who had helped plan the aborted murder attempt. When Jo is invited to sing at the reception, Hank hears her and whistles along from his place of captivity, bringing Ben to his rescue.

***

Hitchcock first considered a remake of his own 1934 film *The Man Who Knew Too Much* as early as 1940, and Sidney Bernstein eventually secured the rights for Transatlantic with a payment of $45,000. It took over twenty years after the release of the original version for the director to begin work on the property as part of his contract with Paramount. The bare bones of the plot did not change from 1934 to 1956. The child of a vacationing couple is kidnapped to keep them from revealing information about an upcoming political assassination in London. And the highlight of both versions is the Albert Hall sequence, which culminates in an aborted murder attempt timed to accompany the clash of cymbals. But aside from this sequence, the details of the story changed a great deal. The vacationing couple was English in the original version and American in the remake; the wife was transformed from an expert marksman to a retired musical star; the kidnapped girl in the original became a boy in the remake; the vacation locale shifted from Switzerland to Marrakech; and the seventy-five-minute black-and-white British version was expanded to a two-hour color VistaVision extravaganza in the 1956 release.

Differences in the endings of the two versions also affected the American censors' reactions to the two films. Whereas the original British version ends in a shootout that upset the Production Code office so much it cut five minutes from the already short film, the 1956 version ends with Doris Day trying to locate her missing son by singing the song "Que Sera, Sera" in the embassy where he is held prisoner. With no terminal shootout to object to, the censors' reaction to the remake was relatively benign.

In reviewing the script for the 1956 version, the Production Code office reminded Paramount that under the Code, "the person kidnapped must *not* be a child."[1] The Code reviewers had raised this issue in 1934, although at that time they were dealing with the completed British film, and it was too late to change such a basic plot element. They did, however, cut out frames that showed the kidnapper placing his gloved hand over the mouth of the abducted child, evidently fearing that the scene might provide too much information to would-be kidnappers.

Censors reviewing the script of the remake were happy to learn that the kidnapped boy would be "somewhat older than seven" (he was eight), which they felt was "all to the good." They also felt that their objection to child kidnapping might be resolved "if it is absolutely clear that the child is held merely as a hostage, with no actual threat to his life." To support this interpretation, the Code office recommended dialogue changes when the British counsel warns the MacKennas there is no guarantee that "the people who took your son . . . will ever give him back to you." They also suggested that the ending scenes where the villain holds a gun to the head of the boy should be rewritten so that "the threat is directed at the father, rather than at the boy."[2]

Hitchcock did only as much as was needed to accommodate the Code admonitions against child kidnapping. He dropped the British counsel's warning that Hank might never be returned and adjusted other dialogue so that neither the kidnappers nor the police ever explicitly state that

Hank's life is at risk. But the implicit threat is always present, driving the plot. The kidnappers warn Ben that "your little boy will be in serious danger" if he passes the message of the dying agent on to the police. The director softens this threat somewhat by having Mrs. Drayton plea for the safety of the boy while he is in her care. But in the closing showdown, the villain holds the gun to Hank's head for a full thirty seconds before turning it on his father.

The censors expressed one element of concern regarding the remake that had not surfaced in their review of the original film. They wanted the plot to make it clear that Drayton is "merely posing as a minister" in a tiny chapel sequence to skirt the Code admonition against a minister being involved in criminal activities. To accommodate this wish, Hitchcock shot scenes with Drayton posing as a minister twice, once with him wearing a Roman collar and once wearing a necktie.[3] The film shows him donning the collar as a disguise as he prepares to address the congregation in the small chapel, but wearing a necktie at all other times.

Although Hitchcock had conceived the assassination attempt in the 1934 film as a Nazi plot, the BBFC policy against offending other nations, and possibly losing foreign revenues, caused the plotters to remain citizens of an anonymous country. In drafting the remake, news of Hungary's drift away from Stalin caused Hitchcock to build the plot around a Russian attempt to assassinate a Hungarian prime minister. In this case, it was Paramount that got cold feet and insisted that no countries be identified in the assassination plot. When the kidnappers drive to the embassy of their employers, the word EMBASSY is spelled out clearly on the entryway plaque, but a light fixture obscures the country's name so that only the first two letters, AO, are visible. *Webster's Dictionary* lists only eight words starting with those two letters, and none of them are names of countries.

François Truffaut raised the issue of the nameless country with Hitchcock. "You went to some trouble, I notice, to avoid mention of a specific country; that might raise censorship problems." Hitchcock acknowledged this. "Of course, I didn't want to commit myself to any country. We simply indicated that by killing the ambassador, the spies hoped to embarrass the British Government."[4]

Critical opinion differs over which of Hitchcock's two versions of *The Man Who Knew Too Much* is superior. The opinion most quoted in this regard is Hitchcock's own. In his 1962 interview with Truffaut, he said,

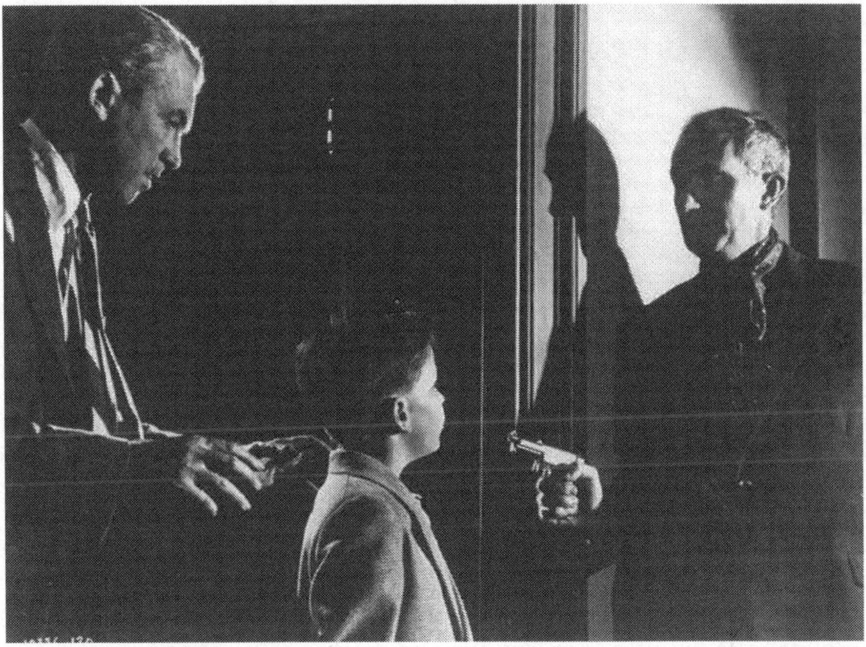

The villain holds a gun on the kidnapped boy, against the suggestions of the Code reviewers. (Courtesy of Jerry Ohlinger.)

"Let's say that the first version is the work of a talented amateur and the second is made by a professional."[5] This answer is generally taken to mean that the director himself preferred the second version. But Hitchcock said different things in different interviews. A 1972 interview with David Castell suggests that he preferred the original version, since he said, "I think it was more spontaneous—it had less logic. Logic is dull; you always lose the bizarre and spontaneous."[6] The director gave a more balanced answer to biographer Charlotte Chandler. "Some of it was better the second time, but some of it was better the first time. The only answer is, I suppose, I'll have to make it a third time."[7]

Several critics compared the 1956 film with its 1934 predecessor. The *London Times* stated its preference for the earlier British version: "In spite of colour, wide screen devices, and even louder sound, the Hitchcock technique has not changed greatly since the days of 1934 when the first *The Man Who Knew Too Much* was a high water mark of British production." The *Times* reviewer found "nothing to prove the value of a director repeating his work."[8] Across the Atlantic, Bosley Crowther offered a positive take on the 1956 version in the *New York Times.* Admitting the "basic absurdity of the plot," he noted that "logic and credibility were never Mr. Hitchcock's strong suits. He depends upon daring deception. And that's what he has in this film. Even in mammoth VistaVision . . . the old Hitchcock thriller stuff has punch."[9]

The film, one of the four Hitchcock ended up owning under his agreement with Paramount, did very well at the box office, bringing in $4.4 million domestically on a $2.5 million budget. Although it was not nominated for Academy Awards in the acting or directing categories, "Que Sera, Sera," the song sung by Doris Day in an attempt to communicate with her kidnapped son, won an Oscar for Best Song. Echoing the *Stage Fright* reaction of Marlene Dietrich in the case of "The Laziest Gal in Town," Doris Day at first was not happy with "Que Sera, Sera," which wound up being one of her biggest hits.[10]

In the end, the Production Code had far more impact on the 1934 British version of *The Man Who Knew Too Much* than on the 1956 remake. While it scissored five minutes from the earlier version, its objections to the remake were easily accommodated by Hitchcock and had little impact on the finished film. The results reflect both the gradual weakening of the Code under Geoffrey Shurlock and Hitchcock's increasing skill in dealing with censorship.

29

The Wrong Man (1956)

Synopsis. *Alfred Hitchcock opens the film personally with a prologue explaining, "This is a true story, every word of it." Stork Club bass player Manny Balestrero (Henry Fonda) lives in Jackson Heights, New York, with his wife, Rose (Vera Miles), and their two young sons. When he goes to an insurance office to borrow money on his wife's life insurance policy, office workers mistakenly identify him as the man who twice held up the office and stole sums of $71 and $200. After witnesses to other local holdups identify him as well, he is arraigned on charges of armed robbery and bail is set at $7,500.*

When his brother-in-law pays the bail, Manny and Rose hire an inexperienced lawyer, Frank O'Connor (Anthony Quayle). As circumstantial evidence mounts against Manny, potential alibi witnesses are found to have either died or moved away, and Rose is institutionalized with a mental breakdown.

Manny's trial starts badly and is aborted when an impatient juror protests at O'Connor's inept cross-examination of a witness and the judge declares a mistrial. While Manny awaits a new trial, the man who actually committed the earlier holdups is caught trying to rob a delicatessen. Manny is cleared, but Rose remains depressed and institutionalized for two years before the Balestreros start a new life in Florida.

***

In June 1953, *Life* magazine published the true story of Manny Balestrero, a New York musician who was unjustly accused of armed robbery and hounded by the legal system until his wife suffered a nervous breakdown. Robert Montgomery subsequently produced a reenactment of Balestrero's trial and disrupted family life for TV, and Warner Bros. purchased the film rights to the story. Hitchcock had promised to do a picture for Warner's in return for its support on *I Confess,* and early in 1955 he took a leave of absence from Paramount to fulfill that obligation. Waiving his salary in return for 10 percent of the gross, he agreed to direct Balestrero's story as *The Wrong Man.*

Hitchcock felt strongly that the film should follow the course of events exactly as they transpired, with no directorial embellishments. He accomplished this by filming in a semi-documentary fashion, shooting in black-and-white in the actual New York locations wherever possible. Although he interviewed many of the participants in the real-life drama and even cast a few in minor roles, he received no cooperation from the New York Police Department, which wanted no part of a story whose main elements were false arrest and mistaken imprisonment.

Hitchcock was so conscious of the need for realism that he abandoned his usual cameo appearance in the film itself, replacing it with a personal appearance in a prologue announcing that everything in the movie is based on fact. In a subsequent interview, he even apologized for a deliberate double exposure near the end of the movie when Henry Fonda's face morphs into that of the real look-alike felon just before the man is captured robbing a delicatessen. The director felt that because the double exposure "never happened in the real story" he was "introducing creative elements into a story that didn't need to be improved upon."[1]

The director's strict attention to detail and real-time pacing produced a grim, unrelenting film unlike any of his others. *The Wrong Man* was also unlike Hitchcock's other films in the reaction it drew from the Production Code reviewers. The censors' page-by-page review of the script elicited only three suggestions, the fewest that they had to offer on any of the director's American films. The suggestions themselves were relatively trivial.

- The toilet fixture should be eliminated from Manny's cell.
- It is unacceptable to show Manny "quite naked."
- The word *geez* should be eliminated.[2]

Hitchcock easily accommodated these suggestions, showing a sink instead of a toilet in Manny's cell, filming Manny as he starts to unbutton his shirt with a gang of naked inmates shown from the waist up in the background, and scrubbing "geez" from the soundtrack.

Hitchcock's insistence on realism led to an argument with Warner Bros. over the film's coda. Following a heartbreaking scene in the sanitarium showing an uncommunicative Rose unable to find any solace in the news of her husband's release, Manny's exit down the institutional halls is covered with the on-screen words:

Manny Balestrero (Henry Fonda) reads a newspaper with an account of the holdup that will change his life.

> Two years later, Rose Balestrero walked out of the sanitarium—completely cured. Today she lives happily in Florida with Manny and the two boys . . . and what happened seems like a nightmare to them . . . but it did happen . . .

These words stay on the screen as the sanitarium hall dissolves into a long shot of a family strolling beneath palm trees before the words fade and "The End" appears over the Warner's logo.

Hitchcock fought against this finish because, in actuality, Rose never completely recovered from her depression. But Warner's need to tack a happy ending onto its grim story outweighed the director's pursuit of realism. The persistence of Rose's mental problems kept the Balestrero family from ever enjoying the advertised happy ending. Manny sued the City of New York and the NYPD for $500,000, but settled out of court for only $7,000. He did receive $22,000 for the rights to his story, but little of this windfall remained after settling the debts incurred for Rose's institutional care.[3]

The bleak, humorless film did poorly at the box office, barely breaking even domestically on a relatively low budget of $1.2 million. Most critics at the time damned the movie with faint praise. *Time* criticized its "completely literal rendering" of the facts.[4] The *New York Times* praised the performances of Henry Fonda and Vera Miles, noting that Hitchcock's "principals are sincere as they enact a series of events that actually are part of New York's annals of crime," but added that the actors "rarely stir the emotions or make a viewer's spine tingle. Frighteningly authentic, the story generates only a modicum of drama."[5]

Hitchcock's French acolytes were quick to anoint the film as a masterpiece. Future film directors Eric Rohmer and Claude Chabrol wrote, "This is a documentary without embellishment, even though the camera that shows it to us is never impassive but always descriptive, narrative, as Hitchcock's camera always is."[6] And another future French director, Jean-Luc Godard, likened Hitchcock's care with individual shots to the "touches" with which the French impressionists enriched their paintings.[7]

Over time, a few American critics have come to agree with the French assessment of *The Wrong Man.* In his review of a lifetime of favorite films, Richard Schickel noted that *The Wrong Man* lacked Hitchcock's usual wit and cheekiness and was relentlessly grim, yet "it was as great as anything he ever did . . . a masterpiece that is essentially without compare in the body of his work."[8]

Perhaps because of its low box-office returns, Hitchcock himself undervalued the film. In his interviews with François Truffaut, he acknowledged that "it wasn't my kind of picture" and suggested that *The Wrong Man* should be filed "among the indifferent Hitchcocks."[9]

Hitchcock told the story straight, with no digressions to increase suspense and no flourishes to worry the censors. Box-office receipts might have been strengthened by a few directorial embellishments and a little of the director's humor and sense of pacing. In the end, though, the lack of the familiar Hitchcock "touches" in the unrelentingly grim story turned away the audiences he usually delighted in manipulating.

30

Vertigo (1958)

Synopsis. *Scottie Ferguson (James Stewart) resigns as a police detective in San Francisco because of a fear of heights that induces vertigo. A former friend, Gavin Elster (Tom Helmore), asks him to shadow his wife, Madeleine (Kim Novak), whom he fears is suicidal. Scottie and Madeleine begin seeing one another after he saves her life when she attempts to drown herself. They fall in love and explore the Bay Area searching for clues to her suicidal tendencies. Their search leads to a church in San Juan Bautista, where Madeleine breaks away and runs up the steep winding staircase leading to the church bell tower. Unable to follow because of his acrophobia, Scottie watches in horror as the love of his life plunges to her death.*

Scottie suffers a nervous breakdown and is nursed back to health by his former fiancée, Midge Wood (Barbara Bel Geddes). One day in the street he sees a redhead, Judy Barton (Kim Novak again), whose face resembles Madeleine's, and he follows her back to her apartment. Judy reluctantly agrees to date Scottie, who persists in trying to remake her in the image of his lost love, asking her to change her hair style and her wardrobe. What Scottie doesn't know is that Judy has played the role of Madeleine before, in an elaborate hoax concocted by Elster to rid himself of his real wife. It was Judy, then Elster's mistress, who had dressed as Madeleine, enticed Scottie, and led him to the bell tower, where she and Elster staged the "suicide" of the real Madeleine as Scottie watched helplessly from below.

Trying to recapture Scottie's love, Judy succumbs to his obsession and submits to the makeover. But she ultimately gives herself away by wearing a necklace she had worn when imitating Madeleine. Realizing he has been duped, Scottie takes Judy back to the murder site, hoping to elicit a confession and relieve his guilt. He overcomes his acrophobia and drags her to the top of the bell tower, where she is startled by the sudden appearance of a nun. Backing away, Judy stumbles into the void as a distraught Scottie watches his love fall to her death a second time.

***

At the time he made *Vertigo,* Hitchcock's power and reputation were on the rise. He'd made a string of successful films for Paramount, his TV show had made him an international celebrity, and the French critics were beginning to take him seriously. At the same time the influence of the Production Code was declining, and Hitchcock used his developing power to take on the Code rule that murderers must be punished.

Vertigo is based on the 1954 French novel *D'entre les morts* (From Among the Dead) by Pierre Boileau and Thomas Narcejac, who also wrote the book that Henri-Georges Clouzot turned into the movie *Les diaboliques. Vertigo* retains much of the source novel's convoluted plot, which strains credibility to the breaking point. The idea that a rich man would hire a friend with a fear of heights to follow a double of the man's wealthy wife so that the double can drop hints of suicidal tendencies and ultimately lead the friend to a location where his fear of heights will cause him to misread the wife's murder as suicide is difficult to comprehend, tricky to recount, and painfully high on the implausibility scale. And the idea that the double would fall in love with the friend and stick around town after the wife's death drives the meter on the scale even higher.

Samuel Taylor, the last in a parade of screenwriters who worked on the film with Hitchcock, acknowledged that the plot is "absurd" and "far fetched" but argued that "the story is honest and true" and that there is "a great deal of depth" in the tale of "a man who is tricked into something that becomes an obsession."[1]

Although Hitchcock and his screenwriters stuck close to the book's plot, they made a few crucial changes in the film's presentation. In addition to shifting the setting from postwar France to San Francisco and changing the wife from a brunette to a classic Hitchcock blonde, they revealed the complicity of the double midway through the movie. In the book, the reader is not told that the woman the obsessed hero is remaking has actually played the role before until the final chapter. And when the book's hero realizes the extent of the double's treachery, he strangles her because she has destroyed the memory of Madeleine.

In the film, as in the book, Scottie is unaware of Judy's previous role as Madeleine until the endgame, when he recognizes Madeleine's necklace and drives them both to San Juan Bautista for the fatal trip up the bell tower. But Hitchcock and Taylor let movie audiences in on Judy's secret as soon as Scottie leaves her apartment the first time through a flashback and what Taylor viewed as the clunky artifice of a confessional letter Judy writes to Scottie. But she tears up the letter when she decides not to run in the hope of winning Scottie's love as herself.[2]

Hitchcock and Taylor worried over the midpoint plot revelation, but defended it as a means of substituting suspense for surprise. Instead of a single shock at the end when the mystery is revealed, the audience spends the second phase of the movie wondering what Scottie will do when he finds out the woman he is remaking as Madeleine has played the role before. It also lets the audience understand, and sympathize with, Judy's reluctance to participate in the transformation. She is faced with a terrible choice—either become someone she's not or risk losing the man she loves.

The filming of *Vertigo* underwent several delays. Principal photography was first postponed by James Stewart's vacation schedule, and then by a series of maladies that left Hitchcock hospitalized and recuperating for the first four months of 1957. While recovering from hernia surgery in January, Hitchcock held the first of a series of meetings with Sam Taylor that deepened and improved *Vertigo*'s script. Taylor introduced the character of Midge as a grounding influence on Scottie, and collaborated with Hitchcock on the early revelation of Judy's role in the murder of the real Madeleine.

Although the schedule delays accommodated these much-needed script improvements, they also led to a significant casting problem. Vera Miles, who was Hitchcock's first choice to play Madeleine, became pregnant in the interim. The news aggravated Hitchcock, who had been grooming Miles as a replacement for Grace Kelly, but was actually welcomed by Paramount's front office, which was able to replace her with Kim Novak, a rising star with much greater box-office recognition. Hitchcock was never comfortable with Novak, whose performance he grudgingly assessed as no better than adequate.[3] But she was a good deal more than adequate, carrying off a difficult dual role in which one of the characters she portrayed was role-playing herself.

The first suggestions for changes in Taylor's completed script came not from the Production Code censors but from Paramount's legal department. They objected to a scene at the inquest following Madeleine's death in which the presiding coroner gives a lengthy speech recounting the dead woman's suicidal tendencies and criticizing Scottie's failure to stop her from leaping to her death. Paramount's lawyers had two objections. First, the coroner's remarks "overstepped the bounds of judicial fairness and propriety." Second, because there was only one coroner in San Benito County, any derogatory depiction of the character in the movie could be taken as a direct slur on a real-life individual and potential grounds for libel. The lawyers also noted that the prospect of libel was further aggravated by one character's verbal description of the coroner as a "son of a bitch."[4]

The legal department suggested the problem might be solved by putting the offending speech in the mouth of a prosecutor or advocate, rather than a coroner acting in a judicial capacity. Hitchcock ignored this advice, leaving the words in the mouth of the coroner, although Sam Taylor modified the speech slightly, shifting some lines and "changing rhythms."[5] He also softened "son of a bitch" to "son of a . . .," an appellation that was eventually cut at the suggestion of the Production Code office.[6]

Taylor later said he suspected that the speech in question, which was designed to highlight and intensify Scottie's feelings of guilt, was written by Hitchcock himself, since its moralizing tone was unlike anything else written by the other screenwriters who had preceded Taylor.[7]

Close on the heels of the lawyers, the Production Code office weighed in on the submitted script. The censors had their own list of demands:

- Eliminate the early banter between Scottie and Midge concerning brassiere design and Midge's love life.
- Eliminate a few "damn its" and a "cat house" reference.
- Avoid photographing any "intimate undergarments" hanging on the cord in Scottie's kitchen following Madeleine's attempted drowning.
- Play down Scottie's embarrassment at having undressed the unconscious Madeleine before putting her to bed and eliminate the pause in Scottie's line, "Not at all. I enjoyed . . . talking to you."
- Omit all indications of sexual relations between Scottie and Madeleine and later between Scottie and Judy.
- Eliminate scenes that are "objectionably lustful" or feature "open-mouth kissing."
- Note that it is "most important that the indication that Elster will be brought back for trial is sufficiently emphasized."[8]

Aside from eliminating a few profanities, Hitchcock ignored most of the censors' suggestions in preparing the final shooting script. At this stage of his career, his reputation was secure, and he was confident in his ability to bargain with the Code office, whose power was beginning to decline. If Code officials asked him to take a piece out of the finished film, he would counter with a give-and-take that allowed him to keep something else in. Eliminating questionable material at the script stage robbed him of bargaining chips once the censors had viewed the finished film.

In their review of the revised shooting script, the censors reiterated their concerns regarding Scottie's embarrassment over undressing Madeleine, the filming of undergarments in his kitchen, and any suggestion of an illicit relationship between Scottie and Madeleine or Judy. The head of the Code office, Geoffrey Shurlock, was so concerned about the intimation of illicit sex that he issued specific directorial instructions to Hitchcock regarding the dissolve following Scottie and Madeleine's prolonged oceanside kiss in a cypress cove, recommending that "the scene should conclude on the couple and not pan away to the pounding waves."[9]

Hitchcock followed this instruction to the letter, ending the scene with a dissolve on Scottie and Madeleine—but only after photographing the pounding waves prominently in the background as the two kiss.

Hitchcock also took extreme care with the first kiss shared by Scottie and Judy in her apartment after he has remade her in Madeleine's image. The "revolving kiss," one of the most famous shots in the director's body of work, depicts Scottie's mixed emotions and memories as the two embrace. The camera appears to circle the pair while the background moves in a slow pan from Judy's apartment to the San Juan Bautista stable where Scottie and Madeleine parted, and back again to the apartment. In actuality, the camera barely moves as the two embrace on a turntable and the moving background is projected on a transparency behind them. As the scene was planned, James Stewart was to lean farther and farther forward, pressing Kim Novak backward as if they were going to lie down together. But movement on the turntable proved to be so awkward that Stewart slipped and fell on the second take, causing a one-hour delay while he visited the studio doctor.[10] When Stewart returned, Hitchcock finally captured the emotional scene, ending with a close-up of the actors' faces instead of a final descent below camera range. Thus any suggestion of subsequent sex was averted, not by the censors' admonitions but by the awkward logistics of the shot itself. Lest there be any doubt about what transpired, though, in the very next scene Judy emerges from the bathroom wearing a fresh evening dress and greeting Scottie with the words, "Hello, my love."

The Production Code stricture that crime cannot be made attractive or go unpunished led the Code office to insist that the script emphasize that the wife murderer Gavin Elster will be brought back for trial.[11] Hitchcock and Taylor made a show of accommodating this dictum by writing a final scene in which Midge is shown listening to a radio news announcement that Elster's arrest and extradition from France are imminent. She shuts off the radio when a grim Scottie walks into her apartment, and she silently fixes him a drink. The two then stare out her window at the lights of San Francisco, still without speaking. Hitchcock filmed this extraneous scene and tacked it on after the heartrending view of Scottie staring down empty-armed from the bell tower. The director wisely cut the extra footage after the first editorial viewing, but was forced to include it in foreign prints to satisfy the censorship boards of other countries. Other countries did not always include the ending, however. In England, at least, it was included in preview showings, but removed in time for the press viewings and public distribution.[12]

The tacked-on ending can be viewed as a bonus feature on the remastered *Vertigo* DVD in the Universal Legacy Series, which includes the comment that Hitchcock was "absolutely correct" in scrubbing it from the domestic release.[13] It's likely that the director never intended the additional scene to be used at all. After reporting on Elster's imminent capture, the radio announcer starts to describe the fate of three University of California sophomores who were caught leading a cow up the steps of their dormitory when Midge turns the broadcast off. This news hardly fits the somber scene that follows, a sign that Hitchcock created it as a sop for the censors and never expected it to be exposed to the light of commercial projectors. Even though it was shown only on foreign screens, the tacked-on scene desecrates the perfect ending of a powerful film and demonstrates the difficulty of strict adherence to the strictures of a censorship code.

Vertigo marked the second Hitchcock movie in a row with a downbeat ending and one of the first in which the unhappy ending was fictional, not dictated by real-life events, as with *The Wrong Man*. In the words of Hitchcock biographer Patrick McGilligan, "For the first time, a Hitchcock love story would end pathetically, with the abject failure of the hero and the death of the leading lady."[14] Hitchcock had always argued that he could

The final shot of *Vertigo*'s domestic release, showing James Stewart staring helplessly down at his dead lover.

make his audience accept an unhappy ending, but he rarely tested this claim in practice.[15] In the case of *Vertigo,* the initial public and critical response suggested he was wrong. The film made a profit, earning $3.2 million in domestic receipts against a $2.3 million cost, but the box-office returns were significantly lower than they had been for any of his other Paramount films except *The Trouble with Harry.*

Critics in the more prominent media outlets tended to be hard on the film. John McCarten in the *New Yorker* called it "far-fetched nonsense," and *Time* rated the movie as just "another Hitchcock-and-bull story in which the mystery is not so much who done it but who cares."[16] Bosley Crowther gave *Vertigo* a positive review in the *New York Times,* calling it "deviously farfetched," but *Newsweek* came down hard on its implausibility, claiming that Hitchcock had "overdone his deviousness, overreached the limits of credibility and . . . in his plot twists, passed beyond the point of no return."[17]

Appreciation for *Vertigo* has grown over time. This has happened with many Hitchcock films, but rarely has the gulf between the initial response and the current acclaim been so great as with this film. *Vertigo* is one of the five films owned by Hitchcock and withheld from recirculation until 1983. Shortly after its rerelease, a few critics, including Donald Spoto and Robin Wood, ranked it as Hitchcock's defining masterpiece.[18] And in 2012, a poll of critics taken every ten years by *Sight and Sound* magazine voted it the best film of all time. Over the years, *Vertigo* has risen steadily in the *Sight and Sound* polls. It is not a cozy film, but one that rewards repeated viewings, and the proliferation of VCRs, DVDs, and streaming has made repeated viewings more and more possible for critics and cinema addicts. By the time of the 2002 poll, the movie trailed *Citizen Kane* for the top spot by only five votes, but in 2012 the number of critics polled by the magazine tripled to 850 and *Vertigo* supplanted *Kane* at the top of the list of all-time greats.[19]

Nonetheless, it's a little difficult for most viewers, even Hitchcock admirers, to accord *Vertigo* the highest pedestal in the all-time pantheon of films. (Critic Richard Schickel, an avowed fan of the director, writes, "I wouldn't go that far.")[20] And for Hitchcock's nemeses, the "plausibles," it isn't even the best Hitchcock film. The implausibility of the plot keeps getting in the way. Hitchcock himself bolstered the argument of the "plausibles" by acknowledging a central flaw in the story: there is no way that the conniving Elster can be certain that Scottie won't make it all the way up the bell-tower stairs on his first try.[21] After all, he makes it on his second try dragging Judy with him. And added to that uncertainty, there's the difficulty of managing the Madeleine look-alike after she has conspired in murder. A man as rich and intelligent as Elster could come up with hundreds of more likely schemes for ridding himself of his wife—hiring a hit man, arranging a fatal accident, or staging a more convincing suicide that doesn't involve a friend with acrophobia.

Film historian and critic David Thomson suggests that anyone troubled by the movie's implausibilities is not a true "creature of cinema" and should stick to novels.[22] *Vertigo* is a compelling film, but it's not too much to expect a modicum of plausibility from a film ranked as the greatest of all time. Roger Ebert's judgment that "*Vertigo* is one of the two or three best films Hitchcock ever made" seems like a more balanced assessment.[23]

The ban on unpunished crime had an adverse impact on more of Hitchcock's films than almost any other Code provision. Starting with *Rebecca*, the rule that evildoers must be punished had seriously weakened such diverse films as *Suspicion, The Paradine Case, Strangers on a Train,* and *I Confess. Vertigo* marked the first case in which Hitchcock managed to deflect its impact, even if most of the overseas market endured the tacked-on ending. Still, it was a major victory, reflecting both the increase in the director's power and the decline of the Code's influence.

31

North by Northwest (1959)

Synopsis*. New York advertising executive Roger Thornhill (Cary Grant) is mistaken for a government agent named George Kaplan by a group of spies led by Philip Vandamm (James Mason). The spies attempt to kill Thornhill by force-feeding him bourbon and sending him off on a treacherous road behind the wheel of a sports car. Thornhill manages to escape with only a DUI charge, but his troubles soon multiply when, trying to locate Vandamm, he is framed for the murder of a diplomat in the United Nations building.*

Thornhill escapes New York by rail headed for Chicago, when he meets a mysterious blonde, Eve Kendall (Eva Marie Saint), who shelters and seduces him in her overnight compartment. In Chicago, Eve sends Thornhill to a desolate Indiana cornfield, ostensibly to meet Kaplan, where he barely escapes strafing by a crop-dusting plane. On the run from both thugs and the police, Thornhill is contacted by an American spymaster, "the Professor" (Leo G. Carroll), who informs him that his doppelganger Kaplan was a fake identity concocted to draw attention from their real operative, Eve Kendall, who has infiltrated Vandamm's organization as his mistress.

Thornhill agrees to continue posing as Kaplan and follows Eve to Vandamm's South Dakota home, which borders on Mount Rushmore. When Vandamm's chief lieutenant, Leonard (Martin Landau), exposes Eve as a spy, Thornhill helps her escape, and Leonard chases them over the presidential faces of Mount Rushmore. Leonard falls to his death and the Professor apprehends Vandamm, leaving Eve and Thornhill to return from their cross-country chase by rail as a married couple.

***

As Hitchcock was readying *North by Northwest* for production, *Variety* noted, "It's open season on the Production Code and the set of morality standards appears to be the target of brickbats from various directions."[1] The relaxation of public standards was accompanied by an added leniency within the Code office as Joe Breen's successor, Geoffrey Shurlock, proved to be much more accommodating to the studios, particularly when dealing with directors he admired, like Hitchcock. As he had in directing *Vertigo*, Hitchcock took full advantage of this leniency in bucking Code recommendations regarding sexuality, marriage, and divorce when filming *North by Northwest.*

North by Northwest came from an original screenplay by Ernest Lehman, who worked closely with the director to incorporate such familiar Hitchcock touches as a wrongly accused man chased cross-country by both the police and a sleek and sinister group of villains. The movie features such justifiably famous set pieces as the crop-duster assault on Cary Grant and the final pursuit of Grant and Eva Marie Saint across Mount Rushmore.

The concept of the movie actually began with the final sequence on Mount Rushmore. "Hitchcock always wanted to do a chase across Mount Rushmore . . . it was a goal we had to get to," Lehman told an interviewer. "Who was getting there, and why, who was chasing whom, and why—that was all a total mystery. Mount Rushmore was a shadowy, distant objective that, in a way, gave impetus to the creating of the movie."[2] After considering a number of geographical plot options, Hitchcock and Lehman decided to start with a murder at the United Nations building in New York and proceed in a northwesterly direction to South Dakota.

The initial letter from the Production Code office to MGM upon reviewing the first ninety pages of the script was that the "material seems acceptable under the requirements of the Production Code."[3] In this and follow-up letters, though, Code officials expressed concern regarding three key issues:

1. The possible homosexuality of Leonard, the Vandamm henchman played by Martin Landau; Code officials noted that the "description of Leonard and the stage directions characterize him as 'effeminate.' . . . If there is any inference whatever in your finished picture that the man is homosexual, we will be unable to approve it under the requirements of the production code."[4]
2. Roger Thornhill's status as a twice-divorced man. In a subsequent letter to MGM, Code administrator Geoffrey Shurlock noted, "We urge and recommend that the dialogue about previous marriages and divorces be eliminated."[5]
3. Any hint that Eve Kendall might be a woman of loose morals; this concern continued throughout the review process. In his initial let-

> ter, Shurlock noted that the "scenes in the dining car and drawing room should be handled in such a way as not to be offensively sex suggestive. . . . The girl's line 'I never make love on an empty stomach' is unacceptably sex suggestive and the exchange should simply be omitted."[6] And in a later letter, Shurlock added, "We do very seriously question the advisability of identifying your leading lady as Vandamm's mistress."[7]

Hitchcock finished principal photography in December 1958 and fought a "running battle" with the Production Code office the following January and February, meeting with the censors, listening to their objections, and horse trading where necessary.[8] In the end, he managed to satisfy their concerns regarding Leonard's effeminacy, Thornhill's divorce history, and the relations between Thornhill and Eve while sacrificing very little of the original script and completed footage.

Martin Landau's portrayal of Leonard is not openly effeminate and contains none of the limp-wristed, offensive stereotypes offered by such character actors as Franklin Pangborn in the 1930s and 1940s. If there is a single word to describe Landau's performance, it is "sinister." Still, there are more subtle shadings of Leonard's character that fulfill the stage directions. Hitchcock had Landau outfitted by Cary Grant's personal tailor, making him one of the best-dressed henchmen in movie history.[9] And the dialogue between Leonard and Vandamm when Leonard suspects Eve is a plant speaks volumes. When Vandamm asks if Leonard has any proof of his suspicions, Leonard replies, "Call it my woman's intuition." Vandamm's incredulous response is "You know what I think? I think you're jealous." When Leonard scowls, Vandamm adds, "No. I mean it! I'm very touched. Very."

So the signs are there for anyone alert enough to pick up on them, strong enough to illuminate Leonard's motives, but subtle enough to slip by the censors and, in all likelihood, a high percentage of filmgoers in the 1950s (including this author as a teenager), who weren't accustomed to seeing homosexuality portrayed subtly. Or, thanks to the Production Code, at all.

Production Code authorities were worried that the somewhat casual attitude Thornhill expresses toward his past divorces might offend Catholic moviegoers. Yet the original script references to the topic were retained as written. When the Professor first asks that Thornhill continue to pretend to be the spy Kaplan in order to deflect suspicion from Eve, he responds, "Now wait a minute, you listen to me! I'm an advertising man, not a red herring. I've got a job, a secretary, a mother, two ex-wives, and several bartenders dependent on me, and I don't intend to disappoint them all by getting myself slightly killed."

In their initial review, the Production Code officials characterized the "ex-wives" reference as "gratuitous" and asked that it be omitted.[10] Far from being gratuitous, Thornhill's marital history is part and parcel of his previous self-centered existence, which makes his ultimate decision to play the red herring and risk his own life to rescue Eve all the more dramatic. Following the Code's suggestion that all references to Thornhill's previous marriages be omitted would erase the primary evidence of the character's growth over the course of the film.

Another reference to Thornhill's rocky romantic past, played for laughs, actually supports the sanctity of marriage. When Eve and Thornhill meet in the forest prior to her unmasking, Eve tells him that one reason she has remained single and was open to the job of spying for her country was "men like you."

When Thornhill responds, "What's wrong with men like me?" Eve answers, "They don't believe in marriage."

As the two embrace, Thornhill defends himself, saying, "I've been married twice," to which Eve responds, "See what I mean?"

Case closed.

Against the Code's wishes, the film explicitly identifies Eve as Vandamm's mistress. One of the Code's other concerns, the dining car repartee in which Eve tells Thornhill, "I never make love on an empty stomach" was, however, excised from the finished film. Hitchcock originally filmed this dialogue as written in the script, but subsequently agreed to overdub the line so that Eve is heard to say "I never discuss love on an empty stomach." Lip readers can still see Eva Marie Saint's lips forming the offending lines, risking whatever depravity might befall them for acquiring that knowledge.

In the spirit of horse trading, Hitchcock swapped the dubbed line in order to salvage the suggestion that Thornhill and Eve spend the night together in her compartment.[11] The upper berth of the compartment, where Thornhill hides from the police searching the train on the way to Chicago, figures in the next-to-last scene in the film, in which Thornhill

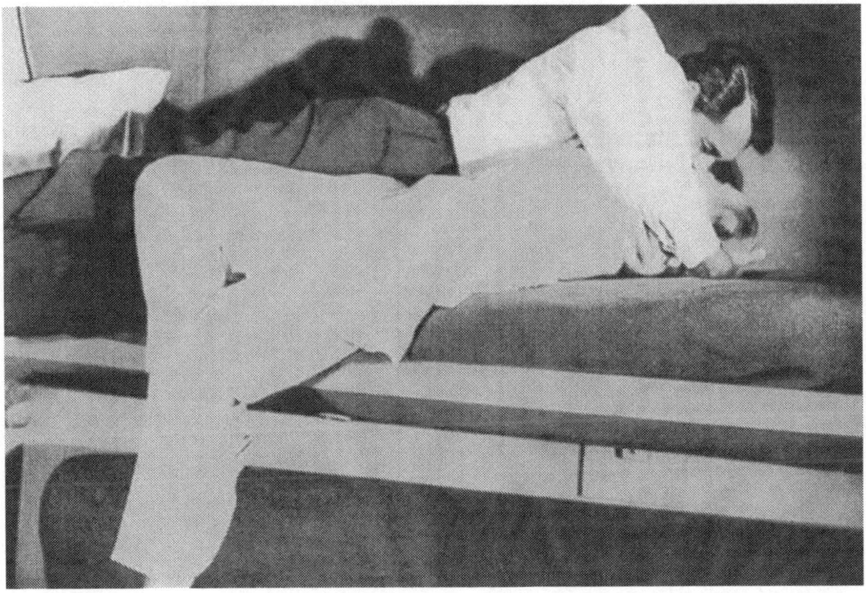

Although Hitchcock honored the Production Code request that Cary Grant and Eva Marie Saint maintain at least a forty-five-degree angle between themselves and the upper berth in the film, this production still shows the couple nearly horizontal.

pulls Eve up into the berth on their return from South Dakota. Eve is dressed in white pajamas, violating another Code request that both parties be in their "day clothes."[12] Code administrator Geoffrey Shurlock suggested that this scene would be acceptable if Thornhill were to say, "Come along, Mrs. Thornhill," as he helps her up, indicating that the pair had been legitimately married since the fracas on Mount Rushmore and thus were on morally solid ground in exercising their berth rite.[13] Hitchcock agreed and looped the welcoming line over a close-up of Eva Marie Saint as she is pulled into the upper berth. Shurlock also insisted that the angle between the couple and the bed not dip below forty-five degrees as they embrace. While Hitchcock honored this suggestion, publicity stills for the scene show Cary Grant and Eva Marie Saint completely horizontal.

The over-dubbed line about making love on an empty stomach wasn't the only bit of racy repartee in the dining room scene. Shortly after Thornhill joins her, Eve tells him, "It's going to be a long night," adding, "And I don't particularly like the book I've started," before pointedly asking, "Do you know what I mean?" It's unlikely that the Code office under

Joe Breen would have let this exchange go by unchallenged, but Geoffrey Shurlock was far more lenient than his predecessor, especially in dealing with premier directors like Hitchcock.

Another example of Code slippage may be found by comparing the controversial kissing scene between Cary Grant and Ingrid Bergman in the earlier film *Notorious* with a similar scene between Grant and Eva Marie Saint in *North by Northwest.* In both scenes, Hitchcock lets his camera linger on the embracing couple, circling the lovers in *Notorious* and watching the lovers themselves circle each other in *North by Northwest.* In *Notorious,* though, he was careful to make sure that no single kiss lasted longer than the three seconds believed to be the Code limit. Over ten years later, in *North by Northwest,* on the other hand, the couples' lips remain locked for as long as sixteen seconds. So long as the protagonists remained "attired in day clothes," per the censors' written request, the length of the kiss did not seem to concern the Code administrators.[14] "In the love scene, neither Cary Grant or myself took off our clothes, and it was a very sexy scene," recalled Eva Marie Saint.[15]

All of this seems very tame by today's standards. One aspect of the Code's morality, though, still appears to be in effect over fifty years later. Whereas male spies like James Bond gleefully hop from bed to bed, reaping secrets as they sow satisfaction, films in which top-billed female characters are asked to obtain intelligence by sleeping with the enemy are still relatively rare, and are primarily set in time of war (for example, *Mata Hari, The Black Book, Head in the Clouds*). Yet Hitchcock successfully sent his heroines into this breach twice, with Ingrid Bergman in *Notorious* and Eva Marie Saint in *North by Northwest.*

Hitchcock openly flouted the Production Code with a last-minute change in the film's final scene. In the shooting script reviewed by Code administrators, the final shot of the film is described as a shot "toward the end of the observation car as the train rolls off into the night."[16] Instead, just before the final negative was completed, Hitchcock requested a shot of the train going into a tunnel, and that blatantly metaphorical shot, appearing just after Roger Thornhill pulls Eve Kendall into the upper berth, fills the final frames of the film. Thus, in the words of film expert Bill Krohn, "The last shot of *North by Northwest* is the most explicit depiction of the bottom-line facts of the sexual act ever pulled off under the Production Code."[17]

When asked about the last-minute switch, screenwriter Ernest Lehman pleaded innocence, saying he knew nothing about it, but wished he had thought of it.[18] Hitchcock himself acknowledged authorship in an interview following the Paris opening of the film. In response to a question on symbols and expressionism, he said, "There are no symbols in *North by Northwest.* Oh yes! One. The last shot, the train entering the tunnel after the love scene between Grant and Eva Marie Saint. It's a phallic symbol. But don't tell anyone."[19]

The Production Code wasn't the only organization to exercise external control over the filming of *North by Northwest.* Both the United Nations and the US Department of the Interior imposed restrictions that shaped the final film. The United Nations prohibited filming either inside the UN building or on its grounds. Hitchcock managed to work around this prohibition by surreptitiously using a camera concealed in a van across the street from UN Headquarters to film a scene of Cary Grant entering the building. Shots within the building, including the scene in which Grant is framed for the knifing of a diplomat, were filmed by using still photographs of the actual interiors to create mock-ups in the MGM studio.

Restrictions imposed by the Department of the Interior proved to be even more limiting. The department refused to allow gunshots or violent scenes either on Mount Rushmore itself or with the monument in the background. Hitchcock agreed to this condition and proposed to solve the problem by creating a studio mock-up and filming the action in the space between the sculpted heads. However, the Department of the Interior would give its permission for the use of a mock-up only on the condition that "only the shoulder, or below the chin line of the presidents' likenesses be used in a close-up of the actors."[20] This last condition made it impossible for Hitchcock to film the gag that had attracted him to Mount Rushmore in the first place. The director had envisioned a scene in which a fugitive hiding in Lincoln's nose would give himself away when he was seized by a sneezing fit. In fact, for a short time, the production was known by the name "The Man in Lincoln's Nose."[21] Even with all its conditions met, the Department of the Interior asked to have its name removed from the credits because, as Hitchcock reported, the reasoning went that "even if nothing was shot on the monument, the public will still think it was shot there."[22]

North by Northwest was an immediate hit with the public and most critics. Although the budget grew from the original $3 million estimate to $4.3 million, the film took in $6 million in North American alone.[23] With one notable exception, critics loved the film. That one exception was Stanley Kaufmann in the *New Republic,* who wrote that the movie starts "promisingly but soon loses us in cliché and preposterousness."[24] Conversely, both the major newsmagazines of the day reviewed it positively, with *Time* calling it "smartly trowelled and thoroughly entertaining" and *Newsweek* finding it shiny, colorful, and "slick, slick, slick."[25] A. H. Weiler wrote in the *New York Times* that it was "suspenseful and delightful," and Hollis Alpert of the *Saturday Review* called it funny and macabre and "much the best Hitchcock that has come along in years."[26] The *Cahiers du cinéma* crowd, whose New Wave directors were the first to take Hitchcock seriously, pronounced it a "masterpiece."[27]

Over time, two of the film's scenes, the crop-dusting sequence and the chase across Mount Rushmore, have come to be listed among Hitchcock's most brilliant set pieces. Although the Production Code initially voiced reservations regarding Leonard's homosexuality, Thornhill's divorces, and the suggestiveness of the scenes between Thornhill and Eve Kendall, few of their objections were reflected in the finished film. In fact, by refusing to let Hitchcock film Cary Grant sneezing in Lincoln's nose, the Department of the Interior probably did more to shape the final product than the toned-down Production Code.

32

Psycho (1960)

Synopsis. *In Phoenix, Marion Crane (Janet Leigh) steals $40,000 from her employer and drives to California to join her lover Sam Loomis (John Gavin), hoping to use the money to clear his debts so they can be married. Encountering a violent storm, she strays from the main road and stops off at a dilapidated motel run by Norman Bates (Tony Perkins), a disturbed young man with a mother fixation. After chatting with Norman, Marion decides to return the money, but before she can leave she is stabbed to death in the shower by a woman seen only in shadow. A horrified Norman wraps the body in the shower curtain, and puts it, along with Marion's luggage (unaware it contains the money), in her car, which he sinks in a nearby swamp. When an insurance investigator, Milton Arbogast (Martin Balsam) comes looking for Marion, he too is knifed and Norman again disposes of the body.*

Marion's lover Sam and her sister Lila (Vera Miles) follow Arbogast to the motel, which Sam searches while Lila explores the home above the motel where Norman lives with his mother. She finds the mummified remains of Norman's mother in the fruit cellar, and is surprised by a knife-wielding Norman dressed in his mother's clothes. Sam arrives in time to save Lila and subdue Norman, who has been living with a split personality since killing his mother and her lover ten years earlier.

***

The shower stabbing of Janet Leigh in *Psycho* is unarguably the best-known sequence in all of Hitchcock's films, and was recognized in a 1990s poll of French movie critics and fans as the single most famous scene in motion picture history.[1] The justifiably renowned scene was inspired by Hitchcock's desire to sidestep the restrictions of the Production Code.

Based on a 1959 novel by thriller writer Robert Bloch, *Psycho*'s script follows the book's basic plot fairly closely. But Hitchcock made two important casting decisions that set the film apart from its source. In Bloch's book, Norman Bates is a short, fat "mama's boy." By casting the tall teen idol Tony Perkins in the role, the director gave the character a level of sympathy and interest that didn't exist in the book.

In both the book and the film, the shower killing of Marion Crane (Mary Crane in the book) occurs early in the story, at the end of chapter 3 in the book and on page 52 of the 133-page initial draft of the script. The casting of Janet Leigh, the top-billed star in the film, in the role of Marion ensures that her character's early death will come as a surprise and that her absence will be more deeply felt. In the book, though, the shower murder culminates in Marion's decapitation. Whether they were influenced by the dictates of good taste or the Production Code's admonition against "undue violence," both Hitchcock and screenwriter Joseph Stefano agreed that they "didn't want to see the woman in the shower having her head cut off."[2]

The film's early focus on Marion Crane represents another departure from the book. The film follows Marion from an early-afternoon tryst with her lover to her murder in the shower, when the focus shifts to Norman Bates, who earns the viewer's sympathy for his attempts to cover up a crime apparently committed by his deranged mother. The book's early focus is on Norman, whom Bloch modeled on a real-life murderer, Ed Gein, a Wisconsin farmer who was accused of butchering at least ten women between 1954 and 1957.

Hitchcock had one picture remaining on his contract with Paramount, and the studio was none too happy about sponsoring a picture involving serial killing, nudity, transvestism, violence, and matricide. When it became apparent that Hitchcock was determined to make the picture, Paramount indicated that it was willing to restructure the director's contract and Hitchcock's agent Lew Wasserman was ready with an innovative proposal. Under Wasserman's proposal, Hitchcock would become the film's producer, with Paramount acting as distributor. Hitchcock would hold the production costs charged to Paramount to an agreed-upon amount by filming on the Universal-International lot with the U-I crew he used in his television productions. As the sole producer, Hitchcock would waive his $250,000 director's fee in return for 60 percent ownership of the negative until Paramount earned a set amount of money from a guaranteed percentage of the gross. Once Paramount had realized that amount, all revenues and ownership rights would revert to Hitchcock. Paramount, which saw *Psycho* as a money loser whose unsavory elements would mar the studio's image as it tried to shift its focus to family musicals, readily agreed to Wasserman's terms, terms that would eventually bring millions to his client.

Free from Paramount's oversight, Hitchcock augmented his TV crew with a few regulars from his movie production team and made plans to film *Psycho* in black-and-white on a tight thirty-six-day shooting schedule. The decision to film in black-and-white was made with one eye on the budget and the other on the Production Code—the director feared that the sight of a nude murder victim soaked in red blood might prove too gruesome for the censors. In addition, Hitchcock had admired the black-and-white thriller *Les diaboliques,* a horror film by French director Henri-Georges Clouzot that featured a bathtub murder and had been released in America to great acclaim in 1955.

In its review of the original *Psycho* script, the Code office found that "while the basic story may be acceptable under the provisions of the Production Code, the present version . . . contains one element . . . which would make it impossible to issue a Certificate on a finished film based on this script." The forbidden element was not the shower scene, which at that point existed only on paper and which the Code office did caution "would have to be handled with the utmost discretion and good taste." Instead, the one script element that "would be unacceptable under the Code" was "the very pointed description of an incestuous relationship between Norman and his mother."[3]

Since Norman and his mother are one and the same person throughout the story, it is hard to imagine what an incestuous relationship might look like and how it might be detected. Luckily, the Code reviewers provided examples of dialogue that they felt clearly established the forbidden mother-son relationship that existed before the mother's death. In Stefano's script, Mother referred to Norman as "ever the sweetheart" while objecting to the way he was "always peeping" and "disgusting me with his love." Moreover, the psychiatrist charged with explaining Norman's condition in the penultimate scene characterizes the mother-son relationship as "more that of two adolescent lovers."[4]

Other Code objections to the script included:

- An excess of profanity.
- The oilman Cassidy's line that bed is "the only playground that beats Las Vegas."

- The suggestion that Norman sees Marion partially nude through a peephole.
- The discussion of transvestism.

Screenwriter Stefano convinced the Code officials to allow the use of the word *transvestite* by citing the dictionary definition, which did not necessarily imply sexual deviance, and arguing that the word was used in the script by a psychiatrist who said clearly that, properly speaking, Norman was not a transvestite.[5] Hitchcock excised the instances of profanity cited by the censors (three *damn*s, two *hell*s, and one irreverent *God*), but retained Norman's peephole voyeurism and Cassidy's objectionable speech so that they could be used as bargaining chips to protect his primary concern, Janet Leigh's shower murder.

The shower scene was well worth protecting. It had taken Hitchcock seven days to shoot the seventy-eight pieces of film that he and George Tomasini would edit down to forty-five harrowing seconds depicting the slashing of Marion Crane. After the movie's release, hundreds of viewers reported that the scene left them too frightened to take a shower, and one distraught father asked Hitchcock for advice after writing that his daughter had been afraid to take a bath after watching *Les diaboliques* and was now afraid to shower as well. Hitchcock responded with the suggestion that the man send the girl out to be dry-cleaned.[6]

The director was not so flippant with the Code censors, who exploded upon viewing the initial cut of the film. They found the shower scene, with its fast-paced sequence of shots, "some impressionistic, some completely realistic, of the girl's nude body" to be clearly "in violation of the Code, which prohibits nudity 'in fact or in silhouette.'"[7]

The shower scene wasn't the only reason the Code office refused *Psycho* its Seal of Approval. Censors also objected to

- The lovemaking in the opening scene, which was "entirely too passionate."
- The oilman's comment on bed as a playground.
- Norman's seeing Marion partially nude through a peephole prior to the knife attack.
- Marion flushing the toilet to dispose of her calculations regarding the stolen funds.[8]

Hitchcock already had his sacrificial pawns lined up for battle when he was informed of the censor's objections. Janet Leigh recalled, "He told me how he had planned all along to manipulate the censors by deliberately putting in things so bizarre, he could come back to them and say, 'Tsk tsk. All right. I'll take *that* out, but you've got to give me this.'"[9]

First to go was the remark the censors had objected to at the script stage. After saying he planned to celebrate his successful real estate deal with a trip to Las Vegas, the oilman Cassidy responds to Marion's comment that she had a headache and would be going home to bed with the pointed observation, "Bed. The only playground that beats Las Vegas." The response was a little too pointed for the censors, and Hitchcock willingly excised it. Since the director cared much less about dialogue than about montage, it's safe to assume he let the remark survive the script review just so he could make a show of removing it from the final print.

Hitchcock had arranged a series of paired shots showing Norman looking through a peephole at Janet Leigh as she undresses. The first pair of shots showed Norman's eye at the peephole, followed by the peephole view of Marion in her black bra and half slip. The second pair showed Norman's eye at the peephole, followed by his view of Marion removing the bra. Hitchcock agreed to replace the bra removal with a shot of Marion in her robe, an apparent victory for the censors.[10] By leaving two peephole shots in, however, the director successfully sidestepped the Code restrictions on voyeurism.

Another Code restriction cautioned against setting scenes in bathrooms. Hitchcock had run into this finicky restriction before, in films as disparate as *The Secret Agent* and *Mr. and Mrs. Smith.* Even when bathroom scenes were allowed, filmmakers were advised not to show toilets. In *Psycho,* Marion Crane not only uses the toilet to dispose of her handwritten calculations of the disposition of the stolen money, but actually flushes it, a sight and sound unheard of in Code-era films. Hitchcock and Stefano managed to salvage the sequence by arguing that it was necessary to the plot. Not only did Marion's use of the flush lever symbolize her remorse, but the surviving scrap of paper became an important clue documenting her presence at the motel.

Most of the images that censors objected to in the shower scene flashed by so fast that viewers couldn't be certain whether or not they were seeing nudity. In one long shot, however, Hitchcock pulled the camera up and back to capture an overhead view of Marion sprawled across the side of the

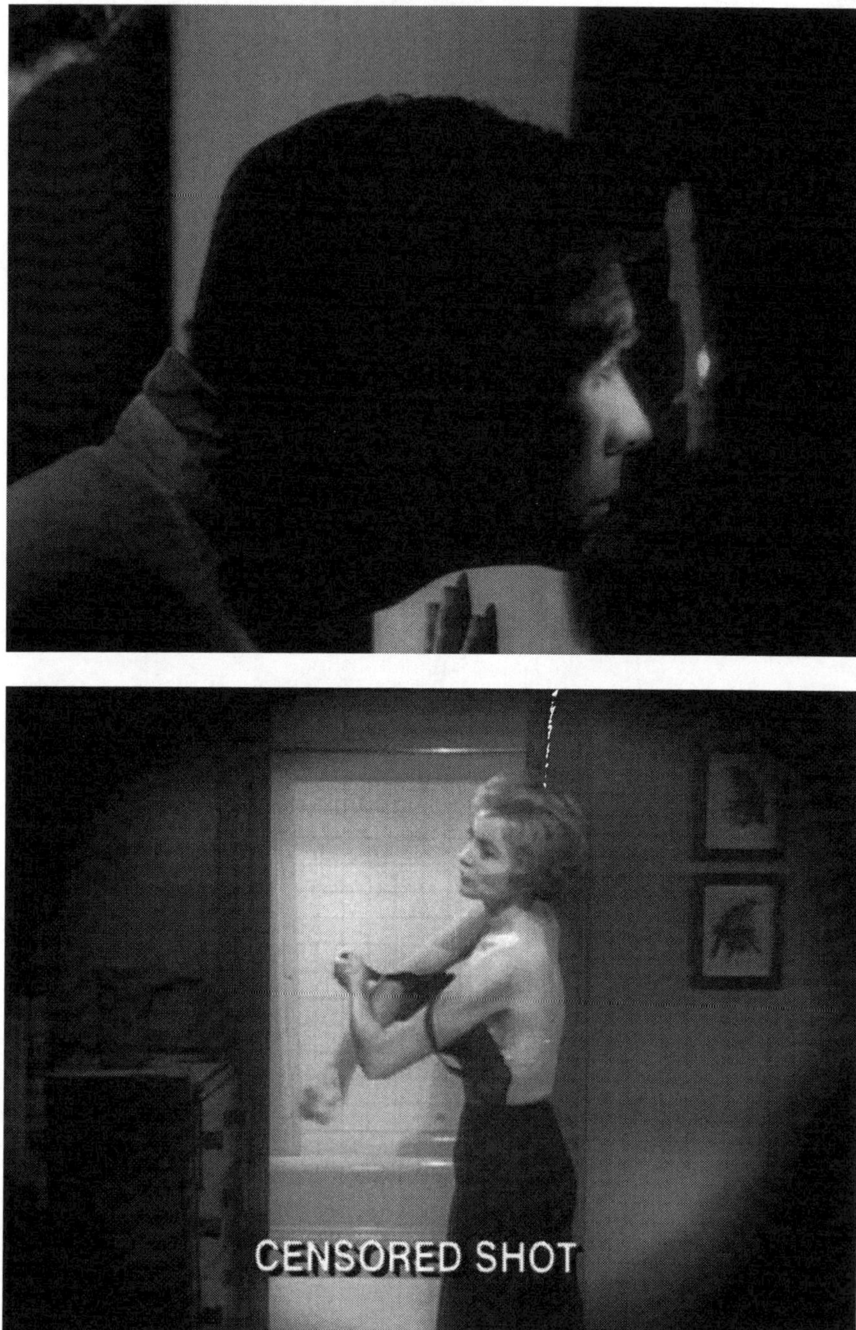

The censored shot of Janet Leigh removing her bra was replaced by a shot of her in her robe, but the forbidden suggestion of voyeurism remained.

tub. In the eyes of screenwriter Stefano, this was the most heartbreaking shot of the sequence because it showed the vulnerability of the victim, whom the viewer "had cared about all through the movie up to this point, and there she was lying there dead."[11] Unfortunately, the shot not only showed the victim's vulnerability but also her bare buttocks, and Hitchcock surrendered it to the censors. The Code reviewers couldn't agree on whether the rapid cuts of the murder itself actually showed nudity or merely suggested it. Three of five initial reviewers insisted they saw nudity; two did not. The Code office sent the film back to Hitchcock, instructing him to remove the nudity. The director apologized profusely, promised to do his best to comply, and sent the sequence back to the reviewers without changing a single frame. This time the three censors who had seen nudity before no longer spotted it, but the two who hadn't seen it now did.

The debate over who had seen what or how much dragged on for nearly a week. Script supervisor Marshall Schlom recalled, "Finally, Mr. Hitchcock said 'I will take out the nudity if you will allow me to keep the two people in bed in the opening scene.'"[12] After the censors refused to agree to this, the director made another offer. If the Code office would allow him to keep the shower scene, he would reshoot the opening lovemaking scene, with the proviso that the censors show up on set to point out any objectionable passages. When the censors failed to show up for the scheduled reshoot, the opening scene was left unchanged. And the Code officials finally agreed that the removal of the one indisputable instance of nudity from the shower scene, the overhead shot of Marion Crane's bare buttocks, was enough to earn the Code's Seal of Approval.

Possibly in deference to the Code decision to give *Psycho* its Seal, the Legion of Decency stopped short of condemning the film, giving it a B rating as "morally objectionable in part for all." Low as its rating was, just one level above "Condemned," it was high enough to represent another victory for Hitchcock over censorship.

With the censors mollified, Hitchcock turned to the marketing of *Psycho.* Concerned that prerelease audiences might reveal the ending and kill the suspense for later viewers, he refused to show the picture in advance to critics and other opinion makers such as columnists, radio commentators, and TV show hosts. This decision flew in the face of conventional industry wisdom and angered a few critics who resented having to stand in line with the general public.

Hitchcock created even more controversy by announcing he'd forbid theaters to seat any audience members after the movie started. At the time of *Psycho*'s release, it was not uncommon for patrons to arrive at the theater any time they wanted. If they missed the beginning, they would simply sit through the remainder of the film and wait for the next showing to watch the part they'd missed. Hitchcock worried that latecomers would wonder why they weren't seeing Janet Leigh, the ostensible star of the film. To forestall this, newspaper and magazine ads insisted that "no one . . . BUT NO ONE . . . will be admitted to the theater after the start of each performance of *Psycho.*"[13] Hitchcock demanded that any exhibitor booking the film enforce this decree.

At first, theater owners were outraged, fearing that frustrated patrons who were turned away would not return, leaving a lot of empty seats. But the exhibitors changed their tune when long lines began to form so that viewers could be sure to see the show from the beginning, and seats were filled when the Paramount mountain announced the start of the film.

Psycho was a box-office hit from the day it opened. Its first US engagements pulled in $9.5 million, and overseas receipts brought in an additional $6 million. Only *Ben-Hur,* the eventual Academy Award winner, did better, but it cost $15 million, as opposed to *Psycho*'s budget of $800,000, making the Hitchcock film easily the most profitable release of the year.

Psycho's popularity helped to bring it four Academy Award nominations: Hitchcock for Best Director; Janet Leigh for Best Supporting Actress; John L. Russell for black-and-white cinematography; and Joseph Hurley, Robert Clatworthy, and George Milo for black-and-white art decoration and set decoration. Not one of them took home an Oscar. It was Hitchcock's fifth nomination without a win. He would never be nominated again.

Critical response at the time varied. *Newsweek* allowed that there were "sporadic chills" and noted that while the "climactic scenes are standardly spooky and contrived," Hitchcock had "milked every drop of excitement from that early stretch—aided and abetted by fine performances from Perkins and Miss Leigh and from a shot of a shower head squirting directly down at the camera."[14]

Several critics mentioned the lack of advance showings and the "see it from the start" requirement in their coverage of the film. At least one reviewer admitted that his opinion was colored by the need to wait in line to see the film in a commercial theater. And Dilys Powell of the *London*

Times spent six paragraphs chronicling the difficulty of getting in to see the film before closing with a paragraph admitting she was "loco about *Psycho.*"[15] Not every critic was "loco about *Psycho.*" Dwight MacDonald denounced the movie in *Esquire* as "a reflection of an unpleasant mind, a mean, sly, sadistic little mind."[16]

A few critics changed their opinion of the film in the wake of the controversy surrounding its first-run showings. Bosley Crowther of the *New York Times* initially described *Psycho* as "old fashioned" and lacking "an abundance of subtlety."[17] But the hullabaloo over the movie caused him to upgrade it to "fascinating" and "provocative" a month after it opened. In a special Sunday piece entitled "An Answer to Those Filmgoers Who Think *Psycho* Should Be Banned," Crowther wrote that Hitchcock invested the film "with conspicuous cinematic artistry in which the power of visual suggestion is used more often than the full-view attack."[18]

Crowther's conversion mirrors the growing appreciation for *Psycho* over the years. *Time,* which had characterized it as "gruesome" and a "creak and shriek movie" upon its release in 1960, was calling it a classic by 1965.[19] And by 2007, *Psycho* was ranked fourteenth on the American Film Institute's list of the one hundred greatest American films of all time.

Psycho's high ranking is due in no small part to Hitchcock's direction of Janet Leigh's murder scene. And the impact of the scene is due in no small part to the constraints the Production Code placed on Hitchcock. Forbidden to show either explicit nudity or the penetrating blade, the director assembled seventy-eight pieces of film that left a lasting impression of violence and vulnerability in the minds of viewers. Years after starring in the shower scene, Janet Leigh reflected on the impact of the Production Code on its popularity. "*Psycho* has endured because of the restrictions they put on us. . . . And because Mr. Hitchcock had to come up with a suspense story without showing what today is normal. He allowed the audience to create what they thought they saw. When the audience becomes a part of the creative process, they aren't going to forget."[20]

33

The Birds (1963)

Synopsis. *Wealthy playgirl Melanie Daniels (Tippi Hedren) meets Mitch Brenner (Rod Taylor), a young lawyer, in a San Francisco pet shop. She is attracted to him and travels to the Bodega Bay home of his mother, Lydia Brenner (Jessica Tandy), where Mitch is spending the weekend, taking with her two small lovebirds for his little sister Cathy as a birthday present.*

As Melanie crosses the bay in a rented motorboat, a lone seagull swoops down on her, gashing her forehead. Alarmed, she is persuaded to spend the night in Bodega Bay, where she finds lodging with Annie Hayworth (Suzanne Pleshette), a local schoolteacher and former flame of Mitch's, who warns Melanie of Lydia's possessive nature.

At the children's birthday party the next day, gulls swoop down on the picnicking children, forcing them to take cover indoors. And that evening, hundreds of sparrows plunge down the chimney of the Brenner home, terrifying the inhabitants.

The inexplicable bird invasions continue, first killing a neighboring farmer and then Annie as she tries to protect a group of fleeing schoolchildren from attacking crows. Downtown Bodega Bay is devastated, and Melanie seeks shelter in the Brenner home with Mitch, Lydia, and Cathy. During a lull in the avian assaults, Melanie explores the home attic, where she is savagely attacked by flocks of birds breaking through a hole in the roof. Mitch rescues her, gathers her and his family into Melanie's convertible, and drives slowly away through an ominous array of birds stretching as far as the eye can see.

***

The Production Code Administration insisted that Hitchcock consult with the American Humane Association throughout the shooting of *The Birds*. The Humane Association's oversight, coupled with the director's decision to finance the project himself—a decision prompted by the financial success of *Psycho*—had a significant impact on the finished film.

The Birds was not released until 1963, three years after *Psycho*, the longest span between pictures in Hitchcock's career to that point. In the interim, the director was busy promoting *Psycho,* attending to his TV show, negotiating to bring Princess Grace of Monaco back into movies, and trying to find a property that could top what had been the best-received film of his career.

Two newspaper stories in the early 1960s led him to that property. While he was preparing for a worldwide tour promoting *Psycho,* Hitchcock read a newspaper account of an incident in which a flock of a thousand birds had plunged down a chimney in La Jolla, California, wrecking the home and injuring the owner. And on his return from the tour, Santa Cruz, California, which was near Hitchcock's Northern California retreat, was invaded by thousands of birds driven inland by fog. The *Santa Cruz Sentinel* headlined, "Thousands of Birds Flounder in Streets" after crashing into cars and homes, creating havoc among the local population.[1]

The two news stories reminded Hitchcock of a Daphne du Maurier novella *The Birds,* which had been published in one of the director's anthologies, *My Favorites in Suspense.* The moody du Maurier story involved an epidemic of murderous avian attacks along the Cornish coast as experienced by a peasant farmer and his family.

Hitchcock already had the film rights to the story and hired Evan Hunter, a successful novelist and mystery writer (under the pseudonym Ed McBain), to produce a screenplay. Hunter transposed the novella's actions from the Cornish coast to Bodega Bay, a small town about sixty miles northwest of San Francisco, and introduced a love story between a spoiled rich daughter of a newspaper owner and a San Francisco lawyer whose mother owns a farm in Bodega Bay.

The only elements of du Maurier's original story that remained intact in the screenplay were the title and the bird attacks. Hitchcock had plunged into the project without knowing exactly how these attacks would be re-created on the screen, but confident that he and his team could work it out. In today's world, the problem could be handled easily with computer graphics, but the creation of realistic bird attacks proved to be more difficult than Hitchcock had anticipated. The director and his team experimented with mechanical birds, hand puppets, miniatures, stuffed birds, blue-screen effects, painted mattes, and plastic replicas before concluding that the only realistic way to approach the problem was to use live birds.

That decision presented a whole new set of problems. Hitchcock's team had to figure out how to catch, train, and film the birds so that their actions and images could be combined with those of live actors without endangering either the birds or the performers. In the end, the production used twenty-five thousand birds, three thousand of which were trained, including thirty seagulls, two thousand finches, seven hundred English sparrows, fifty ducks, and twenty-five ravens.[2]

Getting the bird images to merge on-screen with live actors also proved to be a problem. While some of the shots could be superimposed, in most cases traveling mattes, or painted backgrounds that change from frame to frame, would be needed to blend the images of birds and actors. A blue-screen process for blending moving images had been developed in 1958, but it often produced a blue halo around the foreground figures and would have turned the images of small birds with fast-moving wings into messy blurs. An older system using sodium vapor lamps to separate colors proved to be more successful in combining foreground and background figures without creating annoying halos. This system could replicate the birds' movements satisfactorily, but it was available only through a rival studio, Walt Disney Productions, which had perfected the process. Hitchcock was forced to lease the process equipment and support technicians from Disney for the shooting of *The Birds.*[3]

While the screenplay was being developed, and before Hitchcock had time to turn his attention to casting, he and his wife, Alma, were watching the *Today Show* over breakfast when a slim, attractive blonde in a commercial for Sego, a diet drink, caught his eye. All the blonde did in the commercial was turn her head amiably in response to a young boy's wolf whistle, but it was enough to fascinate Hitchcock. He had his agents contact the girl, brought her to California, scheduled a series of interviews with Universal executives, and within a week had signed Tippi Hedren to a seven-year contract at $500 per week.

Hitchcock outfitted his new protégée in gowns especially designed by Edith Head and personally coached her through an elaborate series of screen tests involving scenes from *Rebecca, Notorious,* and *To Catch a Thief.* Pleased with the results and his new find's personality, he offered her the lead role in *The Birds.* Universal executives objected to giving such an important role to a newcomer with no acting experience or name recognition, but Hitchcock was confident he could groom Tippi Hedren as a replacement for Grace Kelly on his roster of cool blonde starlets.

The Production Code's comments on the initial script of *The Birds* once again reflected the Code's obsession with sex and violence. After suggesting that Melanie wear a bra and full slip instead of the bra and skirt called for in the script, the censors expressed a serious concern "with one aspect of the unusual story—the gruesome details of the several attacks of the birds on the human beings." Fearing that the attacks "could be presented in such a shocking, brutal, and bloody way as to be unacceptable motion picture fare," they cautioned Hitchcock to "carefully consider this particular aspect as you plan, and eventually execute the staging of the action."[4]

In its subsequent review of the revised shooting script, the Code office found the basic story acceptable under the provisions of the Code, reiterated the caution about avoiding "scenes of excessive gruesomeness" and "any offensive exploitation of the girl's nudity," and advised, "In accordance with the Code requirements," the producers should "consult with Mr. James Jack of the American Humane Association as to all scenes in which animals are used."[5]

The Humane Association reviewed the script and added its input to that of the Code, suggesting that a scene showing Mitch stepping around dozens of dead birds should be carefully supervised and filmed with dummy birds.[6] In the long run, the Humane Association had a much greater impact on the filming of *The Birds* than the Production Code censors. Humane Association representatives were on location for all scenes involving live birds, and an aviary was set up to treat any that were injured. Hitchcock reported that concern for the birds sometimes affected the shooting schedules—when, for example, the Humane Association representative would announce, "That's enough, Mr. Hitchcock, I think the birds are getting tired."[7]

Because seagulls are a protected species, the production company had to obtain a permit to catch and train them. The Department of the Interior's Fish and Wildlife Service issued a six-month permit allowing the company to catch and train no more than thirty live heron gulls and retain twenty dead specimens for use in filming. It took two months to reach the full quota of seagulls, and to supplement the supply, the company also began raising gulls from eggs. With only a few days remaining before filming began, the US Fish and Game Department found that the production company had exceeded its quota, levied a fine of $400, and rescinded the permit. This could have been a major setback, but with the help of other bird collectors, Hitchcock's team managed to circumvent the ban, obtain a new permit, and get the gulls needed for filming.[8]

The shooting of the bird attack on the children's party was interrupted when a bird that had been trained to swoop down on the blindfolded birthday girl slipped its leash and escaped to a mudflat far out in the bay. Because the bird's beak had been wired shut to keep it from injuring the children, its handler feared that it would starve if it could not be recaptured. Filming stopped while the handler pursued the bird onto the mudflat and shooed it back to dry land, where another trainer chased it down.

To avoid similar incidents when shooting reverted to the Los Angeles sound stages, cages or polyethylene walls were constructed around the sets to keep the birds from escaping. During the filming of the attack on the Brenner house, the living room set was enclosed by a polyethylene bubble, and fifteen hundred small birds, primarily sparrows, were forced down the chimney into the set. The bubble was designed to contain the birds and keep them from flying off into the catwalks. Even so, a few escaped and roosted in the rafters, where they created sound problems for subsequent films.

During filming, there were rumors that birds were being mistreated on the set, and Humane Association officials wrote supportive letters to the producers debunking these rumors. One such letter affirmed, "As you realize, our representatives have been present during the complete film to date and find that the handling, feeding, and care of the birds has been very good."[9] Humane Association officials also viewed and approved a screening of the finished film. Rutherford Phillips, the executive director, wrote, "There have been a few people who complained about the use of birds in this picture in its various locations. Such reports were based on rumor and misinformation, it is certainly an unusual picture but there was no harm or mistreatment of the birds used in this film."[10]

At least one commentator suggested that it might have been better if Hitchcock and the Code Office had showed less solicitude for the birds and more for the leading lady, who "suffered grievously" under the avian attack staged in the attic of the Brenner house.[11] The attic attack on Melanie, the most savage in the movie, lasts only a minute on the screen, but took a week to shoot and left Tippi Hedren physically and mentally exhausted. She had expected that the scene would involve mechanical birds or superimposed images, but Hitchcock had found mechanical birds to be unsatisfactory early on, and his need for realism required that real birds be used in the attack. As a result, Tippi Hedren sat cowering in a corner for the better part of a week while handlers pelted her with live birds. By Friday, Hedren remembered, "They had me down on the floor with the birds tied loosely to me with elastic bands which were attached through the peckholes in my dress. Well, one of the birds clawed my eye, and that did it. I just sat and cried."[12]

Acting on the orders of her doctor, Hedren took the next week off to recuperate. Some critics of Hitchcock have cited the shooting of the attack to paint the director as an ogre and suggest that he took delight in torturing his actress. Those on the scene, including screenwriter Evan Hunter, disagreed strenuously. Hunter remembered that Hitchcock's thoughts were on montage, on what he needed "to scare the hell out of people. Period." The attic scene was crucial to *The Birds,* just as the shower scene in *Psycho,* which also took a week to shoot, was crucial to that picture. Hitchcock also spent a week shooting the birds' attack on the children's birthday party and the attempted strangling in *Dial M for Murder.* Hedren's hairstylist, Virginia Darcy, who was on hand to look after the actress between takes, adamantly denied that the director unleashed the birds on his actress out of sadism or spite. "Hitch was a perfectionist," she said. "He's not thinking about her, he's thinking about what's on the screen. What he gets on that screen is what counts and everything else dissolves."[13]

One reason that critics may have retrospectively suggested Hitchcock used live birds and prolonged the attic filming out of spite was the subsequent falling-out between the director and his protégée, when she reportedly rebuffed some unsavory sexual demands and asked to be released from her contract. But, in fact, this rift did not occur until the pair's next film together, *Marnie.*

Another misconception, promulgated by Hedren herself, was that the attic scene explained why Hitchcock wanted a neophyte for the role of Melanie—an experienced actress would not have stood for the abuse.[14] But at the time the movie was cast, the script called for the attack to be directed at Annie Hayworth, the character played by Suzanne Pleshette. And Jessica Tandy, the most experienced actress on the set, was also pecked by the bird extras.

Members of Hitchcock's team reported that the director was unusually

Tippi Hedren fends off a bird with her flashlight in the attic attack.

scattered and spontaneous during the filming of *The Birds*.[15] Hitchcock himself told François Truffaut that, although he had always been afraid of improvising on the set, something happened on *The Birds* that he had never experienced. "I began to study the scenario as we went along, and I saw that there were weaknesses in it. The emotional siege I went through seemed to bring out an additional creative sense in me. I began to improvise."[16]

Hitchcock improvised by editing scenes and changing dialogue as the movie was being shot. Exchanges between the townspeople and Mitch and Melanie in the Tides Restaurant as they try to work out the extent and meaning of the birds' attacks were reworked at the last minute. The speech of the hysterical mother who advances on Melanie and blames her for the attacks, shouting, "I think you're the cause of this! I think you're evil! Evil!" was not in the script but improvised on the spot.[17]

The real cause of the birds' attacks perplexed the director and screenwriter throughout the shooting. Du Maurier's novella gives no explanation for the avian invasions, and Hitchcock was adamant that he did not want some "science fiction" explanation. Evan Hunter had addressed the issue in a short speech given by Melanie in the Tides Restaurant following the attack on the schoolchildren. In one late version of the script, the ornithologist, Mrs. Bundy, first makes the case for the birds to Melanie:

> MRS. BUNDY: Birds are not aggressive creatures, Miss. They bring beauty into the world. It is mankind . . .
> WAITRESS (*off*): Three southern fried chickens! Mashed potatoes on all of 'em.
> MRS. BUNDY (*continuing*): . . . insists on making it difficult for life to exist on the planet.
> MELANIE: Maybe they're tired of being shot at and roasted in ovens.

Hitchcock cut Melanie's line and let the waitress's offstage order for fried chicken suggest that the birds are bent on revenge.

The argument for ornithological revenge appears nowhere else in the movie, although it is the basis for a lengthy trailer in which the director addresses the camera in the style of his wry TV prologues and epilogues on *Alfred Hitchcock Presents.* With tongue in cheek, he suggests that birds have no reason to resent the human race, since they should be proud of the way their species brings beauty to mankind, as they did in decorating plumed hats in the era of Charles I. They should also be grateful for being guests of honor at present-day Thanksgiving dinners. Hitchcock's many examples of occasions for ornithological gratitude end when a caged canary pecks at his finger and Tippi Hedren enters the elaborate library set, slams the door behind her, and screams, "They're coming!"

The director's newfound penchant for improvisation extended to the ending of the film. When shooting started, neither Hitchcock nor Evan Hunter was satisfied with the ending, and Hitchcock asked Hunter to write a new one. Hunter complied, composing a scene in which Mitch, Melanie, Cathy, and Mrs. Brenner leave the Brenners' home in Melanie's soft-top convertible, pass through the devastated downtown of Bodega Bay, and endure a final assault in which the birds shred the convertible top before a straight stretch of road allows Mitch to accelerate and outdistance the attackers on the highway to San Francisco.

At one point, Hitchcock considered an ending in which the fleeing family approaches the Golden Gate Bridge, only to find it covered with birds. He was still undecided about the ending when he left Bodega Bay to start shooting in the LA studios, but he left word for his location crew to begin filming Hunter's ending, which showed the widespread devastation in the town of Bodega Bay. To simulate the devastation, the prop man and production designer draped dummies over a derelict boat, overturned cars, splattered blood on buildings, and scattered dead chickens from a local poultry farm all over the roadway, covering them with ketchup. In the words of the storyboard illustrator, "It looked like Armageddon."[18]

It looked too much like Armageddon for the Humane Association observers. When they saw dead chickens all over the road they misinterpreted the scene and became so violent that one woman ripped the jacket off production designer Bob Boyle. That same day, Hitchcock called from Los Angeles to say he'd decided on another ending and wouldn't need scenes of devastation in Bodega Bay after all.[19]

Hitchcock had decided to abandon Hunter's ending for a more unresolved one showing the survivors driving away from their home through roads guarded by birds as far as the eye can see. Hitchcock added to the lack of resolution by choosing not to include a title reading, "The End." When the indeterminate ending became somewhat controversial, Hitchcock wrote an exhibitor explaining, "I did have a further ending with a final attack on the automobile as it raced away, but I cut it out because it was so repetitious that the thing was anti-climactic."[20]

The new ending failed to provide any trace of finality or explanation for the general public. Evan Hunter reported that when he saw *The Birds* in a public cinema, people seemed stunned by the ending and turned to each other, mumbling, "Is it over?" "Is that it?" "Huh?" In creating the indeterminate ending, Hitchcock had uncharacteristically misjudged the reactions of his audience.[21]

The responses of the critics reflected the confusion of the movie audiences. When *The Birds* opened in New York, "many of the newspapers and magazines picked up on Hitchcock's unresolved ending and reacted negatively."[22] Overall, reviews were mixed. The *London Times* said the movie was "brilliantly handled," and the *New York Times* found it "beautifully constructed."[23] On the other hand, the *New Yorker* rated it a "sorry failure," and *Time* called it "silly potboiling."[24] Even those reviewers who liked the film were lukewarm regarding Tippi Hedren's performance. The *New York Times* called her "bland," and the *London Times* found her less appealing than many of those "cool-but-sizzling-underneath blondes that Mr. Hitchcock delights to feature in his films."[25]

The Birds turned a profit, bringing in $5 million domestically against a sizable (for Hitchcock) budget of $3.3 million, but it was nowhere near *Psycho* in popularity or profitability. When asked by *San Francisco Chronicle* columnist Herb Caen if *The Birds* was one of the scariest films he ever made, Hitchcock replied, "Undoubtedly—I paid for it myself, and I am terrified of losing all my money." Hitchcock didn't lose any money, but the financial risks he had undertaken weighed on him throughout the making of the film. Pictorial director Albert Whitlock reported, "All the way through *The Birds* he kept saying, 'I wonder if we haven't taken on too much here.'"[26] The director's worries over his financial risks may have affected his decision to abandon both Evan Hunter's final scenes and his own grandiose image of a bird-covered Golden Gate Bridge for the shorter, less expensive ending.

During filming, Hitchcock went out of his way to heed the Production Code's suggestion and follow the advice of the Humane Association and the Department of the Interior in caring for his twenty-five thousand feathered extras. Starting from scratch, he and his team created special effects that still frighten audiences and can stand up to today's computer-generated images. Unfortunately, the plot didn't measure up to the effects. Years later, Hitchcock said, "Alma had never liked the original idea of doing *The Birds*. She didn't think there was enough story there. Well, she was right. Not enough story, too many birds."[27]

34

Marnie (1964)

Synopsis. *Marnie Edgar (Tippi Hedren) is a compulsive thief who changes identities as she moves from secretarial job to secretarial job. Her only ties are to her mother in Baltimore and a beloved horse, Forio, that she boards at a stable in rural Maryland.*

When she applies for a job at the publishing firm of Mark Rutland (Sean Connery), he recognizes her as the woman who stole money from one of his business associates but, fascinated, hires her anyway. When she disappears with the contents of the company safe, he tracks her down, recovers the money, and blackmails her into marrying him. But Mark soon learns that his new wife is profoundly neurotic, subject to nightmares, terrified of thunderstorms and the color red, and repulsed by sexual contact. When he attempts to take her by force on their honeymoon cruise, she submits, but then tries unsuccessfully to commit suicide.

After the honeymoon, Marnie panics at the sight of a red riding outfit during a fox hunt, causing Forio to bolt and break a leg, so that she is forced to shoot her beloved horse. Distraught, she again tries to rob Rutland's company safe, but Mark stops her. Suspecting her neuroses can be traced to her childhood, Mark forces Marnie to accompany him to her childhood home, where he demands answers from her puritanical mother about the secrets of his wife's childhood.

The mother breaks down and admits she had been a prostitute when Marnie was very young and that Marnie had killed a sailor one night with a poker when she thought he was attacking her mother. The mother took the blame for the killing, claiming self-defense, and Marnie repressed the memory entirely. With the childhood secret revealed, there is hope that Marnie, with Mark's help, will conquer her neuroses.

***

The topic of sexual assault, both on-screen and off, haunted the making of Hitchcock's next film, *Marnie,* which was based on a novel by English author Winston Graham. Hitchcock had acquired the screen rights for

$50,000 prior to the book's publication, envisioning it as a vehicle for Grace Kelly's return to film. Kelly, by then Princess Grace of Monaco, had read the novel and told Hitchcock she was interested. A Monaco palace spokesman announced her return to acting on March 19, 1962, while Hitchcock was filming *The Birds.* Hitchcock's joy was short-lived, though. On June 7, another official palace statement announced that the princess was withdrawing from negotiations to star in the film.

The princess sent a handwritten note to Hitchcock saying that "it was heartbreaking for me to have to leave the picture," adding, in a reference to Hitchcock's oft-quoted line comparing actors to cattle, "I also hate to feel that there are probably many other 'cattle' who could play the part equally as well. Despite that, I hope to remain one of your sacred 'cows.'"[1]

Disappointed, Hitchcock set the project aside for a while, and then eventually offered the title role to Tippi Hedren while *The Birds* was still in production. He explained his decision to François Truffaut during his series of interviews with the French director, which occurred between the wrapping of *The Birds* and the beginning of the *Marnie* shoot. "Once you've started a girl, you must make sure by not letting her go out to some other company. So I must complete my job as Svengali."[2]

Hitchcock had originally tapped Joseph Stefano, who had the screenwriting credit on *Psycho,* to write a treatment for *Marnie,* but when delays made Stefano unavailable for revisions the director turned to Evan Hunter, who had written *The Birds* screenplay. While that film was still in production in 1962, Hunter and Hitchcock had a serious disagreement about a scene that the director considered crucial to the filming of *Marnie.* As Hunter recalled the scene, it takes place "on Marnie's wedding night. The Sean Connery character rapes Marnie. . . . He approaches her, while she is just cowering in the corner and terrified. She's frigid. . . . She's terrified, and he rapes her. I said to Hitch, 'I'm not sure I can recover this character ever again after this moment. I think he's lost to every woman in the audience.' He said, 'No.' He wanted that scene in the film."[3]

At one point in the discussion, Hunter remembered, Hitchcock shared his vision of the scene. He held up his hands as if framing a shot, palms out, fingers together, thumbs extended and touching. Moving his hands toward the screenwriter's face like a camera moving in for a close-up, Hitchcock said, "Evan, when he sticks it in her, I want that camera right on her face!"[4]

Striving for compromise, Hunter recalled, "I went home and wrote two drafts. I wrote one draft the way Hitch wanted it, with the rape. . . . I wrote the other scene the way I thought it should go, where he comforts her and says, 'Don't worry, we'll work this out.' The mistake I made was that I put the rape scene on yellow pages outside of the script and I put my way on white pages in the script. I wrote a long letter to Hitch explaining why my way was a better way to go and that I was certain once he had read my way that he would realize it was the way to go and we could forget all this silly nonsense about a rape. Well, I got fired."[5]

Hitchcock replaced Hunter with playwright Jay Presson Allen, the wife of stage and screen producer Lewis Allen. She had no screenwriting experience, but had successfully adapted the novel *The Prime of Miss Jean Brodie* for the stage. Years later, Allen told Hunter, "Evan, the minute you told Hitch you didn't want to write the rape scene, you bought your ticket back to New York. The only reason he wanted to make that movie was the rape scene."[6]

Allen got along quite well with Hitchcock. She and her husband socialized with the director and his wife, Alma, and spent a weekend at the Hitchcocks' Santa Cruz home, where they celebrated daughter Patricia's birthday. Allen said she never characterized the honeymoon scene as rape with Hitchcock, and Hitchcock, perhaps because she wasn't "one of the boys," never used the word *rape* with her.[7]

Although Hitchcock and Allen never characterized the honeymoon scene as rape with each other, the Production Code Administration wasn't fooled. Following his review of the script, Geoffrey Shurlock wrote Hitchcock's assistant, Peggy Robertson, "As presently described, this marriage consummation scene seems unacceptable. Mark's actions could almost be described as an action of rape. His stripping Marnie nude could not be approved and the subsequent action when she is placed on the bed and he apparently starts to make love to her also is unacceptably suggestive."[8]

Aside from this worry, the Code Office was primarily concerned with language, asking that the screenwriters eliminate the expressions "little bitch," "goddam," "crissakes," and "a running-type futz at the moon," along with Mark's honeymoon speech to Marnie in which he speculates that her thieving ways would eventually have led her "onto your back across an office desk with some angry old bull of a businessman taking what he figured was coming to him."[9]

The next script submitted to the censors accommodated most of the Code Office's suggestions. The expression "little bitch" was changed to "little witch," "for crissakes" became "for Pete's sake," and Mark's speculative future for a thieving Marnie had her merely "cornered in an office by an angry businessman."

The Code Office found the revised version basically acceptable, except for one "goddam" that had survived the rewrite, but it cautioned that the acceptability of the marriage-consummation sequence "will depend on the discretion with which it is presented on the screen. We will be unable to approve any scene of nudity. . . . Also, the action should not go on long enough to suggest that the close-up of Marnie amounts to photographing a woman engaged in intercourse."[10]

Jay Presson Allen said years later that she viewed the honeymoon scene as "just a trying marital situation."[11] And that's the way she wrote it, after allowing Mark to back off and agree to accommodate Marnie's hesitancy on their wedding night. When the confrontation finally comes, it begins violently as a frustrated Mark tears Marnie's nightgown from her body. She freezes as Hitchcock films her first from the shoulders up and then from the thighs down, with the gown puddled around her slippers. Appalled by his own actions, Mark apologizes, takes off his own robe and gently wraps it around Marnie. Then, in accordance with the script, "Gently, but compulsively, he pulls her to him, softly, coaxingly covers her face with kisses . . . it is not just his desire that has overflowed, but his very real love for her. And it is love that dictates the manner in which he takes her, . . . not simply using her, but courting, caressing, desperately urging her response."[12]

And Hitchcock got the close-up he wanted, showing Marnie's face, expressionless, "staring blankly at the ceiling above her" with no flicker of expression as the camera discreetly pans to a view of the ocean through a porthole.[13]

The controversial scene was emotionally wrenching, but showed so little that the Code Office did not find it offensive, passing it at its first screening for the censor. As a practical matter, the scene, as written by Allen, was hardly explicit. Even so, Tony Lee Moral, the author of *Hitchcock*

Hitchcock shows where he wants the camera to cut when Sean Connery removes Tippi Hedren's nightdress in the controversial honeymoon scene. (Courtesy of Photofest.)

and the Making of "Marnie," wrote that Hitchcock had notched another win in his battle with the censors "by depicting rape in a mainstream Hollywood film."[14]

Hitchcock preferred working on a sound stage rather than actual locations, feeling that he had more elements under his control inside a building. As with *The Birds,* he explored different approaches that would enable him to film animals indoors. In the case of *Marnie,* though, the director appeared sluggish and distracted during this phase of the production, and the resulting shots were often less than perfect.[15] He rented a mechanical horse from Disney for close-ups of Tippi Hedren and Diane Baker in the riding scenes and leased a large treadmill from MGM so that the foxhunting scenes could be filmed using actual horses against a rear-projection background. The separation between the riders in the foreground and the background scenery in the process shots looked extremely artificial and was heavily criticized when the film was released, but Hitchcock pronounced himself satisfied with the effect. He wanted to show Marnie riding freely with the wind blowing in her hair and, in the words of production designer Robert Boyle, the director's "main concern was the visceral sensation—the feeling aroused was more important to him than the technological perfection."[16]

The artificiality of studio filming was also evident in the scenes depicting the dockyard street in Baltimore where Marnie grew up. Hitchcock insisted on using a painted backdrop of a large freighter docked at the end of a back-lot street of row houses, even though his production team had scouted suitable sites in Baltimore. Production designer Boyle recalled that they had hired an artist to produce a large flat painting, but that the perspective was off, particularly after a rainstorm "made it all slick so that nothing looked right." "The whole thing was a disaster," Boyle said, "and it looked terrible." After viewing the dailies, he went to Hitchcock and asked him to reshoot the scene, saying that his production team knew how to alter the lighting as well as the texture and perspective of the painting to get a more realistic look. "But Hitchcock wouldn't reshoot it. He would reshoot if Tippi Hedren's hair or dress was awry, but not that."[17]

Unit manager Hilton Green said, "It didn't matter to Hitch that it didn't look realistic; what was important was that it looked realistic to him. That's the impression he was trying to create."[18] But several critics ridiculed the painted backdrop when the film was released. One Hitchcock apologist addressed this criticism by arguing, "*Marnie* is an expressionistic film in many ways; scarlet suffusions over the screen, back projections, and backdrops, artificial thunderstorms, these are expressionistic devices, and one must accept them."[19]

With regard to the backdrop, at least, Hitchcock agreed with the critics. Shortly after the film was released, he told Boyle he'd been right about the painting, that "it didn't look too good."[20] Much later, in an interview at Britain's National Film Theater, an audience member suggested that the distorted image of the ship was "presumably symptomatic of her [Marnie's] troubled childhood." Hitchcock denied this, saying, "We had a lousy scene painter."[21]

While the scene painter made an easy target for blame, Hitchcock had the chance to fix the problem during filming and elected not to. During the second half of *Marnie*'s production schedule, when the process shots were being filmed, Hitchcock was noticeably less affable and seemed disturbed and anxious on the set. According to his biographer Peter Ackroyd, "He was drinking more than ever and often fell asleep after lunch. . . . He was tired all the time and complained of various pains and ailments. . . . He called in specialists, who could not find any specific cause for his problems, and he went for a medical examination twice a week. He told associate Norman Lloyd that 'you might have to finish this one for me.'"[22]

Hitchcock's peace of mind during the filming was also disturbed by his deteriorating relationship with Hedren, who felt that the director's attentions were suffocating and controlling. "He was almost obsessed with me," she told an interviewer twenty years later, "and it's very difficult to be the object of someone's obsession."[23]

Things came to a head publicly in January 1964, after a poll of *Photoplay* magazine readers voted Hedren the Most Promising New Star of the Year. Hitchcock refused to allow her to travel to New York to receive the award on the *Tonight Show,* citing a tight shooting schedule made tighter by the imminent departure of Sean Connery, who had to return to the UK for another film commitment. He was also worried that Hedren's absence from the set might harm her performance by taking her out of the mood he had created for her character. This led to a public row on the set. In the words of Hitchcock's authorized biographer, John Russell Taylor, "This never happened to Hitch. Never. And hard things were said. Afterwards, all Hitch would volunteer was, 'She did what no one is permitted to do. She referred to my *weight.*'"[24] According to some observers, one of the "hard things" said included the words "fat pig."[25] For the remainder of the film, Hitchcock and Hedren reportedly communicated on the set only through third parties. "Would you ask Miss Hedren . . .?" "Would you tell Mr. Hitchcock . . .?"[26]

About two weeks after the argument, Hitchcock summoned Hedren to his office and, according to the actress's memoir, "He suddenly grabbed me and put his hands on me." After repulsing his advances, she asked to be released from her contract. Hitchcock refused, reportedly threatening to ruin her career.[27]

Although no one but the two parties involved witnessed the scene, a few of the director's friends have questioned the accuracy, or at least the interpretation, of Hitchcock's attitudes and actions toward Tippi Hedren. Joan Fontaine, whom Hitchcock isolated and manipulated on the set of *Rebecca* to help shape her performance, suggested that the director may have intended his obsessive attentions and threats to draw a confused and edgy performance from the actress. And Jay Presson Allen doubted that there was ever anything untoward in Hitchcock's approach to Hedren. "Hitch was only trying to make a star out of her. He may have had something like a crush on her, a *crise de coeur,* but there was never anything overt. Nothing. Nothing. He would never in one million years do anything to embarrass himself."[28]

If Hitchcock did try to extend Hedren's contractual obligations to include carnal favors, it is difficult to defend sexual harassment as a Svengali-like directorial technique. Whatever happened behind the closed doors of the director's office, whether it was an innocent misunderstanding, the pathetic lunges of an old man who had missed out on what many directors of lesser status seemed to take for granted, or something darker, it was serious enough to cause the director and his protégée to part ways.

However, the breakup did not occur immediately. Hedren claimed that Hitchcock "never spoke directly to me again," but Hitchcock biographers point out that the director's log books show several meetings with her over the next year to arrange public appearances for the promotion of *Marnie* and perhaps to try to patch things up.[29] Hitchcock continued to pay Hedren's salary of $500 per week, but finally released her from her contract when she refused to appear in one of the *Alfred Hitchcock Hour* telefilms, and over a year after completing *Marnie,* she took a small role in *A Countess from Hong Kong,* Charlie Chaplin's final film.[30]

Even after post-production was complete, Universal still had reservations over one particular passage, Marnie's mother's recollections of her own bartered virginity. "And I wanted Billy's basketball sweater. I was fifteen. And Billy said if I'd let him, I could have the sweater. So I let him. . . . I still got that old sweater. And I got you, Marnie." The shipping of the film's prints had already begun when the Universal front office asked Hitchcock to excise the lines about the basketball sweater. Hitchcock agreed, and his editor made the cuts in the studio's master copy.[31] However, 350 prints had already gone out, and it is the original version that shows up in the DVD produced by Universal at the turn of the century.

With no further incidents, *Marnie* opened in July 1964. It did poorly at the box office, earning $3.3 million in America, a little more than *Vertigo* and just enough to put it in the black. Nor did it fare well with the critics. The majority of American reviewers ridiculed the "expressionistic" process shots and painted backdrops, criticized the lack of suspense, and dismissed the psychological analysis of Marnie's condition as naïve.

Eugene Archer in the *New York Times* wrote that the movie was "at once a fascinating study of a sexual relationship and the master's most disappointing film in years," and went on to speculate, "A strong impression arises that Mr. Hitchcock is taking himself too seriously—perhaps as a result of listening to too many admirers. Granted that it's still Hitchcock—and that's a lot—dispensing with the best in acting, writing, and even technique is sheer indulgence. When a director decides he's so gifted that all he needs is himself, he'd better watch out."[32]

In the *New York Herald Tribune,* Judith Crist dismissed the movie as "pathetically old fashioned and dismally naïve."[33] Edith Oliver in the *New Yorker* called it "an idiotic and trashy movie with two terrible performances," but qualified her judgment by adding, "I had quite a good time watching it."[34]

Looking back from the perspective of the twenty-first century, film historian and critic David Thomson writes, "To put it mildly, the sexual openness of the film is both gloomy and melodramatic—it's as if Hitch sensed that censorship was breaking down, but he was lost in the new liberty. There's also the chance that he felt both his new celebrity and his age and became obsessed with an actress, something he had played with all his life, but handled."[35]

As is true of most of Hitchcock's work, *Marnie*'s critical acceptance has grown since the film's release. During Hitchcock's centennial year in 1999, A *Sight and Sound* magazine panel of top directors ranked *Marnie* number ten among the director's greatest films. On its release in 1964, though, it was Hitchcock's "first outright failure in ten years" and marked both a critical and personal setback for the director.[36]

Marnie was the first film Hitchcock undertook following his career-spanning interview with François Truffaut, and the French director believed that its failure weighed heavily on his subject. "I am convinced that Hitchcock was never the same after *Marnie,* and that its failure cost him a considerable amount of his self-confidence. This was not so much due to the financial failure of the film (he had had others), but rather to the failure of his professional and personal relationship with Tippi Hedren."[37]

Tony Lee Moral concludes, "What is evident from the production history is that whatever happened between Hitchcock and Hedren did not adversely affect the completion of the film or its intrinsic design."[38] However, it certainly left its mark on both parties. Hedren never again achieved the stardom or audience acclaim she had in her two Hitchcock films, and coming at the end of a decade during which the director made "classic after classic without pause," *Marnie* signaled "the start of the weakest period of Hitchcock's career."[39]

35

Torn Curtain (1966)

Synopsis. *An American nuclear scientist, Michael Armstrong (Paul Newman), leaves his assistant and fiancée, Sarah Sherman (Julie Andrews), at a physics conference in Copenhagen and travels to East Germany, where he announces that he is defecting to the Communists. When Sarah follows him, he orders her to return to the United States because her presence will interfere with his real mission, which is to obtain the mathematical formula for an anti-missile system from a Communist professor in Leipzig.*

Sarah refuses to leave, and Armstrong's mission is further complicated when Hermann Gromek (Wolfgang Kieling), his Communist bodyguard, follows him to a farm where the scientist meets with an underground group that will help him escape from East Germany when he completes his mission.

When the bodyguard threatens to expose Armstrong's connection with the underground, Armstrong and the wife of the group leader are forced to kill him. Leaving the wife to dispose of the body, Armstrong and Sarah go to Leipzig, where he tricks the Communist professor into revealing the formula just as the Berlin police discover the murder and set off in pursuit of the Americans. With the help of the underground, they return to East Berlin, where Armstrong attempts to elude the police by shouting, "Fire!" in a crowded theater. He and Sarah escape in the ensuing confusion and travel by freighter to Sweden and safety.

***

When he made *Torn Curtain* in 1966, Hitchcock was sixty-six, the Production Code was thirty-six, and both were in decline. It was the last film the director would make under the watchful eye of the Code, which was replaced in 1968 by the precursor of today's rating system. Hitchcock himself was dispirited at the time. His latest film, *Marnie,* had been a critical and box-office disappointment, and two members of his production team, director of photography Robert Burks and editor George Tomasini, died while *Torn Curtain* was in the planning stages. Hitchcock also broke with his longtime music director, Bernard Herrmann, when Herrmann delivered a somber score instead of the lighter pop and jazz music requested by Universal executives.

The torn curtain of the title is the Iron Curtain, and the film is the first of Hitchcock's postwar espionage thrillers in which the enemy is specifically identified. The Soviet bloc, especially East Germany, is the enemy, just as it was in the ongoing Cold War, and the MacGuffin is a mathematical formula for an anti-missile system that was in the mind of a German scientist under Russian control and could be understood only by the American scientist played by Paul Newman.

Hitchcock was not well served by Newman or the film's other star, Julie Andrews. Universal had insisted on casting big names in the lead roles, and Newman and Andrews were two of the biggest in the mid-1960s. Newman was fresh from successes in *The Hustler, Hud,* and *Harper,* and Andrews had just won an Academy Award for *Mary Poppins* and starred in what was then the top-grossing film of all time, *The Sound of Music.* Unfortunately, Method actor Newman came on board with a fourteen-point letter that covered some directorial ground Hitchcock reserved for himself, and Andrews was so popular she was available only for a short window of time, forcing Hitchcock to begin shooting before he was entirely satisfied with the script.

Both stars were adequate in their parts, although Newman was miscast as a renowned nuclear scientist, and it was only the second nonsinging role for Andrews. "Everybody sat around waiting for her to sing," Hitchcock complained.[1] He also resented the stars' high salaries, griping that the $1.5 million committed to them was "more than we have to pay for the cost of the rest of the picture."[2]

The Production Code office cited three major concerns with the shooting script. In one of the movie's earliest scenes, the censors felt that the "intimacies of lovemaking that are going on between Armstrong and Sarah would seem to be quite unacceptable as written." The Code reviewers also worried that the killing of Gromek, the East German bodyguard assigned to Armstrong, "seems extremely gruesome as described." Finally, they warned that censors in various countries might object to Armstrong's cries of "Fire!" in a crowded theater.[3]

Two of these three concerns resurfaced when the Code censors reviewed the finished film, and they withheld their Seal of Approval on the grounds that, "first, there was an excessively sensual scene of love-making in the bed between Paul Newman and Julie Andrews. Secondly, there were three cries of 'Fire.'"[4]

Hitchcock recut the love scene to the satisfaction of the Code reviewers, who found that "the most glaring" intimacies had been removed and the result warranted a Code certificate.[5] Based on what remains of the scene in the final print, it is difficult to imagine that there was anything "excessively sensual" in it to begin with. The movie opens on a chilly cruise ship in frigid Scandinavian waters. The ship has a defective heating system, and Paul Newman and Julie Andrews are discovered keeping warm in bed under a huge pile of blankets and overcoats. We see close-ups of their heads as they kiss and nuzzle, and from time to time their heads disappear under—but never too far under—the covers. When their heads do disappear, the covers are filmed as an inert pile, with no evident movement underneath. Still, evil is in the eye of the beholder, and what remained on the screen was enough to raise eyebrows. *Censored Hollywood* claims that *Torn Curtain* "got away with intimations of oral sex."[6] Sorry, but the only oral activity that could possibly be discerned in the finished film was mouth to mouth.

Hitchcock was typically coy on this topic. "My sense of propriety didn't seem to meet the approval of the Legion of Decency," he told an interviewer. "They contend that there were premarital occupations going on, and I didn't understand why they said that, because I can't see a thing."[7]

This remark was more than a little disingenuous. While the viewer can't see a thing beneath the inert lump of covers, it is clear that whatever is going on is premarital, since Julie Andrews tells Paul Newman it's customary that "marriage should come before the honeymoon cruise," a remark that the Code office felt highlighted the offensiveness of the sequence.[8]

Hitchcock addressed the Code concern over the three cries of "Fire!" by eliminating two. The remaining cry survived because it was pronounced as *feuer*, the German word for fire, and would sound "slightly garbled" to US audiences. It was therefore acceptable to the Code, which had banned cries of "Fire!" from the screen. It is hard to understand the logic behind this ban. By the time the Code was written, filmgoers were sophisticated enough to discern the difference between screen images and real life and weren't likely to emulate the Parisians at the 1900 World Exposition who ran from the theater at the sight of a life-size locomotive bearing down on them in an early Lumière film. Perhaps the Code authors feared that on-screen cries of "Fire!" might wake up sleeping audience members and send them into a panic.

Code reviewers found the script description of the murder of the bodyguard Gromek "excessively gruesome" and cautioned that "some care and discretion should be exercised in the filming of this scene to keep it within the limits of good taste."[9] If Gromek's murder was gruesome on the page, it was even more gruesome on-screen. It ranks with Janet Leigh's death in *Psycho* as one of the most harrowing murders ever committed to film during the Code years, and was just as intricately designed as the shower scene in the earlier Hitchcock film. In *Torn Curtain,* the bodyguard Gromek confronts Newman and the wife of an underground conspirator in the kitchen of her farmhouse and threatens to expose Newman as a spy. Newman and the wife dispatch Gromek with the tools at hand, stabbing him with a kitchen knife that breaks off in his neck, bringing him to his knees with sharp blows from a shovel, and wrestling him across the floor to the gas stove, where they asphyxiate him by turning on the gas and holding his head in the oven as his hands flail ineffectively above their heads.

The scene plays out with no background music. Bernard Herrmann, who had written the background music for the *Psycho* shower scene, also composed a score to back Gromek's murder, but he and Hitchcock had severed connections before he had a chance to use it, and his successor, James Addison, elected to let the scene play with no backup. Ironically, Herrmann's score was eventually released in its entirety as a standalone recording, and has since come to be regarded as a little-known masterpiece.[10]

Torn Curtain was made at a time when James Bond was becoming popular and the nation's screens were filled with spies and counterspies who dropped as frequently and bloodlessly as targets in a shooting gallery. Hitchcock told François Truffaut that he wanted to avoid the cliché in which "somebody gets killed and it goes very quickly." Instead, he said, "I thought it was time to show that it was very difficult, very painful, and it takes a very long time to kill a man."[11]

Hitchcock succeeded in this aim. Gromek's murder is the high point of the film and a worthy addition to the list of the director's memorable

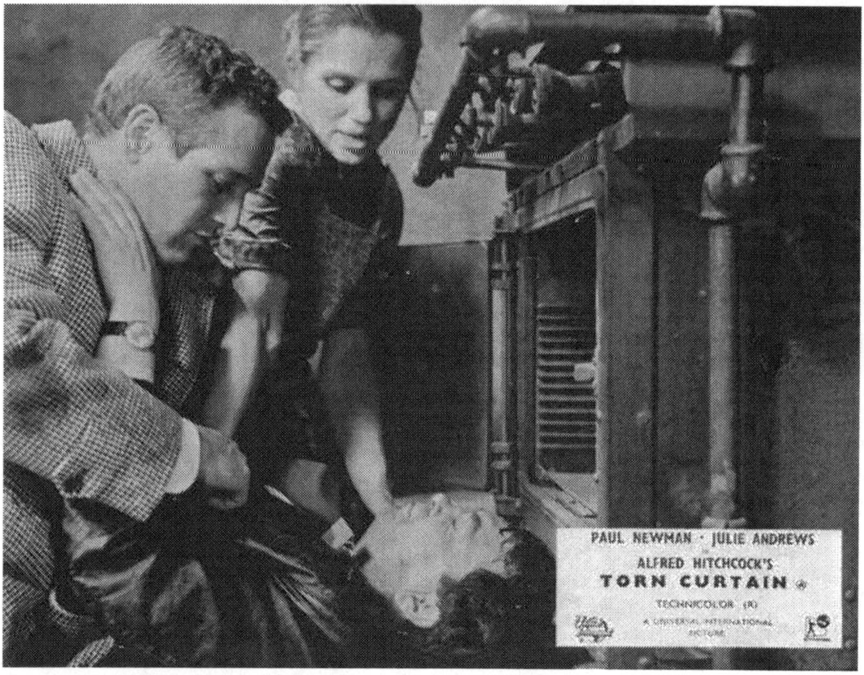

Professor Michael Armstrong (Paul Newman) and a farmer's wife (Carolyn Conwell) use a gas oven to complete the excruciatingly drawn-out murder of the spying East German bodyguard Hermann Gromek (Wolfgang Kieling).

scenes. The sequence is painful and disturbing, and it's unlikely that it would have received a Code Seal of Approval had Joe Breen still been in charge of the Code office. Although the Production Code office passed the scene uncut, the Legion of Decency warned Catholics that the "detailed treatment of a realistically brutal killing" was "questionable on moral grounds."[12]

Reviews of the film were almost universally negative. Richard Schickel in *Life* wrote, "Hitchcock is tired to the point where what once seemed highly personal style is now repetitions of past triumphs."[13] And Bosley Crowther of the *New York Times* found the movie a "pathetically undistinguished spy picture."[14] Even so, the picture turned a profit for Universal, bringing in $6.5 million in North America alone, more than any of Hitchcock's other post-*Psycho* films.[15]

Geoffrey Shurlock may have had cause to regret his leniency with respect to *Torn Curtain*. Shortly after the picture's release, he received a letter of complaint from a moviegoer regarding Gromek's murder and responded with these words:

> One thing I have learned in my thirty-four years connection with the Production Code is never to attempt to defend the indefensible.
>
> The scene you refer to is indefensible, and would have better been left out of the film. By way of off-set, I would like to call your attention to the fact that such cases are rare. We hope to keep them that way—or rarer.[16]

But Shurlock's hope of blocking indefensible scenes was short-lived. Two years later, Jack Valenti, the head of the MPAA, dismantled the Production Code and replaced it with the ratings system.

VII

The Television Years (1955–1965)

Hitchcock and the familiar line image that accompanied the beginning of each weekly airing of *Alfred Hitchcock Presents*.

36

Television Censorship

In the 1950s, the number of US households with television sets grew from 4 million to 48 million, and Alfred Hitchcock became a national celebrity by hosting the weekly half-hour series *Alfred Hitchcock Presents,* which ran from 1955 through 1961, succeeded by the *Alfred Hitchcock Hour* from 1962 to 1965. In some ways, television censorship at that time resembled movie censorship in the 1930s. Like the movie studios in the early 1930s, the television networks of the 1950s had a code, but it was self-administered and largely toothless. But several forces kept the developing TV networks from outraging public decency the way the movie studios had prior to the opening of the Breen office. These forces included the Federal Communications Commission (FCC), local network affiliates, program sponsors, religious and civic groups, social organizations, advertising agencies, blacklists, and finally, viewers who wrote indignant letters to the networks and sponsors.

Television censorship began with government oversight. The FCC was established by Franklin Roosevelt in 1934 to regulate the private use of a limited public resource, broadcast bandwidths. The FCC's purview included the right to prohibit "obscene and indecent" material. Although it could not censor such material in advance, it had the power to issue warnings and fines after the fact, and to refuse to renew the licenses of chronic miscreants.

The FCC considered programming "obscene" if it met a three-pronged test. First, "an average person, applying contemporary community standards, must find that the material, as a whole, appeals to the prurient interest." Second, "the material must depict or describe, in a patently offensive way, sexual conduct." Third, "the material, taken as a whole, must lack serious literary, artistic, political, or scientific value." Material was considered merely "indecent" if it "depicts or describes sexual or excretory organs or activities or terms patently offensive as measured by contemporary community standards." Obscene material was prohibited at all times during the 1950s, but indecent material was permitted outside the hours of 6 a.m. to 10 p.m., on the assumption that children would not be watching during this time.[1]

As community standards changed over time, the criteria for what was considered indecent grew more lenient. In the 1950s and early 1960s, for instance, TV programmers would not show married couples sharing the same bed. Thus, on the *Dick Van Dyke Show,* Rob and Laurie Petrie slept in twin beds for the duration of the show's five-year span. Lucille Ball and Desi Arnaz, although married in real life, also had their twin beds separated by a nightstand in *I Love Lucy.* The first married couple to share a bed on a TV series was Darrin and Samantha Stephens on *Bewitched,* which ran from 1964 to 1972. By the early 1970s, king-size beds no longer raised the eyebrows of TV censors.

The FCC cannot act proactively to censor material, but can only react to complaints once objectionable material has been aired. Over the years, major FCC rulings have been followed by court actions as broadcasters have sought to overturn sanctions and fines. In 1978 the Supreme Court upheld, in a 5-4 decision, the FCC's ruling that George Carlin's classic "Seven Dirty Words" monologue was indecent.

The Supreme Court also supported the FCC in 2009 with a 5-4 decision in *FCC vs. Fox Television Stations Inc.,* a case that arose when the commission sanctioned, but did not fine, NBC following the performer Bono's use of the phrase "fucking brilliant" during the network's Golden Globes Award telecast. The networks argued that the FCC's action was "arbitrary and capricious" since it decided to clamp down on a particular "fleeting expletive" after declining to issue penalties for similar instances in the past. In dissenting, Justice John Paul Stevens contended that not every swear word meant the same thing. "As any golfer who has watched his partner shank a short approach shot knows," Justice Stevens wrote, "it would be absurd to accept the suggestion that the resultant four-letter word uttered on the golf course describes sex or excrement and is therefore indecent. . . . It is ironic, to say the least, that while the FCC patrols the airwaves for words that have a tenuous relationship with sex or excrement, commercials broadcast during prime-time hours frequently ask viewers whether they are battling erectile dysfunction or are having trouble going to the bathroom."[2]

The courts have not always supported the FCC. In 2011, the US Third Circuit Court of Appeals struck down the $550,000 fine the commission levied against CBS in the wake of Janet Jackson's one-second nipple-baring "wardrobe malfunction" during the 2004 Super Bowl halftime show. The court found that the fine, which was occasioned by over five hundred thousand viewer complaints, "arbitrarily and capriciously departed from its prior policy excepting fleeting broadcast material."[3] The ruling did nothing to revoke the $10 million that the National Football League refunded to the program's sponsors.

The FCC's oversight of indecent material focused by definition on "sexual or excretory organs or activities" but paid little attention to other potentially harmful television content, such as violence, criminality, drug use, and alcohol abuse. With the emergence of TV in the early 1950s, Congress held its first hearings on the FCC's responsibilities in these broader areas. The hearings produced no government action, as Congress resolved to rely on the industry's promise to regulate itself through a voluntarily applied code.

As a first step toward self-regulation, the National Association of Broadcasters (NAB) established a Code of Practices for Television Broadcasters in December 1951. The NAB Code was patterned on the Motion Picture Production Code and prohibited many of the same things, including profanity, the negative portrayal of family life, disrespect for God and religions, illicit sex, depiction of drunkenness and addiction, presentation of detailed criminal techniques, and the negative portrayal of law enforcement officers. Compliance with the Code was signaled by the "Seal of Good Practice" displayed during closing credits on most US television programs from 1952 through the early 1980s.

The NAB Code included many of the same bugaboos that filmmakers encountered regarding offensive language, risqué dancing, and the depiction of toilets. Lucille Ball was pregnant during the entire 1952 season of *I Love Lucy*, but the word *pregnant* was never allowed on the air. Instead, the show used euphemisms like "expecting" and "with child" to describe the obvious without risking offense. Elvis Presley's first appearance on the *Ed Sullivan Show* was not censored, but on his third appearance in January 1957, CBS censors cropped out his lower body gyrations, allowing him to be filmed only from the waist up.

And CBS yanked the pilot episode of *Leave It to Beaver* because Wally and the Beav were forced to hide a mail-ordered baby alligator in the family toilet. The network finally allowed the show to be aired after all shots of

The NAB Seal of Good Practice as it appeared in 1958.

the toilet seat were excised. *All in the Family,* which first aired on CBS early in 1970, broke down many TV barriers, including that of potty phobia. In its opening season, Archie Bunker perpetrated a noisy flush off camera, a first for TV, over ten years after Janet Leigh had broken the movie barrier by flushing evidence in *Psycho.*

In practice, the FCC and the NAB Code had less to do with TV censorship than did program sponsors. TV's economic terms gave sponsors "extraordinary power to tailor material to their own tastes."[4] Examples of the tyranny of sponsors could be found everywhere, although they were largely invisible to the viewing public.

- The name of Abraham Lincoln was judged "offensive" on a *Climax!* episode sponsored by the Chrysler Corporation because the Lincoln auto was a Ford product.[5]
- *Playhouse 90,* sponsored by the American Gas Association, eliminated all references to gas chambers from the Nazi trials dramatized on *Judgment at Nuremberg.*[6]

- All references to coffee were deleted by a sponsor who sold tea.
- Hemingway's "Old Man," the story of a crooked jockey, could not be aired because the sponsors insisted that the jockey must be honest.
- The manufacturers of nonfilter cigarettes wanted villains in their shows to be smoking filter cigarettes.[7]
- Chevrolet scratched the line "fording a stream" from a show it sponsored to avoid plugging its rival, the Ford Motor Company.[8]

To make sure that sponsors would not be offended, networks established their own standards departments, adding another hurdle for programming to clear on its way to the public airwaves. The standards departments were staffed by censors who dealt directly with the producers of network shows. In much the same way as the Breen office dealt with movie producers, the network censors would review synopses of upcoming scripts so that the TV producers could head off any problems at the typewriter before incurring the expense of production. The network censors would then review the final show scripts, as well as rough cuts of the filmed product, and would refuse to air any show that failed to make requested changes.[9]

Many of the comments of network censors in the early days of TV mirrored those of their movie counterparts at the time. One network censor found the words *sweat* and *spit* "too graphic," warned that a scene showing models at work "must cover them with utmost discretion," and vetoed a scene of a cigarette being dropped in a coffee cup as a "disrespectful use of the sponsor's product."[10]

Because TV sponsors were attuned to any negative reaction, and television reached a much broader audience than the movies, television content in the 1950s and 1960s was much more susceptible to protests from pressure groups than films. Religious groups were especially terrifying to television executives. The Film Commission of the National Council of Churches reportedly caused NBC to cancel plans for a television play in which a Protestant minister committed adultery. And Jewish groups tried unsuccessfully to block a 1962 telecast of *The Merchant of Venice* starring George C. Scott because of its anti-Semitic portrayal of Shylock.[11]

Ethnic groups were also sometimes successful in pressuring TV executives. When Italian organizations complained that Italians were overrepresented among the Prohibition-era bootleggers depicted on *The Untouchables,* more parts were given to German and Polish villains, and an Italian who played one of Eliot Ness's agents, Paul Picerni, was given a bigger role. "We try to spread it around," the executive producer of the series said. "A Polish heavy one week, a German heavy the next, and so on. After all, you want colorful names for heavies. . . . The colorful names are usually foreign."[12]

TV executives also fielded complaints from professional groups. One executive complained that "it was almost impossible to do a script showing a member of any profession in an unfavorable light without getting a complaint from that professional organization."[13]

The production companies themselves often added another layer of censorship, supplying long lists of "Don'ts" to writers. Screen Gems, a subsidiary of Columbia Pictures, informed the writers of the *Manhunt* series that they must not "show anyone smoking or using tobacco in any form. No matches, no mechanical lighters were to be used. There must be no derogatory mention of any drugs, food, automobiles. No shaving equipment." All of these "Don'ts" were invoked to avoid offending potential sponsors.[14]

In a telling comment on the insidious nature of early television censorship, one advertising executive boasted to Congress that "creative men in television have come to know the whims and desires of sponsors and advertising men so well that they can avoid offense without even being told."[15]

Television producers faced more censors than movie producers and were even more timid about confronting them. Success was measured in terms of sheer audience size, so they first fought to attract more viewers and then fought to keep from losing any of them. In the early days of TV, audience numbers were not segregated by age, gender, or buying power, so it was difficult to gauge the inherent value underlying the gross numbers.

Television came of age at the time of the Red Scare, and, like the movies, it was subjected to blacklisting. Men and women were denied the right to work by faceless individuals who decided, frequently on the basis of little or no evidence, that they leaned too far left politically. Like the movie producers, television producers knuckled under to this craven form of censorship. In the case of television, however, blacklisting was even more difficult to fight. Where Hollywood had only one blacklist, television had many. "Each network had a list. The most important advertising agencies had lists. Some talent agencies had lists. A man could be on one list but not another."[16] Very often, the blacklisted victims were unaware of the problem until they were unable to get jobs on a particular network.

Television personality Gary Moore, who tried to challenge the blacklist, said, "It was like fighting six men in a closet with the lights out—you can't tell who's hitting you." Sometimes performers he requested were deemed unavailable for no stated reason. "I would submit names to the network, as I was required to do, and the word would come back that such-and-such a person was unacceptable. We were never told why." Producer David Susskind reported that during the height of the blacklist he submitted some five thousand names to Young and Rubicam, the advertising agency representing his sponsor, only to find that one-third were rejected and that he was ordered never to reveal to those rejected that the reason was political blacklisting, which persisted into the early 1960s.[17]

In 1968 the Motion Picture Production Code Office was disbanded and the Code was replaced by a rating system. The 1960s also saw a gradual liberalization of what was permissible on the airwaves, and by the early 1970s the ability to segment the TV audience further expanded the parameters of acceptable programming. By the end of the 1970s the NAB Code seemed hopelessly outdated and unenforceable, and in 1983 the Code was suspended as a result of a Justice Department ruling on a suit brought by smaller advertisers who felt that certain elements of the Code were discriminatory.

Just as the advent of TV in the 1950s and 1960s caused the Motion Picture Production Code to loosen its grip on movie content, so the coming of cable television in the 1980s and 1990s caused the broadcast networks to loosen their restrictions on TV programming. In 1990 the NAB issued a new statement of principles that was advisory rather than prohibitive and focused on individual stations. And in 1996, the NAB, acting with the Motion Picture Association of America and the National Cable and Telecommunications Association, developed a rating system modeled after that of the MPAA, composed of six rating categories ranging from TV-Y (appropriate for all children) to TV-MA (designed for adults and therefore may be unsuitable for children under seventeen). The appropriate category is displayed on-screen at the beginning of all rated programs (everything but sports, news, and advertising). The FCC allows for subratings in the case of certain thematic elements that "may call for parental guidance." These are D for suggestive dialogue, L for coarse language, S for sexual content, and V for violence.

The constraints on TV programming have relaxed considerably since the NAB developed the Code of Practices for Television Broadcasters in 1951. Alfred Hitchcock encountered TV censorship during those early years of the Code when restrictions were the tightest and FCC head Newton Minnow characterized the TV landscape as a "vast wasteland."[18] The director was less involved with his TV show than with his movies, but he still managed to sidestep elements of the NAB Code through the clever use of the personal comments he made opening and closing episodes of *Alfred Hitchcock Presents.*

37

Alfred Hitchcock Presents

At a time when most film people considered TV the enemy, Hitchcock's agent Lew Wasserman, the president of Music Corporation of America (MCA), persuaded the director to host an anthology series of crime dramas on television: *Alfred Hitchcock Presents.* The show premiered on CBS in October 1955, and by its second year was one of the ten most popular shows on television. It ran successfully in various forms for a decade, making Hitchcock the most recognized director in the world. It also made him the richest director in the world, since he made far more from his TV series than he ever had as a film director.

The format of the show was deceptively simple. Hitchcock would enter to the show's theme music, Gounod's *Funeral March of a Marionette,* replace the familiar sketch of his profile with the real thing, and introduce both the evening's show and the sponsor's first "intrusive" message with droll, understated humor. The story would begin following the sponsor's message, pause for another commercial at its midpoint, and finish, usually with a twist ending. Hitchcock would return following the ending to wrap up the story and introduce a final message from the sponsor. It was in his opening and closing monologues that Hitchcock was able to steer his stories around the censors' roadblocks.

Hitchcock's appearances brought continuity to the anthology series, and the dry, macabre humor of his introductions and wrap-ups kept the audience returning week after week. The contents of the director's presentations were the work of James Allardice, a successful playwright who had won an Emmy for his work on the first season of *The George Gobel Show.* Allardice was an MCA client like Hitchcock, and the pair hit it off immediately. Hitchcock screened his most recent film, *The Trouble with Harry,* for the author to give him an idea of the kind of understated British humor the director wanted for his TV appearances. Allardice took the lesson to heart and delivered beyond all expectations, writing every lead-in and lead-out for all ten years and 359 episodes of the series. Allardice's premature death following the final season was one reason Hitchcock decided to discontinue the series.

An example of the deadpan irony Allardice infused in Hitchcock's appearances can be found in his introduction of the series' first episode.

> Good evening. I'm Alfred Hitchcock. And tonight I am presenting the first in a series of stories of suspense and mysteries called, oddly enough, *Alfred Hitchcock Presents.* I shall not act in these stories, but will only make appearances, something in the nature of an accessory before and after the fact, to give the title to those of you who can't read, and to tidy up afterwards for those who don't understand the endings. Tonight's playlet is really a sweet little story. It's called *Revenge.* It will follow—oh dear, I see the actors won't be ready for another sixty seconds. However, thanks to our sponsor's remarkable foresight, we have a message that will fit in here nicely.

Hitchcock delighted in spearing his sponsors, whose names he never mentioned, in these preambles. A few examples follow.

> Now, my sponsors would like to bring you an important message. I needn't tell you to whom it is important.

> Our play tonight is a blend of mystery and medicine. It follows this one-minute anesthetic.

> Tonight's story is about a man named Perry and follows after a minute called *tedious.*

> This evening, I shall attempt several feats of legerdemain. One is to make an hour disappear without your realizing it. That will not be easy considering this first minute.

Hitchcock's initial sponsor, Bristol-Myers, bridled at this cavalier treatment at first, but letters from delighted viewers soon convinced the company of the wisdom of Hitchcock's observation that "a knock is as good as a boost."[1]

Hitchcock's appearances soon became the highlight of the series. "The best thing about *Alfred Hitchcock Presents* is Alfred Hitchcock presenting," wrote *New York Herald Tribune* critic John Crosby in his review of the series' opening episode.[2]

The individual episodes were based on short stories by authors like Ray Bradbury, Roald Dahl, Garson Kanin, John Cheever, Ellery Queen, Robert Bloch, H. G. Wells, and Evan Hunter, and featured such established stars as Joseph Cotten, Peter Lorre, Vincent Price, Claude Rains, Gloria Swanson, Laurence Harvey, Claire Trevor, and Mary Astor. The series also featured up-and-coming actors like Walter Matthau, Charles Bronson, Burt Reynolds, Robert Redford, Steve McQueen, Katharine Ross, Robert Duvall, and Joanne Woodward, and served as an early training ground for such directors as Robert Altman, William Friedkin, Sydney Pollack, Arthur Hiller, and Stuart Rosenberg.

Hitchcock himself directed 18 of the 359 episodes in the series, choosing them from a short list prepared by associate producer Joan Harrison. Harrison had accompanied the director from England as his secretary, left to produce films on her own, and then returned to help produce *Alfred Hitchcock Presents.* Norman Lloyd, who had acted for Hitchcock in *Saboteur* and *Spellbound,* joined the production team in 1957 as an associate producer with Harrison.

More than a third of the episodes directed by Hitchcock and others focused on a protagonist who was a murderer. Given the series' penchant for ironic twist endings, the murderer appears to get off scot-free in many of these episodes. This failure of justice ran counter to the provisions of the Motion Picture Production Code and the Television Code adapted by the NAB. To appease the censors, Hitchcock used his post-show wrap-up to assure viewers that, no matter what seemed to have happened in the episode they just witnessed, the guilty parties were eventually punished for their crimes. Hitchcock said of these endgame reversals to his "situation tragedies," "I come on and give some small hint to the effect that the murderer didn't really get away with it at all—Let us call it a small tolerance. I do it simply as a necessary gesture to morality."[3]

Here is how Hitchcock's tongue-in-cheek disclaimers worked when a murderer appeared to escape justice on those episodes he directed himself. In one of the series' most famous episodes, "Lamb to the Slaughter," based on a short story by Roald Dahl, a meek housewife played by Barbara Bel

Geddes fatally bashes her policeman husband with a frozen leg of lamb when he threatens to leave her. She then prepares and serves the lamb to her husband's police colleagues, who smack their lips over the feast and wonder aloud what could have happened to the murder weapon. Hitchcock appears after the camera fades out on the face of a giggling Bel Geddes to assure the viewers that the wife "would have gone scot-free if she hadn't tried to do in her second husband the same way. Unfortunately, he was the forgetful type and had forgotten to plug in the freezer. The meat was as soft as jelly."

In "The Perfect Crime," an arrogant detective, Charles Courtney, played by Vincent Price, is stunned when defense lawyer John Gregory, played by James Gregory, presents him with evidence that he had helped to convict, condemn, and execute an innocent man. To keep this information from going public, the detective disposes of the lawyer in his pottery kiln, and the story ends with the detective displaying a vase "made from a very special kind of clay" in his trophy case. Hitchcock returns to the trophy case himself in the epilogue, notes the absence of the sinister vase, and informs the viewer, "Courtney did not retain his last trophy very long. He was caught. A charwoman knocked over the precious vase, breaking it into pieces, a few of them identifiable as bits of Mr. Gregory . . . Ever since, cleaning women the world over have been knocking over vases, trying to emulate her success."

In "Arthur," a confirmed bachelor and successful chicken farmer, Arthur Wilson, played by Laurence Harvey, avoids marriage to a conniving gold digger by wringing her neck and incorporating her remains in an improved brand of chicken feed of his own devising. When the police, who suspect Arthur of murder, are unable to find a body, Arthur consoles them with gifts of chickens fattened with his new feed. After Laurence Harvey smirks his way to the end of the tale, boasting to the camera of the special ingredients in his chicken feed, Hitchcock comes on to tell the viewer, "There was a very sad end to our story. Because of the excellent bone, meat, and blood meal Arthur Wilson kept supplying them, his chickens grew to enormous size. Then it happened. One day as he shouldered his way through the hungry flock . . . but it's too awful to describe."

In "Wet Saturday," Sir Cedric Hardwicke plays Mr. Princey, whose jealous daughter Millicent has just killed her beau with a croquet mallet after learning he planned to marry another woman. Princey concocts a plan to pin the murder on Captain Smollet (John Williams), who had hoped to marry the murdered beau's fiancée. After rigging evidence against the dull Smollet, Princey enlists his aid in disposing of the body. Princey calls the police, and the story ends implying that the frame-up will succeed. Hitchcock appears following the fade-out to assure the audience that the police weren't fooled. "When the police arrived, Captain Smollet didn't play the game, thus confusing poor Millicent to the extent that she reenacted the crime using her father as the victim. Broke the croquet mallet too."

Hitchcock's episode-closing disclaimers satisfied both the NAB Code and his own network's Bureau of Standards and Practices. There was one episode, however, that no amount of Hitchcock's and Allardice's humor could salvage. The episode was written by *Psycho* author Robert Bloch and was entitled "The Sorcerer's Apprentice." A kind magician, Sadini (David J. Stewart), takes in a homeless, somewhat obtuse boy, Hugo (Brandon de Wilde), as an assistant. Sadini's act features his deceitful wife, Irene (Diana Dors), whom he pretends to saw in half and then magically restore with a wave of his wand. Irene manipulates Hugo into killing her husband, promising the boy that he can take over the act and reinforcing his belief that the magic is all in the wand. After Hugo commits the murder, Irene goes back on her promise, and she is knocked unconscious during a struggle with the boy. Before she wakes up, Hugo decides to practice sawing her in half.

Although NBC refused to air this gruesome episode, it later went into syndication with the other episodes produced in the 1961–1962 season and reached viewers in subsequent airings of the series with no word of dissent.

Sponsor interference in the series itself was minimal, and ultimately ineffective. Al Tennyson, head of television production for the Hollywood advertising agency whose client, Lincoln-Mercury, sponsored Hitchcock's series after the drug company Bristol-Myers, reported that part of his job "was to look over a synopsis of each story in advance of production to see if there was anything in it my client might object to." He noted that his predecessor at Bristol-Myers had done the same thing and "a lot of the synopses I saw at first had already been seen and thrown out by Bristol-Myers." Just about all of these rejected scripts "dealt with people being knocked off with pills and other kinds of medicinals," obviously "a very sensitive area for Bristol-Myers." Tennyson observed that his contribution "was never a

Hitchcock is joined by a scarecrow for an introduction to an *Alfred Hitchcock Presents* episode. He subsequently appeared in the scarecrow's garb.

creative one, simply a monitoring task," and admitted that "over the years we did object to a few shows in which cars figured negatively in the plot."[4] So Bristol-Myers' tenure as censor was short-lived, since Lincoln-Mercury could okay shows the pharmaceutical company had rejected, just as Lincoln-Mercury's objections could be overruled by subsequent sponsors.

The half-hour episodes of *Alfred Hitchcock Presents* were filmed on an accelerated three-day schedule, with one day for rehearsals and two days for filming. Hitchcock filmed his lead-ins and lead-outs in batches of twenty-four over a two-day period four times a year. Allardice's scripts often required Hitchcock to appear in costume, which he did with aplomb, carrying off his comments in settings that included a dead letter office, a butcher shop, and the inside of a bottle, costumed variously as a scarecrow, a Beatles drummer, a surfer, a jack-in-the-box, and other outlandish creations. The settings, costumes, and props may or may not have been relevant to the evening's episode. More often than not, they were, in the words of critic John Crosby, "magnificently irrelevant."[5] And, more often than not, Allardice's words were hilarious.

A few examples:

> (*Dressed as a scarecrow*) My producer has at last found a practical use for my talents. He reasoned that since I've been frightening people for years, why not birds? The job is somewhat restricting, but I have a number of visitors. One little girl and a tin woodsman are quite bothersome. They seem to be under the absurd impression that I'm going to go dancing up the road with them.
>
> This is the end of tonight's story. We would like to show you more, but we seem to have run out of characters.
>
> Here is the ever popular revolver. It is an excellent means of establishing credit in a strange city. It is equally useful in the removal of unwanted or unsightly persons.

Under the terms of the deal cut by Lew Wasserman, Hitchcock received $129,000 per episode of *Alfred Hitchcock Presents,* and the rights reverted to him after the first broadcast. In 1964 Hitchcock sold these rights, along with those for *Psycho,* to MCA in exchange for 150,000 shares of stock, making him the company's third-largest shareholder and, effectively, his own boss.[6]

Lew Wasserman's deal on behalf of *Alfred Hitchcock Presents* not only made Hitchcock financially independent but also made him the best-known director in Hollywood. "Before TV I'd get about a dozen letters per week," the director said. "Now it's several hundred."[7] At the same time, the TV appearances helped him to establish a public image as a droll raconteur and to flimflam the censors with outlandish interpretations of material that might otherwise have been banned. All in all, not a bad deal.

VIII

The Post-Code Years (1968–1980)

Hitchcock with a line of film canisters marking his entire career. (Courtesy of Jerry Ohlinger.)

38

The Decline of the Code

The era of the Production Code Administration officially ended on November 1, 1968, when the MPAA replaced it with a rating system that classified films as G (for general audiences), M (for mature audiences), R (restricted—under sixteen requires accompanying parent or adult guardian), and X (no one under sixteen admitted). Alfred Hitchcock's final three films, *Topaz, Frenzy,* and *Family Plot,* were made under this rating system and free from the strictures of the Production Code Administration. But they were not entirely free from censorship. An R rating could damage box-office receipts, while an X rating could be fatal, and the members of the rating board were only too happy to suggest cuts that could lift a movie's rating from X to R or R to M. Studios still wanted happy endings, and foreign governments still needed to be appeased. In addition, films destined for eventual TV viewing had to meet restrictions at least as strict as those of the Production Code, so that studios often produced two versions of the same film, one for theatrical release and one for television.

The eventual demise of the Production Code Administration was hastened by two Supreme Court rulings. In 1948, in an antitrust decision against Paramount Pictures, the court ruled 8-0 that the major motion picture companies could no longer control the theaters in their distribution system. MPAA members were given five years to divest themselves of their theater chains. Once the studios lost control over the theaters and the power to decide which movies would have access to first-run screenings, it became easier for independently produced movies and foreign films without a Code Seal to get theatrical distribution.

The second Supreme Court decision to impact the Production Code occurred in 1952 in response to the banning of an Italian film, *The Miracle,* directed by Roberto Rossellini. The film starred Anna Magnani as a mentally challenged peasant girl who meets a bearded stranger while herding sheep. She believes the bearded man to be St. Joseph, and falls asleep listening to him talk. She winds up pregnant and is reviled by fellow villagers for claiming she was impregnated by the grace of God, like the Virgin Mary. The short film was condemned by the Catholic Church and banned in New York by the commissioner of licenses, even though it had been approved by the New York Censors' Board. The producers appealed the ban, which was upheld by the state appellate court. After losing another appeal, the producers turned to the Supreme Court, which overturned the ban and ruled that motion pictures are entitled to the guarantees of free speech and free press. This overturned a 1915 Supreme Court ruling that motion pictures were "a business pure and simple," not protected speech under the Constitution. This earlier ruling had opened the floodgates to state and local censorship groups, which began closing in the wake of the 1952 *Miracle* ruling. This ruling also reduced studio fears of federal censorship, which had been one of the prime motivations for the formation of the Production Code Administration in 1934.

Several other factors led to the demise of the Production Code Administration. These included the liberalization of public attitudes in the postwar years; the influx of more explicit foreign films that escaped the need for a Code Seal; the rise of TV and attendant decline in movie attendance, which dropped from 82 million weekly viewers in 1945 to 55 million in 1950 and 30 million in 1960; and the success of Code-defying Hollywood films such as Otto Preminger's *The Moon Is Blue,* a "racy" comedy that today seems incredibly mild and became one of the first major US films to be released without a seal.

In the mid-1960s, two films in particular sounded the death knell for the Production Code. In 1964, Sidney Lumet's movie *The Pawnbroker* tested the Code's ban on nudity. The story of a Jewish Holocaust survivor who runs a Harlem pawnshop and is haunted by memories of his wife and son who did not survive, the film had two brief nude scenes: a fleeting shot of the protagonist's wife, and a slightly longer shot of an African American prostitute who bares her breasts to tempt the pawnbroker. The two scenes were hardly the stuff of sensationalism, but the sight of bare breasts caused the head of the Production Code Administration, Geoffrey Shurlock, to refuse to issue a Code Seal, even though he admired the film itself.

The Pawnbroker's producers appealed the ruling and the Code Review Board, which was composed of a mix of MPAA members, independent producers, and exhibitors, overruled Shurlock. The board announced that while it "upheld and affirmed" Shurlock's decision, it decided to grant a "special exemption" to *The Pawnbroker* on the condition that the producers shorten the scenes that the Code office found unacceptable. The producers cut a few frames from the objectionable scenes, the Code office awarded its seal, and *The Pawnbroker* was released. Perhaps because the scenes in question didn't pander to prurient interests, the film's box-office receipts failed to meet the commercial expectations raised by the controversy, but the Code's strict ban on nudity had been breached.

What *The Pawnbroker* did for the Code ban on nudity, *Who's Afraid of Virginia Woolf?* did for the ban on obscenity. Mike Nichols's film version of Edward Albee's Tony Award–winning play was denied a Code Seal "due to the presence of a good deal of profanity, blunt sexual references, and coarse and sometimes vulgar language."[1] As with *The Pawnbroker,* the film's producers, in this case Warner Bros., appealed the verdict. And, as with *The Pawnbroker,* the appeals board recognized the seriousness of the film (as well as the seriousness of Warner's $7.5 million investment) and made an exception of *Who's Afraid of Virginia Woolf?* The producers made relatively few concessions in winning the Code Seal of Approval. The word *frigging* was deleted, and Elizabeth Taylor's party-opening line "Screw you" was downgraded to "Goddamn you." But most of the play's risqué material, including the parlor game "Hump the Hostess," remained intact. Warner's did make the additional concession that no one under the age of eighteen would be admitted unless accompanied by a parent. In spite of this restriction, the film was a major box-office hit, earning $14.5 million for Warner Bros. and winning five Academy Awards, including Best Actress (Elizabeth Taylor) and Best Supporting Actress (Sandy Dennis).

Martin Quigley, the coauthor of the Production Code, correctly viewed the *Virginia Woolf* decision as the beginning of the end for his creation. In a 1966 *Motion Picture Herald* editorial entitled "The Code Is Dead," he lamented that the "high quality" and "great cost" of *Virginia Woolf* had triumphed over its torrent of "blasphemy, profanity, and obscenity."[2]

To the dismay of Martin Quigley, the Production Code was becoming irrelevant on its way to extinction. From the time of its installation to the late 1940s, it was estimated that roughly 95 percent of all films shown in America bore the Code Seal. By the time *Virginia Woolf* was released in 1966, Joe Breen had been dead for six months, and only 59 percent of the films released in the United States carried the seal.[3]

In addition to the *Virginia Woolf* decision, 1966 saw the appointment of Jack Valenti as head of the MPAA, a position that had been vacant since the death of Will Hays's successor, Eric Johnston, three years earlier. The dapper Valenti had been lured from his position as special assistant to President Lyndon Johnson by an annual salary in excess of $170,000. He took over his new position in time to lead the MPAA Review Board through the *Virginia Woolf* decision and made it his first priority to overhaul the outmoded Production Code and replace it with a rating system designed to guide parents in selecting films for their children.

In the fall of 1966, Valenti unveiled a new Production Code designed to keep movies "in closer harmony with the mores, the culture, the moral sense and the expectations of our society." The revised Code "replaced rules on murder, drug addiction, and nudity with more general rules that prescribed *caution* on scenes of violence, exposure, criminal behavior, and sexual intimacy."[4] In revamping the Code, Valenti took a clear stand against the "odious enterprise" of censorship and gave the Production Code Administration the power to designate certain films as "Suggested for Mature Audiences," a first step on the road to the comprehensive rating system that would replace the Production Code two years later.

39

The Rise of the Rating System

The comprehensive movie rating system arrived in November 1968, when Jack Valenti scuttled the Production Code entirely and replaced it with a four-letter system (G, M, R, and X) designed to provide parental guidance and (in theory, but not in practice) free filmmakers from the interfering scissors of censors. With a few changes, the rating system introduced by Valenti is the one in use today. The M rating was soon changed to PG (for parental guidance), which was more descriptive than the broad M (for mature) label. And, in the 1980s, the rating PG-13 was inserted between PG and R when certain films aimed at young audiences, notably *Indiana Jones and the Temple of Doom,* were judged to contain material too disturbing for children under thirteen. Finally, in 1990, the X rating was replaced by NC-17 (no one under seventeen admitted) because, according to Valenti, "the symbol X had become so stained, so soiled, that it just meant something that was not part of our rating system. So we changed the name to NC-17, using the same criteria for the rating, and then copyrighted NC-17 so someone who has not gotten the rating NC-17 cannot self-apply it. You could self-apply the X."[1]

According to Valenti, the new rating system was strictly for parental guidance and would release filmmakers from the "odious" hands of the censors. But the men in charge of the newly formed Code and Rating Administration were the same censors who had previously enforced the Production Code. Geoffrey Shurlock stepped down when the rating system was introduced, but retained a vote on the Rating Board as a consultant. His place at the head of the fledgling administration was taken by Eugene "Doc" Dougherty, the senior member of the Production Code staff, who had served under both Joe Breen and Geoffrey Shurlock. The Code members who remained in the Rating Administration were used to dealing directly with producers and directors, and continued to perform many of the same activities they had undertaken with the Production Code Administration: examining draft scripts, reviewing finished screenplays, screening films, and sharing their findings with filmmakers.

The seven-member Rating Board had just as much power to affect a movie's box-office receipts as the members of the Production Code Administration. The board was no longer exclusively male, since Valenti added a child psychologist, Dr. Jacqueline Bouhoutsos, when he established the Rating Board. But for the most part, the Rating Board members had been trained in the bargaining tactics of the production Code Administration and continued to use these tactics in their new organization. An NC-17 (previously X) rating was estimated to cause a 50 percent reduction in attendance, while the audience drop associated with an R rating was thought to approach 20 percent.[2] With these stakes, it's only natural that producers and directors would confer with board members to determine what sort of cuts would turn an NC-17 rating into an R, or convert an R rating to PG-13.

To the untrained eye, this sort of dealing between producers and board members looks very much like censorship. At least, that's the way it appeared to Stephen Farber, a young man who had just received an MA in film history from UCLA in 1969 when he was hired, along with another film school graduate, Estelle Changas, to add diversity to the aging Rating Board staff as an intern. Farber served six months of a one-year appointment, left to write a screenplay, and subsequently wrote a controversial book, *The Movie Rating Game,* chronicling his experiences on the board and his criticisms of the newly formed rating system.

He charged, among other things, that board members placed overly harsh restrictions on sex while taking a surprisingly lenient view of violence, and that ratings "often seemed determined by minor elements in a film, a bit of nudity or a four-letter word."[3] But the thing Farber found most disturbing, which contradicted Valenti's claim that the Rating Board acted only to classify and not to censor, was that "in practice, the theoretical distinction between censorship and classification tends to blur. For the rating board does more than simply label films. Films are altered—at all stages of production—because of the interference of the board, and some films are even prevented from being produced, distributed, or exhibited because they are threatened with the highly restrictive X rating." The board's pointed suggestions were not limited to identifying the changes that would have to be made to ensure that a film received an R rather than an X. At the behest of the board, producers also made last-minute edits to obtain an M (or PG) rating instead of an R. According to Farber, "From the very earliest stage . . . film-makers are prodded to tone down their material, and drastic changes often result from the board's threats."[4]

Farber further alleged that "the board has its most direct influence on the content of films when it participates in editing of finished films." He cited the 1969 annual report of the Rating Board, which acknowledged that "102 of the 325 films rated that year—*almost one third*—were re-edited to some extent 'in order to achieve the rating desired by the distribution company.'" The list of reedited films included *Bob & Carol & Ted & Alice, Butch Cassidy and the Sundance Kid, Darling Lili, Goodbye, Columbus, The Happy Ending, If . . ., The Learning Tree, A Man Called Horse, The Reivers,* and *The Wild Bunch.* In other words, "Many of the most highly-respected and popular films reviewed that year were, at the direction of the rating board, secretly re-edited before they were released."[5] By all reports, this sort of interference still goes on, even though the makeup of the review board has changed from Production Code veterans to a group of eight anonymous but "representative" parents under the supervision of an appointed chairperson.[6]

None of the inner workings of the rating system could be known in November 1968, when Jack Valenti announced that the system would replace the Production Code Administration's long-standing censorship role. As a director who had chafed under the Code Administration's restrictions on sex and violence for the thirty-four years of its life, Alfred Hitchcock presumably looked forward to a future free from these restrictions as he prepared his next film, *Topaz.*

40

Topaz (1969)

Synopsis. *In Copenhagen just before the 1962 Cuban missile crisis, a defecting Soviet agent, Boris Kusenov (Per-Axel Arosenius) reveals to CIA agent Michael Nordstrom (John Forsythe) that Russia is establishing a secret liaison with Cuba. Because France has better diplomatic relations with Cuba, Nordstrom asks his friend, French agent André Devereaux (Frederick Stafford), to investigate.*

When Cuban leader Rico Parra (John Vernon) visits the UN, Devereaux manages to steal a copy of a secret treaty between Moscow and Havana. Traveling to Havana, he learns from his mistress, Juanita de Cordoba (Karin Dor), a resistance leader who is also having an affair with Parra, that the Soviets are building missile launchers on the island. She provides Devereaux with film of the launching sites before Parra, learning of her treachery, murders her.

Devereaux is recalled to Paris and reprimanded for cooperating secretly with the CIA. In Paris, he warns a senior government official, Jacques Granville (Michel Piccoli), that the Soviet defector has identified a ring of Russian spies, dubbed Topaz, operating in the upper echelons of the French government. The defector has had contact with one member of the ring, Henri Jarré (Philippe Noiret), but does not know the identity of the ring leader. Jarré is murdered before he can reveal the name of the ringleader, who turns out to be Granville. Devereaux's wife, Nicole (Dany Robin), who has been having an affair with Granville, is able to connect him to the murdered Jarré. When Devereaux exposes Granville as a Soviet spy at an international peace conference, the traitor returns to his home and commits suicide.

***

Topaz, the first film to be undertaken by Hitchcock after the demise of the Production Code, turned out to be a disaster from beginning to end. The absence of the Code did allow the director to accomplish a few things that might previously have been prohibited, but unexpected circumstances prevented him from taking full advantage of its repeal. After the failure of

Torn Curtain, Hitchcock had worked for some time on a project involving a serial killer, but Universal was reluctant to bankroll it. Instead, the studio suggested he adapt *Topaz,* a best-selling espionage novel whose rights Universal had purchased. The terms of the purchase dictated that the novel's author, Leon Uris, would be engaged to write the screenplay. Unfortunately, Hitchcock and Uris did not get along, and the director found the novelist's product unusable. With the start of production looming, Hitchcock turned the writing job over to Samuel Taylor, who had worked with him on the *Vertigo* screenplay. Taylor started from scratch to adapt the convoluted plot of the novel, but the production schedule was so tight that he often found himself preparing scenes just before they were to be filmed. Under these circumstances, Hitchcock was unable to give *Topaz* his usual advance preparation, and the movie suffered as a result.

Although Hitchcock was free from the strictures of the Production Code, at least one Code-like restriction still stood in his way on *Topaz.* The action of the novel was based on a true incident in which the highest reaches of the French government were infiltrated by a band of Soviet spies. Because the true-life incident reflected poorly on the French government, permission to film in Paris was withheld until the US ambassador to France, Sargent Shriver, could promise that Hitchcock would show the government in a good light and make it plain that the evildoers were punished.

Casting also proved to be a problem. Because the complex plot was spread among four locales, Copenhagen, Washington, Havana, and Paris, the leads in the story were split between two roles—the CIA agent who led the action in Copenhagen and Washington, and the French agent who took over in Havana and Paris. To save money, and possibly to avoid the complications he had encountered with top-tier star Paul Newman on *Torn Curtain,* Hitchcock filled these two lead roles with a second-tier American star, John Forsythe, as the CIA agent, and a virtual newcomer, Frederick Stafford, as his French counterpart. Both actors delivered bland, wooden performances. Luckily, the minor roles were competently and memorably performed by established character actors, particularly Per-Axel Arosenius as the Russian defector, John Vernon as the Cuban strongman, and Philippe Noiret and Michel Piccoli as the French traitors.

For years, Hitchcock had filmed bedroom scenes within the rigid confines of the Code, shooting actors fully clothed (*The 39 Steps*), from the shoulders up (*Marnie*), or totally hidden beneath covers (*Torn Curtain*). With the Code restrictions removed, the director anticipated more freedom in filming the key love scene in the *Topaz* script between Frederick Stafford's French agent and the Cuban resistance leader played by Karin Dor. As the cameraman was setting up to film the scene, however, the wardrobe mistress informed Hitchcock that the views of Miss Dor's body would have to be restricted to avoid showing surgical scars. Frederick Stafford followed this news with the information that lung surgery had left a livid scar from one side of his chest to the other. "Very well, then," Hitchcock said, "We shall film the scene from the shoulders up."[1]

In spite of the rushed schedule, casting shortcomings, and other disappointments, Hitchcock still managed to infuse *Topaz* with a few signature touches. The opening scenes depicting the defector's escape from Russian surveillance in a Copenhagen ceramics factory are pure cinema, almost totally free of dialogue. And the overhead shot of Karin Dor's purple gown pooling around her like spreading blood as she falls to the floor after being shot by her Cuban lover is breathtaking. It's a perfect example of Truffaut's observation that in Hitchcock's films, "the love scenes were filmed like murder scenes and the murder scenes like love scenes."[2]

The film's few bright spots were not enough to overcome its lackluster heroes, convoluted plot, and excessive length. But the most troublesome aspect of *Topaz* was the ending. Or, more properly, the endings, since there were three of them to choose from. The first ending filmed by Hitchcock featured a duel between Frederick Stafford's agent and the leader of the spy ring played by Michel Piccoli. The duel takes place at dawn in a deserted soccer stadium with all participants clothed in black. As the two duelists stand twenty paces apart and face off against each other with pistols, a Soviet sniper hidden in the stands shoots the spy, who became expendable once his identity was uncovered.

Preview audiences found much to dislike about the film and hooted down the dueling scene, which they thought was preposterous. Although the duel was filmed as spectacle, the script itself undercut its seriousness. Instead of watching a dramatic challenge from the unmasked spy, the audience learns of the duel through a spirited back-and-forth discussion among the French agent's family members, who view the proposed duel with equal mixtures of incredulity and concern. And Hitchcock violates his own rule of suspense by having the Russian sniper make a sudden surprise appearance to shoot the spy instead of showing him hiding in the stands and preparing his rifle as the duel is set up, so that the audience might worry over the identity of his target.

Studio executives were so concerned over the preview audiences' negative reactions to the duel scene that Hitchcock agreed to film an alternate ending at Orly airport in which the unmasked traitor freely boards a Moscow-bound plane and waves to the French agent Devereaux, who is boarding a nearby flight to Washington. In spite of the fact that this cynical ending mirrored much of what was actually happening at the time, with admitted spies like Philby, Burgess, and Maclean fleeing safely to Russia, no one but Hitchcock was happy with this finish. The French government was unhappy because it showed the spy who had infiltrated its highest reaches leaving with its secrets, the studio was unhappy because the villain gets off scot-free, and Samuel Taylor was unhappy because it betrayed the point of his screenplay, that "the Cold War, and spying, and power politics, destroys lives."[3]

In deference to Universal and Samuel Taylor, Hitchcock composed a third backup ending from existing footage in which a figure is shown entering the unmasked spy's home, followed by a freeze-frame of the door and the sound of a gunshot, suggesting suicide. The image was followed by flashback shots of the characters destroyed by the conflict superimposed on a newspaper headline announcing the end of the Cuban missile crisis.

Hitchcock preferred the Orly airport ending, but Universal argued for the freeze-frame suicide and, in the end, different endings were shown to different audiences. In London, critics saw the freeze-frame ending, while the general public saw the airport ending. American and French audiences viewed the freeze-frame ending. Ironically, this ending would not have been permitted had the Production Code still been in effect, since the Code explicitly forbade suicide as a means of avoiding punishment for one's crimes. The DVD released by Universal nearly forty years later used Hitchcock's preferred airport ending, but included all three endings as a bonus feature.

None of the custom-tailored endings pleased the critics or the public. The lack of recognizable stars hurt the box office, and *Topaz* lost more money than any other Hitchcock film. Reviews were generally scathing. Pauline Kael wrote, "Hitchcock's new film *Topaz,* his fifty-first feature, is the same damned spy picture he's been making since the thirties, and it's getting longer, slower, and duller. . . . Though it is based on the Leon Uris book about the Cuban missile crisis and is therefore said to have some basis in fact, I've seen more believable pictures set in Ruritania."[4] Hitchcock's reputation and the presence of a few memorable moments led several critics to temper their judgment. Richard Corliss in *Film Quarterly* tried to have it both ways. He wrote that *Topaz* was "really two films, inept and effable, poorly acted and well acted, shoddily shot and exquisitely shot, mediocre and transcendent."[5]

Hitchcock himself regarded *Topaz* as a "complete disaster."[6] His third failure in a row, after *Marnie* and *Torn Curtain,* sent the director seeking cover in a familiar setting, London, and in a familiar plot, the story of an innocent man wrongfully accused of murder.

41

Frenzy (1972)

Synopsis: *Richard Blaney (Jon Finch), an embittered, out-of-work ex-RAF pilot, becomes a suspect in the "Necktie Murders" terrorizing London when his ex-wife Brenda (Barbara Leigh-Hunt) is found strangled. The real murderer is his friend, Covent Garden fruit merchant Bob Rusk (Barry Foster), who further implicates Blaney by throttling the former pilot's girlfriend, Babs Milligan (Anna Massey), with a necktie and turning Blaney in to the police while pretending to hide him.*

Blaney is convicted but escapes, intending to murder Rusk, whom he now knows to be the real strangler. He is followed by Chief Inspector Oxford (Alec McCowen), and together they find Rusk's latest victim in his flat and are waiting when the killer, tieless, brings in a trunk to dispose of his new victim's body. Oxford arrests Rusk and clears Blaney.

***

In *Frenzy,* Hitchcock took full advantage of the demise of the Production Code, filling the screen with coarse language, nudity, and a graphic rape scene. The story was based on a 1966 novel, *Goodbye Piccadilly, Farewell Leicester Square,* by Arthur La Bern, which features a sexually impotent psychopath who strangles women in modern-day London. Searching for an accomplished writer to adapt La Bern's novel to the screen, Hitchcock first approached Vladimir Nabokov, who could not make time in his schedule, and settled on playwright Anthony Shaffer, whose hit play *Sleuth* was currently running in New York and London.

The film was shot in London and cast with highly regarded professionals from the London stage whose names were not well known in Hollywood. The lead role of the ex-RAF pilot Richard Blaney went to Jon Finch, who had just finished playing the title role in Roman Polanski's film of *Macbeth.* The acerbic, hard-drinking, irresponsible Blaney is one of the least likable "wrong man" heroes in Hitchcock's films. In fact, the friendly, outgoing murderer Bob Rusk, played by Barry Foster, is a much more appealing character than Blaney. More appealing, that is, until thirty minutes into the film, when the audience sees him strangle Blaney's former wife.

The scene in which Rusk assaults Blaney's ex-wife Brenda is one of the most harrowing in all of Hitchcock's films. The author of *The Encyclopedia of Alfred Hitchcock,* Thomas Leitch, terms it "the most repulsive scene of his career."[1] The scene, which is every bit as disturbing as the shower scene in *Psycho,* took just as much planning and effort as the *Psycho* murder. A monumental feat of editing, it required parts of seven shooting days. Forty-three shots were spliced together into a montage of quick cuts shifting between close-ups of the actors' faces, the tightening necktie, kicking feet, a bare breast that the victim tries to tuck back into her brassiere, and ending on a final freeze-frame of the dead woman's face.

Hitchcock had originally intended to end the sequence with a close-up of blood and saliva coming out of the victim's mouth. Screenwriter Anthony Shaffer told Hitchcock he didn't think that shot should be used. When Hitchcock asked, "Why not?" Shaffer said, "It's disgusting" and they would run the risk of losing the audience if he left that shot in the film. Hitchcock responded, "Nonsense, dear boy," and left the shot in the first rough cut of the film.[2] But it was gone in the second rough cut and the final print, replaced by a freeze-frame of the victim's face with her tongue lolling out.

The "blood and saliva" close-up didn't make the final American cut, but it was included as a bargaining chip in the version sent to the British Board of Film Censors. The BBFC retained its censorship functions long after the Production Code had morphed into the Classification and Rating Association and did not officially become the British Board of Film Classification until 1984. Hitchcock biographer Patrick McGilligan thought it appropriate that the chin spittle shot be "the last red herring of Hitchcock's career," allowing the British censors to demand a few cuts in the rape scene and "pass everything else."[3]

Hitchcock argued that the explicit, repulsive treatment of Brenda's death was necessary. "You need a frank approach to that rape scene," he argued. "Otherwise something very crucial would have been lost: you would not have seen the killer at work." He added, "You can't get the audience to participate in a scene unless you bring them very close to the action."[4]

Having shown the killer's work up close in the murder of Blaney's ex-wife, Hitchcock let the viewers' minds do the work in imagining the death

Bob Rusk (Barry Foster) rapes his friend's ex-wife (Barbara Leigh-Hunt) in what one critic called "the most repulsive scene of [Hitchcock's] career." (Courtesy of Jerry Ohlinger.)

of Blaney's current girlfriend Babs. The director follows with his camera as the killer leads Babs up a flight of stairs to his apartment and opens the door with the words, "You know, you're my kind of woman," the same line that had sealed the fate of his previous victim. As the door closes behind the couple, Hitchcock discreetly withdraws his camera, tracking back down the stairs and out into the busy Covent Garden street where the ambient noise will cover any screams.

After sparing viewers the sight of Babs's death, Hitchcock implicates them in the disposal of her body. The killer stuffs Babs's naked body into a sack half filled with potatoes and hefts the sack into the bed of a produce truck before he misses his monogrammed tiepin and realizes his victim must have clutched it in her hand as she died. To retrieve the pin, he hurries back to the loading dock and clambers into the truck bed just as the driver pulls away. Not only does Hitchcock draw laughs from the macabre situation, he actually has the audience rooting for the psychotic killer as he races against time to free his victim's body from the potato sack and reclaim the incriminating tiepin from her rigor-stiffened fingers by breaking them.

Hitchcock also flouted the departed Production Code in small ways. Early in the film, when Blaney and his girlfriend Babs check into the Hotel Coburg, they sign the register as Mr. and Mrs. Oscar Wilde. The use of fictitious names by unmarried couples seeking hotel accommodations had been a bugaboo for the Code censors on films ranging from *The 39 Steps* through *Spellbound*. In 1970s London, it is unlikely that such a ruse would have been necessary at a hotel as nondescript as the Coburg, but Hitchcock left the anachronistic register signing in the script, presumably for the humor of Wilde's name but, equally likely, as a final nose-thumbing at the strictures of the defunct Code.

Freedom from the Production Code did not necessarily mean freedom from censorship. Hitchcock not only had to satisfy the British Board of Film Censors, he also had to meet the demands of the Code of Practice for Television Broadcasters to facilitate TV showings. To this end, "bastard" was redubbed to "dirty rat" in an early scene, and in the film's closing moments, the scene showing the bare breasts of Bob Rusk's final victim was reshot for TV to provide a print free from nudity.[5]

Reviews of *Frenzy* were overwhelmingly positive. Most echoed the "Hitchcock is back" theme reflected in Richard Schickel's *Life* magazine review entitled "The Return of Alfred the Great." "After flat *Marnie*, mechanical *Torn Curtain*, diffuse *Topaz*, *Frenzy* is like a homecoming, not just to the London where Hitchcock began his career almost a half a century ago, but to that country of the imagination that is uniquely his."[6] John Russell Taylor repeated this theme in the *London Times* under the heading 'Hitchcock Magic Is Intact," in which he concluded that "*Frenzy* is an example of a great director again making a film worthy of his great talents."[7] And Vincent Canby wrote in the *New York Times*, "*Frenzy* is Hitchcock in the dazzling, lucid form that is as much the meaning as the method of his films."[8]

The few negative reviews tended to focus on Hitchcock's taking advantage of the relaxed Production Code, which led to "a good deal of criticism of what some saw as excessive violence or unnecessary nudity."[9] Charles Champlin's review in the *Los Angeles Times* reflected this approach, criticizing the script for its "leaden exposition" and "some questionable explicitness of language, violence, and nudity."[10] A subsequent assessment of *Frenzy* in *The Encyclopedia of Alfred Hitchcock* summed up this concern about the film's explicit content: "If *Frenzy* is Hitchcock with the gloves off, it has made thousands of viewers thankful for gloves."[11]

One of the most negative reviews of *Frenzy* came from a surprising source. Arthur La Bern, the author of the book upon which the film was based, wrote a scathing letter to the *London Times* condemning the film treatment and disavowing any association with it. Bern characterized his viewing of the film as 'a most painful experience." He found Anthony Shaffer's adaptation "appalling," the dialogue farcical, the film itself "distasteful," and announced his "wish to disassociate myself with Mr. Shaffer's grotesque misrepresentation of Scotland Yard."[12]

It's difficult to credit La Bern's claims that he found the film distasteful, since the most disturbing elements of *Frenzy,* the rape/murder of Blaney's ex-wife and the attempt to recover incriminating evidence from the naked body in the potato sack, are both described graphically in the novel. In a subsequent interview, Hitchcock observed that he and Anthony Shaffer had actually "cleaned up" La Bern's story, noting that in the book, "the murderer was found by fingerprints left on a potato: after 'the potato had been stuffed into a questionable area of the victim's body.' "[13]

While the question of whether or not the descriptions of sexual assault are more disturbing in the book or the movie can be reduced to claims and counterclaims between pot and kettle, there is no doubt that Hitchcock and Shaffer's description of Scotland Yard's workings diverge sharply from La Bern's. Chief Inspector Oxford gets far more attention in Hitchcock's movie than in La Bern's novel. The longest scene within the Yard itself shows Oxford eating a full meal at his desk because his wife insists on experimenting with inedible nouvelle cuisine at home. Instead of dull, expository exchanges between Oxford and his sergeant within the confines of the Yard, Hitchcock and Shaffer move the plot along through scenes at the Oxfords' dinner table in which the chief inspector shares details of the case with his wife through gritted teeth as he pokes at her culinary catastrophes. These wry scenes between Chief Inspector Oxford and his wife, which are nowhere in La Bern's book, provide welcome relief from the grim topic of serial sexual assaults.

Movie audiences agreed with the majority of the critics. *Frenzy* would eventually become the biggest earner of any of Hitchcock's films, bringing in $16 million and even outgrossing *Psycho.* The made-for-TV version brought in an additional $2 million for three showings, nearly as much as the cost of the film itself.[14]

For a time, *Frenzy* was billed as "Hitchcock's only R-rated film." Since only three of the director's fifty-three films were released after the MPAA introduced its rating system, this is a relatively meaningless claim. It does indicate, however, that the R rating could be a draw as well as a deterrent. The subsequent rerelease of *Psycho* under the rating system made *Frenzy* only one of Hitchcock's two R-rated films, a claim that never made the ads.

Hitchcock had every reason to be pleased with the critical and box-office response to *Frenzy.* Freed from the restrictions of the Production Code, he made the movie he wanted to make, from a story he selected personally, with a talented and cooperative screenwriter and a thoroughly professional cast of his own choosing. *Frenzy* belongs on any list of the director's finest accomplishments.

42

Family Plot (1976)

Synopsis. *Elderly Julia Rainbird (Cathleen Nesbitt) promises phony psychic Blanche Tyler (Barbara Harris) $10,000 if she can locate the heir to the Rainbird fortune, who was given up for adoption as a child. With the help of her cab driver boyfriend George Lumley (Bruce Dern), Blanche sets out to find the heir, who has changed his name and is posing as a jeweler, Arthur Adamson (William Devane). With the help of his wife, Fran (Karen Black), Adamson has been kidnapping wealthy people and demanding ransom payments in diamonds.*

Following leads to the missing heir, Blanche and George come to the attention of the kidnappers, who assume the pair must be after them for their crimes. To escape detection, the Adamsons hire a henchman to sabotage the brakes of Blanche's car and send her and George down a treacherous mountain road.

Blanche and George survive the downhill trip and Blanche is waiting at the kidnappers' door when they return home with their latest victim, a Catholic bishop they have abducted in the middle of a service. When Blanche spots the bishop's body in the rear of the Adamsons' car, she realizes the pair are criminals and tries to get away. The Adamsons sedate Blanche and lock her in a secret basement room as they drive off to exchange the bishop for the ransom diamond.

The kidnappers return home and hide the new diamond in a stairway chandelier before attempting to dispose of Blanche. George arrives in time to overcome the Adamsons and rescue his girlfriend, who leads him straight to the glass chandelier and points to the diamonds, hidden in plain view. Impressed, George declares that Blanche must really be psychic, but she dispels this notion immediately with a wink at the audience.

***

There is little in Hitchcock's final film, *Family Plot,* that could not have been filmed ten years earlier under the Production Code. The film was based on *The Rainbird Pattern,* a noirish thriller by Victor Canning that tracks two seemingly disparate couples, a fake spiritualist and her cab driver boyfriend who are trying to find the missing heir to the Rainbird fortune, and a kidnapper and his wife. In the book both couples wind up dead, along with the wealthy spinster who hires the spiritualist.

Hitchcock and Ernest Lehman, who wrote the screenplay for *North by Northwest,* turned this dark tale into a wry comedy in which no one dies except a secondary character, the kidnappers' henchman, who wasn't even in the novel. With such a low body count, *Family Plot* is one of the least violent of all of Hitchcock's films.

The comedic tone is carried by the lead couple, the spiritualist and her boyfriend, played by Barbara Harris and Bruce Dern. Hitchcock gave these lesser-known actors freer rein than was his custom, and Harris ran away with the show, channeling the gravelly voice of Sidney Greenstreet in her contacts with the spirit world. The Blanche/George relationship is the one element of the film that might have been whitewashed if the Production Code censors had still been in business. Characterized in the film as "a sex-starved medium," Blanche persists in demanding sexual attentions from George, who at one point announces that he is "going home to my own bed where I can get some sleep." When Blanche objects, asking, "What are you doing? Saving it for a rainy day?" George responds, "You never know when you're going to need it."

Harmless as this exchange sounds, it is the type of sexual innuendo that would have set off alarms in the Production Code office, as would George's complaint while driving that Blanche has him "by the crystal balls," even though he promises a "standing ovation" performance when they get home.

These double entendres, along with a few "goddamns," one "aw, shit," and one exchange in which Blanche answers George's "Christ, no" with "Christ, yes," and the admonition, "Now George, stop blaspheming," are the only elements that might have been questioned by the Code censors. And these elements could easily have been softened or cut without affecting the impact of the finished film. But Hitchcock was finally able to tell the kind of jokes on the screen that he loved to tell privately.

Older critics tended to handle Hitchcock gently, even reverently, while younger critics had less patience with the master. Charles Champlin in the *Los Angeles Times* called *Family Plot* "atmospheric, characterful, precisely paced, intricately plotted, exciting and suspenseful, beautifully acted, and, perhaps more than anything else, amusing."[1] Veteran Vincent Canby described the film in the *New York Times* as "thoughtful, measured in tone and so courtly that we are well into the performances before we realize just how high he's set us up, and with what good humor."[2]

On the other hand, Jay Cocks of *Time* found *Family Plot* "vulgar, lifeless, and maladroit."[3] And *New York*'s acerbic critic John Simon wrote, "Though less pretentious and preposterous than *Torn Curtain* and *Topaz,* less ludicrous than *Marnie,* and less offensive than *Frenzy,* it is still late Hitchcock and not very good. It is nearest in spirit to *The Trouble with Harry* in laughing at itself as it goes along; but laughter and suspense mix as badly as laughter and titillation."[4]

At the box office, the public had no trouble accepting Hitchcock's mix of suspense and humor. *Family Plot* brought in $7.4 million, making a tidy profit on its cost of $3.8 million.

Hitchcock was taken with Barbara Harris's portrayal and suggested the movie end with an unscripted wink at the camera after Harris uses her "psychic" powers to point to the chandelier where the villains have hidden their ill-gotten diamonds. Screenwriter Anthony Shaffer argued against this ending, since the story line had clearly established Blanche as a fake. Hitchcock insisted on the wink, giving Adamson a short speech promising to "go get the new diamond for our chandelier" when he is carrying the drugged Blanche, a giveaway that could explain her final feat of discovery. The wink stayed, and Hitchcock liked it so much he incorporated it in the ad campaign, with his own visage winking out from inside a crystal ball. Since *Family Plot* was Hitchcock's final film, Harris's ending wink turned out to be his own closing wink, acknowledging over fifty years of collaboration with a grateful audience.

Conclusion

By the end of his career, Hitchcock was manipulating the censors as successfully as he manipulated moviegoers. But the harm done by the Production Code was incalculable. Although the censors' prodding stimulated the director's creativity in a few instances, on balance his movies were damaged by their interference.

The destruction of records during World War II bombing raids limits our knowledge of the effects of British censorship on Hitchcock's earliest films, but the director himself observed that the BBFC's concern regarding political and social issues kept him from trying to make films "with some sociological importance."[1] Hitchcock did manage to find ways around the BBFC's censorship while making his British thrillers. He took advantage of the head censor's faulty eyesight by literally getting him to turn a blind eye to the screen when questionable material was projected. Another trick he initiated in Britain was the use of dressing-room dialogue in which women slipped in and out of lingerie while discussing key plot points. Censors were reluctant to remove already-filmed scenes essential to the story, even if they deemed the scanty attire unacceptable. In *The Lady Vanishes,* Margaret Lockwood discusses her impending marriage with two friends in their hotel room while the three young women are undressing, distracting both the audience and the porter bringing them dinner.

Hitchcock successfully imported this ploy to America in a number of films, notably *Rear Window,* in which the censors allowed the director to retain shots they found objectionable of Grace Kelly in a negligee because she is wearing it when a key piece of evidence, the body of a throttled dog, is discovered in the courtyard below James Stewart's apartment.

Production Code reviewers had their greatest impact on Hitchcock's films in the years shortly after he came to America to work for David O. Selznick, a period when the Code was at the height of its power. The Code rule that did the most damage to his films in this period was the admonition that evildoers must be punished. Blind adherence to this rule led to the implausible explanation for the death of the title character in *Rebecca* and the outlandish absolution of Cary Grant's character in *Suspicion,* significantly altering both these films. The rule also forced an improbable conclusion on *The Paradine Case* and kept Farley Granger from fulfilling his half of the criss-crossed murder plot in *Strangers on a Train,* to the dismay of the book's author Patricia Highsmith.

The last Hitchcock film materially affected by the Code reviewers was *I Confess.* By removing the passion from the pre-ordination romance of Montgomery Clift and Anne Baxter, the censors rendered the priest's blackmail all but implausible, and by insisting that the real murderer be punished, they ruled out the original ending, which culminated in the priest's hanging.

The damage done by the need to exact punishment on criminals almost extended to *Vertigo* as well, but by that stage of his career Hitchcock had achieved enough power to overrule a weakened Code. He managed to retain the heartrending ending in which James Stewart stares helplessly down from the bell tower at the body of his lost love, narrowly averting a tacked-on scene in which Barbara Bel Geddes listens to a radio announcement that the wife murderer who had hired Stewart had been apprehended. Although this superfluous and mood-jarring ending was cut from US prints, it was included in most foreign versions to satisfy international censorship boards that justice had been done.

Table 1 lists the number and type of comments logged by the censors on each of the director's American films. Nearly all of his scripts gave rise to complaints about profanity and warnings regarding improper attire. Between 1940 and 1968, Code censors logged an average of 22.5 comments on each of Hitchcock's films. *I Confess* generated the most, at 59. The number of comments decreased as the control of the production Code office passed from Joe Breen to Geoffrey Shurlock in 1954. Under Breen, Hitchcock faced an average of 26.7 comments per film, a number that dropped to 12.5 under Shurlock.

As Hitchcock's reputation increased and the power of the Production Code office declined, the censors' decisions had less and less impact on the director's films. Cuts were still enforced—the censors edited Cole Porter's lyrics in *Stage Fright,* decided which window shades should be drawn in *Rear Window,* and eliminated an overhead shot of Janet Leigh's body from *Psycho*'s shower scene, but these cuts had relatively little impact on the finished films compared with the changes imposed on earlier, Selznick-era films.

YEAR	MOVIE	COST $ MIL	US BOX OFFICE $ MIL	CODE NOTES NO.	SEX					
					RAPE	COUPLES IN BED	ILLICIT RELATIONS	SEDUCTION	IMMODEST ATTIRE	HOMO-SEXUALIT
1926	*THE LODGER*									
1929	*BLACKMAIL*				√					
1930	*MURDER!*									
1932	*NUMBER SEVENTEEN*									
1934	*MAN WHO KNEW TOO MUCH*									
1935	*THE 39 STEPS*					√			√	
1936	*SECRET AGENT*								√	
1936	*SABOTAGE*									
1937	*YOUNG AND INNOCENT*									
1938	*THE LADY VANISHES*						√		√	
1939	*JAMAICA INN*								√	√
1940	*REBECCA*	**1.3**	2	**36**			√		√	√
1940	*FOREIGN CORRESPONDENT*	**1.5**	1.1	**9**					√	
1941	*MR. AND MRS. SMITH*	0.7	1.4	**26**					√	
1941	*SUSPICION*	**1.25**	**1.8**	**13**			√		√	√
1942	*SABOTEUR*	0.8	**1.25**	**22**						
1943	*SHADOW OF A DOUBT*	**0.8**	**1.2**	**7**					√	
1944	*LIFEBOAT*	**1.7**	**1**	**29**					√	
1945	*SPELLBOUND*	**1.7**	**4.7**	**45**			√		√	
1946	*NOTORIOUS*	**2.4**	**4.8**	**50**			√	√		
1947	*THE PARADINE CASE*	4.3	**2.2**	**45**					√	
1948	*ROPE*	**1.5**	**2.2**	**17**						√
1949	*UNDER CAPRICORN*	**2.5**	**1.5**	**20**					√	
1950	*STAGE FRIGHT*	**1.5**	1	**30**				√	√	
1951	*STRANGERS ON A TRAIN*	1.2	**1.8**	**26**			√			
1953	*I CONFESS*	1.6	**2**	**59**			√		√	
1954	*DIAL M FOR MURDER*	0.8	**2.7**	**15**					√	
1954	*REAR WINDOW*	**2.1**	**5.3**	**21**			√	√	√	
1955	*TO CATCH A THIEF*	2.5	**4.5**	**29**			√	√	√	
1955	*THE TROUBLE WITH HARRY*	**1.1**	1.3	**9**						
1956	*MAN WHO KNEW TOO MUCH*	2.5	**4.4**	**14**						
1956	*THE WRONG MAN*	1.2	1.2	**3**					√	
1958	*VERTIGO*	**2.3**	**3.2**	**20**		√	√	√	√	
1959	*NORTH BY NORTHWEST*	**4.3**	**6**	**7**		√	√	√	√	√
1960	*PSYCHO*	**0.8**	**9**	**30**		√	√	√	√	
1963	*THE BIRDS*	3.3	**5**	**4**					√	
1964	*MARNIE*	3	3.3	**14**	√	√				
1966	*TORN CURTAIN*	**5**	**6.5**	**8**		√	√			
1969	*TOPAZ*	**4**	0.8							
1972	*FRENZY*	**2**	**6.5**		√	√	√		√	
1976	*FAMILY PLOT*	**3.8**	**7.4**							
	AVERAGE	**2.0**	**3.1**	**22.5**						
	AVERAGE under Breen			**26.7**						
	AVERAGE post-Breen			**12.5**						

Table 1. Summary of Code Comments on Hitchcock Films. Box-office figures rendered in bold type are from Joel W. Finler's *Hitchcock in Hollywood* (New York: Continuum, 1992). Other figures are from Patrick McGilligan's *Alfred Hitchcock: A Life in Darkness and Light* (New York: HarperCollins, 2003).

VIOLENCE					SOCIAL ISSUES					
EXCESSIVE BRUTALITY	SUICIDE	POISONING	KNIFING	STRANG-LING	FOREIGN AFFAIRS	PROFANITY	DRINKING	RACY DIALOGUE	TOILET PRESENCE	UNPUNISHED CRIME
			√							
√						√				√
			√		√	√		√		
√					√	√		√	√	√
			√			√				
						√				
					√	√		√	√	
√	√					√	√			
						√				√
√					√	√				
						√		√	√	
		√				√	√			√
						√		√		
		√			√	√				
√						√		√	√	
√						√		√		
		√				√	√	√		
	√	√				√			√	√
√						√	√			
						√				
						√		√		
√		√		√		√	√			√
						√				√
√			√	√		√				
								√		
√								√		
						√		√		
√					√	√				
						√			√	
						√		√		√
			√			√		√		
√			√			√		√	√	
√										
√						√		√		
√			√	√		√		√		
√	√									
√				√						

By the time Hitchcock reached his glory years, with *Rear Window, North by Northwest,* and *Vertigo,* censors had relatively little impact on his films. They were still a force to be reckoned with, but he had learned to reckon very well with them, using misdirection, misinformation, hedged promises, and throwaway scenes to protect his visual creations. Often, he deliberately inserted outrageous dialogue or outlandish images in rough cuts as bait so they could be grudgingly surrendered in return for somewhat less outlandish images that he wanted to protect. Other trading chips would be generated by the censors' script reviews. Originally, the Production Code office had intended these reviews as a means of rooting out offensive dialogue and plot developments before they were committed to film. As his career advanced, however, Hitchcock would ignore these preliminary warnings and film the offensive material so it could be bargained away in return for the creative montages he wanted to keep.

In bargaining with the censors, the first element Hitchcock usually surrendered was dialogue. The director told interviewers, "I don't believe in dialogue" and repeatedly sacrificed dialogue deemed objectionable to protect treasured scenes. After dialogue, Hitchcock was also willing to give up logic and plot. He believed that "nothing in the world is as dull as logic," and viewed plot as the sometimes expendable link between key scenes—as, for example, the slender thread joining the crop-dusting sequence in *North by Northwest* to the climax on Mount Rushmore.[2]

"The subject doesn't count," the director said. "You get your satisfaction through style of treatment. I'm not interested in content."[3] Hitchcock's disdain for plot and subject matter may have made him complicit in the damage done to such early American films as *Rebecca, Suspicion,* and *I Confess,* although challenging the censors' insistence on punishing evildoers in some of these instances would have meant going against his studio bosses as well. Certainly the studios' desire for happy endings encouraged their compliance with the Code when a challenge might have meant portraying a popular icon like Cary Grant as a villain or sending an upcoming star like Montgomery Clift to the gallows.

Other lower-level sacrifices to the censors included alleged phallic symbols in *Spellbound* and the use of color in *Psycho,* which Hitchcock filmed in black-and-white because he felt the sight of red blood running down a bathtub drain would be ruled too gruesome.

The last elements to be surrendered in the give-and-take with the censors were lesser scenes and a few frames from offending montages. To save the seduction scene between Cary Grant and Grace Kelly in *To Catch a Thief,* Hitchcock traded away earlier shots of French policemen ogling naughty postcards, cut some of the verbal foreplay in the scene, and made sure the angle between the lovers and the couch never dipped below forty-five degrees, even though the ensuing fireworks left little doubt regarding the scene's conclusion. To save the shower scene in *Psycho,* the director agreed to cut an overhead shot showing Janet Leigh's bare buttocks. At the request of British censors, he also cut a few frames from the brutal rape scene in *Frenzy.* He was philosophical about these cuts, telling the *London Times,* "I am not given to goriness, you know . . . these things are always a matter of degree, and it always depends on whether you do it with taste or not. . . . I did not get seriously censored, because I have enough experience in the business to know what is acceptable."[4] It does not seem to have occurred to Hitchcock that this self-censorship was just another way of surrendering to the dictates of the Production Code.

Table 1 also traces hot-button items identified by the censors through the years of Hitchcock's filmmaking. One of the most incomprehensible taboos was on-screen toilets. Hitchcock first encountered this ban during his British years, when the US Production Code reviewers objected to the mere mention of a toilet, referred to as a "thingummy," in *The Lady Vanishes.* This Code aversion to toilets resurfaced in such diverse films as *Mr. and Mrs. Smith, The Paradine Case,* and *The Wrong Man* until "Hollywood's single most iconoclastic image" was finally overcome with a vengeance in *Psycho.* In the words of Hitchcock biographer Patrick McGilligan, the director won a major victory over the censors with "the sight and sound of the flushing toilet in *Psycho.* . . . As that water flowed, it took away, along with Janet Leigh's notebook pages of financial figuring, years of unhealthy and extreme censorship."[5]

Stabbings are a frequent means of dispatching friends and foes in Hitchcock's thrillers, beginning with *Blackmail,* in which the fatal knifing of Cyril Ritchard is hidden behind a dressing-room curtain. In cases in which knifings were shown on-screen, the Production Code censors typically warned that "every care should be exercised to avoid any objectionable gruesomeness," and producers were advised to take protective shots to guard against subsequent deletions by local and international censor boards. Hitchcock obeyed these admonitions on a series of films, including *The 39 Steps, Sabotage, Dial M for Murder,* and *North by Northwest,* in which blade insertions were rendered bloodless by blithely ignoring physiology or dressing the victims in heavy clothing. This began to change with *Psycho,* even though the knife never actually touched Janet Leigh's bare skin and the blood was shot in black-and-white, and culminated in the full-color stabbing in *Torn Curtain,* which shows a kitchen knife broken off in the neck of the Soviet watchdog Hermann Gromek.

The progressive decline of the Code's influence can also be traced through the treatment of rape in Hitchcock's films. In the words of the Code, rape and sexual assault "should never be more than suggested, and then only when essential to the plot. They should never be shown by explicit method." The first instance of attempted rape in a Hitchcock thriller was discreetly hidden behind a dressing-room curtain in *Blackmail.* Thirty-five years later, Marnie's rape by her husband was unsettling, but hardly explicit by today's standards. Downplayed as "just a trying marital situation" by the screenwriter, it easily passed the Code review at its first showing.[6] Once the Production Code had been dismantled, Hitchcock depicted the true brutality of the act in *Frenzy* in what one author called "the most repulsive scene of his career."[7]

Hitchcock also grew bolder in pushing the boundaries of sexuality and seduction as his career progressed. In *The 39 Steps,* Robert Donat and Madeleine Carroll share a bed while fully clothed and handcuffed together. Even though the pair are at odds with each other and barely exchange any kind words, let alone tender caresses, the Production Code insisted that the scene be cut in all versions exported to the United States. Ten years later, Hitchcock sidestepped the censors in *Notorious* by observing the letter, if not the spirit, of the Code's supposed three-second limit on "lustful kissing" by filming Cary Grant and Ingrid Bergman, upright and fully clothed, in a passionate embrace that lasts nearly three minutes and includes at least twenty kisses—none of which clock in at more than three seconds.

Ten years after filming *Notorious,* Hitchcock overcame Code concerns regarding the seduction scene between Grant and Grace Kelly in *To Catch a Thief* by convincing the censors that the calming effect of background strings in the musical score would offset the orgasmic overtones of the accompanying fireworks display. Grant and Kelly remain fully clothed in the scene, although the Code reviewers cautioned against out-of-frame caressing, insisting that it be "clearly shown that he is simply touching her necklace."[8]

The first instance of a couple in bed together in nightclothes in a Hitchcock thriller occurs when Grant (again) and Eva Marie Saint attempt to perform their upper berth rites in the *Twentieth Century Limited* at the close of *North by Northwest.* Even though the pair had been newly married (by virtue of the dubbed line "Come along, Mrs. Thornhill"), the censors insisted that Hitchcock cut the scene before the angle between the couple and the bed dipped below forty-five degrees. While the censors were insisting on marriage and measuring angles of repose, Hitchcock sent the train whistling through a tunnel in one of the most obvious phallic symbols committed to film during the Code era.

Hitchcock's next movie, *Psycho,* opens with a scene of Janet Leigh, clad only in a bra and half slip, in bed with John Gavin, who is naked from the waist up. The two are completing a midday hotel rendezvous in a manner the Code censors judged to be "entirely too passionate."[9] The admittedly erotic scene was passed, however, when the censors, focusing their attention on Janet Leigh's shower murder, failed to respond to Hitchcock's invitation to show up on the set at an appointed time and oversee the shooting of a more modest version of the scene.

Hitchcock's final film under the Code, *Torn Curtain,* opens with a scene of Paul Newman and Julie Andrews in bed together, presumably (although not obviously) naked under a huge pile of blankets and overcoats, trying to keep warm on a chilly cruise ship in frigid Scandinavian waters. From time to time their heads appear and they kiss and nuzzle in close-up, but when they disappear under the covers, the stacked pile of covers remains inert. The Code had objected that "the intimacies of lovemaking that are going on . . . would seem to be quite unacceptable as written," but these intimacies, whatever they were, never made it from the printed script to the screen.[10]

Topaz, the first film Hitchcock made in the absence of the Production Code, finally offered the director the chance to show more on-screen than close-ups of the heads of couples in bed together. Unfortunately, he was stymied by surgical scars on the bodies of the two leads, Frederick Stafford and Karin Dor, and Hitchcock reluctantly decided to "film the scene from the shoulders up."[11]

As the influence of the Production Code declined, Hitchcock's films grew darker and more explicit. He created scenes, like the shower death in *Psycho,* the marital rape in *Marnie,* Gromek's murder in *Torn Curtain,* and the brutal rape in *Frenzy,* that he never would have considered earlier in his career. On viewing *Frenzy,* the author of *The Encyclopedia of Alfred Hitchcock* wrote, "If *Frenzy* is Hitchcock with the gloves off, it has made thousands of viewers thankful for gloves."[12]

It's certainly true that a few of Hitchcock's films were improved by the Production Code's gloves. To paraphrase Dr. Samuel Johnson, censorship, like the prospect of hanging, can concentrate the mind. Some of Hitchcock's best work was accomplished in an attempt to subvert the censors' oversight. Without the Production Code's rules, there would have been no memorable kissing scene in *Notorious* and no transcendent shower scene in *Psycho.* And Code officials actually improved *Notorious* by demanding that Ingrid Bergman's character be reformed and suggesting that she marry the lead spy, played by Claude Rains, who had once been in love with her. But the harm done by censorship far outweighs its few victories, and longing for more "gloves on" censorship of Hitchcock's work reveals a misunderstanding of the potentially destructive effects of censorship and its overall impact on the director's films.

To that point, it is relatively easy to track the effect of the Production Code on films that eventually made it to the screen. The greatest danger posed by censorship lies in the films that were kept off the screen altogether. Hitchcock dressed up *Foreign Correspondent* as a spy thriller and got the Code Seal of Approval, but he abandoned the original source material, so that Vincent Sheean's *Personal History,* with its warnings about the Nazi threat, never made it to the screen because producers worried about offending the German market.

We know what the censors kept out of Hitchcock's films, but we'll never know what an unfettered Hitchcock might have accomplished, or what the missing pieces cost the moviegoing public. Would the director's career have been different if the BBFC hadn't discouraged films of sociological import? Would a villainous Cary Grant have extended his range enough in *Suspicion* to win the Best Actor Oscar that eluded him throughout his career? Could *I Confess* have been a masterpiece if Montgomery Clift had been allowed to die for the sins of another? Even seemingly inconsequential omissions, such as a censored word or a banished bathroom, might distort an artist's vision and potentially alter the perception of his work.

Toward the end of his career, the Production Code Office was little more than a nuisance to Hitchcock, a nuisance he was able to tolerate, like a tight budget or a Method actor. But the damage done by censors to his early American films can never be undone. And we will never know what other movies he might have made if he hadn't adjusted his own sights to fit within the censors' limits. A great director's work might have been even greater.

Acknowledgments

This book could not have been written without the wide-ranging knowledge and generous assistance of the staff of the Margaret Herrick Library of the Academy of Motion Picture Arts and Sciences in Beverly Hills. Jenny Romero, who is in charge of the library's special collections, was especially helpful. Wayne Billheimer provided an insider's knowledge of the movie business and helped me track down promotional stills in the possession of major studios. Jerry Ohlinger and his staff scoured their files for stills that illuminated the censors' demands, and Mark Coggins applied his knowledge of photography to turn electronic images into illustrations suitable for publication. Sheila York deserves thanks for introducing me to the wonders of the Margaret Herrick Library and bringing her sharp editorial eye and enthusiasm for movies to bear on the manuscript. As part of the final vetting process, Charles Barr gave the text a close reading and provided many useful comments, as did editor Robin DuBlanc.

As always, any blame for misstatements or misinterpretation of the research materials rests with the author. In the interests of sharing the blame, however, I wish to acknowledge the contributions of the Wednesday Night Wine Tasting and Literary Advancement Society, whose members include Sheila Scobba Banning, Anne Cheilek, Mark Coggins, and Ann Hillesland. For nearly twenty years, this group has helped to keep me on time, on target, and in reasonably good taste.

Appendix

Pre-Code "Don'ts" and "Be Carefuls"

In 1927, Will Hays, president of the Motion Picture Producers and Distributors of America, formed a committee of studio heads Irving G. Thalberg (Metro-Goldwyn-Mayer), Sol Wurtzel (Fox), and E. H. Allen (Paramount) to collaborate on a list of "Don'ts" and "Be Carefuls" reflecting items typically challenged by local censorship boards. This was the result:

Resolved, That those things which are included in the following list shall not appear in pictures produced by the members of this Association, irrespective of the manner in which they are treated:

1. Pointed profanity—by either title or lip—this includes the words "God," "Lord," "Jesus," "Christ" (unless they be used reverently in connection with proper religious ceremonies), "hell," "damn," "Gawd," and every other profane and vulgar expression however it may be spelled;
2. Any licentious or suggestive nudity—in fact or in silhouette; and any lecherous or licentious notice thereof by other characters in the picture;
3. The illegal traffic in drugs;
4. Any inference of sex perversion;
5. White slavery;
6. Miscegenation (sex relationships between the white and black races);
7. Sex hygiene and venereal diseases;
8. Scenes of actual childbirth—in fact or in silhouette;
9. Children's sex organs;

10. Ridicule of the clergy;
11. Willful offense to any nation, race or creed;

And be it further resolved, that special care be exercised in the manner in which the following subjects are treated, to the end that vulgarity and suggestiveness may be eliminated and that good taste may be emphasized:

1. The use of the flag;
2. International relations (avoiding picturizing in an unfavorable light another country's religion, history, institutions, prominent people, and citizenry);
3. Arson;
4. The use of firearms;
5. Theft, robbery, safe-cracking, and dynamiting of trains, mines, buildings, etc. (having in mind the effect which a too-detailed description of these may have upon the moron);
6. Brutality and possible gruesomeness;
7. Technique of committing murder by whatever method;
8. Methods of smuggling;
9. Third-degree methods;
10. Actual hangings or electrocutions as legal punishment for crime;
11. Sympathy for criminals;
12. Attitude toward public characters and institutions;
13. Sedition;
14. Apparent cruelty to children and animals;
15. Branding of people or animals;
16. The sale of women, or of a woman selling her virtue;
17. Rape or attempted rape;
18. First-night scenes;
19. Man and woman in bed together;
20. Deliberate seduction of girls;
21. The institution of marriage;
22. Surgical operations;
23. The use of drugs;
24. Titles or scenes having to do with law enforcement or law-enforcing officers;
25. Excessive or lustful kissing, particularly when one character or the other is a "heavy."

Notes

Introduction

1. McGilligan, *Alfred Hitchcock,* 219.

2. Doherty, *Hollywood's Censor,* 109.

3. Alfred Hitchcock, "Some Aspects of Direction," in *Quasimodo to Scarlett O'Hara: A National Board of Review Anthology* (New York: Frederick Ungar, 1982), 396.

4. Jean Domarchi and Jean Douchet, "An Interview with Alfred Hitchcock," *Cahiers du cinéma* 102, December 1959, reprinted in Naremore, *North by Northwest,* 178.

5. Ibid., 500.

6. McGilligan, *Alfred Hitchcock,* 181.

7. Kael, *For Keeps,* 317.

8. Alfred Hitchcock, quoted in closed-circuit press conference moderated by Richard Schickel, NBC Television, Burbank, CA, March 23, 1976, 5, Margaret Herrick Library, Academy of Motion Picture Arts and Sciences, Los Angeles.

9. McGilligan, *Alfred Hitchcock,* 501.

10. Thomson, *The Moment of "Psycho,"* 58.

11. Spoto, *The Dark Side of Genius,* 331.

1. Origins of the Code

1. Leff and Simmons, *Dame in the Kimono,* 94.

2. Keller, *Freedom of the Screen,* 36.

3. LaSalle, "A Short History of the Code," 228.

4. Miller, *Censored Hollywood,* 34.

5. Martin, *Hollywood's Movie Commandments,* 17.

6. Miller, *Censored Hollywood,* 39.

7. Leff and Simmons, *Dame in the Kimono,* 8.

8. Ibid., 6.

9. Doherty, *Hollywood's Censor,* 41.

10. Couvares, *Movie Censorship and American Culture.*

11. Leff and Simmons, *Dame in the Kimono,* 30.

12. Miller, *Censored Hollywood,* 73.
13. Leff and Simmons, *Dame in the Kimono,* 30.
14. Black, *Hollywood Censored,* 162.
15. Miller, *Censored Hollywood,* 82.
16. Doherty, *Hollywood's Censor,* 59.
17. Forman, *Our Movie Made Children,* 140.
18. Doherty, *Hollywood's Censor,* 57.
19. Ibid., 65.
20. LaSalle, "A Short History of the Code," 231.
21. Vizzard, *See No Evil,* 48.
22. Doherty, *Hollywood's Censor,* 67.
23. Black, *Hollywood Censored,* 182.
24. Doherty, *Hollywood's Censor,* 70.
25. Augustus de Morgan, "A Budget of Paradoxes," *Bulletin of the American Mathematical Society* 22, no. 9 (1916): 468–71.
26. Black, *Hollywood Censored,* 190.
27. Ibid., 192.
28. Morris L. Ernst, "Sense and Censorship," *Cinema Arts Magazine,* July 1937, 96.
29. Black, *Hollywood Censored,* 192.
30. Joel W. Finler, *The Hollywood Story* (New York: Crown, 1988), 158.

2. Censors at Work

1. Albert E. Van Schmus, Oral History, 128, Margaret Herrick Library, Academy of Motion Picture Arts and Sciences, Los Angeles.
2. Vizzard, *See No Evil,* 113.
3. Islin Auster, Memorandum to Files, Re: *Rebecca,* July 19, 1938, Motion Picture Producers and Distributors Association Collection, Margaret Herrick Library, Academy of Motion Picture Arts and Sciences, Los Angeles. (This collection is hereafter cited as MPPDA.)
4. Ibid.
5. Frank Walsh, *Sin and Censorship,* 106, 107.
6. Van Schmus, Oral History, 130.
7. Jack Vizzard, Memorandum to Files, Re: *Psycho,* February 22, 1960, MPPDA.
8. Rebello, *Alfred Hitchcock,* 146.
9. Van Schmus, Oral History, 347.
10. Doherty, *Hollywood's Censor,* 75.
11. Miller, *Censored Hollywood,* 91, 92.

12. Ibid., 92.
13. Doherty, *Hollywood's Censor,* 49.
14. Joseph I. Breen, to Mr. David O. Selznick, May 14, 1944, MPPDA.
15. Van Schmus, Oral History, 147.

3. The British Board of Film Censors

1. Sean Clarke, "Explained: Film Censorship in the U.K.," *Guardian,* March 13, 2002.
2. Miller, *Censored Hollywood,* 32, 33.
3. Matthews, *Censored,* 24.
4. Ibid., 40.
5. Ibid.
6. Ibid., 64.
7. Ibid., 61.
8. Ibid., 57.
9. Ibid., 101.
10. Miller, *Censored Hollywood,* 33.
11. Leff, *Hitchcock and Selznick,* 70.
12. Truffaut, *Hitchcock,* 43.
13. Ibid., 64.
14. Ibid., 106.
15. J. Danvers Williams, "The Censor Wouldn't Pass It, Says Hitchcock," *Film Weekly,* November 5, 1938.

4. The British Gaumont Thrillers

1. Truffaut, *Hitchcock,* 87.
2. Joseph Breen to Mr. Vincent G. Hart, January 25, 1936, *The Man Who Knew Too Much* File, Motion Picture Producers and Distributors Association Collection, Margaret Herrick Library, Academy of Motion Picture Arts and Sciences, Los Angeles. (This collection is hereafter cited as MPPDA.)
3. Joseph Breen to Mr. Will Hays, January 26, 1936, MPPDA.
4. Joseph Breen to Mr. Arthur Lee, January 28, 1936, MPPDA.
5. Ibid.
6. Vincent G. Hart to Mr. Arthur Lee, July 2, 1935, *The 39 Steps* File, MPPDA.
7. C. E. Schwengeler to Mr. Vincent G. Hart, July 5, 1935, *The 39 Steps* File, MPPDA.
8. Vincent G. Hart to Mr. Arthur Lee, July 9, 1935, *The 39 Steps* File, MPPDA.
9. Sydney Carroll, review of *The 39 Steps, Sunday Times,* June 9, 1935.

10. Harris and Lasky, *The Films of Alfred Hitchcock,* 53.

11. Vincent G. Hart to Mr. Arthur Lee, July 9, 1935, *The 39 Steps* File, MPPDA.

12. Vincent G. Hart to Mr. Arthur Lee, November 13, 1935, *Secret Agent* File, MPPDA.

13. Ibid.

14. Ibid.

15. Vincent G. Hart to Mr. Arthur Lee, May 15, 1936, *Secret Agent* File, MPPDA.

16. Mogg, *The Alfred Hitchcock Story,* 42.

17. Ivor Montagu to Michael Balcon, May 4, 1936, quoted in Barr and Kerzoncuf, *Hitchcock Lost and Found,* 119.

18. Barr and Kerzoncuf, *Hitchcock Lost and Found,* 119.

19. Vincent G. Hart to Mr. C. E. Schwengeler, December 17, 1936, *Sabotage* File, MPPDA.

20. Truffaut, *Hitchcock,* 109.

21. Conrad, *The Hitchcock Murders,* 12.

22. McGilligan, *Alfred Hitchcock,* 91.

23. F. S. Harmon to Mr. Arthur Lee, January 26, 1938, *The Girl Was Young* File, MPPDA; McGilligan, *Alfred Hitchcock,* 212n.

24. Spoto, *The Art of Alfred Hitchcock,* 66.

25. F. S. Harmon to Mr. Arthur Lee, October 5, 1938, *The Lady Vanishes* File, MPPDA.

26. F. S. Harmon to Mr. Erich Pommer, August 15, 1938, *Jamaica Inn* File, MPPDA.

27. Charles Laughton to Mr. F. S. Harmon, October 18, 1938, *Jamaica Inn* File, MPPDA.

28. Truffaut, *Hitchcock,* 123.

29. Taylor, *Hitch,* 150.

30. McGilligan, *Alfred Hitchcock,* 225.

31. Taylor, *Hitch,* 150.

32. F. S. Harmon to Mr. Budd Rogers, December 22, 1938, *Jamaica Inn* File, MPPDA.

33. Ibid.

34. Truffaut, *Hitchcock,* 122.

35. Condon and Sangster, *The Complete Hitchcock,* 83.

36. Barr, *English Hitchcock,* 241.

37. Leitch, *The Encyclopedia of Alfred Hitchcock,* 157.

5. Hitchcock and Selznick

1. J. Danvers Williams, “The Censor Wouldn’t Pass It, Says Hitchcock,” *Film Weekly,* November 5, 1938.

2. Charles Barr, "'A Marvelously Dramatic Subject': Hitchcock's *Titanic* Project," *Hitchcock Annual* (2000–2001): 100.

3. McGilligan, *Alfred Hitchcock,* 220.

4. Mogg, *The Alfred Hitchcock Story,* 33.

5. Leff, *Hitchcock and Selznick,* xii.

6. Spoto, *The Dark Side of Genius,* 214.

7. Leff, *Hitchcock and Selznick,* 216.

8. Ibid., xii.

6. *Rebecca* (1940)

1. Auster, I, File Memo Re: *Rebecca,* July 15, 1938, *Rebecca* File, Motion Picture Producers and Distributors Association Collection, Margaret Herrick Library, Academy of Motion Picture Arts and Sciences, Los Angeles. (This collection is hereafter cited as MPPDA.)

2. Leff, *Hitchcock and Selznick,* 46.

3. *American Movie Classics Magazine,* July 1997.

4. Leff, *Hitchcock and Selznick,* 46.

5. Joseph I. Breen, File Memo Re: *Rebecca,* August 11, 1939, MPPDA.

6. Ibid.

7. Thomson, *Showman,* 334.

8. Joseph I. Breen to David O. Selznick, September 5, 1939, MPPAA.

9. Ibid.

10. Val Lewton to Joseph I. Breen, September 19, 1939, MPPAA.

11. David Boyd, "The Trouble with Rebecca," in Boyd and Palmer, *Hitchcock at the Source,* 121.

12. Joseph I. Breen to David O. Selznick, September 28, 1939, MPPAA.

13. Boyd, "The Trouble with Rebecca," 121.

14. Judith Anderson, quoted in *The Making of "Rebecca," "Rebecca" Featurette,* Alfred Hitchcock Premiere Collection (Twentieth Century Fox Home Entertainment, Beverly Hills, CA, 2008).

15. McGilligan, *Alfred Hitchcock,* 249.

16. Ibid., 260.

17. Leff, *Hitchcock and Selznick,* 82.

18. James Shelley Hamilton, "*Rebecca,*" in *Quasimodo to Scarlett O'Hara: A National Board of Review Anthology* (New York: Frederick Ungar, 1982), 352.

19. Leff, *Hitchcock and Selznick,* 75.

20. David Thomson, quoted in *The Making of "Rebecca."*

21. Boyd, "The Trouble with Rebecca," 119.

22. Doherty, *Hollywood's Censor,* 109.

23. Ibid.

7. *Foreign Correspondent* (1940)

1. Joseph I. Breen to Gen. Will H. Hays, June 18, 1938, *Personal History* File, Motion Picture Producers and Distributors Association Collection, Margaret Herrick Library; Academy of Motion Picture Arts and Sciences, Los Angeles. (This collection is hereafter cited as MPPDA.)

2. Joseph I. Breen to Mr. Walter Wanger, June 21, 1938, MPPDA.

3. *Variety,* June 30, 1938.

4. McGilligan, *Alfred Hitchcock,* 248.

5. Mark Harris, "Hollywood Propaganda and World War II," interview on Criterion *Foreign Correspondent* DVD (Criterion Collection, 2014).

6. McGilligan, *Alfred Hitchcock,* 272.

7. Ibid., 258.

8. Ibid.

9. Joseph I. Breen to Gen. Will H. Hays, March 18, 1940, MPPDA.

10. Joseph I. Breen to Mr. Walter Wanger, April 1, 1940, MPPDA; Joseph I. Breen to Mr. Walter Wanger, March 18, 1940, MPPDA.

11. Joseph I. Breen to Mr. Walter Wanger, April 1, 1940, MPPDA; Joseph I. Breen to Mr. Walter Wanger, May 31, 1940, MPPDA.

12. McGilligan, *Alfred Hitchcock,* 271.

13. Ibid., 273, 274.

14. Ibid., 274.

15. Ibid.

16. Ibid., 273.

17. Ibid.

18. *Time,* quoted in ibid., 272; Ferguson, *Film Criticism,* 405.

19. Bosley Crowther, "The Screen: *Foreign Correspondent,*" *New York Times,* August 28, 1940.

20. Powell, *Dilys Powell Film Reader,* 44.

21. Mogg, *The Alfred Hitchcock Story,* 67.

22. Simone, *Hitchcock as Activist,* 51.

23. Ferguson, *Film Criticism,* 405.

24. Simone, *Hitchcock as Activist,* 56.

25. Ibid., 57.

8. *Mr. and Mrs. Smith* (1941)

1. Truffaut, *Hitchcock,* 139.

2. Ibid.

3. Joseph I. Breen to Mr. Joseph J. Nolan, August 13, 1940, *Mr. and Mrs. Smith* File, Motion Picture Producers and Distributors Association Collection, Margaret

Herrick Library, Academy of Motion Picture Arts and Sciences, Los Angeles. (This collection is hereafter cited as MPPDA.)

4. Ibid.

5. Joseph I. Breen to Mr. Joseph J. Nolan, August 17, 1940, MPPDA.

6. Ibid.

7. Gottlieb, *Hitchcock on Hitchcock,* 92.

8. McGilligan, *Alfred Hitchcock,* 278; Theodore Strauss, "At the Music Hall; *Mr. and Mrs. Smith,*" *New York Times,* February 21, 1941; John Mosher, quoted in McGilligan, *Alfred Hitchcock,* 278.

9. *Suspicion* (1941)

1. Joseph I. Breen to Mr. Joseph J. Nolan, January 2, 1941, *Suspicion* File, Motion Picture Producers and Distributors Association Collection, Margaret Herrick Library, Academy of Motion Picture Arts and Sciences, Los Angeles (this collection is hereafter cited as MPPDA); Joseph I. Breen to Mr. Joseph J. Nolan, January 14, 1941, MPPDA; Joseph I. Breen to Mr. Joseph J. Nolan, February 3, 1941, MPPDA; Joseph I. Breen to Mr. Joseph J. Nolan, February 6, 1941, MPPDA.

2. McGilligan, *Alfred Hitchcock,* 288.

3. Krohn, *Hitchcock at Work,* 37.

4. McGilligan, *Alfred Hitchcock,* 289.

5. Spoto, *The Dark Side of Genius,* 246; Bosley Crowther, "*Suspicion,* Hitchcock Thriller, at Music Hall," *New York Times,* November 21, 1941; Humphries, *The Films of Alfred Hitchcock,* 69.

6. Chandler, *It's Only a Movie,* 138.

7. McGilligan, *Alfred Hitchcock,* 290.

8. Truffaut, *Hitchcock,* 142.

9. Doherty, *Hollywood's Censor,* 151.

10. *Saboteur* (1942)

1. Ackroyd, *Alfred Hitchcock,* 99; Truffaut, *Hitchcock,* 150.

2. Krohn, *Hitchcock at Work,* 42, 43.

3. Production Code Administration to Mr. Jack Skirball, December 16, 1941, Letter No. 1, *Saboteur* File, Motion Picture Producers and Distributors Association Collection, Margaret Herrick Library, Academy of Motion Picture Arts and Sciences, Los Angeles. (This collection is hereafter cited as MPPDA.)

4. Ibid.

5. Production Code Administration to Mr. Jack Skirball, December 16, 1941, Letter No. 2, MPPDA.

6. Krohn, *Hitchcock at Work,* 46.

7. Production Code Administration to Mr. Jack Skirball, December 16, 1941, Letter No. 1, MPPDA; Production Code Administration to Mr. Jack Skirball, December 16, 1941, Letter No. 2, MPPDA.

8. Production Code Administration to Mr. Jack Skirball, December 16, 1941, Letter No. 2, MPPDA.

9. Production Code Administration to Mr. Jack Skirball, December 16, 1941, Letter No. 1, MPPDA.

10. Production Code Administration to Mr. Maurice Pivar, February 12, 1942, MPPDA.

11. Truffaut, *Hitchcock,* 145.

12. Ibid., 147.

13. Simone, *Hitchcock as Activist,* 83.

14. Krohn, *Hitchcock at Work,* 46.

15. *Nation,* quoted in Mogg, *The Alfred Hitchcock Story,* 76; Bosley Crowther, "The Screen: *Saboteur,*" *New York Times,* May 8, 1942.

16. Dilys Powell, quoted in Mogg, *The Alfred Hitchcock Story,* 76.

11. *Shadow of a Doubt* (1943)

1. Rohmer and Chabrol, *Hitchcock,* 74; Spoto, *The Art of Alfred Hitchcock,* 116; Lindsay Anderson, quoted in McGilligan, *Alfred Hitchcock,* 327.

2. McGilligan, *Alfred Hitchcock,* 327.

3. Truffaut, *Hitchcock,* 153.

4. Joseph I. Breen to Mr. Maurice Pivar, August 26, 1942, *Shadow of a Doubt* File, Motion Picture Producers and Distributors Association Collection, Margaret Herrick Library, Academy of Motion Picture Arts and Sciences, Los Angeles.

5. Ibid.

6. Krohn, *Hitchcock at Work,* 56.

7. Ibid.

8. Chandler, *It's Only a Movie,* 146.

9. Archer Winston, "*Shadow of a Doubt,*" *New York Post,* January 13, 1943.

10. Bosley Crowther, "The Screen: *Shadow of a Doubt,*" *New York Times,* January 13, 1943.

11. *London Times* review of *Shadow of a Doubt,* quoted in Condon and Sangster, *The Complete Hitchcock,* 122.

12. McGilligan, *Alfred Hitchcock,* 327.

13. Truffaut, *Hitchcock,* 151.

14. Ackroyd, *Alfred Hitchcock,* 107.

12. *Lifeboat* (1944)

1. Truffaut, *Hitchcock,* 155.

2. Ibid.

3. Roeder, *The Censored War,* 20.

4. McGilligan, *Alfred Hitchcock,* 338.

5. Ibid., 338, 339.

6. Ibid., 339.

7. Ibid.

8. Joseph I. Breen to Colonel Jason S. Joy, August 4, 1943, *Lifeboat* File, Motion Picture Producers and Distributors Association Collection, Margaret Herrick Library, Academy of Motion Picture Arts and Sciences, Los Angeles (this collection is hereafter cited as MPPDA); Joseph I. Breen to Colonel Jason S. Joy, September 11, 1943, MPPDA.

9. Joseph I. Breen to Colonel Jason S. Joy, August 4, 1943, MPPDA; Joseph I. Breen to Colonel Jason S. Joy, September 23, 1943, MPPDA.

10. Joseph I. Breen to Colonel Jason S. Joy, August 4, 1943, MPPDA; Joseph I. Breen to Colonel Jason S. Joy, September 11, 1943, MPPDA.

11. Joseph I. Breen, telegram to General Will H. Hays, March 3, 1944, MPPDA; Joseph I. Breen to General Will H. Hays, March 6, 1944, MPPDA.

12. Joseph I. Breen to Colonel Jason S. Joy, August 4, 1943, MPPDA.

13. Joseph I. Breen to Colonel Jason S. Joy, August 4, 1943, MPPDA; Joseph I. Breen to Colonel Jason S. Joy, September 11, 1943, MPPDA.

14. Joseph I. Breen to Colonel Jason S. Joy, August 4, 1943, MPPDA; Joseph I. Breen to Colonel Jason S. Joy, September 15, 1943, MPPDA.

15. McGilligan, *Alfred Hitchcock,* 341.

16. Ibid., 351.

17. Ibid., 341.

18. Howard Barnes, "On the Screen: *Lifeboat,*" *New York Herald Tribune,* January 14, 1944.

19. Bosley Crowther, "The Screen in Review: *Lifeboat,*" *New York Times,* January 13, 1944.

20. McGilligan, *Alfred Hitchcock,* 351.

21. Dorothy Thompson, quoted in ibid., 350.

22. Richard Winnington, "*Lifeboat,*" *News Chronicle,* March 19, 1944.

23. David Lardner, *New Yorker,* February 5, 1944, 57.

24. McGilligan, *Alfred Hitchcock,* 353.

13. *Spellbound* (1945)

1. Joseph I. Breen to David O. Selznick, May 19, 1944, *Spellbound* File, Motion Picture Producers and Distributors Association Collection, Margaret Herrick Library, Academy of Motion Picture Arts and Sciences, Los Angeles. (This collection is hereafter cited as MPPDA.)

2. Ibid.

3. Ibid.

4. Joseph I. Breen to David O. Selznick, June 19, 1944, MPPDA.

5. Joseph I. Breen to David O. Selznick, June 30, 1944, MPPDA.

6. Doug McClelland, *The Unkindest Cuts: The Scissors and the Cinema* (London: A. S. Barnes, 1972), 97.

7. Leff, *Hitchcock and Selznick,* 140.

8. Matthew Gale, ed., *Dalí and Film* (New York: Museum of Modern Art, 2007), 178.

9. Leff, *Hitchcock and Selznick,* 157.

10. Ibid., 143.

11. Ibid., 157.

12. Ibid., 154.

13. Whitty, *The Alfred Hitchcock Encyclopedia,* 409.

14. Leff, *Hitchcock and Selznick,* 143.

15. A. R. Allen to Joseph I. Breen, June 10, 1946, MPPDA.

16. Joseph I. Breen to Reginald Allen, June 21, 1946, MPPDA.

17. Leff, *Hitchcock and Selznick,* 159.

18. Bosley Crowther, "The Screen in Review: *Spellbound,*" *New York Times,* November 2, 1946.

19. Leff, *Hitchcock and Selznick,* 169.

20. Agee, *Agee on Film,* 179, 180.

21. Polito, *Farber on Film,* 265.

22. Truffaut, *Hitchcock,* 167, 165.

23. Thomson, *Have You Seen . . . ?* 609.

14. *Notorious* (1946)

1. John Taintor Foote, "The Song of the Dragon," *Saturday Evening Post,* November 12, 1921, 3–5; November 19, 1921, 18–19.

2. Simone, *Hitchcock as Activist,* 121.

3. Leff, *Hitchcock and Selznick,* 195.

4. Ibid.

5. Drew Casper, audio commentary on *Notorious,* Alfred Hitchcock Premiere Collection (Beverly Hills: Twentieth Century Fox Home Entertainment, 2008).

6. Giblin, *Alfred Hitchcock's London,* 220, 221.

7. Leff, *Hitchcock and Selznick,* 203.

8. Joseph I. Breen to David O. Selznick, May 25, 1945, *Notorious* File, Motion Picture Producers and Distributors Association Collection, Margaret Herrick Library, Academy of Motion Picture Arts and Sciences, Los Angeles. (This collection is hereafter cited as MPPDA.)

9. Ibid.

10. Geoffrey Shurlock, File Memo Re: *Notorious,* June 15, 1945, MPPDA.

11. Joseph I. Breen to Mr. William Gordon, July 25, 1945, MPPDA.

12. Leff, *Hitchcock and Selznick,* 200.

13. Ibid., 206.

14. Joseph I. Breen to Mr. William Gordon, September 21, 1945, MPPDA.

15. Joseph I. Breen to Mr. William Gordon, November 29, 1945, MPPDA.

16. Motion Picture Production Code Memo, Re: *Notorious* Deletions Requested, June 26, 1946, MPPDA.

17. William Gordon to Mr. Joseph I. Breen, June 28, 1946, MPPDA.

18. Gardner, *The Censorship Papers.*

19. Ingrid Bergman obituary, *New York Times,* August 31, 1982.

20. Frank I. Nugent, "Mr. Hitchcock Discusses Love, *New York Times Sunday Magazine,* November 3, 1946.

21. McGilligan, *Alfred Hitchcock,* 376.

22. Ebert, *The Great Movies,* 338.

23. Truffaut, *Hitchcock,* 171.

24. Agee, *Agee on Film,* 213–14.

25. Bosley Crowther, "The Screen in Review: *Notorious,*" *New York Times,* August 16, 1946.

26. R. E. Vining to Joseph I. Breen, November 17, 1947, MPPAA.

27. Truffaut, *Hitchcock,* 167.

28. Thomson, *Have You Seen . . . ?* 609.

15. *The Paradine Case* (1947)

1. Joseph I. Breen to Mr. L. B. Mayer, March 12, 1935, *The Paradine Case* File, Motion Picture Producers and Distributors Association Collection, Margaret Herrick Library, Academy of Motion Picture Arts and Sciences, Los Angeles. (This collection is hereafter cited as MPPDA.)

2. Ibid.

3. Truffaut, *Hitchcock;* McGilligan, *Alfred Hitchcock,* 338, 173, 177.

4. McGilligan, *Alfred Hitchcock,* 338.

5. Leff, *Hitchcock and Selznick,* 248.

6. Joseph I. Breen to Mr. David O. Selznick, August 26, 1946, MPPDA.

7. Ibid.

8. Joseph I. Breen to Mr. David O. Selznick, November 23, 1946, MPPDA.

9. Joseph I. Breen to Mr. L. B. Mayer, March 12, 1935, MPPDA.

10. Thomson, *Showman,* 487, 488.

11. Ibid., 486.

12. Finler, *Hitchcock in Hollywood,* 73.

13. Mogg, *The Alfred Hitchcock Story,* 95.

14. Bosley Crowther, "The Screen in Review: *Spellbound,*" *New York Times,* November 2, 1946.

15. Leff, *Hitchcock and Selznick,* 262.

16. Hitchcock and Transatlantic

1. Leff, *Hitchcock and Selznick,* 235.

2. Ibid., 268.

3. Ibid., 266.

17. *Rope* (1948)

1. Laurents, *Original Story By,* 124.

2. McGilligan, *Alfred Hitchcock,* 406.

3. Walter Srebnick, "Working with Hitch: A Screenwriters Forum with Evan Hunter, Arthur Laurents, and Joseph Stefano," in Gottlieb and Allen, *The Hitchcock Annual Anthology,* 19.

4. Ibid.

5. Joseph I. Breen to Mr. Alfred Hitchcock, September 4, 1946, *Rope* File, Motion Picture Producers and Distributors Association Collection, Margaret Herrick Library, Academy of Motion Picture Arts and Sciences, Los Angeles. (This collection is hereafter cited as MPPDA.)

6. Ibid.

7. Stephen S. Jackson to Mr. Fred Ahern, December 15, 1947, MPPDA.

8. Ibid.

9. Stephen S. Jackson to Mr. Fred Ahern, December 22, 1947, MPPDA.

10. Stephen S. Jackson to Mr. Victor A. Peers, January 28, 1948, MPPDA.

11. Victor A. Peers to Mr. Stephen S. Jackson, January 28, MPAA.

12. David Sterritt, "Morbid Psychologies and So Forth: The Fine Art of *Rope,*" in Boyd and Palmer, *Hitchcock at the Source,* 164.

13. McGilligan, *Alfred Hitchcock,* 412.

14. Leff, *Hitchcock and Selznick,* 272.

15. Ibid., 273.

16. Ibid., 272.

17. *Time,* quoted in Sterritt, "Morbid Psychologies and So Forth," 159.
18. *Hollywood Reporter,* August 26, 1948.
19. Bosley Crowther, "The Screen," *New York Times,* August 27, 1948.
20. *Hollywood Reporter,* August 26, 1948.
21. Bosley Crowther, "The Screen," *New York Times,* August 27, 1948.
22. McGilligan, *Alfred Hitchcock,* 420.
23. Ibid.
24. Ibid.
25. Thomas M. Pryor, "Censorship Ties *Rope* in Knots," *New York Times,* November 21, 1948.
26. Ibid.
27. Arthur Laurents, quoted in *Rope Unleashed,* documentary accompanying *Rope* DVD (Universal City, CA: Universal Studios, 2000).

18. *Under Capricorn* (1949)

1. Truffaut, *Hitchcock,* 185.
2. Mogg, *The Alfred Hitchcock Story,* 102.
3. Spoto, *The Art of Alfred Hitchcock,* 175.
4. Truffaut, *Hitchcock,* 184.
5. Spoto, *Notorious,* 246.
6. Ibid.
7. Truffaut, *Hitchcock,* 189.
8. Joseph I. Breen to Mr. Victor A. Peers, July 14, 1948, *Under Capricorn* File, Motion Picture Producers and Distributors Association Collection, Margaret Herrick Library, Academy of Motion Picture Arts and Sciences, Los Angeles. (This collection is hereafter cited as MPPDA.)
9. Victor A. Peers to Joseph Breen, July 30, 1948, MPPAA.
10. Doherty, *Hollywood's Censor,* 287.
11. Vizzard, *See No Evil,* 146.
12. Ibid., 147.
13. Spoto, *Notorious,* 279.
14. Mogg, *The Alfred Hitchcock Story,* 102.
15. Doherty, *Hollywood's Censor,* 289.
16. Spoto, *Notorious,* 294.
17. Ibid., 296.
18. Vizzard, *See No Evil,* 148, 149.
19. Doherty, *Hollywood's Censor,* 290.
20. *Hollywood Reporter,* quoted in Truffaut, *Hitchcock,* 185, 186.
21. Harold Barnes, quoted in McGilligan, *Alfred Hitchcock,* 437; Bosley

Crowther, "The Screen in Review: *Under Capricorn,*" *New York Times,* September 9, 1949.

22. Mogg, *The Alfred Hitchcock Story,* 102; *London Times,* October 5, 1949.

19. Hitchcock and Warner Bros.

1. McGilligan, *Alfred Hitchcock,* 469.
2. Ibid., 464–65.
3. Joel W. Finler, *The Hollywood Story* (New York: Crown, 1988), 238.
4. McGilligan, *Alfred Hitchcock,* 465.

20. *Stage Fright* (1950)

1. Joseph I. Breen to Mr. J. L. Warner, April 8, 1949, *Stage Fright* File, Motion Picture Producers and Distributors Association Collection, Margaret Herrick Library, Academy of Motion Picture Arts and Sciences, Los Angeles. (This collection is hereafter cited as MPPDA.)
2. Joseph I. Breen to Mr. J. L. Warner on draft *Stage Fright* script, April 26, 1949, *Stage Fright* File, MPPDA.
3. Ibid.
4. Joseph I. Breen to Mr. J. L. Warner, November 16, 1949, *Stage Fright* File, MPPDA.
5. Joseph I. Breen to Mr. J. L. Warner, February 13, 1950, *Stage Fright* File, MPPDA.
6. McGilligan, *Alfred Hitchcock,* 436.
7. Joseph I. Breen to Mr. J. L. Warner, February 28, 1950, *Stage Fright* File, MPPDA.
8. Vizzard, *See No Evil,* 106, 107.
9. Joseph I. Breen to Mr. J. L. Warner on draft *Stage Fright* script, April 26, 1949, *Stage Fright* File, MPPDA.
10. Krohn, *Hitchcock at Work,* 111.
11. McGilligan, *Alfred Hitchcock,* 431.
12. *London Times* review of *Stage Fright,* quoted in Condon and Sangster, *The Complete Hitchcock,* 168.
13. Rohmer and Chabrol, *Hitchcock,* 105.
14. Richard Schickel, Commentary on *Stage Fright* DVD (Warner Bros. Home Video, 2007).
15. Truffaut, *Hitchcock,* 189.
16. Joseph I. Breen to Mr. J. L. Warner on draft *Stage Fright* script, April 26, 1949, MPPDA.

17. *London Times* review of *Stage Fright,* quoted in Condon and Sangster, *The Complete Hitchcock,* 168.

18. Bosley Crowther, "The Screen in Review; *Stage Fright,*" *New York Times,* February 24, 1950.

21. *Strangers on a Train* (1951)

1. Wilson, *Beautiful Shadow,* 168.

2. Geoffrey M. Shurlock, File Memo Re: *Strangers on a Train,* June 30, 1950, *Strangers on a Train* File, Motion Picture Producers and Distributors Association Collection, Margaret Herrick Library, Academy of Motion Picture Arts and Sciences, Los Angeles. (This collection is hereafter cited as MPPDA.)

3. Truffaut, *Hitchcock,* 194.

4. Williams, *Raymond Chandler,* 271.

5. McGilligan, *Alfred Hitchcock,* 245.

6. Williams, *Raymond Chandler,* 272.

7. Truffaut, *Hitchcock,* 193.

8. McGilligan, *Alfred Hitchcock,* 445.

9. Williams, *Raymond Chandler,* 276.

10. Joseph I. Breen to J. L. Warner, October 9, 1950, MPPDA.

11. Geoffrey M. Shurlock, File Memo Re: *Strangers on a Train,* October 27, 1950, MPPDA.

12. Joseph I. Breen to J. L. Warner, November 7, 1950, MPPDA.

13. Ibid.; Joseph I. Breen to J. L. Warner, November 26, 1950, MPPDA.

14. McGilligan, *Alfred Hitchcock,* 442.

15. Alfred Hitchcock, quoted in "Making of *Strangers on a Train*: A Hitchcock Classic," special DVD edition (Burbank, CA: Warner Bros., 2004).

16. Chandler, *It's Only a Movie,* 196.

17. McGilligan, *Alfred Hitchcock,* 449.

18. Krohn, *Hitchcock at Work,* 117.

19. Joseph I. Breen to J. L. Warner, October 9, 1950, MPPDA.

20. Manny Farber, *Nation,* July 28, 1951, 77.

21. Spoto, *The Art of Alfred Hitchcock,* 189; Ebert, *The Great Movies II,* 428.

22. Farber, *Nation.*

23. Powell, *The Dilys Powell Film Reader,* 45, 46.

24. Bosley Crowther, "The Screen in Review; *Strangers on a Train,*" *New York Times,* July 4, 1951.

25. Wilson, *Beautiful Shadow,* 170.

26. Hiney and MacShane, *The Raymond Chandler Papers,* 142.

27. MacShane, *The Life of Raymond Chandler,* 177.

28. Truffaut, *Hitchcock,* 198, 193.

22. *I Confess* (1953)

1. Geoffrey M. Shurlock, File Memo Re: *I Confess,* December 16, 1948, *I Confess* File, Motion Picture Producers and Distributors Association Collection, Margaret Herrick Library, Academy of Motion Picture Arts and Sciences, Los Angeles. (This collection is hereafter cited as MPPDA.)

2. Jack Vizzard, File Memo Re: *I Confess,* April 10, 1952, MPPDA.

3. McGilligan, *Alfred Hitchcock,* 245.

4. Martin Quigley to Sidney Bernstein, April 6, 1952, MPPDA.

5. McGilligan, *Alfred Hitchcock,* 459.

6. Ibid.

7. Joseph I. Breen to Alfred Hitchcock, July 24, 1952, MPPDA.

8. Ibid.

9. Joseph I. Breen to Jack Warner, August 29, 1952, MPPDA.

10. Joseph I. Breen to Alfred Hitchcock, July 24, 1952, MPPDA.

11. Jack Vizzard to Martin Quigley, April 18, 1952, MPPDA.

12. Joseph I. Breen to Alfred Hitchcock, July 24, 1952, MPPDA; Joseph I. Breen to Alfred Hitchcock, August 6, 1952, MPPDA; Joseph I. Breen to Alfred Hitchcock, August 12, 1952, MPPDA.

13. Truffaut, *Hitchcock,* 204.

14. Ibid., 203.

15. Ibid.

16. Bosley Crowther, "The Screen in Review; *I Confess,*" *New York Times,* March 23, 1953.

17. Condon and Sangster, *The Complete Hitchcock,* 178.

18. "*I Confess,*" *Hollywood Reporter,* February 5, 1953.

19. Mogg, *The Alfred Hitchcock Story,* 116.

20. McGilligan, *Alfred Hitchcock,* 466.

21. Ibid.

22. Rockett, *Irish Film Censorship,* 123.

23. *Dial M for Murder* (1954)

1. Truffaut, *Hitchcock,* 209.

2. Bosley Crowther, "The Screen in Review; *Dial M for Murder,*" *New York Times,* May 29, 1954; Peter Bogdanovich, quoted in *Hitchcock and Dial M.* documentary accompanying *Dial M for Murder* DVD (Burbank, CA: Warner Home Video, 2004).

3. Bogdanovich, quoted in *Hitchcock and Dial M.* documentary.

4. Joseph I. Breen to Mr. Jack Warner, June 25, 1953, *Dial M for Murder* File, Motion Picture Producers and Distributors Association Collection, Margaret Her-

rick Library, Academy of Motion Picture Arts and Sciences, Los Angeles. (This collection is hereafter cited as MPPDA.)

5. Ibid.

6. Joseph I. Breen to Mr. Jack Warner, August 4, 1953, MPPDA.

7. Dixon, *The Early Film Criticism of François Truffaut,* 54–55.

8. Crowther, "The Screen in Review; *Dial M for Murder.*"

9. Truffaut, *Hitchcock,* 209.

10. Bogdanovich, *Hitchcock and Dial M.* documentary.

24. Hitchcock in Ascendance

1. Doherty, *Hollywood's Censor,* 293, 297.

2. Ibid., 308.

3. Miller, *Censored Hollywood,* 166.

4. Doherty, *Hollywood's Censor,* 327.

25. *Rear Window* (1954)

1. Joseph I. Breen to Mr. Luigi Lurachi on draft *Rear Window* script, November 20, 1953, *Rear Window* File, Motion Picture Producers and Distributors Association Collection, Margaret Herrick Library, Academy of Motion Picture Arts and Sciences, Los Angeles. (This collection is hereafter cited as MPPDA.)

2. Ibid.

3. Ibid.

4. Curtis, "The Making of *Rear Window,*" in Belton, *Alfred Hitchcock's "Rear Window,"* 30.

5. Eugene Dougherty, File Memo in Re: *Rear Window,* November 27, 1953, *Rear Window* File, MPPDA.

6. Ibid.

7. Eugene Dougherty, File Memo in Re: *Rear Window,* February 15, 1954, *Rear Window* File, MPPDA.

8. Ibid.

9. Ibid.

10. McGilligan, *Alfred Hitchcock,* 489.

11. Eugene Dougherty, File Memo in Re: *Rear Window,* February 16, 1954, *Rear Window* File, MPPDA.

12. Jack Moffitt, review of *Rear Window, Hollywood Reporter,* July 13, 1954; Bosley Crowther, "The Screen in Review: *Rear Window,*" *New York Times,* August 5, 1954.

13. John McCarten, "Hitchcock Confined Again," *New Yorker,* August 7, 1954, 50–51.

14. Thomson, *Have You Seen . . . ?* 714.

15. Ibid.

26. *To Catch a Thief* (1955)

1. McGilligan, *Alfred Hitchcock,* 500.

2. DeRosa, *Writing with Hitchcock,* 98.

3. Joseph I. Breen to Mr. Luigi Luraschi, May 6, 1954, *To Catch a Thief* File, Motion Picture Producers and Distributors Association Collection, Margaret Herrick Library, Academy of Motion Picture Arts and Sciences, Los Angeles. (This collection is hereafter cited as MPPDA.)

4. Joseph I. Breen to Mr. Luigi Luraschi, July 9, 1954, MPPDA.

5. McGilligan, *Alfred Hitchcock,* 501.

6. Joseph I. Breen to Mr. Luigi Luraschi, July 9, 1954, MPPDA.

7. Geoffrey Shurlock to Mr. Luigi Luraschi, February 24, 1955, MPPDA.

8. McGilligan, *Alfred Hitchcock,* 501.

9. Alfred Hitchcock, quoted in Moral, *Alfred Hitchcock's Moviemaking Master Class,* 111.

10. Joseph I. Breen to Mr. Luigi Luraschi, July 9, 1954, MPPDA.

11. *New Yorker,* quoted in Harris and Lasky, *The Films of Alfred Hitchcock,* 171.

12. Bosley Crowther, "Screen: Cat Man Out *To Catch a Thief,*" *New York Times,* August 5, 1955.

13. Harris and Lasky, *The Films of Alfred Hitchcock,* 173.

14. Truffaut, *Hitchcock,* 223.

27. *The Trouble with Harry* (1955)

1. Joseph I. Breen to Mr. Luigi Lurachi on draft *Trouble with Harry* script, August 5, 1954, *Trouble with Harry* File, Motion Picture Producers and Distributors Association Collection, Margaret Herrick Library, Academy of Motion Picture Arts and Sciences, Los Angeles.

2. Ibid.

3. Ibid.

4. Krohn, *Hitchcock at Work,* 150.

5. Condon and Sangster, *The Complete Hitchcock,* 204.

6. Bosley Crowther, "Whimsical Film from Hitchcock," *New York Times,* October 18, 1955.

7. Condon and Sangster, *The Complete Hitchcock,* 204.

8. DeRosa, *Writing with Hitchcock,* 158.

28. *The Man Who Knew Too Much* (1956)

1. Geoffrey Shurlock to Mr. Luigi Luraschi, April 29, 1955, *The Man Who Knew Too Much* File, Motion Picture Producers and Distributors Association Collection, Margaret Herrick Library, Academy of Motion Picture Arts and Sciences, Los Angeles.

2. Ibid.

3. Krohn, *Hitchcock at Work,* 159.

4. Truffaut, *Hitchcock,* 228.

5. Ibid., 94.

6. Finler, *Hitchcock in Hollywood,* 110.

7. Chandler, *It's Only a Movie,* 229.

8. *London Times* review of *The Man Who Knew Too Much,* quoted in Condon and Sangster, *The Complete Hitchcock,* 210.

9. Bosley Crowther, "The Screen in Review: *The Man Who Knew Too Much,*" *New York Times,* May 17, 1956.

10. McDevitt and San Juan, *A Year of Hitchcock,* 268.

29. *The Wrong Man* (1956)

1. Gottlieb, *Alfred Hitchcock Interviews.*

2. Geoffrey Shurlock to Mr. Jack L. Warner, January 19, 1956, *The Wrong Man* File, Motion Picture Producers and Distributors Association Collection, Margaret Herrick Library, Academy of Motion Picture Arts and Sciences, Los Angeles.

3. Lou Lumenick, "A Case of Mistaken Identity Ruined a Man's Life—And Inspired Hitchcock," *New York Post,* February 7, 2016.

4. Mogg, *The Alfred Hitchcock Story,* 139.

5. A. H. Weiler, "Screen: New Format for Hitchcock; Suspense Is Dropped in *The Wrong Man,*" *New York Times,* December 24, 1956.

6. Rohmer and Chabrol, *Hitchcock,* 146, 147.

7. Godard, *Godard on Godard,* 49.

8. Schickel, *Keepers,* 200.

9. Truffaut, *Hitchcock,* 242, 243.

30. *Vertigo* (1958)

1. Samuel Taylor, "A Talk by Samuel Taylor," in Raubicheck and Srebnick, *Hitchcock's Released Films,* 288.

2. Ibid., 294.

3. Gottlieb, *Hitchcock on Hitchcock,* 2:229.

4. Luigi Luraschi, Memorandum Re: "From among the Dead" to Mr. Alfred Hitchcock, July 11, 1957, *Vertigo* File, Motion Picture Producers and Distributors Association Collection, Margaret Herrick Library, Academy of Motion Picture Arts and Sciences, Los Angeles. (This collection is hereafter cited as MPPDA.)

5. Taylor, "A Talk by Samuel Taylor," 290.

6. Geoffrey Shurlock to Mr. Luigi Luraschi, September 18, 1957, MPPDA.

7. Taylor, "A Talk by Samuel Taylor," 290.

8. Geoffrey Shurlock to Mr. Luigi Luraschi, August 1, 1957, MPPDA.

9. Geoffrey Shurlock to Mr. Luigi Luraschi, September 18, 1957, MPPDA.

10. McGilligan, *Alfred Hitchcock,* 557.

11. Geoffrey Shurlock to Mr. Luigi Luraschi, August 1, 1957, MPPDA.

12. Charles Barr, "*Vertigo,*" 2nd ed., BFI Film Classics (London: BFI, 2003), 75.

13. Foreign Censorship Ending, *Vertigo* DVD bonus feature, Universal Legacy Series (Universal City, CA: Universal Studios, 2008).

14. McGilligan, *Alfred Hitchcock,* 448.

15. Truffaut, *Hitchcock,* 106.

16. John McCarten, "The Current Cinema," *New Yorker,* May 26, 1958; *Time,* quoted in McGilligan, *Alfred Hitchcock,* 564.

17. Bosley Crowther, "*Vertigo,* Hitchcock's Latest," *New York Times,* May 29, 1958; *Newsweek,* quoted in McGilligan, *Alfred Hitchcock,* 564.

18. Spoto, *The Art of Alfred Hitchcock,* 265; Wood, *Hitchcock's Films Revisited,* 108.

19. Ian Christie, "Chronicle of a Fall Foretold," *Sight and Sound,* September 1, 2012.

20. Schickel, *Keepers,* 202.

21. Truffaut, *Hitchcock,* 247.

22. Thomson, *Have You Seen . . . ?* 943.

23. Ebert, *The Great Movies I,* 477.

31. *North by Northwest* (1959)

1. *Variety* (1957), quoted in Doherty, *Hollywood's Censor,* 327.

2. John Brady, "An Interview with Ernest Lehman," in *The Craft of the Screenwriter* (New York: Touchstone Books, 1982), 198–206.

3. Geoffrey Shurlock to Mr. Robert Vogel, August 21, 1958, *North by Northwest* File, Motion Picture Producers and Distributors Association Collection, Margaret Herrick Library, Academy of Motion Picture Arts and Sciences, Los Angeles. (This collection is hereafter cited as MPPDA.)

4. Ibid.

5. Geoffrey Shurlock to Mr. Robert Vogel, October 16, 1958, MPPDA.

6. Geoffrey Shurlock to Mr. Robert Vogel, August 21, 1958, MPPDA.

7. Geoffrey Shurlock to Mr. Robert Vogel, September 19, 1958, MPPDA.

8. McGilligan, *Alfred Hitchcock,* 573.

9. Mogg, *The Alfred Hitchcock Story,* 147.

10. Geoffrey Shurlock to Mr. Robert Vogel, October 2, 1958, MPPDA.

11. McGilligan, *Alfred Hitchcock,* 574.

12. Geoffrey Shurlock to Mr. Robert Vogel, October 16, 1958, MPPDA.

13. Geoffrey Shurlock, January 28, 1959, memo, cited in Krohn, *Hitchcock at Work,* 216.

14. Geoffrey Shurlock to Mr. Robert Vogel, October 16, 1958, MPPDA.

15. Eva Marie Saint, quoted in Moral, *Alfred Hitchcock's Moviemaking Master Class,* 112.

16. Krohn, *Hitchcock at Work,* 216.

17. Ibid., 217.

18. Ernest Lehman, Audio Commentary on *North by Northwest,* 50th Anniversary DVD edition (Warner Bros. Entertainment and Turner Entertainment, 2009).

19. Alfred Hitchcock, quoted in Jean Domarchi and Jean Douchet, "An Interview with Alfred Hitchcock," *Cahiers du cinéma,* December 1959, reprinted in Naremore, *North by Northwest,* 182.

20. Philip Kemp, "Famous Locations," in Mogg, *The Alfred Hitchcock Story,* 74.

21. Krohn, *Hitchcock at Work,* 204.

22. Alfred Hitchcock, quoted in Domarchi and Douchet, "An Interview with Alfred Hitchcock," 178.

23. McGilligan, *Alfred Hitchcock,* 573, 575.

24. Stanley Kaufmann, *New Republic,* August 10, 1959, 23.

25. *Time,* August 17, 1959, 78, 80; McGilligan, *Alfred Hitchcock,* 575.

26. McGilligan, *Alfred Hitchcock,* 575.

27. Luc Moullet, *Cahiers du cinéma,* December 1959, reprinted in Naremore, "*North by Northwest,*" 195–97.

32. *Psycho* (1960)

1. Leigh and Nickens, "*Psycho,*" 3.

2. Walter Srebnick, "Working with Hitch; A Screenwriter's Forum with Evan Hunter, Arthur Laurents, and Joseph Stefano," in Gottlieb and Allen, *The Hitchcock Anthology,* 36.

3. Geoffrey Shurlock to Mr. Luigi Luraschi, November 23, 1959, *Psycho* File,

Motion Picture Producers and Distributors Association Collection, Margaret Herrick Library, Academy of Motion Picture Arts and Sciences, Los Angeles. (This collection is hereafter cited as MPPDA.)

4. Ibid.

5. Taylor, *Hitch,* 254.

6. Condon and Sangster, *The Complete Hitchcock,* 245.

7. Jack Vizzard, File Memo RE: *Psycho,* February 22, 1960, *Psycho* File, MPPDA.

8. Ibid.

9. Rebello, *Alfred Hitchcock and the Making of "Psycho,"* 145.

10. Laurent Bouzereau, *The Making of "Psycho,"* documentary accompanying Collector's Edition *Psycho* DVD (Universal City, CA: Universal Studios, 1999).

11. Leigh and Nickens, *"Psycho,"* 75.

12. Rebello, *Alfred Hitchcock and the Making of "Psycho,"* 146.

13. Ibid., 149.

14. *Newsweek,* June 20, 1960.

15. Powell, *The Dilys Powell Film Reader,* 50.

16. Dwight MacDonald, quoted in McGilligan, *Alfred Hitchcock,* 600.

17. Bosley Crowther, review of *Psycho, New York Times,* June 17, 1960.

18. Bosley Crowther, "An Answer to Filmgoers Who Think *Psycho* Should Be Banned," *New York Times,* August 25, 1960.

19. McGilligan, *Alfred Hitchcock,* 600.

20. Leigh and Nickens, *"Psycho,"* 75.

33. *The Birds* (1963)

1. Ackroyd, *Alfred Hitchcock,* 210.

2. Moral, *The Making of Hitchcock's "The Birds,"* 104.

3. Ibid., 105, 106.

4. Geoffrey Shurlock to Miss Peggy Robertson, November 21, 1961, *The Birds* File, Motion Picture Producers and Distributors Association Collection, Margaret Herrick Library, Academy of Motion Picture Arts and Sciences, Los Angeles. (This collection is hereafter cited as MPPDA.)

5. Geoffrey Shurlock to Miss Peggy Robertson, February 8, 1962, MPPDA.

6. Moral, *The Making of Hitchcock's "The Birds,"* 182.

7. Ackroyd, *Alfred Hitchcock,* 216.

8. Moral, *The Making of Hitchcock's "The Birds,"* 99–101.

9. Ibid., 182.

10. Rutherford Phillips, letter of January 28, 1963, quoted in ibid.

11. Gardner, *The Censorship Papers,* 96.

12. McGilligan, *Alfred Hitchcock,* 628.

13. Moral, *The Making of Hitchcock's "The Birds,"* 141, 142.

14. McGilligan, *Alfred Hitchcock,* 628.

15. Ibid., 626.

16. Truffaut, *Hitchcock,* 290.

17. Krohn, *Hitchcock at Work,* 262.

18. Moral, *The Making of Hitchcock's "The Birds,"* 144.

19. Ibid., 144, 145.

20. Ibid., 146.

21. Ackroyd, *Alfred Hitchcock,* 220.

22. Moral, *The Making of Hitchcock's "The Birds,"* 198.

23. *London Times,* August 29, 1963; Bosley Crowther, review of *The Birds, New York Times,* April 1, 1963.

24. Brendan Gill, *New Yorker,* and *Time,* April 5, 1963, quoted in McGilligan, *Alfred Hitchcock,* 639.

25. Crowther, review of *The Birds; London Times,* August 29, 1963.

26. Moral, *The Making of Hitchcock's "The Birds,"* 108, 109.

27. Ackroyd, *Alfred Hitchcock,* 220.

34. *Marnie* (1964)

1. Gottlieb and Allen, *The Hitchcock Annual Anthology,* 24.

2. Moral, *Hitchcock and the Making of "Marnie,"* 19.

3. Gottlieb and Allen, *The Hitchcock Annual Anthology,* 24.

4. Moral, *Hitchcock and the Making of "Marnie,"* 37.

5. Gottlieb and Allen, *The Hitchcock Annual Anthology,* 24.

6. Ibid.

7. Moral, *Hitchcock and the Making of "Marnie,"* 45.

8. Geoffrey Shurlock to Miss Peggy Robertson, October 7, 1963, *Marnie* File, Motion Picture Producers and Distributors Association Collection, Margaret Herrick Library, Academy of Motion Picture Arts and Sciences, Los Angeles. (This collection is hereafter cited as MPPDA.)

9. Ibid.

10. Geoffrey Shurlock to Miss Peggy Robertson, November 7, 1963, MPPDA.

11. Jay Presson Allen, quoted in *The Trouble with Marnie,* DVD bonus material, Marnie Collector Edition (Universal City, CA: Universal Studios, 2000).

12. Moral, *Hitchcock and the Making of "Marnie,"* 45.

13. Ibid., 46.

14. Ibid., 121.

15. Harold Melniker, cited in ibid., 97.

16. Robert Boyle, quoted in ibid., 96.
17. Robert Boyle, quoted in ibid.
18. Hilton Green, quoted in ibid., 99.
19. Robin Wood, quoted in *The Trouble with Marnie.*
20. Robert Boyle, quoted in ibid.
21. Ackroyd, *Alfred Hitchcock,* 232.
22. Ibid., 229.
23. Moral, *Hitchcock and the Making of "Marnie,"* 100.
24. Taylor, *Hitch,* 272.
25. Ackroyd, *Alfred Hitchcock,* 230.
26. Taylor, *Hitch,* 272.
27. Hedren, *Tippi,* 72.
28. Ackroyd, *Alfred Hitchcock,* 230.
29. Hedren, *Tippi,* 73; McGilligan, *Alfred Hitchcock,* 649.
30. Ackroyd, *Alfred Hitchcock,* 231.
31. Moral, *Hitchcock and the Making of "Marnie,"* 121.
32. Eugene Archer, review of *Marnie, New York Times,* July 23, 1964.
33. Judith Christ, quoted in Moral, *Hitchcock and the Making of "Marnie,"* 146.
34. McGilligan, *Alfred Hitchcock,* 655.
35. Thomson, *Have You Seen . . . ?* 525.
36. Ackroyd, *Alfred Hitchcock,* 231.
37. Truffaut, *Hitchcock,* 327.
38. Moral, *Hitchcock and the Making of "Marnie,"* 108.
39. McDevitt and San Juan, *A Year of Hitchcock,* 330.

35. *Torn Curtain* (1966)

1. Laurent Bouzereau, *Torn Curtain Rising,* bonus feature on *Torn Curtain* DVD (Universal City, CA: Universal Pictures, 2006).
2. McGilligan, *Alfred Hitchcock,* 664.
3. Geoffrey Shurlock to Mr. Alfred J. Hitchcock, August 13, 1965, *Torn Curtain* File, Motion Picture Producers and Distributors Association Collection, Margaret Herrick Library, Academy of Motion Picture Arts and Sciences, Los Angeles. (This collection is hereafter cited as MPPDA.)
4. J. A. Vizzard, memo to *Torn Curtain* File, March 30, 1966, MPPDA.
5. Ibid.
6. Miller, *Censored Hollywood,* 208.
7. Budge Crawley, Fletcher Markle, and Gerald Pratley, "I Wish I Didn't Have to Shoot the Picture: An Interview with Alfred Hitchcock," reprinted in LaValley, *Focus on Hitchcock,* 25.
8. Geoffrey Shurlock to Mr. Alfred J. Hitchcock, August 13, 1965, MPPDA.

9. Ibid.

10. Jack Sullivan, "A Different Way to Master Suspense," *Wall Street Journal,* July 23–24, 2016.

11. Truffaut, *Hitchcock,* 311.

12. Geoffrey Shurlock to Mr. Robert Vogel, October 16, 1958, MPPDA.

13. Richard Schickel, "A Slight Touch of Hitchcock," quoted in McGilligan, *Alfred Hitchcock,* 675.

14. Bosley Crowther, review of *Torn Curtain, New York Times,* July 31, 1966.

15. Mogg, *The Alfred Hitchcock Story,* 147.

16. Geoffrey Shurlock to Mr. A. F. Marshall, December 5, 1966, MPPDA.

36. Television Censorship

1. Federal Communications Commission, Frequently Asked Questions: Obscenity, Indecency & Profanity, https://www.fcc.gov/reports-research/guides/obscenity-indecency-profanity/faq.

2. Justice John Paul Stevens, dissenting, in *FCC vs. Fox Television Stations Inc.,* Supreme Court Docket No. 07–582, April 28, 2009.

3. United States Court of Appeals for the Third Circuit, *CBS Corporation vs. Federal Communications Commission,* Docket No. 06–3575, November 2, 2011.

4. Keough, *Flesh and Blood,* 310, 311.

5. Schumach, *The Face on the Cutting Room Floor,* 244, 245.

6. Burns, *Invasion of the Mind Snatchers,* 81.

7. Schumach, *The Face on the Cutting Room Floor,* 249, 244, 247.

8. John McCarty and Brian Kelleher, *"Alfred Hitchcock Presents,"* 32.

9. Schumach, *The Face on the Cutting Room Floor,* 249.

10. Ibid.

11. Ibid., 250, 251.

12. Ibid., 251.

13. Ibid.

14. Ibid., 250.

15. Ibid., 247.

16. Ibid., 235.

17. Ibid., 234, 238.

18. Ibid., 243.

37. *Alfred Hitchcock Presents*

1. McCarty and Kelleher, *"Alfred Hitchcock Presents,"* 35.

2. McGilligan, *Alfred Hitchcock,* 529.

3. McCarty and Kelleher, *"Alfred Hitchcock Presents,"* 45.

4. Ibid., 33, 34.
5. Ibid., 41.
6. Ibid., 13.
7. Ackroyd, *Alfred Hitchcock,* 177.

38. The Decline of the Code

1. Tropiano, *Obscene, Indecent, Immoral, and Offensive,* 141.
2. Martin Quigley, quoted in Leff and Simmons, *The Dame in the Kimono,* 264.
3. Farber, *The Movie Rating Game,* 12.
4. Tropiano, *Obscene, Indecent, Immoral, and Offensive,* 90.

39. The Rise of the Rating System

1. Andy Klein, "Censorship and Self Regulation," in Keough, *Flesh and Blood,* 313.
2. Peter Travers, "The Ratings Game," in Keough, *Flesh and Blood,* 350.
3. Stephen Farber, quoted in Tropiano, *Obscene, Indecent, Immoral, and Offensive,* 96.
4. Farber, *The Movie Rating Game,* 2, 57.
5. Ibid., 57.
6. Kirby Dick, *This Film Is Not Yet Rated* (Santa Monica, CA: Chain Camera Productions, 2006).

40. *Topaz* (1969)

1. McGilligan, *Alfred Hitchcock,* 692.
2. François Truffaut, quoted in Charles J. Rzepka and Lee Horsley, eds., *A Companion to Crime Fiction* (Malden, MA: Wiley-Blackwell, 2010), 546.
3. McGilligan, *Alfred Hitchcock,* 693.
4. Kael, *Deeper into Movies,* 79.
5. Richard Corliss, quoted in McGilligan, *Alfred Hitchcock,* 694.
6. Ibid.

41. *Frenzy* (1972)

1. Leitch, *The Encyclopedia of Alfred Hitchcock,* 113.
2. Anthony Shaffer, in *The Story of "Frenzy,"* bonus materials on *Frenzy* DVD (Universal City, CA: Universal Studios, 2000).
3. McGilligan, *Alfred Hitchcock,* 711.

4. Foery, *Alfred Hitchcock's "Frenzy,"* 139.

5. Ibid., 61, 62.

6. Richard Schickel, "The Return of Alfred the Great," *Life,* June 2, 1972.

7. John Russell Taylor, "Hitchcock Magic Is Intact," *London Times,* May 23, 1972.

8. Vincent Canby, review of *Frenzy, New York Times,* June 22, 1972.

9. Foery, *Alfred Hitchcock's "Frenzy,"* 122.

10. Charles Champlin, "Hitchcock's Special Place," *Los Angeles Times,* July 14, 1972.

11. Leitch, *The Encyclopedia of Alfred Hitchcock,* 115.

12. Foery, *Alfred Hitchcock's "Frenzy,"* 123.

13. McGilligan, *Alfred Hitchcock,* 701.

14. Ibid., 709.

42. *Family Plot* (1976)

1. Charles Champlin, quoted in Mogg, *The Alfred Hitchcock Story,* 181.

2. Vincent Canby, quoted in McGilligan, *Alfred Hitchcock,* 730.

3. Jay Cocks, quoted in ibid.

4. Simon, *Reverse Angle,* 236, 237.

Conclusion

1. J. Danvers Williams, "The Censor Wouldn't Pass It, Says Hitchcock," *Film Weekly,* November 5, 1938.

2. Jean Domarchi and Jean Douchet, "An Interview with Alfred Hitchcock," *Cahiers du cinéma,* December 1959, reprinted in Naremore, *"North by Northwest,"* 178, 500.

3. Leff, *Hitchcock and Selznick,* 266.

4. Whitty, *The Alfred Hitchcock Encyclopedia,* 60.

5. McGilligan, *Alfred Hitchcock,* 219.

6. Jay Presson Allen, quoted in *The Trouble with Marnie,* DVD bonus material, Marnie Collector Edition (Universal City, CA: Universal Studios, 2000).

7. Leitch, *The Encyclopedia of Alfred Hitchcock,* 113.

8. Joseph I. Breen to Mr. Luigi Luraschi, May 6, 1954, *To Catch a Thief* File, Motion Picture Producers and Distributors Association Collection, Margaret Herrick Library, Academy of Motion Picture Arts and Sciences, Los Angeles. (This collection is hereafter cited as MPPDA.)

9. Jack Vizzard, File Memo RE *Psycho,* February 22, 1960, *Psycho* File, MPPDA.

10. Geoffrey Shurlock to Mr. Alfred J. Hitchcock, August 13, 1965, *Torn Curtain* File, MPPDA.

11. McGilligan, *Alfred Hitchcock,* 692.

12. Leitch, *The Encyclopedia of Alfred Hitchcock,* 115.

Selected Bibliography

Ackroyd, Peter. *Alfred Hitchcock: A Brief Life*. New York: Doubleday, 2015.

Agee, James. *Agee on Film: Reviews and Comments*. New York: McDowell, Obolensky, 1958.

Allen, Richard. *Hitchcock's Romantic Irony*. New York: Columbia University Press, 2007.

Allen, Richard, and Sam Ishii-Gonzales, eds. *Alfred Hitchcock Centenary Essays*. London: British Film Institute, 1999.

———. *Past and Future Hitchcock*. London: Routledge, 2004.

Auiler, Dan. *"Vertigo": The Making of a Hitchcock Classic*. New York: St. Martin's, 1998.

Barr, Charles. *English Hitchcock*. Moffat, UK: Cameron & Hollis, 1999.

———. *"Vertigo."* London: British Film Institute, 2002.

Belton, John, ed. *Alfred Hitchcock's "Rear Window."* Cambridge: Cambridge University Press, 2000.

Black, Gregory D. *Hollywood Censored*. New York: Cambridge University Press, 1994.

Boyd, David, and R. Barton Palmer, eds. *Hitchcock at the Source*. New York: SUNY Press, 2011.

Burns, Eric. *Invasion of the Mind Snatchers*. Philadelphia: Temple University Press, 2010.

Chandler, Charlotte. *It's Only a Movie: Alfred Hitchcock, a Personal Biography*. New York: Simon & Schuster, 2005.

Chandler, Raymond, *The Raymond Chandler Papers*. Edited by Tom Hiney and Frank MacShane. New York: Atlantic Monthly, 2000.

Condon, Paul, and Jim Sangster. *The Complete Hitchcock*. London: Virgin, 1999.

Conrad, Peter. *The Hitchcock Murders*. New York: Faber & Faber, 2000.

Couvares, Francis G. *Movie Censorship and American Culture*. 2nd ed. Amherst: University of Massachusetts Press, 2006.

Curtis, Scott. "The Making of *Rear Window*." In *Alfred Hitchcock's "Rear Window,"* edited by John Belton. Cambridge: Cambridge University Press, 2000.

DeRosa, Steven. *Writing with Hitchcock*. 2nd ed. New York: CineScribe Media, 2011.

Deutelbaum, Marshall, and Leland Poague, eds. *A Hitchcock Reader*. Ames: Iowa State University Press, 1986.

Doherty, Thomas. *Hollywood's Censor: Joseph I. Breen and the Production Code Administration.* New York: Columbia University Press, 2007.

Ebert, Roger. *The Great Movies.* New York: Broadway Books, 2002.

———. *The Great Movies II.* New York: Broadway Books, 2005.

Farber, Manny. *Farber on Film.* Edited by Robert Polito. New York: Library of America, 2009.

Farber, Stephen. *The Movie Rating Game.* Washington, DC: Public Affairs, 1972.

Ferguson, Otis. *The Film Criticism of Otis Ferguson.* Edited by Robert Wilson. Philadelphia: Temple University Press, 1971.

Finler, Joel W. *Hitchcock in Hollywood.* New York: Continuum, 1992.

Foery, Raymond. *Alfred Hitchcock's "Frenzy."* Lanham, MD: Scarecrow, 2012.

Forman, Henry James. *Our Movie Made Children.* New York: Macmillan, 1934.

Gardner, Gerald. *The Censorship Papers: Movie Censorship Letters from the Hays Office, 1934 to 1968.* New York: Dodd, Mead, 1987.

Giblin, Gary. *Alfred Hitchcock's London.* Baltimore: Midnight Marquee, 2006.

Godard, Jean-Luc. *Godard on Godard.* New York: Da Capo, 1972.

Gottlieb, Sidney, ed. *Alfred Hitchcock Interviews.* Jackson: University Press of Mississippi, 2003.

———. *Hitchcock on Hitchcock.* Berkeley: University of California Press, 1995.

———. *Hitchcock on Hitchcock.* Vol. 2. Berkeley: University of California Press, 2015.

Gottlieb, Sidney, and Richard Allen, eds. *The Hitchcock Annual Anthology.* London: Wallflower, 2009.

Gottlieb, Sidney, and Christopher Brookhouse, eds. *Framing Hitchcock.* Detroit: Wayne State University Press, 2002.

Harris, Robert A., and Michael S. Lasky. *The Films of Alfred Hitchcock.* Secaucus, NJ: Citadel, 1976.

Hedren, Tippi. *Tippi: A Memoir.* New York: HarperCollins, 2016.

Humphries, Patrick. *The Films of Alfred Hitchcock.* Greenwich, CT: Portland House, 1986.

Kael, Pauline. *Deeper into Movies.* Boston: Little, Brown, 1973.

———. *For Keeps.* Boston: Atlantic Little, Brown, 1973.

Keller, Laura Whitten. *Freedom of the Screen.* Lexington: University Press of Kentucky, 2008.

Keough, Peter, ed. *Flesh and Blood: The National Society of Film Critics on Sex, Violence, and Censorship.* San Francisco: Mercury House, 1995.

Kerzoncuf, Alain, and Charles Barr. *Hitchcock Lost and Found.* Lexington: University Press of Kentucky, 2015.

Krohn, Bill. *Hitchcock at Work.* London: Phaidon, 2000.

LaSalle, Mick. "A Short History of the Code." In *Dangerous Men,* appendix 2. New York: Thomas Dunne Books, 2002.

Laurents, Arthur. *Original Story By: A Memoir of Broadway and Hollywood.* New York: Applause, 2001.

LaValley, Albert J., ed. *Focus on Hitchcock.* Englewood Cliffs, NJ: Prentice-Hall, 1972.

Leff, Leonard J. *Hitchcock and Selznick.* New York: Weidenfeld &Nicholson, 1987.

Leff, Leonard J., and Jerold L. Simmons. *The Dame in the Kimono.* New York: Grove Weidenfeld, 1990.

Leigh, Janet, and Christopher Nickens. *"Psycho": Behind the Scenes of the Classic Thriller.* London: Pavilion Books, 1995.

Leitch, Thomas, *The Encyclopedia of Alfred Hitchcock.* New York: Checkmark Books, 2002.

MacShane, Frank. *The Life of Raymond Chandler.* New York: E. P. Dutton, 1976.

Martin, Olga J. *Hollywood's Movie Commandments.* New York: H. W. Wilson, 1937.

Matthews, Tom Dewe. *Censored.* London: Chatto & Windus, 1994.

McCarty, John, and Brian Kelleher. *"Alfred Hitchcock Presents."* New York: St. Martin's, 1985.

McDevitt, Jim, and Eric San Juan. *A Year of Hitchcock.* Lanham, MD: Scarecrow, 2009.

McGilligan, Patrick. *Alfred Hitchcock: A Life in Darkness and Light.* New York: HarperCollins, 2003.

Miller, Frank. *Censored Hollywood: Sex, Sin, and Violence on Screen.* Atlanta: Turner, 1994.

Mogg, Ken. *The Alfred Hitchcock Story.* Dallas: Taylor, 1999.

Moral, Tony Lee. *Alfred Hitchcock's Moviemaking Master Class.* Studio City, CA: Michael Wiese Productions, 2013.

———. *Hitchcock and the Making of "Marnie."* Rev. ed. London: Rowman & Littlefield, 2017.

———. *The Making of Hitchcock's "The Birds."* Harpenden, UK: Kamera Books, 2013.

Naremore, James, ed. *"North by Northwest."* New Brunswick, NJ: Rutgers University Press, 1993.

Nugent, Frank I. "Mr. Hitchcock Discusses Love." *New York Times Sunday Magazine,* November 3, 1946.

Powell, Dilys. *The Dilys Powell Film Reader.* Oxford: Oxford University Press, 1992.

Raubicheck, Walter, and Walter Srebnick. *Hitchcock's Rereleased Films.* Detroit: Wayne State University Press, 1991.

Rebello, Stephen. *Alfred Hitchcock and the Making of "Psycho."* New York: Dembner Books, 1990.

Rockett, Kevin. *Irish Film Censorship.* Dublin: Four Courts, 2004.

Roeder, George H., Jr. *The Censored War.* New Haven: Yale University Press, 1993.

Rohmer, Eric, and Claude Chabrol. *Hitchcock: The First Forty-Four Films.* Translated by Stanley Hochman. New York: Frederick Ungar, 1979.

Schickel, Richard. *Keepers.* New York: Knopf, 2015.

Schumach, Murray. *The Face on the Cutting Room Floor.* New York: William Morrow, 1964.

Simon, John. *Reverse Angle.* New York: Crown, 1982.

Simone, Sam P. *Hitchcock as Activist: Politics and the War Films.* Ann Arbor, MI: UMI Research Press, 1985.

Spoto, Donald. *The Art of Alfred Hitchcock.* 2nd ed. New York: Anchor Books, Doubleday, 1992.

———. *The Dark Side of Genius: The Life of Alfred Hitchcock.* Boston: Little, Brown, 1983.

———. *Notorious: The Life of Ingrid Bergman.* New York: Harper Collins, 1997.

———. *Spellbound by Beauty.* New York: Harmony Books, 2008.

Strauss, Marc Raymond. *Hitchcock Nonetheless.* Jefferson, NC: McFarland, 2007.

Taylor, John Russell. *Hitch: The Life and Times of Alfred Hitchcock.* New York: Pantheon Books, 1978.

Thomson, David. *Have You Seen . . .?* New York: Knopf, 2008.

———. *The Moment of "Psycho."* New York: Basic Books, 2009.

———. *Showman: The Life of David O. Selznick.* New York: Knopf, 1992.

Tropiano, Stephen. *Obscene, Indecent, Immoral, and Offensive.* Milwaukee: Limelight, 2009.

Truffaut, François. *The Early Film Criticism of François Truffaut.* Edited by Wheeler Winston Dixon. Bloomington: Indiana University Press, 1993.

———. *Hitchcock.* Rev. ed. New York: Simon & Schuster, 1985.

Van Schmus, Albert E., Oral History with Albert E. Van Schmus. Margaret Herrick Library, Academy of Motion Picture Arts and Sciences, Los Angeles.

Vizzard, Jack. *See No Evil.* New York: Simon & Schuster, 1970.

Walker, Michael. *Hitchcock's Motifs.* Amsterdam: Amsterdam University Press, 2005.

Walsh, Frank. *Sin and Censorship: The Catholic Church and the Motion Picture Industry.* New Haven: Yale University Press, 1996.

Whitty, Stephen. *The Alfred Hitchcock Encyclopedia.* Lanham, MD: Rowman & Littlefield, 2016.

Williams, Tom. *Raymond Chandler: A Life.* London: Aurum, 2012.

Wilson, Andrew. *Beautiful Shadow: A Life of Patricia Highsmith.* New York: Bloomsbury, 2003.

Wood, Robin. *Hitchcock's Films Revisited.* New York: Columbia University Press, 1989.

Index

Page numbers in italics refer to illustrations.

Index

Screen Classics

Screen Classics is a series of critical biographies, film histories, and analytical studies focusing on neglected filmmakers and important screen artists and subjects, from the era of silent cinema through the golden age of Hollywood to the international generation of today. Books in the Screen Classics series are intended for scholars and general readers alike. The contributing authors are established figures in their respective fields. This series also serves the purpose of advancing scholarship on film personalities and themes with ties to Kentucky.

Series Editor

Patrick McGilligan

Books in the Series

Olivia de Havilland: Lady Triumphant
Victoria Amador

Mae Murray: The Girl with the Bee-Stung Lips
Michael G. Ankerich

Hedy Lamarr: The Most Beautiful Woman in Film
Ruth Barton

Rex Ingram: Visionary Director of the Silent Screen
Ruth Barton

Conversations with Classic Film Stars: Interviews from Hollywood's Golden Era
James Bawden and Ron Miller

You Ain't Heard Nothin' Yet: Interviews with Stars from Hollywood's Golden Era
James Bawden and Ron Miller

Von Sternberg
John Baxter

Hitchcock's Partner in Suspense: The Life of Screenwriter Charles Bennett
Charles Bennett, edited by John Charles Bennett

Hitchcock and the Censors
John Billheimer

My Life in Focus: A Photographer's Journey with Elizabeth Taylor and the Hollywood Jet Set
Gianni Bozzacchi with Joey Tayler

Hollywood Divided: The 1950 Screen Directors Guild Meeting and the Impact of the Blacklist
Kevin Brianton

He's Got Rhythm: The Life and Career of Gene Kelly
Cynthia Brideson and Sara Brideson

Ziegfeld and His Follies: A Biography of Broadway's Greatest Producer
Cynthia Brideson and Sara Brideson

The Marxist and the Movies: A Biography of Paul Jarrico
Larry Ceplair

Dalton Trumbo: Blacklisted Hollywood Radical
Larry Ceplair and Christopher Trumbo

Warren Oates: A Wild Life
Susan Compo

Improvising Out Loud: My Life Teaching Hollywood How to Act
Jeff Corey with Emily Corey

Crane: Sex, Celebrity, and My Father's Unsolved Murder
Robert Crane and Christopher Fryer

Jack Nicholson: The Early Years
Robert Crane and Christopher Fryer

Anne Bancroft: A Life
Douglass K. Daniel

Being Hal Ashby: Life of a Hollywood Rebel
Nick Dawson

Bruce Dern: A Memoir
Bruce Dern with Christopher Fryer and Robert Crane

Intrepid Laughter: Preston Sturges and the Movies
Andrew Dickos

Miriam Hopkins: Life and Films of a Hollywood Rebel
Allan R. Ellenberger

John Gilbert: The Last of the Silent Film Stars
Eve Golden

Stuntwomen: The Untold Hollywood Story
Mollie Gregory

Saul Bass: Anatomy of Film Design
Jan-Christopher Horak

Hitchcock Lost and Found: The Forgotten Films
Alain Kerzoncuf and Charles Barr

Pola Negri: Hollywood's First Femme Fatale
Mariusz Kotowski

Sidney J. Furie: Life and Films
Daniel Kremer

Albert Capellani: Pioneer of the Silent Screen
Christine Leteux

Ridley Scott: A Biography
Vincent LoBrutto

Mamoulian: Life on Stage and Screen
David Luhrssen

Maureen O'Hara: The Biography
Aubrey Malone

My Life as a Mankiewicz: An Insider's Journey through Hollywood
Tom Mankiewicz and Robert Crane

Hawks on Hawks
Joseph McBride

Showman of the Screen: Joseph E. Levine and His Revolutions in Film Promotion
A. T. McKenna

William Wyler: The Life and Films of Hollywood's Most Celebrated Director
Gabriel Miller

Raoul Walsh: The True Adventures of Hollywood's Legendary Director
Marilyn Ann Moss

Veit Harlan: The Life and Work of a Nazi Filmmaker
Frank Noack

Harry Langdon: King of Silent Comedy
Gabriella Oldham and Mabel Langdon

Charles Walters: The Director Who Made Hollywood Dance
Brent Phillips

Some Like It Wilder: The Life and Controversial Films of Billy Wilder
Gene D. Phillips

Ann Dvorak: Hollywood's Forgotten Rebel
Christina Rice

Michael Curtiz: A Life in Film
Alan K. Rode

Arthur Penn: American Director
Nat Segaloff

Claude Rains: An Actor's Voice
David J. Skal with Jessica Rains

Barbara La Marr: The Girl Who Was Too Beautiful for Hollywood
Sherri Snyder

Buzz: The Life and Art of Busby Berkeley
Jeffrey Spivak

Victor Fleming: An American Movie Master
Michael Sragow

Hollywood Presents Jules Verne: The Father of Science Fiction on Screen
Brian Taves

Thomas Ince: Hollywood's Independent Pioneer
Brian Taves